The Elegiac Mode

Poetic Form in Wordsworth
and Other Elegists

THE ELEGIAC MODE

Poetic Form in Wordsworth
and Other Elegists

By ABBIE FINDLAY POTTS

Cornell University Press

ITHACA, NEW YORK

Copyright © 1967 by Cornell University

First published 1967

Selections from poems by D. H. Lawrence ("The Best
of School," "The Punisher," "Last Lesson of the After-
noon," "The Wild Common," "Letter from Town: on a
Grey Morning in March," "A Baby Asleep after Pain,"
"Come Spring, Come Sorrow," "Corot," "Michael An-
gelo," "He-Goat," "River Roses," "A Young Wife,"
"Hymn to Priapus," "In the Dark," "Mutilation," "I Am
Like a Rose," "Why Does She Weep?" "Sinners," "Birth
Night," "Paradise Re-Entered," "Spring Morning," "The
Song of a Man Who Has Come Through," "Manifesto,"
"Going Back," "Craving for Spring," "The Ship of
Death," "Lightning," "The Attack," "The Deepest Sensu-
ality," "Sense of Truth," "Demiurge," "The Work of
Creation") are from *The Complete Poems of D. H. Law-
rence*, Vols. I and II, edited by Vivian de Sola Pinto and
F. Warren Roberts; copyright 1920 by B. W. Huebsch,
Inc., copyright 1923, 1933, 1948, and 1951 by Frieda Law-
rence; reprinted by permission of The Viking Press,
Inc., New York, and of William Heinemann Limited and
Laurence Pollinger Limited, London, and the estate of
the late Mrs. Frieda Lawrence.

Library of Congress Catalog Card Number: 67–12093

PRINTED IN THE UNITED STATES OF AMERICA
BY VAIL-BALLOU PRESS, INC.

In memory of

LANE COOPER

1875-1959

Acknowledgments

THE late Professor Abbie Findlay Potts wrote this volume on elegiac form to stand—along with her two earlier books on tone and mode, *Wordsworth's "Prelude"* and *Shakespeare and "The Faerie Queene"*—as the last in her "trilogy on literary form." She had completed the manuscript and had packaged it for mailing to the Press just before she died in February 1964.

Grateful acknowledgment is made by the publisher to friends of Dr. Potts who helped to prepare the manuscript for the printer: to Helen D. (Mrs. Robert K.) Richardson, who acted as liaison between Cornell University Press and other friends assisting with the volume; to Professors Carl R. Woodring and Jack Stillinger, who gave careful attention to the text; to Professor Alice P. Comparetti, who checked many of the quotations; to Professor Vivian C. Hopkins, who reviewed the copy editing; to Professors Jeremy Ingalls and Dearing Lewis, who contributed much in the course of proofreading; and also to Dr. Ruth Morris Bakwin, who has given generous assistance.

Contents

ELEGY IN OUR TIME

The Elegiac Mode

Poetic Form in Wordsworth
and Other Elegists

incaedua silva . . .
. . . nemoralibus umbris— . . .
venit odoratos Elegeia nexa capillos,
    et, puto, pes illi longior alter erat.
forma decens, vestis tenuissima, vultus amantis,
    et pedibus vitium causa decoris erat. . . .
            si memini, limis subrisit ocellis— . . .
non sum materia fortior ipsa mea.
                                —Ovid *Amores* iii, 1

(Out from the grove Elegeia, her hair in a fillet and fragrant,
   Walking with long step and short, alternate, came into view.
Shapely she was, lightly clad; on her face was the look of a lover;
   Flawed in her gait, still she seemed fairer because of the flaw. . . .
If I remember her rightly, she smiled with her eyes glancing side-
      ways. . . .
Love is my matter, said she, I am no stronger than love.)

   Elegy is the form of poetry natural to the reflective mind. It *may*
treat of any subject, but it must treat of no subject *for itself;* but
always and exclusively with reference to the poet himself. As he
will feel regret for the past or desire for the future, so sorrow and
love become the principal themes of elegy.
                        —Coleridge, *Table Talk,* October 23, 1833

Prologue

THIS book is the fourth in a series of studies of literary form. My critical edition of the *Ecclesiastical Sonnets* of William Wordsworth (1922) represented the sonnet as the variously adaptable stanza for an epic poem. In *Wordsworth's Prelude: A Study of Its Literary Form* (1953) I examined the formal constituents of an autobiography. And in *Shakespeare and The Faerie Queene* (1958) I compared the ethical action of Spenser's romance and Shakespeare's drama. The present study of elegiac form is not a history of elegiac literature; here I propose a more particular review of elegies and similar meditative poems familiar to Wordsworth when he wrote the Lucy and Matthew ballads of 1799. In such a review I hope to distinguish genuine elegy from the mortuary idyll and lyric melancholia of the late seventeenth and the eighteenth centuries, that woebegone flood of verse no more characteristic of Wordsworth in A.D. 1799 than of Solon, Xenophanes, Simonides, Callimachus, or Propertius in centuries B.C. Although there is scant magic in a term, the Greek and Latin connotation of "elegy" can be often enough illustrated from Wordsworth's writing to justify the classical perspective on the development of his style. Moreover, if the term itself be cleared of its spurious associations, it will serve as an admirable clue into and out of the labyrinthine maze of letters in the century that he initiated.

To that end, after some consideration of the behavior of classical elegy, in which the eye of the elegist was first caught by ἠέλιος, the sun, and thus duly oriented to a life of discovery on earth, I plan to substantiate from English literature also the hypothesis that, beyond its minor sorrows, elegy is the poetry of skeptical vision and that its most characteristic formal trait is revelation. Originally the elegist, however dismayed, perplexed, or unhappy, wrote toward light rather than darkness; we may most surely recognize elegiac form in its successive *anagnorises*.

And if there be a kind of imagination that, by virtue of its meditative power, its "genuine insight," refines the feeling of lyric, enhances the outlines of idyll, and gives intenser meaning to the action of epic and drama, or even, as with the seer Blake, transforms discovery into prophecy, it might well be called the elegiac imagination. It looks toward and then looks beyond gnomic and didactic poetry. Restless and challenging, it makes and unmakes ethical codes, ritual, and liturgy. It rearranges even as it disturbs the patterns of civil government and ecclesiastical hierarchy. Although its themes are the puzzles of life and the riddle of death, it settles down neither in the tavern nor in the churchyard. Since its form is revelatory, without it life would look like a mere aggregate of things and persons and events, and death would seem hollow. With it, personality and destiny take on shape and color, meaning and value. In this sense may we not speak of Wordsworth and Yeats as elegiac poets with the same assurance that we speak of Sophocles and Shakespeare as dramatic poets, of Homer and Milton as epic poets?

Again, writers and scholars of a day when *Ash Wednesday* goes unique and nameless may find the term "elegy" an index of its function and a convenient tool for categorizing several other unclassified works both in verse and prose composed or evaluated in our own century. For instance—as Professor Ruth Temple reminds me—when Virginia Woolf was "making up" her book, *To the Lighthouse,* she wrote: "I have an idea that I will invent a new name for my books to supplant 'novel.' A new ———— by Virginia Woolf. But what? Elegy?" Search into the nature of the elegiac imagination may prove rewarding for other writers, too, and for other scholars, in fields where I have no commission to labor.

Horace's dictum (*De Arte Poetica* 75 ff.) that elegy is the medium of complaint, *querimonia,* or of gratitude for granted prayers, *voti sententia,* and Dante's belief (*De Vulgari Eloquentia* II, iv) that it is the style of the unhappy and is to be expressed in the lowly vernacular do little more than recognize feeling as the motive for composition. The genre has been and may still be other than a poem in a regretful mood about a sepulchral theme. Beyond discussion of its history and materials and its relation to the lyric dirge and the idyllic epigram or inscription and the gnomic sentiment, it invites study of its own peculiar tone. How in its clear-eyed meditations, its "effort to see," did it, does it, help solve the riddle of human personality— ἀνὴρ ἀγαθός or *docta puella*—or illumine the mysteries of the universe?

I am not unaware of the central importance of "illumination" to students of myth, analysts of the psyche, theologians dealing with the soul, mystics and metaphysicians, and scientists who, like Father Pierre Teilhard de Chardin most recently, believe that the history of the living world can be summarized as the elaboration of ever more perfect eyes within a cosmos in which there is always something more to be seen. The part played also in literature by the metaphors of light and darkness has been noted by the scholars of every age. In a restricted area, I shall be content to study those traits of authentic elegy that characterize the art of William Wordsworth and a certain few of his successors.

My indebtedness to classical scholarship will be noted in passing. The richly enumerative studies made by Professor John W. Draper of the English funeral elegy and the rise of English romanticism (1929) have ably defined one voluminous section of the genre, what the *Lexicon* of Suidas in reference to the poetry of Simonides called θρῆνοι (dirges), ἐγκώμια (eulogies), ἐπιγράμματα (inscriptions), παιᾶνες (hymns of praise), as distinguished from δι' ἐλεγείας (elegiacs). Professors Amy L. Reed (1924) and Eleanor M. Sickels (1932), respectively, have sketched the background of Gray's *Elegy* and portrayed the gloomy egoism of the years preceding the Lucy poems. In *The Poetry of Meditation, A Study in English Religious Literature of the Seventeenth Century*, Professor Louis L. Martz has related elegy to devotional exercise and the stern discipline of the soul toward holiness. These books make it unnecessary for me to refer in detail to poems appropriating the title of elegy without quite performing its function as understood by the writers of antiquity who first practiced it. The prior line in the tradition is, I submit, the more fruitful. My argument, therefore, will exhibit Matthew as ἀνὴρ ἀγαθός and Lucy as *docta puella*, the schoolmaster-sage-poet and the luminous woman. As in the earlier days of elegy, both are *personae* for the speculative adventures they invite.

At the center of the essays I have placed several chapters based on new evidence or evidence considered anew. Dealing with Wordsworth's poetry written from 1799 to 1814, these constitute addenda to my books on *The Prelude* and *Ecclesiastical Sonnets*, which were published under scholarly duress to be helpful to others. Now, somewhat more tentatively, I have tried to enlighten and please myself. I hope that any readers who may in slight degree be enlightened and pleased along with me will be tempted to carry the argument further, with evidence either pro or con.

It was Professor Northrop Frye who first aroused my interest in *anagnorisis;* and for my initial study of elegy I was helped by conversations with the classical scholars Elizabeth Hazelton

Haight of Vassar College and Mary V. Braginton of Rockford College. Another former colleague, Dr. Susan M. Savage, has carefully checked references to Greek and Latin texts and my interpretation of them. The comment of Professor Stephen M. Parrish of my Alma Mater, Cornell University, helped to keep me on the path, and in the final reaches of my argument the studies of Hardy and Yeats have profited by challenge and suggestion from Professors Katherine Haynes Gatch and Marion W. Witt. Finally I owe a great debt to Professor Carl R. Woodring of Columbia University, who has read the whole manuscript with careful attention to my argument and valuable comment on my evidence.

Here, too, I gratefully recall from many years ago my teachers of Greek and Latin, Edward Edwards, Jr., and Arthur F. Gardner; and, at Cornell, George P. Bristol. Since Cornell's Lane Cooper was the wise teacher who introduced me to Wordsworth's poetry and since he died when my book was in process, it is fitting that his name should appear on my dedicatory page.

Again I acknowledge the generosity of Dr. Ruth Morris Bakwin, who has enabled me to publish studies that, however modest, may shed light on matters as yet not clearly perceived. To the librarians of the New York State Public Library in Albany and Russell Sage College Library in Troy I express my thanks for frequent kindness and continuing hospitality. Mrs. Janice Chilcott Merson has assisted me in preparing the typescript.

ABBIE FINDLAY POTTS

ELEGEIA

CHAPTER I

Flute Song

WHEN song surrendered its musical instruments and became poetry, poets still clung to their metaphors of the lyre and trump, the pipe and flute. Although we now speak of lyric poetry with scant regard for the lyre and of pastorals with little heed for the shepherd's pipe, and although we expect no call of the clarion to begin the latest historical novel, we in our time also crave a musical frame for our various doings—gun shots for our Westerns and a plaintive organ for our romances, dinner music for our parties and haunting melodies for our advertisements. And however little the disc we play or the tape-recording we hear tallies with the rhythm or sense of our quiet talk or solitary reverie, we often converse to music and meditate to music.

Any student of literary form will recognize such changes in taste even as he must account for the persistence of old patterns of feeling. But how puzzled, even bewildered, the Muses themselves would be were they confronted with our discourse that is not poetical and our poetry that is not musical! All the circumstances of their art have become strange. The idyllic merriment of comic Thalia and the dramatic actions of tragic Melpomene, so long shaped by the stage, are exaggerated and distorted on the screen; and the orchestra beats out an ever more monotonous accent for the once variously elegant dancer, Terpsichore. Perforce Calliope and Clio, the Muses of epic poetry and history, tune their legends and chronicles to the beam of a radio, and the celestial music of Urania survives only as a faint overtone for the roar of rockets and for bombs bursting in air. Even sadder, what used to be delicately sung has been during our era more and more entrusted to mute wood pulp and rag tissue. Thus reduced, pulpy and ragged, the so-called "poems" of today lure their readers into an easy chair rather than piping them outside upon an athletic field or a picnic ground for a race or a stroll, a game or a gambol. Strait-jacketed by the margins on a page, the three Muses of song are most distraught. Euterpe, trying to be "pure," has abandoned her lyre. Erato has fallen in love with a crooner. And Polyhymnia, sacred poetry, repeats herself in humdrum stereotypes to the sound of an organ more eagerly sought in the cinema than in the cathedral.

Where is the Muse with the flute? Herself nameless and the handmaiden of her more celebrated sisters, she never quite made the first nine; but when these same nine sisters languish, she has been known to assume their duties and skills for her own. Where is she now, the Muse of elegiac poetry, the speculative Muse, the Muse with the flute? That she was in Paris during the early summer of 1910 we learn from the greatest elegist of our century, Rainer Maria Rilke, who seems to speak for her in his address to the ancient Greek double-flute:

> O cross-way of my mouth, O lips-uniter,
> O flute, that parts my breath for me in two.[1]

Flute song, elegiac poetry, began in Ionia about the seventh century B.C. After a pastoral infancy there the elegiac Muse

[1] Rainer Maria Rilke, *Poems 1906 to 1926,* tr. with an Introduction by J. B. Leishman (London, 1957), p. 121; quoted by permission of Hogarth Press, Ltd.

went on to share the heroic enterprises of men with Calliope and
originally led them into battle; with Erato she partook of their
banquets and amorous adventures. She could poke fun like
Thalia and clarify sorrow like Melpomene. In spite of her uneven gait and glance sideways she was as graceful as Terpsichore
and as candid as Clio. She was as eager for pleasant harmonies
as Euterpe. Above all, she was faithful to Urania and the lights
overhead and stood often by Polyhymnia to speak for the truth
within.

Whenever down the slipshod centuries she and her flute have
been audible, she has allied herself with her sister Terpsichore
in those precise choral gestures, arsis and thesis, that accompany
the metrical lift and fall of the foot in patterns made by the active body. She hides behind balladry, takes over at horse races,
and cannot resist pageantry whether secular or religious, learned
or lewd. She understands rhythm as we understand it: rhythm
in *verse* when it turns and re-turns with its "words dancing";
and rhythm in *prose* with its "words walking straight ahead."
She would approve our desire for freedom of phrase even in
the kind of poetry we call "discourse" and warns us against
critics so lacking kinaesthetic awareness that they attempt by
their sharp judgments to drive a wedge between verse and prose.
She would be the first to remind us that Aeneas does not need
to see his mother dance, that he can always recognize her by
the way she walks—*et vera incessu patuit dea.*

And when Terpsichore, dancing, lapses in energy or gentil-
ity, the Muse with the flute pipes on, sorrowing, challenging,
questioning. Her traits as we rehearse them make her out to be
just the guide we need for our poetic renascence in the twentieth
century. Inside or outside of our books, on her way through
the thickets and jungles and marshes of our mass media, she goes
where her sisters dare not venture. We cannot dispense with
her vigor and independence in love and thought, her goodly
walking and stalking rhythms, her hunger for affairs and enterprises, her skeptical comment on all that has been and is and

should not be. She deserves a new book in her honor and will not fail modestly to belittle it. First, let us invoke her: Elegeia!

Next, in order to estimate the accomplishment of the elegiac imagination in that country and century of Wordsworth so like our own, let us briefly review the traces of elegy in earlier, even the earliest, times. Through the distichs of the Ionian Mimnermus and the Umbrian Propertius and their fellows from the seventh to the first century before Christ, we are enabled to hear for ourselves the characteristic rhythms of elegiac poetry, flute song. In later chapters we shall go on to inquire about the interests and themes of the elegist and his recurrent images and metaphors. Then, coming to Wordsworth's various elegiac ballads, stanzas, and odes, we shall be provided with the wherewithal for a keener enjoyment of them. In particular we shall ask and try to answer the question: why did this poet use the ballad metre for his elegies on Lucy and Matthew? Is there in the ballad tradition some special reminiscence of, or analogy with, the affecting melody of the flute as invented by Pallas Athene (Ovid's guess), played rebelliously by Pan and Marsyas, and—with better evidence to prove it—cherished by the ancient peoples of the Fertile Crescent and the Eastern Mediterranean? [2]

Here we are concerned with elegy's flute not as a musical instrument, an item in the history of music, not even as a literary theme or poetical allusion. It is always possible to ask, but we are not likely to receive a reply to our question about the actual notes played by the flutist in accompanying the elegiac distichs of Mimnermus and Archilochus. Did the αὔλημα, the music of the flute, mark out the melody of the αὐλῳδία, the song which it accompanied? Or was this instrument of Dionysus used for an obbligato or for variations and counterpoint? Answer who can.

[2] For curious information about the flute in legend, literature, and music, consult H. Macaulay Fitzgibbon, *The Story of the Flute* (2d ed.; London and New York, 1928). See also Freya Stark, *Ionia: A Quest* (New York, 1954), p. 85.

Nevertheless, we may propose a kinship in quality and an associative value between the various functions of the meditative poem and the "sweet desolation—balmy pain" which Keats imagined in the strain Pan heard "along the reedy stream." [3] Whether the pierced reed from Lake Aulocrene in Phrygia, the Egyptian flute found in the tomb of the Lady Maket of about 1450 B.C., or the classical αὐλός was earliest, whether the single pipe or double flute was more convenient for the performers of elegy, must be left to the expert; we shall chiefly consider the resonance in the mind of those who heard sung the elegiac distichs of Callinus, Archilochus, Mimnermus, Tyrtaeus, Solon, Xenophanes, Theognis, Simonides, Callimachus or, as recited in Latin, the elegiac couplets of Catullus, Tibullus, Propertius, and Ovid.

This elegiac distich, the flute song itself, took form as a first line of dactylic hexameter and a second line of what Sir Maurice Bowra [4] describes as "two and a half dactyls followed by another two and a half":

$$- \cup \cup \,|- \cup \cup \,|-_\wedge \,||- \cup \cup \,|- \cup \cup \,|-_\wedge$$

This second line is no mere pentameter shortened from a hexameter out of which Ovid's Cupid has dropped one metrical foot to soften it for his amorous purposes. With its syncope and strong caesura at the end of the first trimeter and its catalexis at the end of the second trimeter it offers an opportunity for many sorts of doubling phrase to secure emphasis by repetition or contrast. Although the habit of classical verse is quantitative, not accentual, the usually fourteen-syllabled minor line of the elegiac distich is in some ways comparable with the old fourteener of English verse. Except that the former is dactylic and divides into seven and seven and the latter, the ballad measure, is iambic and divides into eight and six, both can and do use

[3] Quoted by Fitzgibbon, *op. cit.*, p. 2.
[4] C. M. Bowra, *Early Greek Elegists* (Cambridge, Mass., 1938). Georg Luck, *The Latin Love Elegy* (London, 1959), p. 20.

pause and syllabic equivalence for a wide variety of rhythmic effects. And when dactyls, spondees, and trochees are substituted at the beginning of an otherwise iambic ballad line, a hovering rhythm not unlike that of the elegiac pentameter results—if a poet studies flute song and balladry together.

Two such poets were Coleridge and Wordsworth in the last few years of the eighteenth century. Coleridge, however, was cultivating the classics with somewhat more obvious relish: his correspondence of 1792 indicates that he would be examined in Easter week "on the last book of Homer and Horace's [De] Arte Poetica." [5] That spring he was writing a Greek ode, and in 1793 he translated into English heroic couplets the Latin elegiac couplets from the *Carmina Quadragesimalia*, composed a Latin quatrain, *Ave atque Vale*, and wrote the *Lines on an Autumnal Evening* with its echoes of Greek epigrammatic verse. There are reminiscences of Horace in 1795 and of Ovid, Pindar, and Aeschylus in 1796. [6]

Meanwhile, Wordsworth as a youth had been making those translations of Catullus later to be appropriated by Coleridge and sent to the *Morning Post* (1798). [7] He had translated Virgil and imitated Anacreon, Moschus, Horace, and Juvenal. [8] However widely read both young men were in English poetry— thanks to Wordsworth's father and his master, William Taylor, and to Coleridge's master, James Boyer—their formal schooling was classical. Neither seems to have been much interested in the exact reproduction of Greek and Latin metres in English poetry, but both were familiar with classical rhythms and with

[5] *Collected Letters of Samuel Taylor Coleridge*, ed. Earl Leslie Griggs (Oxford, 1956), I, 20 ff.

[6] In *The Poems of Samuel Taylor Coleridge*, ed. Ernest Hartley Coleridge (London, 1912), consult the notes for the years 1787–1800.

[7] Jane Worthington Smyser, "Coleridge's Use of Wordsworth's Juvenilia," *PMLA*, LXV (June, 1950), 419–426.

[8] *The Poetical Works of William Wordsworth*, ed. E. de Selincourt and Helen Darbishire (Oxford, 1940–1949), I, 366–374; quoted by permission of The Clarendon Press, Oxford. This edition is hereafter cited as *P.W.*

their propriety for various subjects and moods. When and how would this knowledge invigorate and enrich their original verse?

During his earliest years as poet, and especially from 1797 to 1800, Coleridge was not only the wide and sagacious reader which John Livingston Lowes, Arthur Nethercot, and others have proved him to be but also an unresting experimenter with English metres and rhythms, rhymes, and stanzas. Wordsworth, too, under the influence of English poets from his fourteenth year onward, had tried his hand at many and diverse English metrical forms. Before the two poets fused their literary experience and enthusiasms in 1795, both had been at work on the different uses of pentameter—in blank verse, sonnets, and heroic couplets; and both had attempted the Spenserian stanza, Coleridge with a poem for Sara and an address to Joseph Cottle (1795) and Wordsworth with his *Female Vagrant* (1793-1794). Moreover, both had exercised themselves in the four-foot line, whether for couplet, quatrain, stanza, or irregular ode. Their verses were prevailingly iambic but, when in the Miltonic vein of *L'Allegro* and *Il Penseroso*, now and again substituted a trochee or spondee at the beginning of the line: witness Wordsworth's *Beauty and Moonlight* (1786), *The Vale of Esthwaite* (1787), and *Inscription . . . Windy Brow* (1794); and Coleridge's *Absence* and *Happiness* (1791) and *The Sigh* and *The Kiss* (1794). Wordsworth's adaptations of Catullus (1786 and 1795-1797) have several initial trochees and spondees, as we should expect. These are even more frequent in his Horatian *Ode to Apollo* (1789-1790) and they determine the rhythm of *From the Greek* (1794). Witness also Coleridge's *Ode in Manner of Anacreon* (1792) and his *On a Lady Weeping* (?1790) from the Latin of Nicolaus Archius. The latter is trochaic throughout, as are his imitations of Casimir (1794) and *To an Unfortunate Woman* (1797). Up to 1797, despite their classical education, neither young poet reproduced in English the dactylic pattern of the elegiac distich. As yet in their writing there is no clear echo of flute song.

Nevertheless, it is appropriate to notice further that the alternation of a longer with a shorter line in the classical distich has an obvious kinship with native patterns familiar to Wordsworth and Coleridge. For instance, with Poulter's measure, the rhymed couplet uses for its first line an alexandrine and for its second line a fourteener. It is appropriate, also, to recall that this fourteener when resolved into the common ballad measure of eight and six had been for centuries the staple of English balladry and minstrelsy. Indeed, the ballad as Coleridge and Wordsworth were about to renew it is a kind of English flute song. And it would be Wordsworth's felicitous decision to adopt its metrical form for elegy in his Lucy and Matthew ballads of 1799.

We must observe, also, that both poets were early familiar with the minstrelsy of Burns among their immediate predecessors, more so than with the trochaic marvels of Blake. Not less likely is their knowledge of Cowper's hymns and Wesley's psalmody. Wordsworth revered both Collins and Chatterton, as did Coleridge. We may doubt that they had studied Robert of Gloucester's *Chronicle* and those *Saints' Lives* which, says Saintsbury, have " 'all the bones' of the full-swinging ballad metre"; [9] nor was it necessary for them to know that Phaer had translated Virgil's hexameters and Golding had translated Ovid's elegiacs into English fourteeners; [10] already they knew the

---

[9] George Saintsbury, *A History of English Prosody* (3 vols.; London, 1906), I, 67–68. Saintsbury (I, 404–405) is well aware that "you may find something very like the fifteener-fourteener in Greek from one point of view, and in early Latin from another . . . [But] is the affiliation worth making? . . . *It is suggestion at most that these foreign or ancient patterns give*" (my italics).

Again, Saintsbury's belief that the fourteener may have been a form of "this old alliterative stuff" (I, 406) shortened by way of octosyllabic couplets in French romances and Latin hymns into a minor line, "an agreeable sort of partner to the major," accords with our understanding of the second line of the classical elegiac couplet as *mollis:* a softening of the first line of dactylic hexameter by the dropping of one foot.

[10] Henry Burrows Lathrop, *Translations from the Classics into English from Caxton to Chapman, 1477–1620* (University of Wisconsin Studies in Language and Literature, Number 35, Madison, 1933), pp. 109–113. Professor Lathrop has detailed the failures of those translators who kept

rhythms of Chaucer's *Sir Thopas* and Spenser's March and July
Eclogues and were not out of reach of the influence of carols,
hymns, and such Latin parcel-songs as *Velut maris stella.*

Yet it was above all the "ineffably beautiful" common measure
of the seventeenth century [11] with its "marvelous spiritualizing"
that helped both young men to avoid the sentimental flattening
of the mock balladry of the eighteenth century. Jonson had
translated the prose *Letters* of Philostratus into "Drink to me
only with thine eyes"—more akin to flute song even than his
octosyllabic *Elegy* or his *Epitaph on S.P.*, which lacks a syllable
in its shorter lines. Although the echoes of flute song can be
heard in the initial four lines of each stanza of Donne's trochaic-
iambic *Song*—

> Sweetest love, I do not go
>   For weariness of thee,
> Nor in hope the world can show
>   A fitter love for me—

he chose to write his *Elegies* in the heroic couplet. And Théophile de Viau, his contemporary across the Channel, used for
his *Élégies* the alexandrines which reverse the classical elegiac
rhythm into iambs:

> En la plus belle ardeur où je puis voir Caliste,
> Mon âme y sent toujours quelque chose de triste.

It may be that Robert Herrick most nearly recalls the temper
and metre of the minor kind of erotic elegies of Alexandria and

---

too close to ancient rhythms. Of their partial successes he says (p. 109):
"The fourteen-syllable line is our most ancient meter, and seemed in
the sixteenth century the most natural one. It is the meter of Orm, of
Robert of Gloucester, and of the ballads, and it is 'the common meter'
of hymns." Also it is "the meter of Phaer and Golding and Chapman's
Iliad" (p. 110). "The verse can be noble and moving, as in Southwell's
Burning Babe; but it cannot fall from this height without flatness, and
hence is most effective in short lyric. The verse can be tender, as in a
number of ballads, but again lacks flexibility in changing its mood, and
therefore in gentle as in noble emotion is best suited for lyric composition. Its characteristic is motion; its special quality is energy."

[11] Saintsbury, III, 335.

Rome: "Gather ye rosebuds while ye may"; "Sweet western wind, whose luck it is"; "Bid me to weep, and I will weep" (*To Anthea*); "Good morrow to the day so fair"; *To the Water Nymphs*—

> Reach with your whiter hands to me
>   Some crystal of the spring,
> And I about the cup shall see
>   Fresh lilies flourishing.

His daisies are exhorted to

> Stay but till my Julia close
>   Her life-begetting eye,
> And let the whole world then dispose
>   Itself to live or die.

That Herrick knew Latin elegy well we may infer from his approximation of the elegiac rhythm in a pledge to Ovid, Catullus, Propertius, and Tibullus, the chief Latin elegists:

> Then this immensive cup // Of aromatic wine
> Catullus I quaff up // To that terse Muse of thine.
> Round, round the roof does run // And being ravished thus
> Come I will drink a tun // To my Propertius.

To make more likely our hypothetical association in Wordsworth's mind between the ballad measure and elegy we need not look to these singing elegists of the seventeenth century alone, even less to Gray's melodious pentameter quatrain in the eighteenth century; Milton's Latin *Elegies* and not least his elegiac couplets written for Leonora singing in Rome had been flute song at its most ingratiating and thoughtful:

> Quid mirum? Leonora tibi si gloria major,
>   Nam tua praesentem // vox sonat ipse Deum
>   . . . . .
> Quod si cuncta quidem Deus est per cunctaque fusus,
>   In te una loquitur // caetera mutus habet.

Quid mirum! The most highly regarded elegy in English literature would now and then repeat those cadences, especially in
the dying fall of its short lines: "So may some gentle Muse";
"Temper'd to th'Oaten Flute"; "Shall now no more be seen";
"Nor in the glistering foil"; "But now my Oate proceeds."
And has it been noticed that behind the pentametrical lines of
Lycidas a triple phrasing is often possible, reminding us not
only of the three syllables in the dactylic foot and of the triple
emphasis in each half of the minor line of the classical distich
but of the triple structure of the distich itself with its hexameter
followed by the two halves of its pseudopentameter?—what
Georg Luck in his recent study of Latin elegy compares to a
waltz rhythm. Witness:

Hence	with denial vain	and coy excuse . . .
Meanwhile	the Rural ditties	were not mute . . .
Thee Shepherd,	thee the Woods,	and desert Caves . . .
Alas!	What boots it	with uncessant care . . .
To sport	with Amaryllis	in the shade . . .
That strain I heard	was	of a higher mood . . .
What hard mishap	hath doom'd	this gentle swain?
Next Camus,	reverend Sire,	went footing slow . . .
What recks it them?	What need they?	They are sped . . .

Thus, most subtly, the threes modify the fives.

It would be impossible to assess the respective influence of
their classical training and their English reading in the trochees,
spondees, and dactyls of the great narrative ballad of Coleridge
and the elegiac ballads of Wordsworth. Saintsbury has observed
that "something like the later English vacillation between iambic
and trochaic rhythm . . . is already apparent [as early as in the
Canute Song]." [12] Thanks to "the delight in prosodic liberty"
evolved by those spinsters and knitters in the sun, crooners of
lullabies, sighers of love ditties, haunters of taverns, mutterers
of political lampoons, pious souls, mourning or petitioning,
which Saintsbury is at great pains to categorize,[13] Coleridge

[12] *Ibid.*, I, 30.   [13] *Ibid.*, I, 297.

would supply for the common ballad measure, that "daisy of
metres," [14] its crowning facility and grace. Thanks also to the
minor line of the elegiac couplet, when he and his friends
Southey and Wordsworth reached for the ballad, that "life-
buoy of English poetry," [15] they grasped at classical elegiac
rhythms as well. Both strains can be heard in their literary experiments of 1797–1799.

Already Coleridge and Wordsworth had written poems in
the ballad stanza, *abcb* and *abab*. On March 23 and 24, 1787,
Wordsworth set down the ballad of Mary and William in Esthwaite's Vale; and the seven beats of the old fourteener can be
heard in Coleridge's *The Rose* and his imitation of Ossian
(1793), in his imitation from the Welsh (?1794), and also
(1794) in *Epitaph on an Infant* and *To Miss Brunton*. The
spondaic tendency in such phrases as "slow-waving," "Cease,
restless gale," "Thus, faithful maiden," reveals power to modify
the monotonous iambic line. And, finally, the early experience
of both poets with *rime couée*, tailed rhyme, gave promise of
further power to amplify the melodies of the short ballad stanza.
Coleridge had used this tailed rhyme effectively in his *Easter
Holidays* (May 12, 1787) and later in *Shurton Bars;* Wordsworth, in his *Septimi Gades* (1794), an adaptation of Horace
Odes ii, 6. Small wonder that the spondaic stress in that one of
the Lucy elegies which begins

> Three years she grew in sun and shower,
>
> Then Nature said, "A lovelier flower
>
> On earth was never sown;
>
> This Child I to myself will take;
>
> She shall be mine, and I will make
>
> A Lady of my own."

evokes memories of other than iambic rhythms.

In 1797 Coleridge had translated the Latin elegiac couplets

[14] *Ibid.*, II, 144.   [15] *Ibid.*, I, 299.

of the Reverend W. L. Bowles (an inscription for Richard Camplin, 1792, in Nether Stowey Church) but—alas!—into the heroic couplets of the age of Donne and the age of Pope. The lovely flute of *The Rime of the Ancient Mariner* (1798) was not yet audible; such sweet sounds were yet to be heard. Nevertheless, in 1795, not too long before, he had been listening while the Reverend W. J. Hort taught a young lady some song-tunes on his flute. What his ear heard his pen described as follows in the rhythm if not the syllabic count of the minor line of the classical elegiac distich:

> Hush, ye clamorous Cares! be mute!
>   Again, dear Harmonist! again
> Thro' the hollow of thy flute
>   Breathe that passion-warbled strain:
> Till Memory each form shall bring
>   The loveliest of her shadowy throng;
> And Hope, that soars on sky-lark wing,
>   Carol wild her gladdest song.

Master Hort's pupil will, he begs, "raise the Poet's kindred strain / In soft impassioned voice, correctly wild."

The description of flute music as "thrilling tones, that concentrate the soul" might well serve to characterize the metrical art of Coleridge and Wordsworth during the years of their close collaboration on balladry. And where better can we observe the working of this kind of "magic spell" than in a review of what Coleridge did to the script of *The Three Graves*?

Says De Selincourt: "The discovery of these stanzas [*The Three Graves*, Part II, in a notebook] . . . partly in W.'s hand and partly in that of Mary Hutchinson, who was staying at Racedown in the early months of 1797, proves them to be W.'s composition. Presumably he wrote Part I also." [16]

In Part II (and in Part I as we have it in Coleridge's *Poems*, 1893, from an autograph MS) the iambic beat of the old four-

[16] *P.W.*, I, 374.

teeners is well-nigh invariable, except for a few possible spondees: "Stretch out"; "There, there"; "Small need"; "What passed"; "Ye shall"; "fast-rooted"; "She is my child"; "Thou daughter"; "Sweet love"; "All pale"; "No dog"; "Unblest"; and, in a few lines added by Coleridge, "Three times," "Called home," and "This spade." The otherwise monotonous rhythm of Parts I and II may be the reason why a discouraged Wordsworth handed this particular script over to his friend.

According to Barron Field, Wordsworth had given Coleridge the subject of his *Three Graves* but considered that Coleridge's Parts III and IV were "shocking and painful, and not sufficiently sweetened by any healing views." [17] Whatever we think of Coleridge's handling of plot and character, however, into his undeniable Parts III and IV has gone somewhat of the flutelike quality we associate at its finest with *The Ancient Mariner* and *Christabel*, yet to be written. Trochees, spondees, and dactyls are numerous and extra lines permit a phrasal grouping into threes, in the direction of the elegiac pattern:

O Edward   you are   all to me
I wish   for your sake   I could be
    More lifesome and more gay.

The iambs are yielding to anapests or to the remembered dactylic cadence of flute song:

And she went   oftener   than before
And Mary   loved her   more and more
    She managed all the dairy.

There are trochaic and spondaic modifications such as:

        On the hedge-elms in the narrow lane
        Still swung the spikes of corn.

Spondees now and again follow spondees: "so five months passed"; "No ice, no snow"; "Yea, both sweet names." Rocking

17 *Ibid.*

rhythms reminiscent of, even if shorter than, the minor line of the elegiac couplet are to be found: "So having prayed, steady and slow." Many lines begin with seeming dactyls or trochees substituted for iambs: "Giddy she seemed, and sure there was"; "Lingering he raised his latch at eve." As yet, the iamb has the last beat but it is hard put to make its stand. A new hovering rhythm prevails.

This rhythm is well within the "infinite . . . adaptabilities" of that common measure which, according to Saintsbury, "is perhaps the most definitely English . . . of all metres." [18] It is also within the gift of the classical rhythm of

$$- \cup \cup \,|- \,\cup \cup \,|-_\wedge \,||- \,\cup \cup \,|- \,\cup \cup \,|-_\wedge$$

which gives the proper swing of flute song. The articulation of the dactyl permits the flutist a nicer fingering than the jog trot of the unvaried iambic stress.

Now, in the four-foot lines of *Christabel*, begun in 1797, Coleridge believed that he was versifying "on a new principle: namely, that of counting in each line the accents, not the syllables. Though the latter may vary from seven to twelve, yet in each line the accents will be found to be only four." [19] Coleridge's "new principle" was, of course, not new, and his four-beat line was in the very nature of the English accentual tradition, which permitted a wide variety of equivalent substitutes for the iamb. But as a Latin scholar he felt the need of a verse permitting more syllables and more various quantitative effects, a line calling more frequently for the dactylic and spondaic rhythm which had been characteristic of the elegiac fourteener. May we suggest that what he did was to restore flute song to modern English literature?

In *The Ancient Mariner* supremely, the reader is set free from the obvious syllabic schemes of the eighteenth century and from the eighteenth-century idea of balladry, even from

[18] Saintsbury, I, 247–248.
[19] *The Poems of Samuel Taylor Coleridge,* p. 215.

the common ballad metre itself. The rebellion begun by Burns, Blake, and Southey is most urgent in the *Rime* of Coleridge, where we frequently hear the music of dactyl and trochee at the beginning of the line: "Merrily did we drop"; "Nodding their heads"; "We were the first"; "Water, water, everywhere"; "Lay like a load on my weary eye"; "Swiftly, swiftly flew the ship." Not infrequently we observe the relaxing influence of the anapest: "By thy long grey beard and glittering eye"; "Instead of the Cross the Albatross"; "Thro' the holes of his eyes and the hole of his mouth"; "For the sky and the sea, and the sea and the sky." Again, not unlike shortened or syncopated elegiac pentameters, come the rocking rhythms: "Day after day, day after day."

Moreover, and here we can be insistent, in the metrical art of Wordsworth, too, the pattern of two strong beats in the middle of the fourteener is not alien to the pattern of the two long emphases in the middle of the minor line of classical elegy. Nor does the definite caesura within both major and minor lines of the elegiac distich—a likely device to allow the flutist to take breath—fail to add its influence toward a hovering rhythm in English elegiac balladry. From this introduction of a hovering rhythm we can foresee what came to pass when for his Lucy and Matthew elegies of 1799 Wordsworth adopted the ballad metre as modified by Coleridge: an endless variety of effects. Witness the following stanza reminiscent of both English and classical measures:

> Strange fits of passion have I known
> And I will dare [pause] to tell
> But in the Lover's ear alone
> What once to me [pause] befell.

Those who prefer to accent more vigorously on an iambic base may question such a distribution of stresses; but to one reader at least this permissible scansion evokes a memory of the dactylic swing and the emphasis, middle and end, of flute song as heard in Ionia, Athens, and Sparta, and in Rome.[20] For instance, the Ionian Mimnermus telling about rosy-fingered Dawn, who forsook ocean to climb the skies:

Ὠκεα/νὸυ προλι/ποῦσ᾽ // οὐρανὸν/ εἰσανα/βῆ

or the Spartan Tyrtaeus, about the good man and war:

οὗτος ἀ/νὴρ ἀγα/θὸς // γίγνεται/ ἐν πολέ/μῳ

or Solon, the Athenian lawgiver, singing a song instead of making a speech:

κόσμον ἐ/πέων ᾠ/δὴν // ἀντ᾽ ἀγο/ρῆς θέμε/νος

or Xenophanes, the most thoughtful of the Greek elegists, as he recommends auspicious fables and pure stories:

εὐφή/μοις μύ/θοις // καὶ καθα/ροῖσι λό/γοις.

We may instance, also, those fourteen-syllabled minor elegiac lines for which Propertius invoked his flute, *tibia*, to celebrate *his* Lucy, Cynthia. She had all the graces of Venus, all the skills of Minerva (i, 2, 30):

Omnia quaeque Venus // quaeque Minerva probat.

For her lover she was the beginning and the end (i, 12, 20):

Cynthia prima fuit, // Cynthia finis erit.

His love for her would be at the last what it was at the first (ii, 20, 34):

Ultima talis erit // quae mea prima fides.

[20] Cf. Bowra, *Early Greek Elegists*. Texts for the Greek elegists may be found in *Elegy and Iambus* and *Lyra Graeca*, both texts ed. and trans. J. M. Edmonds, in the Loeb Classical Library (Cambridge, Mass., 1961 and 1934–1952 respectively); quoted by permission of Harvard University Press. The elegies of Propertius are quoted from the text given in the Loeb Classical Library, ed. and trans. H. E. Butler (Cambridge, Mass., 1952); quoted by permission of Harvard University Press. English translations, except as otherwise noted, are my own.

And when he says to her (ii, 18B, 33–34): "Since you have no other brother and no other son,"

Frater ego et tibi sum ∥ filius unus ego,

our ear has a premonition of what Wordsworth would say to Matthew many centuries later (*The Fountain* 61–62):

"And Matthew, for thy children dead ∥
I'll be a son [pause] to thee!"

And, although Wordsworth was a classical student familiar with the elegies of Catullus, Tibullus, Propertius, and Ovid, and although he had adapted many lines of Juvenal for the English ear, we may grant that without Coleridge's delicate modulations of the septenaries in the common ballad measure, and his equally magical reshaping of the four-foot verse in the stanzas of *Christabel,* his more conservative friend might have stopped with *Lucy Gray,* and with *We Are Seven, Expostulation and Reply,* and *The Tables Turned,* the only three poems in authentic common measure contributed by Wordsworth to *Lyrical Ballads,* 1798. There are other ballad-like poems in the first edition of this epoch-making volume; but they are mainly octosyllabic, although the stanzas of *To My Sister, Simon Lee, Anecdote for Fathers,* and *Lines Written in Early Spring* have trimeters for the final line of the stanza, and *The Thorn, The Mad Mother,* and *The Last of the Flock* have occasional three-foot lines. All of Wordsworth's stanzaic poems in 1798, however, profit by the substitution of trochees for iambs here and there at the beginning of the line.

When Coleridge, William, and Dorothy departed from Nether Stowey for their trip to the Continent in 1798, Coleridge left behind him, along with the unfinished *Christabel,* a fragment to be entitled *The Ballad of the Dark Ladie,* its stanzas in octosyllabic triplets with a final trimeter; but the ballad is mainly iambic and lacks the metrical variety of *The Ancient Mariner.* In the year ahead his poems would become more and more "occasional," suggested by his experience and his reading in Germany; some of these as offered to the *Morning Post* and *Annual Anthology* are slight or insignificant. His interest in metrics, however, continued. This becomes clear from the *Hexameters* he sent to the Wordsworths in a letter from Ratzeburg during the winter of 1798–1799. It is likely that his Catullian *Hendeca-Syllables, The Homeric Hexameter,* and *The Ovidian Elegiac Metre* also belong to this year:

> In the hexameter rises the fountain's silvery column;
> In the pentameter, aye, falling in melody back.[21]

Translated from Schiller, this pattern for flute song may well have encouraged Wordsworth to modify further the ballad rhythms he was reviewing in Percy's *Reliques,* which he had bought at Hamburg en route for Goslar. We know that the 1799 septenaries of the elegiac ballads about Lucy and Matthew increasingly exhibit the rhythm of flute song.

> "O Mercy!" to myself I cried,
> "If Lucy should be [pause] dead!"

[21] As early as October 24, 1794, Coleridge was recommending R. F. P. Brunk's *Analecta Veterum Poetarum Graecorum* (1772–1776) to Francis Wrangham (*Letters,* I, 121). For the *Critical Review* of February, 1797, he reviewed Bishop Horsley's tract *On the Prosodies of the Greek and Latin Languages* (*ibid.,* I, 318). In early December, 1798, he wrote to Wordsworth concerning Greek and Latin hexameters: *"we read all the spondees as iambics or trochees"* (*ibid.,* I, 450). On September 29, 1799, he referred to his translation of Psalm 46 into hexameters, "allowing trochees for spondees as the nature of our language demands" (*ibid.,* I, 532). Recently Dr. David Erdman has attributed to Coleridge a review of *Musae Etonienses,* published in the *Critical Review* for November, 1796. His argument and the review may be read in the *Bulletin of the New York Public Library,* LXIII (September, 1959), 449–454. The review refers to the versification of Ovid and Tibullus. That Coleridge was sensitive to elegiac meter during these years may also be illustrated from his joke on "elegiac Pens," "villains with uneven legs," in a letter of October 8, 1799. There is an alternate reading of Coleridge's pentameter in Huntington MS HM 12123: "In the pentameter still falling melodious down."

Here, as in some of the verses of *The Ancient Mariner*, the
rhythm seems to hover as between iambic and trochaic-dactylic-
spondaic.

> Nor, England! did I know till then
> What love I bore [pause] to thee.

Lucy is now

> Rolled round in earth's diurnal course,
> With rocks, and stones, and trees.

> She lived unknown, and few could know
> When Lucy ceased to be;
> But she is in her grave, and [pause] oh,
> The difference [pause] to me!

From our spondaic wanderings we return to our iambic base.
The Two April Mornings and *The Fountain* have a similar
elegiac melody, and Matthew meditating on the dead Emma,
like Wordsworth meditating on the dead Matthew, is in the
tradition and at times the rhythm of classical flute song. The
poet begins from an iambic base—

> A village schoolmaster was he,
> With hair of glittering grey;
> As blithe a man as you could see
> On a spring holiday.

When the schoolmaster has been challenged to explain his "so
sad a sigh" and when his meditative effort begins, the spondees
throng into the verse:

> Yon cloud with that long purple cleft
> Brings fresh into my mind
> A day like this which I have left
> Full thirty years behind.

Then, the sigh having been explained and the identity of personal relationship asserted, again the trochees and the iambs are balanced to give the impression of an eternal poise:

> Matthew is in his grave, yet now,
> Methinks, I see him stand,
> As at that moment, with a bough
> Of wilding in his hand.

Similarly in *The Fountain:* as the poem goes from narration to meditation, it goes from the iambic of balladry to the spondaic or trochaic or dactylic of elegy. When Matthew is urged—

> "Sing here beneath the shade,
> That half-mad thing of witty rhymes
> Which you last April made!"—

and when he replies—

> "No check, no stay, this Streamlet fears!"—

or when, thinking back to his childhood, he observes that

> "the same sound is in my ears
> Which in those days I heard";

or when he grieves that

> "the wiser mind
> Mourns less for what age takes away
> Than what it leaves behind";

or, finally, when his witty rhymes cease with the conviction that time is demented and music is at a loss—

> the crazy old church-clock,
> And the bewildered chimes:

then we have heard echoes not only of balladry but also of flute song.

In the second edition of *Lyrical Ballads*, 1800, along with the

Lucy and Matthew elegies just described, we have the more elaborate stanzaic form of *Ellen Irwin*, the trochaic *To a Sexton* and *Song for the Wandering Jew*, the octosyllabic quatrains of *Matthew* (the *Address* on Matthew, similarly paced, with an occasional trimeter, was not published until 1842), the anapaestic *Farmer of Tilsbury Dale*, *Poor Susan*, and *Written in Germany*, and the decasyllabic *Hartleap Well*. Wordsworth was trying various possible patterns for his elegiac ballads. But in the tailed rhyme of *Ruth*, as in "Three years she grew," he had developed elegy as flute song to a point where it would lose its haunting similarity to the fourteen-syllabled minor line of the classical elegiac couplet. Thereafter, he would be found experimenting with the octosyllabic iambic quatrain of *A Poet's Epitaph* and thence would proceed to the pentameter of his sonnets and his blank verse or to those lyric stanzas in which Helen Darbishire has heard echoes of Elizabethan lyric. The shift from pure elegy to gnomic and epigrammatic form, or into the self-revelatory epistle or monologue, had been a tendency of classical elegy also. In Wordsworth's *Ruth*, although it is an elegiac love story rather than a lament, the meditations give point to the events; almost as if to acknowledge the development of poetic metaphor from pipe to flute, Wordsworth wrote of his forlorn maiden as follows:

> And, coming to the Banks of Tone,
> There did she rest; and dwell alone
> Under the greenwood tree . . .
> That oaten pipe of hers is mute
> Or thrown away; but with a flute
> Her loneliness she cheers.

"This flute, made of a hemlock stalk," was surely for Wordsworth as for Ruth the symbol of elegiac feeling.

According to the researches of Francis James Child (1882) and Bertrand Harris Bronson in his collection of *The Traditional Tunes of the Child Ballads*,[22] balladry was song and often

---

[22] Two vols.; Princeton, 1959–1962.

song and dance. Postponing to a later chapter any discussion of analogies actual or metaphorical in the culture of the later nineteenth and the twentieth centuries, we may again remind ourselves of the enterprise and social fortunes of flute song in its initial advance from Ionia to the western world. Not the sedentary harp—not even Coleridge's Aeolian harp, indolent and passive—not the lyre of Byron among the Romantics, not the unaccompanied verses of the Victorians will content the latter-day poetic imagination. Poetry in its renascence as in its youth reaches for the flute.

It was the flute that in antiquity accompanied almost every scene of life, public and private: festivals of Artemis and Dionysus, Jewish deathbeds, Roman oratory; Olympic chariot racing, Etruscan boxing, rowing at sea; the weddings, banquets, and funeral rites of all ancient culture.[23] However irrecoverable the actual melodies or rhythms of those flutes to whose tune Cleopatra's silver oars "kept stroke" and Antony's "Alexandrian feast" on Pompey's galley off Misenum reeled "till the world [went] round," the associations of the instrument in literature have pointed authoritatively to a distinct sort of personal or social feeling. This feeling runs the gamut of human experience from love to grief; and generally even if not invariably it arouses thought, speculative thinking as distinguished from that conceptual or logical thinking which is the province of gnomic poetry or discursive writing.

As a shepherd's pipe the flute underlies the Psalms of David and the Idylls of Theocritus; and those who have been delighted with the woodcuts in Spenser's *Shepheardes Calender* will have noticed the flutist or piper exhibited at the head of the April, August, and November Eclogues. Elegiac pastorals need a book of their own; yet the shepherd's pipe as a meditative rather than idyllic instrument can be briefly instanced in Blake's poet "Piping down the valleys wild, / Piping songs of pleasant glee" —songs which a child would weep to hear—and in Keats's

[23] Fitzgibbon, *op. cit.*, p. 10.

pipes which "Pipe to the spirit ditties of no tone," in his melodist "For ever piping songs for ever new."

In myriad such instances the metaphorical flute takes its place beside the metaphorical harp. There were "flowtours" in *The Romance of the Rose* (763) as Chaucer translated it, and some offside "discordaunce" from the Floytes of Wikket-Tungue; in *The Hous of Fame* the Father of English poetry heard music played not only on the harp by Orpheus, Orion, Chiron, the "Bret Glascurion," but piping on "many a flowte and liltyng horn, / And pipes made of grene corn." When, with more dignified rhythm, flute song became ethical and social criticism in Spenser's *Teares of the Muses*, Clio's "trump of gold," Euterpe's "warbling pipe," Calliope's "golden Clarion"—"all their learned instruments"—would be broken; and Erato would bid the gentle spirits in "Venus' silver bower" turn their eulogies "into elegies" to mourn the debasing of love.

To play a recorder, "this pipe," is "as easy as lying," says Hamlet; in it "is much music, excellent voice." The speculative Hamlet himself is, as a recorder, to be sounded from his lowest note to the top of his compass, but Rosencrantz and Guildenstern have no skill to play upon him. We may wonder who played the instruments in Milton's Hell when the fallen angels marched

> In perfect Phalanx to the Dorian mood
> Of Flutes and soft Recorders—

a passage echoing in Coleridge's *Religious Musings* (237–239) (about Benjamin Franklin's electric experiment):

> Such a phalanx ne'er
> Measured firm paces to the calming sound
> Of Spartan flute!

Shades of Tyrtaeus!

There is an "Essay on Elegies" printed in *The Universal Museum and Complete Magazine* (III, in 1767) and attributed by

Professor Arthur Sherbo to Dr. Johnson.[24] The Essay reveals
what was one characteristic argument of the eighteenth century
toward a more precise definition of elegy and its distinction
from pastoral and from ode. The elegiac muse is "the natural
companion of distress," her object being "the immediate feelings
of the heart." The author states that "elegy has often extended her
province, and the moral contemplations of the poet have worn
her melancholy garb"; he seems not to have known how wide

[24] See *Bulletin of the New York Public Library*, LXIII (January,
1959), 21–22. William Shenstone's "Prefatory Essay on Elegy" may have
been known to Wordsworth, who admired his *Schoolmistress*. Shenstone
says: "Elegy, in its true and genuine acceptation, includes a tender and
querulous idea; . . . it looks upon this as its peculiar characteristic, and
so long as this is thoroughly sustained, admits of a variety of subjects,
which by its manner of treating them it renders its own." Again, "There
is a truly virtuous pleasure connected with many pensive contemplations, which it is the province and excellency of Elegy to enforce." I
quote from *The Works of the British Poets with Lives of the Authors*,
by Ezekiel Sanford, Vol. XXIV (Philadelphia, 1819). Shenstone dis-
approved of heroic couplets for elegy; he approved of heroic metre
with alternate rhyme. His lines, however, are burdened with the dissyllabic adjectives which only Gray might successfully assimilate. His
Delia and Cynthia echo the loves of Tibullus and Propertius, although
the total effect of his elegies is far from classical in spite of his "doric
pipe" and "vocal reed." A decade after Gray's *Elegy* (1751) James
Beattie's *Triumph of Melancholy* with another Delia appeared in the
heroic metre with alternate rhyme. Beattie also wrote elegies in the
heroic couplet. Wordsworth was an admiring reader of both poets;
fortunately for his elegies he disregarded their metrical patterns for the
ballad measure nearer to the flute song of antiquity. Possibly, too, the
flute he heard as a boy over the waters of Windermere still echoed in
his ears (*Prelude* II, 164–174). He would recall Goldsmith's tour, flute
in hand, through Flanders, France, and Italy in 1756. In 1790 he himself
had listened to "amourous music" on Lake Como and to the lulling
"pastoral pipes" of the Swiss; although in his account of the tour he
quoted the " 'Spartan fife' " from Collins and had M. Ramond in mind
for a reference to the traces of "primaeval Man" marching "with his
flute, his book, and sword," his experience with pipe and flute was substantial as well as literary (*Descriptive Sketches*, 1793, pp. 115, 277,
331, 529–533).

and diverse an area she originally commanded. He notes that
after Mr. Gray alternate rhyme has been used, but he allows
that "the couplet is equally proper for this kind of poetry." He
adds, "Nor shall I doubt to place our English ballads such as
have been written by Rowe, Gay, and the natural, easy Shenstone, in the rank of Elegy." Later in this book we shall have
occasion to relate Wordsworth's Lucy poems to ballads of the
eighteenth century. Here we may underline the astuteness of
the essayist in detecting the association between balladry and
elegiac poetry. "In short, whatever the subject is, the language
of this species [elegy] should be simple and unaffected, the
thoughts natural and pathetic, and the numbers flowing and
harmonious."

At the end of the eighteenth century the author of *John
Gilpin* and the Olney Hymns is an especially happy instance
of such language, thoughts, and numbers. Cowper died two
years after *The Ancient Mariner* was published. In training,
temper, and accomplishment he may be compared with his two
more famous successors: all three were elegists in the best sense
of the word, that is, meditative or speculative poets. In no respect are they more alike than in their fondness for the accents
of balladry, in particular the common measure. Why, then, does
Cowper fail to suggest the magical and lilting rhythms of *The
Ancient Mariner*? He is faithfully and monotonously iambic.
The rare trochees and rarer spondees do not often suffice to lift
his homely fables out of the submissively meditative pattern into
speculation for its own sake. Yet no poet was more familiar
with classical elegy. He had translated Milton's Latin *Elegies*,
but into heroic couplets. In his translations from the classics now
and again he used the common measure which we have compared with the minor line of the elegiac distich; and in his
translation of Moschus teaching Cupid we, too, learn

> How reed to reed Pan first with osier bound,
> How Pallas form'd the pipe of softest sound,

> How Hermes gave the lute, and how the quire
> Of Phoebus owe to Phoebus' self the lyre.

Among the gods, then, it is Pan and Pallas who sponsor flute song, leaving the harmonious lyric to Hermes and Phoebus.

It remains only for us to ask what elegy gives to literature corresponding to the gift of the flute to the orchestra. The answer comes by way of opera: in *Isis*, Lully's lament of Pan for the death of Syrinx; Jacopo Peri's *Eurydice;* Gluck's *Orpheo* or Mozart's *Magic Flute.* Whether the flute serves to play an obligato for song or cantata of Bach or Handel or Haydn or itself to sing as member of the choral orchestra, it is archetypically elegiac. Bach's organ was actually a chorus of flutes. One modern composer, Dr. Ermanno Comparetti, writes that the flute gives a "velvety, weightless quality for a scene of serenity, beauty, reflection; . . . it represents . . . celestial moods." Other composers and critics have used similar epithets: elegant, stately, gracious, limpidly sweet and clear, soft, passionate, mellifluous; in the lower register, mournful, desolate, mysterious; in the middle register, mild, plaintive, poetic, melancholy; in the upper register, brilliant, bright, gay, larklike. Are there, then, poems for which these adjectives would be likewise appropriate? Is there, then, some such quality or strain in literature, too?

But elegy is more than flute song. We must go on.

CHAPTER II

The Form of Elegy:
Anagnorisis

TO the Greeks we refer not only for *elegy* as flute song but for many other precise generic terms: *drama* and *epic, idyll* and *character, bucolic* and *georgic,* and *lyric.* Whenever the Greek word is familiar, it serves our critical purposes better than its Latin equivalent, the edges of which are apt to be blunted by non-literary usage. *Rhetoric,* for instance, is a more exact term than "composition" or "discourse" or "oratory"; *praxis,* than "action"; *mythos,* than "plot." Indeed, in the terminology for rhetorical and poetical devices elaborated by Latin grammarians the Greek terms are sometimes the best or only ones we have: *metaphor, metonymy, synecdoche, irony,* the leading *tropes;* not to mention *hyperbole* and *litotes,* and such rare birds as *catachresis* and *homoeoteleuton.* Surely *mimesis* is a more telling name for poetry than "imitation." And what should we do without *symbol?*

Therefore, we hope to be justified in borrowing from the Greek poetics for convenient use in our study of elegy the word *anagnorisis,* variously translated as "recognition," "revelation," "discovery," or "disclosure." One primary instance of *anagnorisis* can be cited from Aristotle's *Poetics,* where it is associated with the *peripeteia* in order to assist a mere change of fortune into an involved action. The lexical meaning of ἀναγνωρίζειν is given as "to recognize or come to the knowledge of a person or thing" (for drama, "so as to produce a dénouement"), "to reveal oneself," "to cause to recognize," "to recognize a rule in a new instance." So wide a range of possible applications recommends it to serve us as well as it served the Greeks.

For there is a vast body of revelatory and self-revelatory literature both classical and modern needing more objective analysis. This body forms a noble tradition all the way from Greek queries about the nature of man and society, Latin probings into the nature of love, and Christian search for the Divine Nature, as well as through the mazes of romantic introspection and into the jungle of contemporary autobiographical writing. What does all this have in common?

Judging from the evidence to be offered in these essays, the common factor in speculative poetry is its outcome in discovery; and thus its distinctive trait is *anagnorisis*. *Anagnorisis* would be a mere synonym for discovery were it not for Aristotle's elaboration: discoveries are made by mark or token, arbitrarily by announcement, through the display of feelings aroused by memory, by reason or inference, fictitiously by false inference or intended deceit, or—best of all—out of the nature of previous events or antecedent discoveries (*Poetics*, XVI). His category is most often employed by students of drama; but although *anagnorisis* crowns the plot of dramatic and epic poetry and rewards the logic of didactic poetry, it is the very goal of elegiac poetry, determining the whole precedure.

The usual symbol of such poetry is light out of darkness. Moreover, whereas drama and epic are primarily concerned with action and didactic poetry with dogma, elegy is the poetry of skeptical and revelatory vision for its own sake, satisfying the hunger of man to see, to know, to understand. Whether the reader be purged or indoctrinated, he must be enlightened. In its latest as in its earliest guise elegy labors toward human truth as its end in view.

Three Greek verbs help us to a homemade distinction between the kinds of vision used actually and metaphorically by poets in their apprehension of light.

First, ἰδεῖν, meaning to perceive or observe, and thus fathering idyllic, imagist, and symbolic poetry with its ideas (ἰδέαι) as visual impressions. Hence, too, come visions, what the eye sees or the mind thinks is seen or imagines as possible to be seen.

Second, there is θεωρεῖν, to see such particular sights in their universal relationship or enhanced association: witness the encyclopedias of wise men, the summaries and epitomes of theologians, the hypotheses of scientists and the concepts of metaphysicians, and ultimately the philological schemata of critics. Akin to such theoretic patterns are the efforts of cosmological poets from Lucretius and John of Patmos on, efforts to consider such *scibilia* and to transform them into memorable shapes. But only when these shapes appear aesthetically valid to writers or readers do they become successful gnomic poetry.

Third, σκοπεῖν, σκέπτεσθαι, which means to peer into. This is not only the procedure of the astronomer with his telescope and the physician with his stethoscope and fluoroscope and the biologist with his microscope, but of the imaginative thinker whose intellectual eye ranges rebelliously through universal darkness toward some new scintilla of light from a world of yet undiscovered meaning and value. Such skeptical vision is the characteristic trait of the elegist as distinct from the idyllist or the theorist.

These functions of the eye do not, of course, dictate to the idyllic, the gnomic, or the elegiac poet his respective forms; yet they record as variously opportune for his creative enterprise what is seen as the result of a mode of seeing. Upon this he must ultimately work his own will in the expression of poems individually as well as formally distinct.

Next, in order to define our immediate problem, let us consider what kinds of *anagnorisis* result from the exercise of these three modes of vision. First, *Discovery of likeness or unlikeness:*

This phenomenon is like that phenomenon, actual or imagined. Out of such comparable appearances arises the fabric of correspondences furnishing a poet's metaphors all the way from Mimnermus to Baudelaire and Yeats. Here elegy finds itself associated with idyll.

Second, *Discovery of idea:* This or that actual phenomenon or these or those actual phenomena leads or lead to an abstraction or noumenon resident above, beyond, or within the world of concrete particulars. Such a discovery, however otherwise richly freighted or clearly pointed, makes use of abstract nouns chiefly. These abstract nouns may be personified or allegorized or symbolized: witness the δίκη, Justice, of Solon or Plato; the Joy of the early Romanticists; the Beauty of the Symbolists, and Rilke's "Death, that friendly Death." Here elegy is associated with gnomic poetry.

Third, *Discovery of identity and community:* This is this and none other, with all its pertinent associations in and out of space and time. Propertius discovers that Cynthia is Cynthia even after death and that their love is naught else but itself. Discovery of identity is properly recognition, equating the name and the thing or revealing the thing in the name: οὗτος ἐκεῖνος, this is the very man. "Rabboni!" And, again Rilke: "Erde, du liebe." "Earth, you darling!" Therewith the springs of feeling are opened and elegy becomes lyric.

"Oh! the difference to me!" This cry is the index of lyrical elegy. Whether the feeling of the elegist follows an event or accompanies an entreaty or argument, whether it is called forth by a situation or a character, it is above all personal. Nevertheless, elegy does not symbolize itself as feeling alone; it is a procedural form and must get on with its task of thought. Nor does it operate through the abstract propositions and logical enthymemes of gnomic poetry; it is speculative rather than sententious. It is not mere reverie or musing. And although it is akin to autobiography, epistle, and dramatic monologue or dialogue and shares their revelatory nature, its emotions and passions

spark and propel thought rather toward vision than toward action. In short, the difference which is "the difference to me,"
however often it may appear to be an inconclusive regret or a
riddling premise, always implies that the poet himself is sincerely
and deeply enough concerned to set his wits to work.

In its ardors, its speculations, and its discoveries elegiac literature is often a challenge to accepted habits and trite patterns;
the energy that goes into elegiac form has always been powerful, sometimes fierce or wayward. So was it in Ionia with the
first three known Greek elegists at the beginning and into the
middle of the seventh century B.C. From what is left of their
writing we observe that Archilochus poked fun at heroic pre-
tensions and resisted military routine; Callinus of Ephesus scorned
the slack, lazy young men of his city; and Mimnermus of
Colophon, worrying about painful old age, γῆρας ὀδυνηρὸν καὶ
ἀργαλέον,[1] mourned because the generations of men flourish and
vanish as leaves in the rays of the sunlight. Youth, the fruit of
the tree, ἥβης καρπός, is ripe only so long as it takes the sun to
flash across the earth to its setting—notice thus early the solar
image, ὅσον τ᾽ ἐπὶ γῆν κίδναται ἠέλιος. Energy on its way from
heat to revelatory light will be the prevailing metaphor of elegiac
musing and always under the temptation to be easily satisfied
with mere creature warmth. Witness Mimnermus again, whose
answer to seasonal transience was casual pleasure, τὴν σαυτοῦ
φρένα τέρπε, satisfy your own desires; and hence his metaphorical tree is seen to provide scions for the spreading foliage of
self-indulgence in pleasure and lamentation ever after him. His
verses were commended by Propertius, the most ardent of the
Latin elegiac writers, and they anticipate our own prolific he-
donism.

In those post-Homeric centuries of social change, when life

---

[1] Greek phrases are quoted from *Anthologia Lyrica*, ed. Eduardus
Hiller and O. Crusius (Leipzig, 1913). Translations from the Greek are
my own. Greek text and translation are conveniently accessible in *Elegy
and Iambus*, edited and translated for the Loeb Classical Library in two
volumes by J. M. Edmonds (London and New York, 1931).

was being channeled variously into new forms both artistic and civic, elegy made the most Protean literary adjustment. Just because it considered the intimate affairs of mankind on the battlefield behind the lines, in the banquet hall between the courses, and in the agora or market place after the speeches, it became the matrix of all kinds of rebellious comment. Epic poetry and epinicial ode came to rest in their respective public domains under the care of professional rhapsode and choragos; drama and philosophy were on their way to take over the amphitheater and the academy. Meanwhile elegiac poetry was busily at work from Ionia to Sparta to Athens, shaping itself as the speech of the poet to a special audience on an urgent matter. As with us in a culture where radio and press are paid to relay the events of hot and cold war and athletic peace, and entertainers are paid to amuse or deceive us, and scholars are paid to teach us but poets must still go hungry if they speak their minds to their intellectual cronies, likewise with the wandering Archilochus and his Ionian fellows and followers while they improvised their topical verses. In art there is always an irreducible minimum, the meditations of him whom now we might call the common man, were he not so uncommon.

But the organizing principle was at work toward *anagnorisis.* The Spartan Tyrtaeus for whom εὐνομίη, Good Order, was a passion, helped to intensify the repute in elegy of ἀρετή, Manly Virtue, and to enhance the notion of the Good Man, ἀνὴρ ἀγαθός, whom many centuries later Wordsworth would entitle "the Happy Warrior." Rebuking the shirker, exhorting the citizen, preaching discipline, and thus winning the Second Messenian War, Tyrtaeus is the earliest forerunner of such as Wordsworth in the Napoleonic era and that host of western writers who aroused or interpreted a patriotic citizenry during the First and Second World Wars. And, most notably, although Solon of Athens enjoyed the works of Aphrodite, ἔργα κυπρογενοῦς, of Dionysus, and of the Muses, the ardors of love and wine and verse were not enough for him; he loved politics, too. And the voicing of this love in the earliest poetry Athens produced illustrates the first great reach of the elegiac imagination from the activities whereby mankind survives to the exercises through which humanity prevails. Singing, Solon directs his well-ordered words against folly, pride, excess, bigheadedness, μέγαν νόον, disorder, δυσνομίη, baseness, κακότητα. Through the Muses he begs fortune, a good name, wealth honestly gained, and contentment; and even as he warns that the mind of the immortals is not to be probed by mortals, he gives honor to the craftsman, poet, seer, and physician, because their knowledge is trustworthy and their motives are unselfish. Solon's passion for justice and rightdoing, δίκη, informed his elegies with those ethical and political issues of which Greek culture is the abiding poetical instance, an elegy of elegies, second only to the meditations of Christendom. Thanks in no small part to the concern of Tyrtaeus and Solon, Hellas became the scene of the sternest conflict, the most enduring love, and the noblest vision of the pagan world. The Greek *anagnorisis* had been honestly earned.

Phoebus himself had made his wishes clear to the city—Φοῖβος γὰρ περὶ τῶν ὧδ' ἀνέφηνε πόλει—and the sun god was a hard taskmaster. In the *Nanno* of Mimnermus, six of whose few surviving verses mention the sun, we are reminded that Ἥλιος is destined to labor all his days, πόνον ἔλλαχεν ἤματα πάτν. And from the *Smyrneis* of the same poet a papyrus commentary quotes lines saying of a warrior that he ran forward like a swift sunbeam, ὅτ' αὐγῇσιν φέρετ' εἴκελος ἠελίοιο. In this same energetic temper at Sparta, Tyrtaeus was feverishly anxious to interrogate doctrine and to debate alternatives: what will be victorious? what will be fitting?

Originally, then, the elegy was no mere lament, not even when it praised the dead. Sing as elegists might about doleful miseries and cureless ills, κήδεα στονόεντα καὶ ἀνήκεστα κακά—a partial concern unhappily emphasized by the Alexandrians and Romans and given currency by Horace and Dante—their prime hero was rather (in the words of Callinus when Ephesus was attacked by the Cimmerians) a lofty tower to all who looked upon him, πύργον . . . ἐν ὀφθαλμοῖσιν. And by the same token, the first *anagnorisis* or discovery of Ionian elegy was of the worth and daring of the human spirit. Quickly throw off this womanish sorrow, γυναικεῖον πένθος, exhorted Archilochus, and bear up, dare to hold out, τλῆτε.

While Solon was, in our phrase, sublimating courage and love by giving them a social and political connotation, Xenophanes, a countryman of Mimnermus but exiled from his native Colophon, used elegiac distichs to challenge the anthropomorphic religious tradition. In a period of uncertainty and surmise the elegist, too, must work toward a new vision of truth. That Xenophanes became and remained an agnostic among believers illustrates the skeptical power of the elegiac imagination. Current ideas of physical health he extended in the direction of their moral analogues: for instance, his thought leapt from cleanliness of body to purity of habit. This advance from one level of experience to another furthered the metaphorical scope and daring of elegy and in the refinement of its thought bore witness to heightened energy. Henceforth, the ἀρετή of the warrior and athlete would bow to the ἀρετή of the citizen and poet. The spur of Phoebus still goaded the elegist, but on from ardor to enlightenment. In his *Lives of the Philosophers* Diogenes Laertius says that Xenophanes is mentioned by Timon as making a God unlike man and more thoughtful than thought, νοερώτερον ἠὲ νόημα.

Sir Maurice Bowra[2] observes that the elegiac couplets of Xenophanes, as distinguished from his hexameters, were concerned "more with feelings . . . than with views, more with the application of principles than with principles themselves." Thus, even within the rudiments of elegy are displayed what Samuel Taylor Coleridge in 1794 called "energic Reason and a shaping mind."[3] And we foresee that ritual, dealing with life and death and hence in its nature partly elegiac, will always need the meditative Muse to purify and exalt its ceremonials, both its agonies and its triumphs. In the very highest reaches

[2] Bowra, *Early Greek Elegists*, p. 107.   [3] *Lines on a Friend*, 40.

of literature the elegist must with undiminished zeal go on to provide the liturgy with what Wordsworth in 1822 described as "the intensities of hope and fear . . . and passionate exercise of lofty thoughts." [4]

In this busy future for elegiac meditation, so clearly foreshadowed in the distichs of Xenophanes, poets would never forget what he told them of a subjective kind of God and a universe fully alive, which sees all over, thinks all over, hears all over, οὖλος ὁρᾷ, οὖλος δὲ νοεῖ, οὖλος δέ τ' ἀκούει. Nor is it strange that while Ionian poetry was thus struggling toward wholeness of sight and sound and thought, Ionian physicists were eager to discover what was the primary substance of things. In this kindred effort, says Sir Maurice, "prose was born." [5] The evidence that early discursive verse and discursive prose were siblings, alike creations of the speculative and theoretic mind, justifies a hope that in our time as well critics will not insist upon their divorce. For both of them discovery is the aim, the theme, and the method. Every curious century and every attempt to reduce to order and meaning whatever it is that sees all over, thinks all over, and hears all over harks back for its personal values to the daring thought of Xenophanes, ἐμὴν φροντίδα.

The elegies gathered under the name of Theognis early in the fifth century B.C. reveal the gloom rather than the sunshine of cultural shift; the writers have become skeptical of skeptics, but the mood is still anxious and eager. It may be that, even as elegy is always in danger of abandoning itself to the warmth of desire or the comfort of sorrow, it is continually tempted by the security of stock generalizations: maxims, epigrams, and other furniture of gnomic or didactic writing. Moreover, assumptions and principles stiffening into doctrine can better be handed down from father to son or from mentor to disciple. Witness the authentic poems of Theognis himself, which exhort his young friend Cyrnus to maintain the aristocratic code, a conservative warning that would seem to blunt the characteristic drive of elegiac meditation toward always better things—better men,

[4] *Ecclesiastical Sonnets* 3.19.1–3.   [5] Bowra, *op. cit.*, p. 107.

better states, better hypotheses, truer truth. But when the shrewd counsel of the older friend to the young one is shaken by the facts of change and infidelity, the penetrating eye does not rest: "Thou hast not deceived me, lad; for I can see right through thee," γάρ σε διώμμαι.

This crux of disillusionment after good advice would be repeated many times in many lands, wherever and whenever poets, growing wise, would grow cautious and therefore be contemned as lost leaders; but now and again Theognis transcended his maxims, hoping for praise from ever new men, to the music of the clear-sounding flute, αυλίσκοισι λιγυφθόγγοις. Out of arbitrary doctrine the poet comes into the optative mood and dares to star not only Cyrnus but elegy itself among the constellated Muses, high over the boundless sea and the whole land. This spurt of passion with a resultant lift of the spirit is another salient feature of Greek elegy and lends charm to the codes it recommends and the persons it stellifies. The Graces of Theognis who sang at the wedding of Cadmus, "What is fair is dear, and what is not fair is not dear," are of a kind with the angels of Wordsworth's *Vernal Ode* (1817), bearing witness that what was fair in Antiquity is still fair today.

> Mortals, rejoice! The very Angels quit
> Their mansions unsusceptible of change,
> Amid your pleasant bowers to sit,
> And through your sweet vicissitudes to range.

Other bright mediating forms in British elegy from the phoenix in Old English poetry to the phoenix of Yeats and Lawrence do not come much short of epiphanies; and the angels of Rilke and Alberti still range through our sweet and bitter vicissitudes.

Of the Greek elegists, Wordsworth is most explicit about him whom he called "pure Simonides,"

> the tenderest Poet that could be,
> Who sang in ancient Greece his moving lay.[6]

[6] "I find it written" 1, 12–13 (1803); *Upon the Same Occasion,* 54 (1819); *Essay on Epitaphs* (1810). Poetical kinship of Simonides and

Although Simonides in the fifth century B.C. used the elegiac distich frequently in reference to the dead, death is rarely conceptionalized by him or abstracted from person or event; through many of his sepulchral epitaphs the dead man speaks in his proper person, with life's normal accent. The best of the Greek memorial epigrams are not dirges; as in the Lucy and Matthew poems of Wordsworth many centuries later, their tenderness has been transformed into human ethos. Latent pathos becomes a dauntless imperative: supremely in the eleven famous words on the tomb of the Spartans slain at Thermopylae, where in spite of disaster the weapon seemingly fallen from the hand of the dead warrior reaches its target through the inscription of the living poet:

> ὦ ξεῖν', ἀγγέλλειν Λακεδαιμονίοις, ὅτι τῇδε
> κείμεθα, τοῖς κείνων ῥήμασι πειθόμενοι.

Wordsworth has been noted by J. W. Mackail, *Lectures on Greek Poetry* (London, 1926), pp. 124–125. What remains of the poetry of Simonides is to be found in the Loeb Classical Library, *Lyra Graeca*, trans. and ed. J. M. Edmonds (London and New York, 1931), pp. 246–417. Whether Wordsworth knew Simonides by repute through Theocritus or Plutarch or Quintilian or had read him in some version of the Anthology, for instance, the *Analecta* of R. F. P. Brunck, he echoes the judgment of Theocritus that the Cean is a divinely inspired singer, θεῖος ἀοιδὸς ὁ Κήϊος; and he agrees with the phrase of Plutarch, ὁ τῶν μελῶν ποιητής, and with the description by Quintilian, *iucunditate quadam commendari potest; praecipua tamen eius in commovenda miseratione virtus, ut quidam in hac eum parte omnibus eius operis auctoribus praeferant* (*Lyra Graeca*, II, 254, 260, 270–272). Wordsworth's copy of John Chetwind's *Anthologia Historica* carries the familiar anecdote (p. 447): "Simonides having buried a dead body whom he found on the shore, was admonished by him, that he should not sail the next day. He did not, but saw his company drowned." In gratitude Simonides wrote (*Lyra Graeca*, II, 374):

> Οὗτος ὁ τοῦ Κείοιο Σιμωνίδεω ἐστὶ σαωτήρ,
> ὃς καὶ τεθνηὼς ζῶντ' ἀπέδωκε χάριν.

Here lies the savior of Simonides of Ceos. Even when dead he repaid the kindness of the living.

>Go, passer-by, tell our tale to our Lacedemonian kinsmen:
>Here we lie, true to their laws; just as they bade, we obey.

Those Athenians who have striven to set freedom on the heights of Hellas lie low at Platea; but their renown does not grow old, οὐδὲ τεθνᾶσι θανόντες. And in the epitaphs for the Greeks dead at Marathon that Hellas might not be enslaved, the eagle-eyed future emerges once again in true elegiac fashion from the dedication and struggle of the now ashen past. So it had been ever since Tyrtaeus sang: "Although the hero is underground, he is reborn deathless," ἀλλ᾽ ὑπὸ γῆς περ ἐὼν γίγνεται ἀθάνατος.

Nevertheless, the epigrammatic form of the elegiac inscriptions and epitaphs of Simonides illustrates the tendency of all speculative writing to become aphoristic: "Dying they died not, for the manly worth that took them down to the house of Hades leads them up again in honor"—the strong hope demands a valid reason. Thus always, as years burden the spirits of long-lived poets, the "moving lay" and the vivid utterance are followed by fruitful lesson or tidy maxim. Such is the revelatory pattern of many of Wordsworth's sonnets:

>Say what is honour? 'T is the finest sense
>Of justice which the mind can frame;

"The Form remains, the Function never dies" of "Afterthought" at the end of *The River Duddon;* and throughout the *Ecclesiastical Sonnets,* never more explicitly than in "Aspects of Christianity in America":

>Transcendent over time, unbound by place,
>Concord and Charity in circles move.

Honor, Justice, Form, Function, Concord, Charity: from the ancient to the modern world travel what are sometimes called in reference to the ethical universals of classical culture "hypostatized abstracts." [7]

[7] T. B. L. Webster, *Art and Literature in Fourth Century Athens* (London, 1956), pp. 8–9.

In its Ionian origin elegy had been neither gnomic nor didactic, neither rhetoric nor dialectic; but it had given energy to all forms by virtue of its unfailing drive into the realm of thought and its power to transcend past, present, and future. In the writings of the more philosophical elegists it led away from old habits and records of personal feeling in war and feast, in love and death, toward intensely curious speculations about the whole fabric of human relationship. That elegy on its dynamic way from Ionia to Sparta to Athens to Alexandria was lifted into serene poise by the tender poet of Ceos before it came to rest in "Alexandrianism" helps us to understand not only Wordsworth's advance from elegiac ballads to sonnets and sententious or dialectic blank verse but also, in a nineteenth century A.D. which resembled somewhat the fourth century B.C., the decline from "Romanticism" to "Victorianism."

And we may make yet another cross reference to the nineteenth century A.D. when we read that at the beginning of the fourth century B.C. "the vital movement of intelligence and imagination passed into prose" [8]—the prose of orators, historians, scholars, scientists, philosophers, critics, essayists, writers of dialogue and comedy. Thereupon, in the third century B.C., after Athens had been subjected to a powerful new Macedonia, elegy was encouraged to revert to its prior function, becoming anew the foster mother of whatever "dealt or professed to deal, with life . . . directly." [9] Not less surely in the times of Victoria, the elegist would become a realist. From the prose speculations of Carlyle, for instance, or the elegiac adventures of Newman and Arnold, or the researches of Spencer and Darwin and Huxley and Mill, English literature would go on to the riddling actualities of Hardy and the seemingly actual fables of Shaw. Finally, we may compare the new movements burgeoning in France and England at our modern *fin de siècle* with the elegiac development at the end of Antiquity under the supervision of scholars centered at the great Alexandrian library of Callimachus,

[8] See Mackail, *op. cit.*, p. 178.   [9] *Ibid.*, p. 205.

himself in the tradition of the elegists Antimachus of Colophon and Philetus of Cos. The distichs of Callimachus of Alexandria by way of the Greek teachers of Augustan Rome would echo in the distichs of Catullus and Propertius and re-echo in the poems of Arnold and Clough

However frequently such future Latin or English elegy might clarify its observations with *epyllia*, little stories, and *idyllia*, little sketches of nature or human character, it would not develop into either epic or idyll. However preoccupied it might be with amorous feeling, it would resist the temptation to sing only. Its comment might often be aphoristic but its personal solicitude inclined it to a skeptical, not a dogmatic procedure. In its restless and discursive moods during the Augustan epoch at Rome and the Victorian period in England, as in the earliest Ionic and the latest Hellenistic periods, elegy went on trying to keep poetry in touch with life. Indeed the elegiac imagination may be recognized most surely whenever the words of literature walk very straight ahead, *prorsus,* or turn their comings and goings, *versus,* most sparely and regularly. That will be a sign that the writer is, as we have pointed out, deeply concerned, sincerely curious.

Of all the many instances of concern in literature, that of the poet for his beloved is likely to seem most intense, and the discoveries of one person about the personality of another person, about personality itself, are most likely to lift poetry above lyric or idyll or epyll. Here elegy impinges upon and lends its characteristic energy, its warmth and light, to the epistle and the dramatic monologue. In such verses as were composed about the fires of Venus (*Veneris ignes*) and man as a flame (*ignis homost*) [10] in that halcyon dawn when humankind was poised between its pagan past and its Christian future, the Latin elegists

---

[10] For phrases quoted from Aeditius and Licinus, forerunners of Catullus, see Elizabeth Hazelton Haight, *Romance in the Latin Elegiac Poets* (New York, 1932), pp. 17, 19; Archibald A. Day, *The Origins of the Latin Love-Elegy* (Oxford, 1938), pp. 102–106.

probed the personality of lover and beloved as relentlessly and
deftly as do the best writers of our own curious and facile pseudopagan days. The awkward Polonian term used by some classical scholars—"subjective-erotic elegy"—does scant justice to the
poetry, say, of Sextus Propertius.[11]

In our estimate of Wordsworth's elegiac writing we may pass
by the tempestuous Catullus, who hated and loved (*odi et amo*),
the delicately sentimental Tibullus, and him whom Propertius
called lascivious Ovid, because already we are prepossessed by
the notoriety of their themes. Let us, rather, search for the form
of Latin elegy in the four *Libri* about Cynthia, there to discover what elegiac secrets Propertius knew when he transformed physical desire so memorably into personal truth. More
than Lesbia, Delia, or Corinna, Cynthia on the Tiber resembles
her better-known contemporary, Cleopatra on the Nile, as what
Shakespeare would call a "lass unparallel'd." Lacking the lofty
associations of the Christian maid and mother and the other-
worldliness of the Dantean Beatrice and the ethical propriety of
the classical Penelopes and Cornelias, the unwed Roman courte-
san so variously subject to the indignities of time stands out with
unforgettable energy and brilliance at the closing of the portals
of the pagan world. Another ordinary harlot? No, says her
lover, Troy might fitlier have burned for Cynthia than for
Helen.

How did Propertius work to this end? [12] First, his concern
is undeviating, no matter how fickle his actions. We are never in
doubt, because he is never in doubt, that, in spite of breaches

[11] In *Homage to Sextus Propertius* (1934) and *Mauberley* Ezra Pound
for our own country echoes this Latin poet.

[12] The text of Propertius is quoted from the edition of H. E. Butler,
the Loeb Classical Library (Cambridge, Mass., 1952). The catalogue of
Wordsworth's library (*Transactions of the Wordsworth Society*, No.
6, pp. 247, 251) lists editions of the Latin elegists in his possession,
including the elegies of Propertius. Our present knowledge of the
elegiac ancestry of Propertius is admirably set forth in *The Latin Love
Elegy*, by Georg Luck (London, 1959), especially Chaps. I–III.

in her faith and in his, for him she is the incomparable one. She is no ideal lady; she is forever Cynthia with her flaws and graces upon her. Like the moon for whom she is named, she has her phases; but when she is most radiant it is because she has dissipated all the miasmic regrets and fruitless complaints with which lesser ladies are beclouded by lesser poets. *Sed tamen obsistam* (II, xxv, 15) is the burden of her lover's elegiac song. *Huius ero vivus, mortuus huius ero* (II, xv, 36). *Ultima talis erit quae mea prima fides* (II, xx, 34). This is no temporary resolve; it is the principle of the lover's being: *mi fortuna aliquid semper amare dedit* (II, xii, 18). We must note, too, that such concentration on his sole beloved allows a gradual refinement in his elegiac procedure. While he meditates upon her beauty, he will probe into her nature, her inner, even her inmost truth. Thus he supplies his poems with an elegiac action distinct from dramatic action but not less cogent.

Briefly stated, but to be illustrated at greater length, the steps in his procedure are four. In Book I, Cynthia is revealed as an actual person; in Book II, as a literary theme; in Book III, as a particular among universals; in Book IV, by way of a memory and a dream, as her eternal self. Within the clarifying and intensifying focus of the lover's thought we behold the form of Cynthia, yes, but also the form of the elegiac imagination. The object to be contemplated is challenged by the subject contemplating it until, in a series of revelations, *anagnorises*, we are shown its actual, its symbolic, its representative, and, at last, its quintessential nature. For this reason the poet must frame a constantly more rigorous test for the object of his love.

Meeting Cynthia in Book I, the *Cynthia monobiblos* (ca. 26 B.C.), at once we have the shock of actuality. Almost two millennia before Wordsworth saw Lucy as a lady of Nature's own, with natural impulses and natural restraints, vital, stately, silent yet sportive and gleeful, graceful, fair as a star yet fresh as a rose in June, Propertius had seen within his Cynthia a natural woman rather than the sophisticated artifice she appeared to others. He did not so much wish to say "my mistress goes forth with her hair beautifully dressed, clad in Coan silk, fragrant with myrrh of Orontes" as "why does she need to spoil her natural beauty with anything money can buy?" *Crede mihi*, believe me, *non ulla tua est medicina figurae*, nothing can improve your good looks. Love himself is not in love with make-up. Wild ivy is the more fair, arbutus from lonely caverns is the lovelier, brooks flow the more alluringly over nature's pebbles. No art helps birds to sing more sweetly. Then, in a series of those negations by which every artist is helped to his affirmation: not by art did Phoebe win Castor or Hilaira, Pollux.

Rarely does Propertius make a picture of Cynthia, a still life, an amorous idyll; he will have us attend to her matchless energy. When she is startled from sleep by the sedulous moon to look upon his drunkenness, she comes alive like a fury to scorn him because he arrives languid when the stars are wan, *exactis sideribus*. Or she interrupts him at his banquet with other women, who flee from her anger with torn hair and tunics in disarray (IV, viii, 61). She is not wont to be angry gently, *molliter irasci non solet* (I, v, 8); but when she bids him stay, it is scarcely worth his while to study in Athens or grow rich in Asia.

Theirs is no merely physical passion. The poet is not content to show her whiteness, her hair, her eyes; he values more her dancing, her lyre-playing, her versifying. She is a *docta puella;* she likes to study and converse; but above her Socratic wisdom, above her power to explain the causes of things, above her songs sung to the Athenian lyre, her lover values in a scale of ascending graces her sophistication in love.

With every experience of her there is a new discovery. From her tears he learns the cost of his infidelity; and from his own suffering he becomes aware that what gives pain can also inspire poetry. From his success in love—*Cynthia rara mea est* (I, viii A, 42)—he discovers that possession brings on ever more bitter slavery: *acrius illa subit, . . . si qua tua est* (I, ix, 26). Love's doctrine from the experience of love is no slight thing: *non nihil egit Amor* (I, x, 20). These discoveries are not Christian; but we think ahead to Abelard and his shining Heloise and to the lovers of Provence.

From such emotional discipline, with the heightened awareness it brings, the lover must face a sterner ordeal in the accidents of space and time. Distance—Cynthia absent at Baiae—causes him to fear; a journey can change a woman's heart, *mutat via longa puella* (I, xii, 11). She is even farther away when she bars her door against him, but a barred door confirms his devotion. Dismay over her intrigues with other men compels self-examination. When thoughts of death intrude, he resolves that even in the dark underworld he shall be known as Cynthia's lover, *semper tua dicar imago* (I, xix, 11). Yet, recognizing the limitations of this world and the inadequacies of all man-made otherworlds, the Latin elegist will not deprive death itself of its actuality: bone will grind on mingled bone in that last embrace. Thus a great love crosses the boundary of death, spurns the shores of destiny, *traicit et fati litora magnus amor* (I, xix, 12).

No modern writer, not even Eliot, has more ably demolished space or driven time closer to the verge of eternity (II, xxi, 19–20):

> Nos quocumque loco, nos omni tempore tecum
> sive aegra pariter sive valente sumus.

In every place, at every hour, in sickness and in health! One troth, one day will set the lovers free, *ambos una fides . . . una dies* (II, xx, 18). Ends are as unnecessary as beginnings, *Cynthia prima fuit, Cynthia finis erit* (I, xii, 20). Faithful love transcends time, *non satis est ullo tempore longus amor* (I, xix, 26). Thus ends a book which began with the cry of woe, *miserum me!*

What, then, is left for the elegist to do once the *Cynthia monobiblos* has been composed?

In a second chastening or humiliating book, *turpis . . . liber*

alter (Book II, *ca.* 24–23 B.C.), he starts off with a reference to
Cynthia as the occasion for a mighty tale, *maxima de nihilo
nascitur historia* (II, i, 16). The actual beloved will serve as a
symbol, redeeming in successful poetry a love that otherwise
might lead to complete wreckage. The book ends with a proud
statement that Cynthia has indeed been glorified by Propertius
as Lesbia by Catullus, Quintilia by Calvus, Lycoris by Gallus.
Meanwhile, we expect and are furnished with striking revelations of artistry in plotting an elegiac action. Interrogation becomes more challenging. Negation and affirmation are subor-
dinated to the experience of and the delight in choice. Cross
reference and allusion increase. The mind leaps more easily to
analogous situations: for instance, Cynthia's varied accomplishments remind the poet of the variety in the activities of mankind. Legend repeats that love is always irresistible, incurable;
so, Propertius and Cynthia will in their turn illustrate a human
truth. The gods themselves, wanton, condone wantonness; the
goddesses in their adventures yield to Cynthia, whose vagaries,
for this reason, her lover will reverently endure. Even scandal
about her will furnish a theme for admirable poetry. If her lover
be jealous of one like Lais, Thais, Helen, he can justifiably point
to Homer's Trojan War as proof that great actions arise from
little jealousies. As a revelation of elegiac method, this is all very
astute.

Then there is change itself, which invites irony—and Chaucer
would later make the most of this opportunity. *Omnia vertuntur*
(II, viii, 7). Mutability in circumstances gives added lustre to
persistence in love. Marriage and fatherhood are lesser relationships. Should he marry, to her his wedding-flute, *tibia*, would
sound more sorrowful than a funeral trumpet, *tuba* (II, vii, 11–
12). If, in the ups and downs of expediency, Achilles grieved
for Briseis, it is to be assumed that love rightfully triumphs over
Propertius. He welcomes sharper agonies; Cynthia will read the
verses which detail his suffering—Cynthia as critic!—and, when
he goes to his burial, it will be with three little books as a gift

for Persephone. On his urn two verses will tell the truth about
him (II, xiii A, 35–36):

> qui nunc iacet horrida pulvis,
> unius hic quondam servus amoris erat.

One love and one only! In a poem as in life, the elegist may
waver but cannot desist.

Concentration is secured, also, amid varied circumstances.
One joyful night outweighs months of disregard and is thus enhanced by contrast. Lovers must ever and anon scorn each the
other to bring on the renewal of love. Though his faithless beloved has made him the joke of the town, he may win repute as
the only one to gather up her bones on her final day. Presenti-
ments of age and death are used to constrain his theme within the
limits of elegiac art—*incipe iam augusto versus includere torno*
(II, xxxiv, 43). He dreams that she is drowning (II, xxvi);
she is ill and he calls on Jupiter to save her; *vivam, si vivet; si
cadet illa, cadam* (II, xxviii, 42). For her there will come a long
night without a dawn, *nox tibi longa venit, nec reditura dies*
(II, xv, 24); but death waits for everyone, *mors quemque manet.*
This favorite device of elegists from Tibullus, fearful of losing
Delia, even to Habington, fearful of losing Castara, and Wordsworth, fearful of losing Lucy, has the effect of illuminating the
life of the beloved. In two sequent elegies Propertius calls Cynthia his light, *mea lux* (II, xxviii A, 59; xxix, 1). And as the book
ends he refuses to judge one like Helen or Venus herself, like
Oenone, Lesbia, Pasiphaë, or Danaë. Enough that he among the
bards of Rome has surpassed the singers of Greece. Yes, *cedite
Romani scriptores, cedite Grai!* The fame of Propertius will be
safe with that of Catullus, Calvus, and Gallus.

Propertius has not been afraid to trust Cynthia against a rich
traditional background; all legend becomes a resonant sounding
board for her adventures, and all the mythical charmers who still
survive in the memory of man must make way for her. Trans-
figurations (II, xxviii) suggest her lofty destiny: if for Io and

Ino and Callisto, why not for other beloved women? Thus he draws her literary life from the roots of antecedent culture through an elegiac device which centuries later will heighten and enrich the meditations of Wordsworth, Pound, and Eliot. Notice the ironic turn Wordsworth gives to the Latin poet's wish to stellify his beloved: Lucy, too, was

> Fair as a star when only one
> Is shining in the sky;

and before her death

> She seemed a thing that could not feel
> The touch of earthly years;

but it is her humble destiny to be "rolled round . . . / With rocks, and stones, and trees" in the "diurnal course" of earth, not in the eternal courses of the stars. Here, tragic inference lurks behind elegiac treatment.

Are there any further rungs on this ladder of personality, a ladder that reaches toward Cynthia as the men of our time reach for the moon? In the elegiac process of intensification the task of Book III (*ca.* 22–21 B.C.) is the universalizing of its theme. Cynthia becomes representative of all that is or can be loved; and her poet becomes representative of all loving poets. Recalling the maxim, *omnia post obitum fingit maiora vetustas* (III, i, 23), after death all things are magnified by their antiquity, he assumes a point of elegiac view not only above but outside of time. Speaking of himself as *sacerdos*, priest, he turns away from war and heroic poetry. He had thought to be another like Homer, poet of the Trojan War, *meque*—me, too! But he is now convinced that he must celebrate the rites of love rather than the triumphs of hate. Love is the God of Peace, *Pacis Amor est;* he will offer to his beloved the immortality to be won only in lofty verse. Thereupon, his elegiac sights will be raised from romantic love to the love and study of nature and a devoted search into the authenticity of legend and myth. Behind the corpse of the storm-tossed Paetus, behind the brawls of the love-maddened

Cynthia, there is something else at work. That profounder calm is only hinted at in fair weather between tempests and in kindness between torments. He will become *haruspex* to detect what is constant in power and passion. And yet he does not wish to surrender the excitement of storms: *in te pax mihi nulla placet* (III, viii, 17–18, 34). Here we are reminded of Wordsworth's "central peace subsisting at the heart / Of endless agitation" (*Excursion* IV, 1146–1147).

Throughout this argument, instances provide illustration for Propertius' theme, and his generalizations follow naturally on evidence. His lines bear witness, *testis* (III, xi, xvii, xix, xxii), a sure sign that he is working in the service of principles.

Thus, solicitous about the eternal aspect of quiet and disquiet, he concludes that all things are not equally fit for all men, *omnia non pariter rerum sunt omnibus apta* (III, ix, 7): sculptor, painter, charioteer, runner—each follows the seeds of his own nature, *naturae . . . semina . . . suae* (III, ix, 20), one for peace, another for war. By this charitable assumption he can the more easily account for the tumults of Cynthia and his own obstinate devotion. From the specular mount of an elegist thus accredited in his own right he describes the birthday of his beloved as if to project it into an ever-desirable future. The devices by which he makes us aware of futurity are, first, his frequent optatives, for instance (III, x, 5–6):

> transeat hic sina nube dies, stent aere venti,
> ponat et in sicco molliter unda minax;

second, the many imperatives, *surge, discute, finge, indue, relinque, pete;* third, the magnificent hortatory phrases that crown the elegy: let the banquet proceed, let the flute blow itself hoarse for the midnight dance, let the wanton words ring free, and, finally, let the birthday be consummated in the solemn rite of newborn love. Thus, Cynthia has been wished, ordered, and exhorted into the future.

But the poet's most effective apology for Cynthia is not in the

negation of all that dims her lustre or in the meditative queries
which settle or unsettle her being or even in wishes, commands,
and hopeful exhortations. With some daring, it must be confessed, the poet justifies their story by the representative example
of the heroes and heroines of legend and by the myths of gods
and goddesses. A Cleopatra will be mastered only by an Augustus. Granted that the Galla of Postumus and the Penelope of
Ulysses are chaste wives, the greed which seduces many women
can be paralleled—even justified—by the greed of the state
itself, its avid commerce and its preciously guarded merchandise.
Felix agrestum, happy the country folk!—here the myth of the
Golden Age takes over. But now, *at nunc*, with the loss of piety
all men and women worship gold and what it buys. As *haruspex*
Propertius will speak out: mighty Rome herself is bought and
sold, undone by her prosperity. When human errors, civic or
personal, are thus illustrated by their great legendary and mythical analogues, the pardon craved by lover and beloved cannot
be withheld. Propertius and Cynthia have been etched in terms
of universal truth; their love is understandable, even pardonable.

Meanwhile, in Book III, the level of concern has been lifted
from the personal to the civic plane, and there is new light
on the scene. In an elegiac metaphor which we shall observe
more closely when we come to English elegy, the lover will
dare darkness because *luna ministrat iter, demonstrant astra
salebras* (III, xvi, 15). When Marcellus dies, he departs from
this human life starward, *ab humana cessit in astra via* (III, xviii,
34). Light, we infer, is the reward of stern effort and the rigorous application of energy: *non datur ad Musas currere lata via*
(III, i, 14).

Furthermore, out of the experience of circumstantial change
and infidelity the meditative mind arrives at the idea of compact.
Thoughts of the lustful Pasiphaë, Tyro, Myrrha, Medea, Clytemnestra, Scylla, suggest the possible resolution that Propertius
and Cynthia shall be true. To this end in a series of periphrastic

gerundives the poet goes on to invoke moon and sun, Luna and Phoebus, as witnesses (III, xx, 15–16):

> foedere sunt ponenda prius signandaque iura
> et scribenda mihi lex in amore nova.

The need for a new law in love—and this more than a millennium before Dante's *Vita Nuova*—is surely a momentous discovery in a third book of Elegies.

Since love furnishes ever anew the food for its own increase, to relieve the burden of his torment the lover will travel to Athens for the study of Plato, Epicurus, Demosthenes, and Menander. There—another valid discovery for a third book of Elegies—he will clear his soul of error, *animum emendare* (III, xxi, 25). In such temper and by similar effort the energies of great Rome herself should be kept true or restored—sublimated, we might say. With such penetrating thought akin to dramatic reversal in the sequences of a play the elegist has driven his argument through into a hope for civic renovation.

Moreover, with his wounds healing he has discovered good sense, *Mens Bona.* In the farewell to his beloved, who will soon grow old as other women do, he prays for her the universal fate: that she be brought to repentance when she is scorned as she has scorned others. It is right that she suffer the outcome of her beauty, *eventum* (III, xxv, 17–18); only thus will she discover herself. This is the essential matter of the thoughtfully pagan end of Book III.

But this is not the end of the elegiac vision. For another book (not earlier than 16 B.C.) there remain the memory of Cynthia living and the dream of Cynthia dead—both translated most effectively by Professor Highet.[13] When an elegist must present for his ultimate discovery the quintessence of his theme, whether it be personal or civic fidelity or infidelity, he will get not only

[13] Gilbert Highet, *Poets in a Landscape* (New York, 1957), pp. 84–86, 94–97.

at the idea of it but at the heart of it. In the tradition of the αἴτια of Callimachus, and as if anticipating the *Fasti* of Ovid, Propertius glances aside from personal love to find a proper perspective against the background of Roman legend. Not less than Alcides on the Palatine and the Feretrian Jupiter, must his memory of Cynthia take its place with memories of Romulus and Iulus, Vertumnus, Arethusa, Tarpeia, and Augustus and Cleopatra at Actium. In this way he can exhibit the rages of his beloved so as to give them grandeur and yet show them somewhat less than great.

And what of death: is its revelatory power clearer than that of remembered life? Horos the stargazer reads the horoscope of Propertius: though one girl will elude him forever, he must go on with his elegies, *at tu finge elegos* (IV, i, 135). Although his poetry be *fallax*, artful, because of it the poet is immortalized, allowed to stand free of the accidents of circumstantial life with its corruptibility and the limitations of time with its boundary in death.

Can Cynthia likewise surmount the final challenge in the last reach of the elegiac vision toward personal truth? The Latin poet accomplishes this task with the help of a dream, an anagoge. Although in their visionary dreams mediaeval writers will allegorize or idealize the dead maiden beyond actual appearance and out of all resemblance, and in the twentieth century pseudo-pagan dreaming will reduce personality to lower or lowest subconscious terms in an irony or anticlimax, in the elegiac dream of Propertius (IV, vii) Cynthia becomes more like herself. The ravages of fire are upon her and her beryl ring has been burned from her finger but her hair and eyes are the same, her breathing life and voice appear unchanged, and her scornful power exhibits itself with undiminished grace. Let such other erring ladies as Clytemnestra and Pasiphaë, or such virtuous wives, *sine fraude maritae*, as Andromeda and Hypermnestra, cure the passions of life with the tears and lamentations of death; Cynthia is silent, she will not reveal the perfidy of her lover. And, as in life, her demands are immediate and peremptory. The memorial verses he writes for her must be brief, so brief that anyone who passes her column cannot fail to read: Here in the soil of Tibur lies *aurea Cynthia,* golden Cynthia.

Wordsworth, too, the poet of starry Lucy, Cynthia's literary namesake, will in his time confess himself helpless before the last unsolved riddle of elegy:

> She died, and left to me
> This heath, this calm, and quiet scene;
> The memory of what has been,
> And never more will be.

And standing by the tomb of his schoolmaster, Matthew, he will ironically echo two words of Propertius, *aurea Cynthia,* when he asks:

> can it be
> That these two words of glittering gold
> Are all that must remain of thee?

In poetry, however, death does not end all, *letum non omnia finit* (IV, vii, 1–2). These shades, *Manes,* are something, *aliquid,* says Propertius; "to this day," as Wordsworth expresses it, "some maintain" that Lucy Gray "is a living child."

> O'er rough and smooth she trips along,
> And never looks behind;
> And sings a solitary song
> That whistles in the wind.

Propertius with his terrible dream has anticipated Wordsworth with his "sweet dream," his "slumber" sealing the spirit.

The English elegiac ballads are simpler than the Latin elegies; they do without the elaborate background of legend and the literary resonance; their energy is more quietly intensified, and their pantheon has become Nature alone. Nevertheless, Lucy with her "thoughts" is in the tradition of the *docta puella* of Propertius; and in both series the poet probes his experience for its inmost truth. Moreover, throughout Matthew's preoccupation with the accidents of space, time, and circumstance we are reminded of the similar anxieties of Propertius: Matthew refusing to accept any other in the place of his Emma echoes the undeviating protestations of the Latin poet; and Matthew's envy of the blackbirds who never "wage a foolish strife with Nature" is a pseudopagan reminiscence of what with the classical elegists had been perforce compliance with the assumptions of pre-Christian doctrine. Finally, both poets associate a Lucy or Cynthia with tempestuous Nature (the snowstorm in Lucy Gray; the dream of Cynthia's drowning); both emphasize the eagerness of an exile to return to his native land; both prefer beauty of thought and beauty of movement to more obvious charms; and both relate their loved ones to the courses of the heavenly bodies: sun, moon, and stars.

Yet over the Christian centuries poetry has made a new and subtler discovery—spiritual? psychological?—as the upshot of its elegiac adventure. Let Propertius in his dream describe the ivy binding the delicate bones of Cynthia with its twining tendrils, *mollia contortis alligat ossa comis* (IV, vii, 80); Wordsworth will write of his own trance as follows:

> Matthew is in his grave, yet now,
> Methinks, I see him stand,
> As at that moment, with a bough
> Of wilding in his hand.

This extended review of the poems on Cynthia as works of elegiac art illuminates also the later MSS of Wordsworth's *Prelude*, MS W and onward, when the autobiography has become a "meditative history" rather than a history of feelings alone and when "Nature" more and more has assumed the character of a beloved instead of a schoolmistress. With both writers we observe the elegiac imagination on the stretch, as it were. In their record of apocalyptic experience both advance by way

of "spots of time" to revelations of civic or religious truth. Both
weigh the career of lover with the possible career of patriot
and finally choose elegiac speculation over dramatic action.
Finally, both poets conceive of themselves and their beloveds,
Cynthia or Nature, as representative; and thus poetry, the poet,
and the poetic theme are universalized. What in their imagination has become manifest is the inner truth of life-as-it-is, B.C.
and A.D. Love, transience, the anxieties and conflicts of men
and women, the puzzles of sense and spirit, the nature of creation and dissolution: this is the list of elegiac themes. Here, too,
in the work of either poet we may find illustrated with supreme
finesse the whole armory of elegiac devices: unremitting concern evident in the proud negations and fierce interrogations—
even more in the hortatory goads and challenges; the rich habit
of allusion, the wide scope of cross reference, and, chiefly, the
high celestial imagery. Epyllia, little stories of a romantic cast,
adorn the spare thinking and help toward ever more representative discoveries. And all situations are immediately, simply, and
daringly confronted without impertinent fantasy or phrase-
making.

Coming to Shakespeare's neopagan Sonnets from the distichs
of the Latin elegists, we feel a strange sense of identity within
the differences. What has been said of Propertius' elegiac themes
and devices may be repeated for the erotic meditations of Shakespeare, except that the Sonnets are not throughout concerned
with the same literary person. The devotion of the lover is
equally intense. The mode of address is identical. The themes
are the same: love, mutability, disillusionment in life, and the
poet's challenge to death. The same devices appear: sharp interrogation (8, 18, 65); prophecy (55); exhortation (1–19); the
promise of fame and immortality through the verse of the lover
(18, 19, 63); the universalizing of the actual situations with
matchless power and clarity (64, 68). On the contrary, although
the Sonnets describe in greater and greater detail outward ap-

pearance or behavioral characteristics, they scarcely probe into or reveal the inner nature of the beloved. The imagery is rich and varied but the scope of legendary and mythical allusion is limited to Phoebus, Adonis, Helen, Mars, Saturn, Philomel, Siren, Cupid, and Diana; and the personification of Time, Fortune, and Death abstracts from the theme what might otherwise be an inner grace. As the drive of thought is less persistent, so are the discoveries rarer and less climactical. As a series the Sonnets fall into the casual arrangement of Catullus or Ovid rather than follow the rigorous organization of Propertius.

When all this is said, more is still to say. Here is the evidence of elegiac imagination at the crossroads between skeptical and ethical forms of expression, between vision and action as distinct literary patterns—with action sure to win. Emotions are being exercised for their own sake as lyrical monodramas or for their propulsive power in creating situations (78 ff.); the poet is preparing himself to delineate *dramatis personae* (66). Circumstances are etched unforgettably and they invite deeds (50, 51); into the laments crowd social and civic references. Throughout the Sonnets in their canonical sequence "Time's thievish progress to eternity" is illustrated by reference to the professional concerns of mankind: astronomy (14), acting (23), law (46), architecture (55), painting (83), floriculture (95, 98, 99), history (106), prophecy (107), music (127), usury (134), housewifery (143), medicine (147). Poetical rivalry and professional prestige tremble on the verge of drama. All these themes woven firmly into the texture of his love constitute a kind of arras for the virtual performance of his erotic action. Especially do the Sonnets to his mistress recall the Cynthia of Propertius: her tyrannous demeanor, the torment, the bitter excuses (139), his negations—"I do not love thee with mine eyes" (141). Yet here, too, the series is felt to be not so much a single meditative adventure as the alternation—recalling Catullus—between hate and love (145, 149). The final sonnets come to rest neither on the sublimated stage of civic glorification nor in the lofty heaven of ultimate discovery. Except for the masterful elegiac sonnet 146, in which alone we get a hint of Christian faith, there is little probing into the inmost significance of love or personality.

Wordsworth thought highly of Shakespeare's Sonnets (Essay, Supplementary to the Preface, 1815), but there is no clear evidence that he had come under their influence before he rediscovered Milton's sonnets in 1802 and launched into a series of poems gnomic or elegiac in the Miltonic vein rather than the near-dramatic Shakespearean. The poem of Wordsworth most clearly illuminated by the Shakespearean elegiac series is, again, the autobiographical *Prelude*. In it we find paralleled the intense concern, the distillation of personal experience into "spots of time"—always the authentic mode of elegy—the importance of breed; the love affair with Nature encompassing all the ups and downs of personal devotion; [14] disillusionment; the revelation of personal growth made in the light of a noble friendship; the echoes of professional and civic life (in Academe and library and revolutionary forum rather than in the theatre); and the amazing facility of language working its cumulative effects into phrasal patterns rarely equalled. The Sonnets lack the civic references characteristic of Propertius and Wordsworth; for Shakespeare that would be the proper task of drama. Both Elegies and Sonnets miss the note of confident faith and reconciliation on which the Autobiography ends. But Cynthia, the Dark Lady, and Nature are limned ever more memorably as the imagination of each poet drives toward a discovery important for the cultural prepossessions of his own age. In these three elegiac poems, pagan, neopagan, and—shall we say?—pseudopagan, the energies of original elegy have been transformed into penultimate light. We have been oriented in this

[14] Abbie Findlay Potts, *Wordsworth's Prelude: A Study of Its Literary Form* (Ithaca, New York, 1953), pp. 209–211.

world. Wordsworth's contemporary, the classicist Goethe, writes the first of his Roman elegies to tell us clearly what this not quite final discovery is:

doch ohne die Liebe
Wäre die Welt nicht die Welt, wäre denn Rom auch nicht Rom.

Without love nothing would be what it is. Yet, at the very end of his life, Goethe was heard to whisper: "Mehr licht!"

CHAPTER III

Lucy (Light)
as Elegiac Symbol

DARKNESS and light as symbols of speculative adventure are frequent in the Christian Era, notably in the literature of the Middle Ages. The chthonian and celestial deities of Antiquity were not to yield entirely to Lucifer and Christ; yet they underwent a transformation in which the mediaeval image of divine power, like the Pauline version of the divine message, owed a debt to both Greece and Judaea. But before we investigate the elegiac writing of those elder classicists of England who were also Christians, let us pause for a brief glance at biblical elegy. The Old Testament is a record of the search for light; the New Testament bears witness to that light as found.

"In the beginning" darkness was associated with emptiness and formlessness. Therefore the first command of Holy Writ— "Let there be light"—was the biblical archetype of elegies, and in the disclosure of His own nature and function the Lord God was the primal elegist. Without declaring the serpent to be the first skeptic, we note that because of him and his devices "the eyes of [Adam and Eve] were opened"—with what disastrous mythic results we know too well. Whether such knowledge of good and evil be a proper discovery or not, the peripety was swift, and none but a Divine Poet could have driven the action through to a symbolic covenant. Thus Noah's rainbow, whereby God and Man were reconciled, became the first light-bringing scriptural symbol; and the second, at the Lord's behest discovered by Abram to signify the multitude of his progeny, was the star-studded heaven. Only the greater light, the sun to rule by day, and the lesser light, the moon to rule by night, were prior to the rainbow and the stars as luminous agencies, or looked upon as symbols revealing Divine Power.

Of the many later instances of the Lord apparent to his creatures in the Old Testament none is more closely associated with the human ordeal than that witnessed by Job. After Satan —not yet called Lucifer—had been allowed to drive the Man of Uz to the full expression of elegiac feeling by way of the symbols of darkness and light, the chastened victim cried out: "I have heard of thee by the hearing of the ear: but now mine eye seeth thee." Since, however, Job is a seer rather than a doer and the change of fortune in his affairs is not a true peripety, this magnificent book remains more an elegy than a drama. Furthermore, those rhapsodic seers who, like Isaiah, would "walk in the light of the Lord," were kept—short of action— peering ahead toward the dawn of their yet unaccomplished Day, when "the eyes of the blind [should] be opened and the ears of the deaf [should] be unstopped." "Look, ye blind, that ye may see."

What was to be seen by the men of the Old Testament is scarcely ever spiritual light on the face of a woman—although Esther is a "star"; it is invariably the undifferentiated glory of the countenance of the Lord Himself or a beam to announce his coming agent, the Messiah. In order to see such lights the scriptural doctrine taught and the scriptural action urged the cleansing of the doors of perception, most often by tears. This cleansing is the prime use of the Book of Psalms.

Cradled in the same Eastern neighborhood with classical elegy but culturally earlier, the Hebrew psalmody of the Old Testament was more opulent in its expression of feeling and more docile in its expression of thought. All the Psalms are intense and all deal with lofty themes, many are speculative, and several are considered by biblical scholars [1] to be proper elegies, on the assumption that an elegy is a lament for personal or national disaster. From the first Psalm, which declares the pleasure of the blessed man to be in meditation on the law of the Lord, to Psalm 119, Ruskin's favorite, in which the psalmist cries out: "O how love I thy law! / It is my meditation all the day!" there is no trifling. Although the more skeptical psalms resemble classical elegy in the lift of energic reason into successive discoveries, the Ultimate Discovery of the Hebraic elegist, the luminous Face or Countenance of the Lord, is always foreseen (21, 27, 36); accepted doctrine is rarely challenged except for an occasional reproach when succour is delayed (19, 88, 89); nor is the singer eager for new experience (131):

> Lord, my heart is not haughty, nor mine eyes lofty,
> Neither do I exercise myself in great matters,
> Or in things too wonderful for me.

Most often wrought into lyric, idyllic (23, 104), and doctrinal forms (119), running the gamut from personal abasement to national triumph, including litany and liturgy, the Psalms reveal the wide scope of human anxiety and relief; but their beatitudes are rarely probed, their prayers are not tentative, nor their praises judicious. The psalmody is choral in the form of hymn or anthem or it enumerates the divine characteristics by rote. To be sure, Hebraic elegy shares with Hellenic elegy dismay over the vanity and brevity of earthly life (39, 90) and regret that it cannot drive beyond the phenomenon of death; but the Psalmist seeks security rather than revelation, and his meditative thought, such as it is, drives on from comfort to comfort rather than from discovery to discovery. He exclaims and supplicates

---

[1] E.g., Richard G. Moulton, *The Modern Reader's Bible* (New York, 1915), pp. 806, 812, 813, 818, 819, 865.

and threatens. He sees visions and is puffed up in his own conceit (18, 26). He protests love of the Lord as unremittingly as Propertius would protest love of Cynthia. It is only when he asks those rare questions—"What is man that thou art mindful of him?"—or meditates upon the power and providence hidden behind earthly and celestial appearances (104) that we detect any clear generic likeness to Greek and Latin elegy.

If Christianity be a poem, as some have considered it, "the greatest poetical structure of all time," it, too, has certain elegiac traits: the curious and unremitting search for enlightenment, a dialectic of this world and the other, and as its *anagnorisis* the apocalypse, literary and ecclesiastical, of Divine Power. Nevertheless, the historical form of the Christian story is more than elegy; it exhibits also choices, ordeals, and peripeties of action, and therefore its analysis may be left to the interpreters of dramatic form. Here we may observe with due reverence that the poetic temper of Jesus was distinct from that of the churchmen who founded an institution upon his life and death. His teaching had much in common with the themes and methods of an eastern Mediterranean world trained in the doctrine of ἀνὴρ ἀγαθός; and although this best brother of man prayed for an earthly kingdom like that in heaven, his tropes were not celestial, of the sun, moon, and stars. Instead, he referred to what goes on within, to the darkness of the inner eye and its light, to the ordinary blindness that forgets to put oil in lamps and the Pharisaic blindness that guides the blind into ditches. Thus, he transformed the clearest trait of Hellenic elegy, skeptical challenge, into the evocation of the human spirit out of its human bondage. In him above all there was nothing "covered" that should not be "revealed." As son of man, he was to be his own sign, symbol, and parable. And thus he became the exemplar for elegiac vision even as he pointed the way to dramatic action.

However familiar the Latin or English psalter had been to English poets before Wordsworth, the copious emotional fervor and the verbose diction of the songs of David—so congenial to Milton—are less easily detected in the Lucy and Matthew poems of 1799 than in the strophes of the Thanksgiving Odes of 1814 and 1816 or in similar passages of *The Excursion*. What does appear in the elegiac ballads is the original, spare, nonmystical kind of concentration Jesus always gave to what was at hand. At this stage of his poetical career Wordsworth was a gospeller, neither a psalmist nor an ecclesiast. He could speak of a lantern, a spinning wheel, rod and line, basket, church clock and chimes as the Man of Galilee had spoken of the humble properties on his own scene, the candle and lamp, flax and old clothes, fish nets and fishhooks and fishers of men, bushel basket, cups and platters, keys and pennies. Such is the authentic procedure of the elegist in any century.

Not until he must review Bede for his *Ecclesiastical Sonnets* (1821–1822) [2] did Wordsworth become a penetrating student of the Christian Middle Ages. The iambs of the early Latin hymnographers even as they shifted into long meter with a trochaic beat would have echoed, perhaps idly, in his ears from the services of the Anglican Church; but classical elegy would be more familiar to him than mediaeval Latin verse written in elegiac distichs.[3] He might have heard or read at Cambridge some of the trochaic rhythms of those goliardic clerks whose

[2] Abbie Findlay Potts, *The Ecclesistical Sonnets of William Wordsworth: A Critical Edition* (Ithaca, New York, 1922).

[3] Such as Maximian's love elegies and the occasional elegies of Ausonius and Paulinus of Nola and of Alphanus at Monte Cassino; also, Hildebert's Roman elegy and Alcuin's *De Clade Lindisfarnensis Monasterii. A History of Later Latin Literature*, by F. A. Wright and T. A. Sinclair (New York, 1931), mentions or quotes the elegiac writing of Rutilius (pp. 69–70), Sedulius (p. 73), Fortunatus (p. 111), Theodulf (p. 147), Serton of Wilton (pp. 303–304), and the *Speculum Stultorum* of Nigel Wireker (p. 307). According to Mackail, *op. cit.*, p. 205: "The chief intellectual occupation of the Middle Ages, it has been said with some truth, was writing enormous quantities of bad Latin verse; and the bulk of that verse was in elegiacs." This comment should be balanced by the more sympathetic researches of Helen Waddell, Philip

Latin gibes or laments have haunted the campus even to our day—*ubi sunt qui ante nos?*—and from his Italian tutor, Agostino Isola, he would have gleaned much additional lore about the classics or the Latin poetry derivative from them. But there is no evidence that he assimilated those poems either in Latin or in the Continental vernacular languages that copy the lewd or skeptical tone of classical elegy; nor does he refer to the songs of the troubadours of Provence who made way for the *Vita Nuova* as surely as Mimnermus made way for Xenophanes. Although Wordsworth read Italian and would recognize the *Divina Commedia* as a sublime representation of love and in the climb up the Purgatorial Mount to the Eternal Light an elegiac action second only to the life of Jesus and the history of the Christian Church, Dante's fictions were distasteful to him. He must have known Renaissance elegies in Latin—those of Milton, for instance; and the sublimation of love attempted by writers of sonnets in sequence was congenial to him—several of the Italian sonnets of Michelangelo he translated in honor of the "heavenward course" of the soul to seek "beyond the visible world . . . Ideal Form, the universal mould."

> The wise man, I affirm, can find no rest
> In that which perishes: nor will he lend
> His heart to aught which doth on time depend.
> 'Tis sense, unbridled will, and not true love,
> That kills the soul; love betters what is best,
> Even here below, but more in heaven above.

Such Platonic convictions are rarely evident in the elegies of 1799–1800 except through the glass of seventeenth-century metaphor, to be discussed a little later. Soon, however, the poet

---

Schuyler Allen, and Ernst Robert Curtius. It would be helpful to know that Wordsworth was familiar with the elegiac metres of Boethius, or that he had read the elegies of Politian and Bembo, Italian writers of the Renaissance; but of this we cannot be sure.

of Lucy will accept the challenge of Spenser and Milton; and the polarity of their thought, helpful in his elegiac *Ode, Intimations of Immortality*,[4] will tempt him, also, to distinguish heaven from earth and thus fall between them as an heir to that fruitless debate between phenomenal and noumenal worlds out of which so many English poems have been composed. We know, somewhat regretfully, that, except for his elegiac autobiography, *The Prelude*, and his elegiac *Excursion*, from 1802 on he became more and more the neoplatonic sonneteer, the idyllist, or the somewhat-less-than-Christian apologist. Yet, like Goethe, he never gave up his search for light.

Granted that elegy is, as our study has encouraged us to believe, the clear seeing, clear sounding form of passionate meditation, the aim of elegiac composition is the refinement of human understanding in a series of revelations about the nature of human life and human destiny. If, then, Jesus may be thought of as the Representative Elegist and his message as the Ultimate Discovery, succeeding elegists would ring true or false in view of what he knew and thought and said and was. To such poetical vision Wordsworth refers when he tells us that all great poetry is religious. Like the sermons and parables of the first Modern Man and the elegies of the nearly contemporary but ancient Propertius in another part of the Roman world, our English and American elegiac writing is most satisfying when the poet speaks humbly and simply, and, in complete dedication, about what is at hand, driving his revelatory action ever deeper and deeper within its cosmic frame.

We are thus brought to consider the *anagnorises* and pertinent symbols of English elegy itself.

At the end of his *Elegy to the Memory of an Unfortunate Lady* Alexander Pope asks:

[4] See Abbie Findlay Potts, "The Spenserian and Miltonic Influence in Wordsworth's *Ode* and *Rainbow*," *Studies in Philology*, XXIX (October, 1932), 607–616.

> Is there no bright reversion in the sky
> For those who greatly think or bravely die?

The answer is yes. The evidence for English literature stretches
from the assumed Cynewulfian *Phoenix* to the visionary *Pearl*
and Chaucer's dream in *The Book of the Duchess* through
Spenser's *Astrophel* and Donne's *St. Lucie's Day* and the *Anni-
versaries*, on past Habington's *Castara* and under Young's elegiac
panorama of the celestial heavens to Blake's *Thel* and Wordsworth's Lucy poems: and thenceforward by way of *Adonais*
and *In Memoriam* to the thoughtful and luminous writing of
Arnold, Hopkins, Yeats, and Eliot, the constellated metaphors
of Dylan Thomas, and the mythic sunshine of Wallace Stevens.
A title from the last-named, *The World as Meditation*, reminds
us that elegy is still meditative poetry, looking for its symbols
of bright reversion upward to the skies, to the sun, the moon,
or the stars.

In Old English heroic literature, for instance *Widsith* and
Beowulf, "settled glory" may be found "underneath the stars";
but the gleeman in Heorot cannot see beyond the actual sun
and moon set "as lights to lighten the dwellers in the land."
In the world of the Seafarer, too, "the shadows of night [be-
come] darker." Nor can the Wanderer understand "wherefore
or why [his] heart should not grow dark in [him]"; pondering
"this dark life well," he asks unavailingly:

> Where is the horse and the rider?
> Where is the giver of gold?
> Where be the seats at the banquet?
> Where be the hall-joys of old?

With their better understanding of the Christian message the
poets Caedmon and Cynewulf begin to represent the lot of
man more cheerfully. Has not God made the bright heavens
for a roof over the bairns of men? Is the Son of God not the
sun of righteousness, "bright beyond the stars"? On Doomsday
will the purging fires, the falling stars, not make way for the

radiant countenance, the shining face of the Lord of might, that Lord "brighter than the sun unto the blessèd"? [5]

Such lyric and idyllic treatment of darkness and light does little more than embellish accepted doctrine; for a sterner probing into the destiny of man we must look to the prose of Aelfric (*Homily* I):

Consider carefully the sun, in which there are . . . heat and light; the heat dries, and the light illumines. The heat does one thing, and the light another, and although they cannot be separated, the heating pertains, nevertheless, to the heat, and the illumination to the light. In like manner, also, Christ alone assumed humanity, and not the Father nor the Holy Ghost; yet they were always with Him in all His works, and in all His course. [6]

Beyond pagan lament and Christian interpretation there is in the literature of our early ancestors one poem not content with describing a situation already in view; it explores a regenerative procedure. Shaping death and life into a vertical action, it may be said to bear upon it the mark of the classical elegist. Actually *The Phoenix* is an amplified version of the elegiac couplets of Lactantius, his *Carmen de Phoenice*. [7] Whether written by Cynewulf or another, the first 380 lines of the Old English text follow the 170 lines of the Latin elegiac text. The Cynewulfian poet translates *unica Phoenix* as "fugel . . . se anhaga . . . deormod drotaŏ," which Albert S. Cook again translates, into present

[5] See the translations of Henry Morley, Chauncey B. Tinker, LaMotte Iddings, and Albert S. Cook in *Select Translations from Old English Poetry*, ed. Albert S. Cook and Chauncey B. Tinker (Boston, 1902).

[6] See the translation by Mary W. Smyth, *Select Translations from Old English Prose*, ed. Albert S. Cook and Chauncey B. Tinker (Boston, 1908), p. 157.

[7] *L. Coelii sive Caecilii Lactantii Firmiani Opera Omnia quae exstant ad optimas editiones collata praemittitur notitia literaria studiis Societatis Bipontinae* (1786), II, 435–440. J. Wright Duff and Arnold M. Duff, in their edition of *Minor Latin Poets* for the Loeb Classical Library (Cambridge, Mass., 1934), pp. 643–665, give an account of the Phoenix in literature from Hesiod on.

English, as "dauntless solitary." This dauntless solitary with the incomparable song is the first elegiac bird in English literature and may be studied as one model for native elegiac song.[8]

Based on the couplets of Lactantius, lines 1–380 are partly idyllic, for instance in the picture of the traditional ever-blooming, ever-fruitful island of a Paradise whose forests stand ever green. Like all paradises before and after it, that glorious land never changes, is subject to no evil. With the entrance of the Phoenix itself, however, in both Latin and Old English texts the action is declared: upon the eternal scene the rhythm of death and life will be projected in an effort to discover and reveal the nature of the re-creative process. The Phoenix will die and will be reborn as a symbol of solar energy, heat and light.

The Latin phrases show with emphasis what are the circumstances of bright reversion: *in primo . . . oriente, aeterni maxima porta poli, hic solis nemus est.* Phoebus and Aurora preside; and, when the first rays of dawn appear, the satellite of Phoebus (*satelles*) flies toward the sun and begins to sing a kind of flute song that outdoes all other flute songs. Says Lactantius (ll. 47–50):

> Quam nec aedoniae voces, nec *tibia* possit
> Musica Cirrhaeis assimulare modis.
> Sed neque olor moriens imitari posse putatur,
> Nec Cyllenaeae fila canora *lyrae*.

Never was flute or lyre able to match it. The English poet expands this passage as follows:

Never was trump, nor horn, nor thrill of harp, nor any voice of man on earth, nor organ, nor strain of melody, nor wing of swan, nor any of the harmonies which God hath created for the cheer of men in this sad world, like unto that descant.[9]

The Phoenix alone knows the secrets of Phoebus; and after a thousand years have bowed him down he leaves his Paradise

[8] *Early English Text Society*, No. 104, *The Exeter Book*, ed. Israel Gollancz, Part I (London, 1895), pp. 200–241.

[9] Cook and Tinker, *Poetry*, pp. 147–148.

for a wilderness to the west and there undergoes the complicated process of rebirth. In so doing he becomes the type not only of doctrinal resurrection but, we may suggest, of the re-creative process as universally exhibited, not least in the arts and literature. For his nest on the top of the loftiest of trees the Bird of the Sun collects or gathers delightful herbs with sweet odors. Wordsworth will name this stage of the poetical adventure recollection in tranquillity. Next, combustion takes place: the Phoenix kindles. We note that the enkindling fire comes from celestial light. Excepting Caedmon's song, rather a lyric than an elegy, is there in English letters any earlier account of the poet's task, indeed of the problem of any or of all new life?

Or of the poetical labor yet to come? The new form follows upon incineration of the old. "The ashes . . . cohering to a ball" (L., *in massam cineres in morte coactos;* O.E., "yslan . . . lucan togaedere geclungne to cleowenne") become the vehicle of new life. Thence the seed, the apple, the beautiful animate worm, the eaglet, the eagle, and finally the re-formed Phoenix "wrought round with flesh" (L., *inde reformatur, qualis fuit ante figura;* O.E., "swyle he aet frymd waes . . . eal edniwe eft acenned"). Thereupon the bird returns to the Earthly Paradise, bringing along "both bones and embers, the relics of the pyre" —the precious text? All takes place under the canopy of heaven.

Lactantius does not know—nor does the English poet— whether the Phoenix be male or female, neither or both. The Latin had ended in a truly elegiac riddle:

> Ipsa sibi proles, suus est pater, et suus heres,
>   Nutrix ipsa sui, semper alumna sibi.
> Ipsa quidem, sed non eadem; quia et ipsa, nec ipsa est,
>   Aeternam vitam mortis adepta bono.

Since *avis* is a feminine noun, the Phoenix is an *alumna.* Cook translates the English text to mean "He is his own son, his kindly father and again the heir to his ancient inheritance."

Here we are not concerned with the last half of *The Phoenix*, which goes on to interpret this record of bright reversion as resurrection, thus turning the elegy into a familiar sermon or lesson; its author was the first of a long line of English poets who would be, in Wordsworth's phrase, "teachers or nothing." On the other hand, the Latin poet, although a father in the African Church (*ca.* 300) and called "the Christian Cicero," saved his preaching for his prose and in his verse stopped short of doctrine. Whatever the truth about spiritual or poetical re-birth, we may agree with both poets that the Phoenix is "not dull . . . nor sluggish, not heavy nor torpid, . . . but nimble and swift and full of light, beauteous and charming, and glori-ously marked." *Sed levis, et velox, regali plena decore;*

> Ac he is snel and swift and swiþe leoht
>   wlitig and wynsum   wuldre gemearcad.

So all Phoenixes should be, and all elegists who look, fly, and sing toward the sun.

Although Wordsworth would be familiar with the meta-morphosis of the Ovidian Phoenix (Book XV), there is no reference to Lactantius in his prose; and it is not likely that he had read the *Carmen de Phoenice* or *The Phoenix*. But his birds, too, under the cope of heaven are in their own way elegiac, symbols of bright reversion. The "singing-bird" that the death-marked sailor had left behind him to "pipe its song in safety" for his bereaved mother; the redbreast that recalled to "the pale-faced Child" "sweet thoughts of angels hovering nigh" and to "old folk" legends of an "ancient church . . . filled with light"; the green linnet that leads "the revels of the May"; the cuckoo telling "a tale / Of visionary hours"; poor Susan's thrush and the caged turtledove, lyrists both, and the skylark, elegist, "ethereal minstrel! pilgrim of the sky"—

> Type of the wise who soar, but never roam;
> True to the kindred points of Heaven and Home—

all share traits with the Phoenix. It is Wordsworth's Bird of Paradise, "the Sun's Bird," most "unearthly" of all Nature's "feathered progeny," that distinctly resembles the traditional Phoenix and best recalls "the truth by some faint trace / Of power ethereal and celestial grace"—

> So richly decked in variegated down,
> Green, sable, shining yellow, shadowy brown,
> Tints softly with each other blended,
> Hues doubtfully begun and ended;
> Or intershooting, and to sight
> Lost and recovered, as the rays of light
> Glance on the conscious plumes touched here and there.

Not less colorful among the Phasianidae had been our Old English Phoenix, the father—if not mother—of English elegiac birds:

In front the bird is gay of hue, with play of bright colors about the breast; the back of his head is green, curiously shot with crimson; his tail is splendidly diversified, now dusky, now crimson, now cunningly splotched with silver. The tips of the wings are white, the neck green below and above. . . . About his neck is the brightest of collars, woven of feathers, like the orb of the sun. . . . In appearance the bird is every way most like, as books relate, to a peacock.

The author of *The Phoenix,* translating the elegiac couplets of Lactantius, was only a little younger than, and in the line of, Alcuin, himself the pupil of Egbert, who was pupil of Bede, who wrote a treatise on metrics. All are important leaders in that Latin culture which fostered English scholarship and poetry in the eighth, ninth, and tenth centuries; and before we go on from theological elegists to elegiac laymen we may remember ever so briefly Alcuin's *Farewell to His Cell.* Here he had been surrounded by trees with whispering branches, bushes with flowering twigs. Here the voice of the teacher had been heard reverently interpreting wise books. And yet

Nil manet aeternum, nil immutabile vere est,
  Obscurat sacrum nox tenebrosa diem.[10]

Out of the shadowy night obscuring the holy day Alcuin and his
fellows through the Christian ages could only cry in the optative:
Christum nos semper amemus. Oh, might He, snatching our
hearts *ad caelum*, make us all His! Such bright reversion to the
caelum as imagined by early Christendom takes place under the
same sky that arched over Propertius and his Cynthia, indeed
over Jesus Himself. Yet the mediaeval procedure whereby that
heaven could be transcended was somehow different; human
life in the Middle Ages had become less simple than it was
either for the Roman or the Galilean. How much less simple,
Abelard bears witness, inheriting as he did from both Alcuin and
Propertius. A Latin love song for Heloise in the *Carmina Burana*
is attributed to Abelard; it reminds us that her name is a derivative of the Greek word for sun (ἥλιος, ἠέλιος), and thus allies
her with many a classical beloved:

> Cujus nomen a Phoebea
> Luce renitet
> Et pro speculo
> Servit polo, illam colo
> Eam volo nutu solo
> In hoc saeculo.[11]

If Heloise had her name from solar light in the mediaeval
trochaic rhythm which closest approximates the minor line of
classical flute song even as it faintly anticipates the septenarius
of the English ballad, Dante's Beatrice of the *Vita Nuova*
(XXXI, XXXIII, XLI) with a statelier rhythm carried on the
revelatory process in terms of light. The light of her humility,
luce de la sua umilitate, was in due process transformed into a

[10] From *A Primer of Mediaeval Latin*, ed. Charles H. Beeson (Chicago,
1925), pp. 319–320.
[11] Philip Schuyler Allen, *Mediaeval Latin Lyrics* (Chicago, Illinois,
1931), p. 107.

luce d'amor characteristic of the angels in heaven. Dante's use of light is, indeed, the brightest of all reversions.

The two outstanding Middle English elegies both mention the bird of Phoebus, the phoenix. Chaucer's *Book of the Duchess* (982) compares Blanche to "the soleyn fenix of Arabye," and the author of *The Pearl* (430) calls the Virgin Mary "Fenyx of Arraby." [12] First to *The Pearl* (*ca.* 1370, more than half a millennium after *The Phoenix*). It is one of the most elaborately bright reversions in English literature and, like its forerunners, dependent upon light for the symbolic beauty of its "precious perle wythouten spot." The poet recounts one of those dreams in which the spirit penetrates truth as visual glory. The incredible gleam on the rocks—"The lyght of hem myght no mon leven"—the crystal cliffs, the trees with indigo blue trunks and burnished silver foliages, shining intensely in a shimmering sheen, the precious oriental pearls instead of gravel on the ground: compared with all this splendor sunbeams are but dark and dim. Birds of flaming colors, music of the cithern, fair vegetations, river banks of bright beryl—Cynthia had only one beryl ring—and streams paved with glittering gems of emerald and sapphire like "stremande sternez" glittering in the welkin of a winter's night: all appeared desirable.

> Bot the water watz depe, I dorst not wade,
> And ever me longed a[y] more and more.

The country beyond is always "loveloker"; unfortunately, it is across the brook. How to get over the stream to the Ultimate City? Well, the eye can pierce where the foot cannot go. Otherworldly values must be referred to visual experience; the puzzle of life and death and new life can be solved only by the progressive sharpening of poetic vision. An elegiac adventure is indicated.

[12] A conveniently abbreviated version of *The Pearl* is given in *A Literary Middle English Reader*, ed. Albert Stanburrough Cook (Boston, 1915), pp. 441–453. Cook's text is taken from the edition of Charles G. Osgood (Boston, 1906).

When the poet sees his lost maiden with face like ivory and unbound golden hair, clad in gleaming white tunic, pearl-adorned and crowned with pearls, in her ideal beauty he recognizes her personal identity: recognition or *anagnorisis* thus becomes the first high accomplishment of this elegiac adventure, too. The longer she is gazed upon, the more fully she is known: a second elegiac accomplishment. Awe takes the place of desire and, when the maiden approaches the brink of the stream to greet the poet, the understanding is alerted. With her help his merely emotional laments and his self-pity are clarified. In the final and supreme *anagnorisis* of the adventure he learns that seeing only with the hungry eyes, the intent to appropriate what one loves for one's own, and the will to have one's own way are untrustworthy; that meekness and devotion are necessary for joy; and that to belong wholly to the Lord is "the rote and grounde of alle . . . blisse." The winning of spiritual value by the gradual refinement of feeling through purification by fire (*The Phoenix*) or revelation by light (*The Pearl*) is the sure mark of the elegiac imagination in our Christian era. Here, too, in merry England the elegiac form is discovery and elegy is the poetry of skeptical vision.

A few years before *The Pearl* had consummated mediaeval elegy the known visual clarity of dreams enabled Chaucer, the forerunner of modern elegy, to make credible even as he immortalized his Good Fair White in an elegiac poem which reflects many of the modes of light. First, we note the windows "ful clere" of the room in which the dream begins, the "many glade, gilde stremes" of the sun, "the welken . . . fair, / Blew, bryght, clere"—"Ne in al the welken was no clowde." [13] Outside, on the path of thick green grass, there are seven times more flowers than "in the welken sterres bee." At every turn Chaucer encourages us to glance up, orients us toward the dawn,

[13] For the quotations from Chaucer, see *The Works of Geoffrey Chaucer*, ed. F. N. Robinson (2d ed.; Boston, 1957); quoted by permission of Houghton Mifflin Co.

toward morning, radiance in Maytime, toward resurgence and resurrection. His knight "clothed all in blak" lamenting a lost lady nevertheless remembers her as full of light. She has "surmounted" others

> as the someres sonne bryght
> Ys fairer, clerer, and hath more lyght
> Than any other planete in heven,
> The moone, or the sterres seven.

And "be hyt never so derk" her lover thinks he sees her evermore.

Although amplified by idyllic and courtly passages, Chaucer's elegiac dream ends sparely enough:

> "She ys deed!" "Nay!" "Yis, be my trouthe!"
> "Is that youre los? Be God, hyt ys routhe!"

Some three hundred years later a similarly curt statement of loss reappears as a refrain to punctuate Donne's *First Anniversary*, an elegy on the untimely death of Mistress Elizabeth Drury. Five times we are told: "shee, shee is dead; shee's dead." [14] Yet Donne in his time will do more than announce the death of a lady and underline her virtues. To brighten her reversion he must anatomize the miseries of a world without her. While the elegiac Muse still lives, he may not quite "consent the world is dead"; it is obsessed, however, by hectic fevers, agues, decay, corruption, disorder, and deformity. His lady would have given it "forme" and "frame." Although this poet himself must "walk in blacks," he will try to cast his eyes up to the heavens. But there, as if to rebuke human arrogance, "the free–borne Sun" has been "impal'd within a Zodiake" and

> of the Starres which boast that they do runne
> In Circle still, none ends where he begun.

[14] For the quotations from Donne, see Vol. I of *The Poems of John Donne*, ed. Herbert J. C. Grierson (Oxford, 1912), p. 237, l. 183; p. 253; and *passim*.

Even the colors of the "various Rainbow" are decayed, for

> shee, in whom all white, and red, and blew
> (Beauties ingredients) voluntary grew, . . .
> Shee, shee, is dead; shee's dead.

The *Second Anniversary*, dealing with the progress of the soul of Elizabeth Drury, is more clearly dependent upon celestial images:

> Up, up, my drowsie Soule, where thy new eare
> Shall in the Angels songs no discord heare; . . .
> Up to th' Apostles, who did bravely runne
> All the Suns course, with more light than the Sunne.

Donne gives us a Paradise somewhat in the luminous manner of Dante's *Paradiso* and Spenser's *Hymns* of Heavenly Beauty and Love:

> Shee to whose person Paradise adher'd,
> As Courts to Princes, shee whose eyes ensphear'd
> Star-light enough, t'have made the Southe controule,
> (Had shee been there) the Star-full Northerne Pole,
> Shee, shee is gone; she is gone.

It would seem that when, over four hundred years after Chaucer and nearly two hundred years after Donne, another English poet exclaimed "If Lucy should be dead!" he was setting Nature's Lady by the side of Heloise, Beatrice, Margaret, the Lady Blanche, and "Mistress Elizabeth" in the heaven of bright reversions. Sportive as the fawn, silent and calm as mute insensate things, stately as the floating clouds, graceful as the storm she may be; but to her also "the stars of midnight shall be dear." The last line of Wordsworth's most plangent elegy is at the heart of all elegiac musing: the light has gone out;

> [Lucy] is in her grave, and, oh,
> The difference to me!

Whether this "difference" be symbolized as a presentiment when "the bright moon" drops "behind the cottage roof" or as sorrow that beclouds a star sole "shining in the sky," the belovèd for whom "the stars of midnight" were dear is still under the domination of the sun, still

> Rolled round in earth's diurnal course,
> With rocks, and stones, and trees.

Later, in *Elegiac Stanzas*, Wordsworth longs for the power —though he survives the longing—to add to what he has seen "the light that never was, on sea or land." Almost invariably his meditations about whatever troubles the heart take from his predecessors the form of the multitudinous facets of light out of darkness. Witness, in chief, his elegiac *Ode, Intimations of Immortality*, with its argument akin to Donne's "pure life of immortality," the world as "a stage," the body as "a prison" and earth "our prison's prison." Not merely to describe in light or deplore in darkness what he has lost does the lover unburden his heart—as in an idyll or lyric; rather he must think his way, lift his spirit out of what is dim and shadowy into what is clear albeit sober-colored. Less capriciously than Donne's *Second Anniversary*, Wordsworth's *Ode* binds the days "each to each by natural piety." Read with Donne in mind, the phrases "there hath past away a glory from the earth," "shades of the prison-house," "man's mortality," "something that is gone," are echoes from seventeenth-century elegy. Read with Chaucer's *Book of the Duchess* in our eye, "the glory and the freshness of a dream" and "the sunshine [as] a glorious birth" take us back to the fourteenth century. In Chaucer's "smale foules," "his houndes" and little "whelp," his founes, soures, bukkes, does, roes, squirelles, we are freshly aware of the literary overtones enriching the "joyous song" of Wordsworth's birds, the holiday of his "every Beast." Chaucer's groves were "ful of bestes," but his "grete trees" will in Wordsworth's imagination become "a Tree, of many, one."

> Oh evil day! if I were sullen
> While Earth herself is adorning,
> This sweet May-morning.

Wordsworth seems to be balancing the May "dawning" of
Chaucer's "sweven in ryme" against Donne's "sullen Writ."
Without disregarding either he will shape an elegiac form of
his own:

> My heart leaps up when I behold
> A rainbow in the sky.

Between the death of the Lady Blanche and that of Elizabeth
Drury many fair ladies had died but few of them had won from
great poets such bright literary reversions—surely not in Spenser's *Daphnaida* (1591) for "the noble and vertuous Douglas
Howard," daughter of Viscount Byndon and wife of Arthur
Gorges, Esquire. This poet, like Chaucer before him and Donne
after him, gives us "a sory wight . . . clad all in black" on a
"gloomie evening"; but the grief of Alcyon for his Daphne remains unillumined, and his curses and hates have naught to do
with challenging thought or a lifted spirit:

> Let Bagpipe neuer more be heard to shrill,
> That may allure the senses to delight;
> Ne euer Shepheard sound his oaten quill
> Vnto the many, that prouoke them might
> To idle pleasance: but let ghastlinesse
> And drery horror dim the chearfull light,
> To make the image of true heauinesse.

The "chearfull light" is effectively dimmed;

> And euer as I see the starres to fall,
> And vnder ground to goe, to giue them light
> Which dwell in darkn, I to minde will call,
> How my faire Starre (that shinde on me so bright)
> Fell sodainly, and faded vnder ground;
> Since whose departure, day is turnd to night,
> And night without a Venus starre is found.[15]

[15] *The Poetical Works of Edmund Spenser*, ed. J. C. Smith and E.
de Selincourt (London, 1912), pp. 527–534.

Nor in *Astrophel*, another "dolefull plaint," does Spenser attempt an elegiac action with a bright reversion for its peripety. Although the dead Stella becomes the starry center—Starlight—of the flower Astrophel into which "this paire of lovers trew" is transformed, "the fairest star in skie, / As faire as Venus or the fairest faire," does not keep her place in the heavens. On the other hand, when Clorinda's plaint for Astrophel ends at the "mournfull hearse," she has, at least, asked the timeless question: "Ay me, can so diuine a thing be dead?"

> Ah no: it is not dead, ne can it die,
> But liues for aie, in blisfull Paradise:
> Where like a new-borne babe it soft doth lie.
> In bed of lillies wrapt in tender wise.
> And compast all about with roses sweet,
> And daintie violets from head to feet.[16]

In these elegies, however, Spenser is the lyric or idyllic poet, more eager to express and delineate woe than to probe into the puzzle of life and death.

Indeed, between the century of Chaucer and the century of Milton and Donne, it would seem that the times were not prevailingly elegiac. Visionary and romantic literature, chronicles and ballads, the study of classical epic and eclogue, and the mighty drive of lay drama with its interest in codes and manners and the formal traits of Senecan tragedy and Plautine comedy had not encouraged elegiac speculation on the part of authors or readers. The period was vigorously active and tirelessly observant; religious and ecclesiastical issues were debated but scarcely probed. All writing had the strongly didactive overtones to be expected from the effort of writers to fuse the Christian and classical elements in their culture: all was, as it were, being taught or recommended, not least the legends of Spenser

[16] *Ibid.*, pp. 546–560. The lilies, roses, and violets will reappear in Wordsworth's *To a Sexton;* and the "bed of lillies," ironically transformed, was the bed on which Troilus longed to wallow in Shakespeare's most elegiac drama.

and the histories of Shakespeare. There existed, to be sure, falls
of princes and ruins of time, ballads recounting disastrous events,
"tragic pageants," dirges and laments and complaints uttering
personal sorrow; but these provoked feeling rather than thought.
The vast sonnet literature, except for that of Shakespeare, was
mainly gnomic and idyllic, concerned with glib generalizations
and sketches of personal beauty. It remained for Donne to re-
vitalize the skeptical elegy, for Milton to illustrate the elegiac
nature of religious doctrine, and for their fellows to extend song
until it should include the full range of meditation.

Until Milton joined them, no other writer had attained the
disciplined power and expressive skill of Spenser and Shakespeare. And may we not conclude that the work of these three
giants is most surely comparable when touched by the elegiac
imagination? Actions become more meditative and hence more
challenging as King Lear follows King Arthur and Lucifer follows King Lear. Images and metaphors betoken feelings fraught
with profounder and loftier concern. And the discoveries, romantic or dramatic or epic, reveal what is more universally important. It is most appropriate, then, that the stern polarity of
darkness and light should control Milton's theme in his elegiac
monody, *Lycidas.* Even in dire personal and civic disaster the
encouragement of Phoebus helps to associate the loss of Edward
King with the solar rhythm: "the day-star in the Ocean bed"

> anon repairs his drooping head,
> And tricks his beams, and with new spangled Ore,
> Flames in the forehead of the morning sky.[17]

[17] Milton's Latin *Elegiarum Liber* reports Charles Diodati and himself
as Phoebicoli, disciples of Phoebus. In the third elegy Phoebus had
submerged his chariot in the waters of Tartarus; and in the fifth elegy
as the Delian Apollo he returns with the spring: *Delius ipse venit.* In
the spring, treachery, slaughter, and violence recede with the darkness.
Cynthia returns, and Phoebus bids Aurora get up out of bed. See *The
Poetical Works of John Milton,* ed. H. C. Beeching (1910), pp. 42, 122,
126, 130, 324.

Nor shall we forget that the action of Milton's epics is also concerned with the dark change of one Lucifer, who originally

> in the happy Realms of Light
> Cloth'd with transcendent brightness [did] outshine
> Myriads though bright.

Therefore, the ordeal whereby the Messiah established Himself as "our Morning Star" reflects the primal command of Milton's God in the seventh book of *Paradise Lost*, "Let there be light."

We are not surprised, therefore, that the familiar elegiac Muse of Milton's contemporaries should be a Lucy (*lux, lucis*) under shadow of death, or that the hue of seventeenth-century elegies should be, if not sombre, at least sober-colored. In their insistence that love be made clear and that desire be made pure, elegies of this period are most true to the tradition, classical, Christian, and native; and they eddy around the satisfaction of desire and the clarification of love in all the many patterns of ethical and theological vision. It was no accident that Donne the preacher put revelation to the uses of Donne the elegist nor that Milton the epic poet prayed that what was dark in him might be illumined, nor that what is possibly the greatest elegy in our tongue would be shaped up into a rebuke for "blind mouths."

Light was the seventeenth-century symbol for love of all kinds: love immanent in sexual act and love transcendent in religious rapture. Huddled together near Milton and Donne and Quarles and Herbert and Vaughan we discover an array of preachers too little read for their contribution to letters and on the other side a group of lewd and purblind writers too familiar in any age—all in search of heat and light, of love and vision.

> If ever any beauty I did see,
> Which I desired and got, 'twas but a dream of thee.

The human beloved of the elegiac school to which we are referring appeared under her various names of Lucia (Herrick, Waller, and Carew for Lucy Hay), Lucasta (Lovelace for Lucy

Sacheverell), Idea (Drayton for Lucy, Countess of Bedford, whom Donne and Jonson also addressed), Lucasia (Katherine Philips for Anne Owen), and—of special importance for our present study—the Castara of William Habington (Lucy Herbert), who with Lyly's Cynthia and Sidney's Stella may be an ancestor not only of Wordsworth's Lucy but of Shaw's Candida, shining one. In this tradition, whenever the beloved is not Lucia or Stella she answers, with Jonson's and Carew's mistress, to the name of Celia, heavenly one:

> Come, my Celia, let us prove,
> While we can, the sports of love.

"While we can"? Transience as prevailing theme of these elegiac songs is reflected from Greek and Latin elegy and supplies the shadow of this lovely light. *Carpe diem.* Now is the time for mirth. Gather we rosebuds while we may. "Fair daffodils, we weep to see / You haste away so soon." But, oh! the heavy change, now thou art gone. And hence Donne allows us a generalization:

> Thus times do shift, each thing his turn does hold;
> New things succeed, as former things grow old.

Quarles darkens even as he illustrates the shadows cast by the sun: "light-in-vain-expecting eyes." Dryden exclaims: "Ah, fading joy!" Therefore we may expect that the wanton and libertine will justify themselves in their infidelity and inconstancy and proceed to wallow (the word is Shakespeare's, and Donne's) in the lily beds. The sentimental lovers will count the roses on funeral wreaths, hover over the lifeless violets, and, while pacing the churchyard, dissolve their death wish into elegiac tears. But the more eagle-eyed, we can be sure, will rather fix their gaze on the sun.

In the poetry of Donne images of the sun rising, the shadow trodden underfoot when the sun is at noon, the sun always "elder by a year," the eclipse, suggest the wide variety of solar metaphors and the stance of the century toward vision. Cowley's *Hymn to Light* and her lusty "husband Heat" further illustrates this predilection. The Horatian Marvell, whom Wordsworth knew best of the three, also contributed to the greatest elegiac ode of the early nineteenth century. When Marvell wrote to the same effect—

> The soul, that drop, that ray
> Of the clear fountain of eternal day,
> Could it within the human flower be seen,
>   Remembering still its former height,
>   Shuns the sweet leaves and blossoms green;
>   And recollecting its own light,
> Does in its pure and circling thoughts, express
> The greater heaven in a heaven less— [18]

his soul "recollecting its own light" foreshadowed Wordsworth's soul with "shadowy recollections"; and Marvell's "clear fountain of eternal day" flowed into Wordsworth's "fountain-light of all our day," "master-light of all our seeing." Finally, Marvell's "pure and circling thoughts [that] express / The greater heaven in a heaven less" may have suggested Wordsworth's "thoughts too deep for tears" given by "the meanest flower that blows"—the Wordsworthian irony for Marvell's "flower" whose "sweet leaves and blossoms green" are shunned by the seventeenth-century soul homesick for its "greater heaven." As Marvell spoke of the "former" "height" of the soul, Wordsworth speaks of a child's "heaven-born freedom on [his] being's height." This close association of Marvell's *On a Drop of Dew* and Wordsworth's elegiac *Ode* illustrates with emphasis the effort of all elegists to lift their love of anything from its brief earthly moment to its consummate heavenly rapture, pre-

[18] The pertinent texts for these and many other similar allusions may be found in *Seventeenth Century Prose and Poetry*, ed. Robert P. Tristram Coffin and Alexander M. Witherspoon (New York, 1929).

natal or postmortal. It also reveals in fresh light Wordsworth's fidelity to the appearances of earth itself: he does not disjoin earth and heaven: his is no double vision.

The single vision that concentrates itself in an intense upward look is best symbolized by Henry Vaughan's spark (*Silex Scintillans*) and rewarded by his "great ring of pure and endless light" (*The World*), from which also are reflected Wordsworth's "celestial light," his "clouds of glory," and his "radiance . . . once so bright." Vaughan more hopefully than any of his contemporaries transformed the realm of death into a world of light. Addressing God as "immortal Light and Heat," he has consummated love most fruitfully in terms of divine revelation and restoration:

> O knowing, glorious Spirit: when
> Thou shalt restore trees, beasts, and men,
> When thou shalt make all new again,
> Destroying only death and pain,
> Give him amongst Thy works a place
> Who in them loved and sought Thy face!

Wordsworth's staunch refusal to surrender the pansy at his feet, the blessed creatures, the babe on his mother's arm, the happy shepherd boy, and man, earth's foster child, and to disown the fountains, meadows, hills, and groves in which he delighted, echoes Vaughan's similar devotion to nature's "creatures" and his constant effort to interpret the mystery of nature's

> hieroglyphics quite dismembered
> And broken letters scarce remembered.

Quite different, then, from dramatic discovery, which most often peers backward or forward through time, the elegiac vision seeks its fulfilment in an intense moment out of time. Whereas seventeenth-century writers symbolized their moment variously as the sun at noon, the taper at midnight, the drop of dew or the teardrop, the pulley, compasses, or scales, the kiss in the cup, the glowworm in the grass,

> Silver, or gold, or precious stone,
> Or star, or rainbow,

their common saint appears to be St. Lucy, and—to borrow a phrase from Donne—their day was indeed St. Lucy's Day. Two centuries later their moment of vision would be known as Wordsworth's "spot of time," three centuries later Pater would translate it into the exquisite moment of the aesthetes, and still more recently Whitehead speaks of a "drop of experience," until by now the clear fountain of eternal day has again become something "out of this world"—even in slang we have our perfect moment.

Although Dante with his One Simple Light was not the first and Eliot will not be the last to express love through the symbol of light and darkness, it is Wordsworth's "visionary gleam" in "every common sight" that still flashes most familiarly in our eyes; and it is through his phrases that we know best the radiance of seventeenth-century writers and their vertical yearning —upward or downward, newborn day or setting sun, sunshine or moonshine, rainbow or embers—all along the scale of energy as fire and love as light. Long before the obvious applications in literature of the Freudian hypothesis of subconscious as distinct from superconscious, still longer before we tried to reach the moon, our elders had run the gamut of literary love longing. However disguised or subverted modern love may at times appear, any poem which sublimates it must be in its own characteristic way a kind of elegiac Hymn to Apollo or even an echo of Plato's elegiac distichs: "Thou gazest at the stars, my star; would I were Heaven, that I might gaze at you with many eyes!" "Even as you shone once the Star of Morn among the living, so in Death you shine now the Star of Eve among the dead." νῦν δὲ θανὼν λάμπεις Ἕσπερος ἐν φθιμένοις.[19]

We must concede that in the seventeenth-century account of

[19] *Elegy and Iambus*, ed. and trans. J. M. Edmonds (London and New York, 1931), II, 4–5.

creation Raphael made epic and didactic out of the primal and quintessential elegy; yet no one whose memory encompasses Genesis, *Paradise Lost,* Dante's deep and towering exposition of darkness and light in the *Commedia,* and Blake's design for the momentous struggle between radiantly obedient Michael and sullenly rebellious Lucifer needs to be at a loss to recognize the part played in western letters by the elegiac imagination.

In ages highly skeptical, therefore, when the scientist is probing phenomena rather than recording them or theorizing about them, it does not surprise us that elegy and the elegists become increasingly dependent on that other and kindred myth of death and rebirth in the sequence of earthly winter and spring and the cycle of vegetative growth, the push of plant life down into this very earth that it may shoot upward again into this very air. Trees of knowledge and trees of life both have their elegiac associations, never more fruitful than in the northern countries where the leaves fall and the imagination is likewise deciduous. Between Yggdrasill with its root in Mimir's well of wisdom and Eliot's prickly pear near the dry, empty pool the elegiac vegetation is thick. Coleridge's critical writing and Wordsworth's Growth of a Poet's Mind (*The Prelude*) are both forms of elegy extended into meditative autobiography by way of the metaphor of growth under the sun. And many are the idylls and dramatic and heroic actions flourishing in terms of the cycle of vegetation as dominated by the rhythms of the heavenly bodies. Idyll, however, is stable and drama's mobility is horizontal: both are determined by the accidents of earth, fair or foul; the heavens above preside over elegy.

That may be why elegy almost always suggests vertical power; for its spatial characteristics and its frame of direction it assumes an outer pattern of downward and upward tendencies and tensions. This pattern can be detected especially in the drive of a boldly conceptual mind—for instance, that of Father Pierre Teilhard de Chardin—down into the phenomenal roots of thought and up "out of this world" into noumenal branches to create philosophical elegy, even the pure poetry of metaphysical thought itself. Or, again, the probing and peering of the inductive scientist and the interpretative scholar, before they arrive at their gnomic generalizations or essential statements of character, are elegiac. Both aim at discovery even as both temporarily end in riddling hypotheses or didactic challenges; in both, an emotion proper to their purpose has supplied a proper motive; and although their joy in discovery is hard won and contingent, their tentative efforts take on the symbolic form of theory or wisdom.

The dirge, the funeral ode, the sepulchral or threnetic epigram, the epitaph, although often concerned with death as a fact, more often invite tears and regret than meditation: they are prevailingly lyric or gnomic. The authentic elegist is preoccupied rather with his diagnosis of whatever is dead or sterile, or bloated, disproportionate, corrupt, death-dealing. His writing has a somewhat stronger affiliation with Blake's prophecies and Meredith's comic genius than with Popian satire. He has too much at stake to destroy what he is trying to understand. Therefore, he delegates the ethical actions necessary for cure to the dramatist and the codes which maintain health to the teacher. He does not look through the eyes of the crowd nor speak formally in parliaments; but he is, nevertheless, the best of patriots.

Such a one was William Blake, several of whose minor "prophecies," when studied in a setting of earlier elegiac writing, appear to be themselves elegies, both in their interrogative procedure and skeptical purpose. They probe rather than predict or assert. The most notable predecessor, in 1789, of the Lucy poems, in 1799, of Wordsworth is Blake's *The Book of Thel*, with its Greek title derived from θέλειν (to wish or will), its Hebraic imagery, and its Christian message: "Everything that lives / Lives not alone nor for itself." The motto of *Thel*—

> Does the Eagle know what is in the pit?
> Or will thou go ask the Mole?

> Can Wisdom be put in a silver rod?
> Or Love in a golden bowl?——

prefaces an investigation of the power to soar and delve with
the discovery of the many and monstrous hardships in the way
of those who would realize themselves, exchanging the "shining
lot" of merely seraphic imagination for the permanent identity
of human life, its humility, its duties, its sleep of death. As the
youngest of the Seraphim in the Vale of Har, Thel bemoans her
transience. Yet "Why should Thel complain?" ask the Lilly of
the valley clothed in light, and the glittering little Cloud, scatter-
ing its bright beauty through the humid air. These reveal to the
plaintive seraph their uses and destiny and try to comfort her.
Even the matronly Clod of Clay, who cherishes the helpless
worm, has an inalienable crown, although of herself and her
dignity she knows not and cannot know;

> I ponder, and I cannot ponder; yet I live and love.

With this elegiac remark she invites Thel to enter her house of
Clay. Then come, fast and furious, the old elegiac queries in a
voice of sorrow from Thel's own imagined grave plot:

> Why cannot the Ear be closed to its own destruction?
> Or the glist'ning Eye to the poison of a smile?

Why? . . . Why? . . . Why? . . . Why? . . . Why? . . .
Why? [20]
    In the theme of transience, in the barrage of questions, and in
the metaphors of light and darkness once again in great poetry
we recognize the traits of elegy. And when Thel, frightened by
the exigencies and perils of human existence, makes the great
refusal and, shrieking, escapes the house of Clay and flees back
unhindered until she comes to the vales of Har, we have a bright
reversion, to be sure, but a reversion in a minor key. Blake is of

[20] *Selected Prose and Poetry of William Blake,* ed. Northrop Frye
(New York, 1953), pp. 101–105; quoted by permission of Random
House, Inc.

course, an ironist as well as an elegist; Wordsworth as an elegist
will be a realist; but they have made the same humble discovery.
Thel's sympathy with "watry bow" and "parting cloud," with
lowly flower and helpless worm and humble Clod will be written more sparely in the story of Lucy, Child of Nature, friend
of fawn and "mute insensate things," floating clouds, willow,
stars, rivulet, and green field. Lucy will persist, however; Lucy
will continue to be

> Rolled round in earth's diurnal course
> With rocks, and stones, and trees.

Were there a possibility that Wordsworth had seen Blake's
poem, his own would appear to be, if not a retort or an answer,
at least a chiming echo. Moreover, when we place Thel and
Lucy side by side, we observe that the echo is the echo of flute
song: the one poem, in the old fourteen-syllabled line with its
seven beats; the other, in the common measure of balladry with
the same seven beats. Both remind us of the hovering minor line
of the classical distich with its usual fourteen syllables. Finally,
and chiefly, we can now foresee the poles between which elegy
will revolve for centuries to come, with the same old queries and
the same inescapable discoveries.

Such wide-ranging investigation as the elegist undertakes is
to be expected in darkly ominous periods of cultural shift,
whether the country be Ionia and Greece five centuries before
Christ or imperial Rome at the beginning of Christendom,
Dante's Italy at its height, Newton's England in the seventeenth
century, or our own puzzled West on the threshold of a new
kind of space age in an old kind of space. The thrust and reach
and plunge of our culture in these uneasily Christian centuries
suggests that, whatever distinguishing name we give to our literature, the elegiac imagination will supply its generic and metrical patterns. The celestial luminaries will swing ever more in
their literary orbit. Light and its shadows, life and its shadow—
death or whatever is deadly or about to die—change, transience,

evanescence: these will still constitute the theme of elegiac poetry, what it is about. They will also determine the form of
elegy, how it comes into being. It may dive with the submarines
and climb with the rockets, but it will still push its roots down
into earth with the trees and always it will rise and set and rise
with the sun and the moon and the stars.

That Wordsworth is one strong link between the elegiac
poetry of our classical and Christian past and the elegiac imagination of our strangely impending future is an hypothesis to be
studied with care. In the following chapters let us set forth his
problems and procedure; we may be able to rescue from current
disregard evidence valuable for poets not yet in vogue. Behind
the rhetorical clarity of his most discursive meditations there
resides a sure sense of the elegist's function as it was understood
by Solon, Xenophanes, and Simonides, and by Dante, and by
Milton and his contemporaries, and by Blake.

AN ELEGIST IN THE MAKING:
WILLIAM WORDSWORTH

CHAPTER IV

Elegy and
Love Lyric

Lucy and William

ALTHOUGH for the survival and renewal of the race the consummation of desire bears a value less mournful than death, for
poetic musing it is not less enigmatic and challenging. And many
are the speculations based upon it, both ecstatic and elegiac.
Within desire itself all sorts, fluctuations, and degrees of feeling
operate toward satisfaction; and within the varying symbolic
forms of love—concupiscent or worshipful, profane or sacred—
the poet propels us toward a moment of vision that may be in-
tellectually lucid but must be aesthetically rich. We are made to
see into life in order that we may love it. Thus, as Donne says,
"to brave clearness all things are reduced."

Not in the same rank with Donne, Marvell, and Vaughan but
a sentimental elegist of no mean power, the William Habington
who loved Lucy Herbert affords us in his verse more obvious
if less distinguished evidence of the symbolism of love as light.
Elsewhere,[1] the possible influence of his Holy Man on Wordsworth's Poet of *The Prelude* has been considered. Here, let us
suggest that his poems about his mistress and wife Lucy made

[1] Potts, *Wordsworth's Prelude*, pp. 203–217.

some small contribution to Wordsworth's Lucy poems; in pre-figuring the later Lucy of a later William, *Castara* teaches us something about the working of the imagination when it deals apprehensively with the possible death of the beloved.

Habington's description of a mistress warrants consideration:

> A mistress is as fair as *Nature* intended her, helped perhaps to a more pleasing *grace* by the sweetness of education, not by the slight of Art. . . . *Advice* and her own fears *restrain* her. . . . Her youth expresseth *life* enough, without the giddy *motion* fashion of late hath taken up. . . . She knows *silence* in woman is the most per-suading oratory.

He refers to virtue as "often tenant to a cottage"; and, to dis-avow mean motives for his love, in addressing Lucy's parents Habington wishes that his Castara were

> The daughter of some mountain cottager,
> Who with his toil worn out, could dying leave
> Her no more dower, than what she did receive
> From bounteous nature.[2]

Likewise, Wordsworth makes his Lucy a lady of *Nature's* own; *Nature* is an *overseeing* power to kindle or *restrain* her; in the *motions* of the storm she sees *grace* that moulds her form by *silent* sympathy; *Nature* endows her with the *silence* of *mute insensate things;* the thoughts which *Nature* gives to her will rear her form and swell her bosom with vital feelings of delight. This providential or overseeing influence of Nature on Lucy, and especially the phrase, "A lovelier flower on earth was never sown," are possible echoes from Habington's lines on Nature (*How Happy though in an Obscure Fortune*):

> She who apparels lilies in their white . . .
> She who in damask doth attire the rose . . .
> She who in purple clothes the violet:

[2] William Habington, *Castara*, 1634–1640, ed. Edward Arber (London, 1870), p. 46. Hereafter cited as Arber. In passages quoted the spelling has been modernized.

> If thus she cares for *things even void of sense,*
> Shall we suspect in us her *providence?* [3]

Habington's "violet . . . unmarkt i' th' shaded vale" and Wordsworth's "violet . . . half-hidden from the eye" have not escaped comment; and *The Description of Castara* shows her to be indeed a Lucy:

> Like the violet which alone
> Prospers in some happy shade:
> My Castara lives unknown,
> To no looser eye betrayed. [4]

Castara is the "star" [5] by which the poet's thoughts do move, and Lucy is "fair as a star." Welcomed by Ovid's Corinna of the Tiber, Petrarch's Laura of the Arno, and Sidney's Stella of the Thames, Habington's Lucy of the Severn would be, says her William, a fourth "star" in the heavenly constellation. A fifth star might well be Wordsworth's Lucy "beside the springs of Dove."

Violets, however, are frequent in the verse of the seventeenth century, for instance in Herrick's poetry, and stars, as in the poems of Waller. More distinctive for their relation to the "Lucy" series are those poems in *Castara* which anticipate the death of the beloved: *To Castara in a Trance; To Death, Castara Being Sick;* and *To Castara upon the Death of a Lady,* where the violet and star are again found together. [6] Most nota-

[3] Arber, p. 76.

[4] *Ibid.,* p. 53. Lienemann (*Die Belesenheit von William Wordsworth,* p. 30) notes this parallel but none of the many others between Habington and Wordsworth. Cf. also Goldsmith's *Deserted Village,* 329–330.

[5] Arber, pp. 17, 75 (*To Castara, Praying: His Muse Speaks to Him*); but (*Domine Labia Mea Aperies,* p. 115) Habington's Holy Man will not "set the purple of the violet" in a woman's veins or illuminate a woman's eyes with "bright stars."

[6] Although Wordsworth's Young Lady who had been reproached for taking long walks in the country (*P.W.,* II, 287) has been tentatively assigned to the year 1801, the poem may have been written while he was familiar with Habington's Castara, "venturing to walk too far in the neighbouring wood" (Arber, p. 43).

ble for its likeness to Wordsworth's line "If Lucy should be dead!" is Habington's *Upon Thought Castara May Die:*

> If she should die, (as well suspect we may,
> A body so compact should ne'er decay)
> Her brighter soul would in the moon inspire
> More chastity, in dimmer stars more fire.[7]

As might be expected, Habingtonian "translunary" fire would become with Wordsworth an actual English fire beside which the dead Lucy once turned her wheel. Although Habington and Wordsworth both use Nature's sun, moon, and stars to bridge the gap between the mysterious poles of love and death, the "bright" soul of Castara has had an unnatural influence upon the celestial bodies; on the other hand, to Wordsworth's Lucy, more simply, "the stars of midnight" have been dear and to Lucy's lover "the descending moon" has suggested thoughts of her death as a natural event. When Lucy dies, she still lives in the mind of her lover. The difference is to him.

From his songs of "frail love" Habington went on to sing the "chaste chemic art" whereby frail love "is calcined to piety." From his love of Nature's Child in "Three years she grew" Wordsworth would advance through apprehensions about Lucy, and sorrow over her loss, to love of Nature herself and what in his lines composed on the banks of the Wye he had called

---

[7] Arber, p. 27. Note the reference to the moon, with which cf. the "sinking," "descending," "bright" "evening-moon" of "Strange fits of passion."

The two stanzas of Wordsworth's "A slumber did my spirit seal" remind the reader of Habington's "holy death that murders sense" and "crowns me with a victory / So heavenly, all / That's earth from me away doth fall" (*Labia Mea*). In the same poem he has warned us that "*time* controls / Our pride, whose *motion all things rolls*." These very words occur to Wordsworth:

> No *motion* has she now, no force; . . .
> *Rolled* round in earth's diurnal course (cf. "time")
> With rocks, and stones, and trees (cf. "all things").

Waller has a comparable image (*Works*, ed. 1729, p. 59). Cf. also among other variations on the ruins of time Suckling's *Fragmenta Aurea*.

"warmer love," "far deeper zeal / Of holier love"; and thence, in a phrase reminiscent rather of Spinoza than of Habington, he would arrive at "intellectual love" or imagination.[8] Whatever term he uses, he does not fail to recapitulate such raptures of the seventeenth century as dignify Habington's *Perfection of Love*, in which that earlier William and his beloved forsook the earth and traveled to the pure and glorious sphere where they could "fix like stars for ever":

> Our souls on earth contracted be;
> But they in heaven their nuptials *consummate*.

Moreover, it was in this same seventeenth-century figure that Wordsworth would chant "the spousal verse" on the great consummation of his love for Nature herself (Prospectus to *The Recluse*).

In renouncing the dull sublunary flame of carnal love and the trivial activities of courtly and worldly life for the calcined love proper to a recluse, holy man, or poet, Habington would not be an entirely trustworthy guide for the Poet of *The Prelude*, who was no mere anchorite. William Wordsworth's retreat to Grasmere with Dorothy in 1799 began a sterner and more active career than William Habington's settlement with Lucy Herbert at Hindlip in the early seventeenth century. And Habington's quaint lip service to Nature is a dim forerunner of Wordsworth's deep-hearted love of and loyalty toward her. It is in Habington's lines to Castara's father that we first read a message from Hindlip thoroughly congenial to the mature recluse at Grasmere. This message is also a peremptory announcement from the seventeenth century of what will henceforth be "real" in theme and procedure for other English poets in the elegiac tradition:

> Enjoy at home what's real; here the Spring
> By her aerial quires doth *sing*
> As sweetly to you, as if you were laid

[8] See for this term Spinoza, *Ethics* V, *passim* and especially propositions 33–37.

> Under the learn'd Thessalian shade.
> Direct your eye-sight *inward*, and you'll find
> A *thousand regions* in your *mind*
> Yet undiscovered. Travel them, and be
> Expert in home cosmography. . . .
> Man's a whole world within himself.[9]

Elegy is not only calcined love longing; It is home cosmography: the world as come true in the chief discoveries of the inner life.

In some such way the scene was set for *The Prelude*, too. Wordsworth and Coleridge, prophets of Nature, would instruct others by singing

> how *the mind of man* becomes
> A *thousand* times more beautiful than the earth
> On which he dwells, above this Frame of things . . .
> In beauty exalted, as it is itself
> Of substance and of fabric more divine.

All this belongs to autobiography as an outgrowth of elegiac speculation. "The proud miracle of verse," as Habington called it in his sixth *Elegy* on his friend Talbot, would not only reconcile death and love; all the mere happenings of experience would be transformed into a vision of constellated and perdurable stars.

Words, to be sure, grow old-fashioned or acquire new meanings. Images change as a poet's experience is enlarged and diversified. However skillfully deployed, the artifices and metaphors of Habington, even of so great a poet as Donne, are congenial to one generation, quaint to another, and, it may be, burdensome to a third. When Donne uses eyes to "epitomize" countries, towns, and courts, and his less penetrating contemporary, Habington, assures us that "all blessings are epitomiz'd in Love," both run the risk of disregard from a posterity who

[9] Arber, p. 93. Habington refers to "inward war" and "inward grace": both are elegiac themes for him as for Wordsworth and, in our time, Rainer Maria Rilke.

would not know what an epitome is. Just where does poetic diction begin and end? Or is its end in its beginning? Wordsworth's rocks and stones and trees, his floating clouds, mountain springs, rivulets, his motions of the storm, and his stars of midnight may well be the most enduring symbols for those "vital feelings of delight" aroused in and by the beloved maiden, so soon to look her last on the green fields of England—he does not say that her eyes have epitomized the landscape for him.

Nevertheless, the best of Habington's elegiac writing invokes what is never out of date. The sun for him, too, shines on a scene in the mind of man that is thoroughly consonant with Wordsworth's speculative travels through the "haunt, and the main region" of his own song. The love elegies of both poets advance toward the same *anagnorisis:*

> But tell me (glorious Lamp) in thy survey,
> Of things below thee, what did not decay
> By age to weakness? I . . . have seen
> The rose bud forth and fade, the tree grow green
> And wither, and the beauty of the field
> With Winter wrinkled. Even thyself dost yield
> Something to time, and to thy grave fall nigher.
> But vertuous love is one sweet endless fire.[10]

Matthew

More dismaying than any break in a personal relationship is the break in an institutional or cultural tradition, where the death of the teacher, the poet, the ruler, whom too often we take for granted, suddenly leaves us bereft of the kind of vision without which our human life is dark indeed. Whether the keen-eyed or keen-minded friend were Milton's Lycidas, Jonson's Shakespeare or Cleveland's Jonson, King's or Carew's Dr. Donne, Marvell's Cromwell, or that poet and painter Mistress Anne Killegrew whom Dryden memorialized, the elder writers never slighted their dedicated persons. Toward these as toward

[10] Arber, p. 80.

a threatened or a dead beloved the elegists turned humbly, and many were the verses indited to those who might now be irreverently called "eggheads."

It need not surprise us, then, to find that Wordsworth, a close student of seventeenth-century lyric, was aware of the enhanced value of the schoolmaster as a man among men who can ameliorate conditions arising from human ignorance and error. His elegiac ballads of 1799–1800, which concern the puzzle of life and death, time and eternity, show him at work in a genre for which the Holy Man of William Habington may well have served as his chief model. For instance, *The Address to the Scholars of the Village School of* —— (although composed in 1798, it was not published until 1842) with its Dirge for the dead schoolmaster, the other poems on Matthew, the lines *Written in Germany*, *A Poet's Epitaph*, and *Ruth* reflect not only personal experience but careful study of elegiac literature and a growing skill in making names, images, and phrases suggest more than they assert.

Matthew, the schoolmaster, is that "soul of God's best earthly mould," with whom Wordsworth had debated the respective value of Nature and Books (1798). Now that he is dead, he rests a "prisoner of the ground." But these are "idle words," says the poet; he will, rather, bring to the "little noisy crew" of children the farewell blessing of their "common Friend and Father," their Master; and he will compose a "Dirge" of rhymes, however "homely in attire," and ill agreeing "with learned ears." This dirge he addresses to Matthew's former scholars: Shepherd, Angler, Woodman, blind Sailor, half-witted Boy, sick man, and those who have been "bold Settlers on some foreign shore." The list is the familiar elegiac catalogue. All will "deplore" their teacher, but for the bereaved young disciple and the other children "sorrow overcharged with pain" will be "lost in thankfulness and praise"; when the Dirge is changed by the "Orphan Quire," it "will make a touching melody."

In this we are reminded of an elegiac parlance definitely pre-Wordsworthian, and as definitely echoing the seventeenth cen-

tury. Habington, for instance, speaks in his seventh elegy [11] on
Talbot of "well-tuned quires" and "some maimed seraphic
quire," two out of many instances. This word, with another
favorite of Habington, "orphan," reappears in Wordsworth's
"Orphan Quire"; Wordsworth and Habington both use the
pretentious term "deplore." Further, Wordsworth's list of de-
ploring scholars recalls Habington's in the seventh elegy on
Talbot; and Habington's "we dare all the sick humours of a
foreign air" may be compared with Wordsworth's "bold Settlers
on some foreign shore."

But the Address is just the sort of humble modification of
Habington's *Laudate Dominum de Coelis* (David) which we
might expect from Wordsworth. Habington's Eternal Father
and Wordsworth's earthly "common Friend and Father,"
the "Dominum" and the "Master," make a parallel finely
illustrative of both poets, like and unlike as they are.
Habington's "enamored souls" agreeing "in a loud symphony"
to give expression to their "flame" come forth in Wordsworth's
diction as a "little noisy crew" raising their voices "with one
accord" in a dirge which "love prompted" him to make.[12]

[11] *Ibid.*, p. 108.

[12] It is even more curious that Wordsworth's metrical point of departure for this first written elegy on Matthew is the stanza of Habington's *Cupio dissolvi*, which will be used also, and more skillfully, in
Ruth (1799). De Selincourt and Darbishire print a sample from an
early draft of the *Address* (*P.W.*, IV, 451):

> Among the distant stars we view
> The hand of God in rain and dew
>   And in the summer heat;
> Our Master's humble works we trace
> All round his happy native place
>   In every eye we meet.

Habington had designed the lyric pattern as follows (Arber, pp. 143–
144):

> The cunning of astrologers
> *Observes* each motion of *the stars*,
>   Placing all knowledge there:
> And lovers *in their mistress' eyes*
> Contract those wonders of the skies,
>   And seek no higher sphere.

Nevertheless, Wordsworth has not assimilated his elegiac debt successfully enough to make feasible in 1800 the publication of the *Address* with its Dirge on Matthew. It still sounds too much like Habington, too little like himself. In *Matthew, The Two April Mornings*, and *The Fountain*, however, the later elegist, by the help of his imagination and his theory that the feelings give importance to the situation, swings free of the artful diction of such as Habington and of the sententious yoke of death and time. These poems are no mere dirges; the elegies of two previous centuries have been completely transmuted.

The character of Matthew is sketched in words familiar to those who have read the antithetical *characters* of the seventeenth century with their emphasis on confident friendship, happiness in prosperity, and resolution in adversity. In Wordsworth's schoolmaster there may be a more particular echo of Habington's Holy Man who "is ever merry," who "cheerfully entertains" poverty, paying to it neither "a sigh" nor "a wrinkle"; that pair of friends, Matthew and Wordsworth, "travelled merrily." And Matthew beside his daughter's grave reminds us of Habington's Holy Man who "is not frighted with [death]: since it not annihilates, but unclouds the soul."

In lieu of the traditional symbol, the sun, at first Wordsworth reads Matthew's name in "two words of glittering gold." "Can it be . . . / That these two words . . . / Are all that must remain of thee?" he asks. His answer adopts Habington's favorite figure of the soul purified from dross to ore: Matthew is "tempered . . . clay." [13] But Matthew is more than that, and Wordsworth goes on to seek a loftier symbol. For *The Two April Mornings* he skillfully combines images also characteristic of Habington. The part played by the sun, the streams, the sky, the mountain, the slope of springing corn, and the earth opening to devour the pride of mountain and vale is identical in Wordsworth's poems and in *Et Exultavit Humiles*; [14] and Hab-

---

[13] *Cupio dissolvi, Et fugit velut umbra* (Arber, pp. 144, 122–123).
[14] *Ibid.*, pp. 138–139.

ington's fruits, flowers, corn, and vines which "nere fail" are partly responsible, it would seem, for the immortal "bough of wilding" (59–60) in Matthew's hand and now in Wordsworth's mind when he recalls their walk at sunrise on that second of two April mornings. As Matthew preserved his daughter Emma in his devoted love, so Wordsworth preserves Matthew and the bough of wilding in his loyal memory.

The crux of their conversation had been suggested as follows:

> "Our work," said I, "was well begun,
> Then from thy breast what thought,
> Beneath so beautiful a sun,
> So sad a sigh has brought?"

Solar beauty provoking sorrowful meditation is the authentic mark of the elegy from Mimnermus to Paul Valéry; it has never been more clearly set forth as a theme than in Habington's *Love's Anniversary, to the Sun*. His assurances that

> as the *same*
> Thy *lustre* is, as then, so is our *flame;*
> Which had *increast*, but that by *love's* decree,
> 'T was such *at first*, it ne're could greater be [15]

reappear in Wordsworth's lines (1800) on the anniversary of the death of Matthew's Emma:

> The self-*same crimson* hue
> Fell from the sky that April morn,
> The *same* which now I view! . . .
> And yet I loved her more,
> For so it seemed, than till that day
> I e'er had loved before.

Thus Wordsworth agrees with Habington: although the sun itself yields "something to time," "vertuous love" is indeed "one sweet endless fire."

The theme of Wordsworth's *The Fountain* is that of Habing-

[15] *Ibid.*, p. 80.

ton's *Recogitabo tibi omnes annos meos* (Isaiah). The imagery is
not unusual; it would reflect the metaphorical habit of any of
the numerous poets who have described fountain and brook,
even were personal experience inadequate to account for it; but
Matthew's unwillingness to sing old border song, or catch, or
witty rhymes may be adapted from Habington's Job, *Versa est
in luctum cythara mea* with its "ill-strung harp" and "the empty
fallacies of mirth" of one whose "root's in earth." [16]

Matthew, however, relents and again becomes poet, singing
the witty rhymes about "the crazy old church-clock," Wordsworth's concrete image for Job's "omnes annos meos" and
Habington's "past years." After all, it is time that is crazy, not
the man of mirth. Having sublimed or calcined the experience
of death under the sun of two April mornings, Wordsworth
goes on to dissipate the thralldom of time under the symbol of
the water at his feet. In Matthew's words:

> No check, no stay, this Streamlet fears;
> How merrily it goes!
> 'T will murmur on a thousand years,
> And flow as now it flows.

The schoolmaster, survivor of all "his kindred laid in earth," is
not "enough beloved"; but when his friend offers to "be a son"
to him,

> At this he grasped my hand and said,
> "Alas! that cannot be."

As love admits of no diminution, it accepts no substitution.

---

[16] *Ibid.*, p. 117. See Wordsworth's rhyme (49–52):
> If there is one who need bemoan
> His kindred laid in earth,
> The household hearts that were his own;
> It is the man of mirth.

To learn what Wordsworth does to seventeenth-century diction compare
Habington's "feathered music" with "blackbird . . . lark . . . carols" (37–39); "whose parents coffined lie" with "his kindred laid in
earth" (50); "flattered by all" with "my life has been approved" (54).

Thus, although the *Address, Matthew, The Two April Mornings,* and *The Fountain* all concern death, in this series, as it develops, the physical aspect of dissolution is little by little surmounted. The power of the imagination has shaped the feelings of Matthew for Emma and William for Matthew into something superior to accident; in this simple way Wordsworth's elegies are relieved of the funeral gloom which Habington seems never quite able to dispel. Instead of resorting to an abstract "aeternity," as Habington would call it, Wordsworth has come into the deathlessness and timelessness of art.

Moreover, when Habington declares that

> Art cannot regain
> One *poor* hour lost, nor rescue a small *fly*
> By a *fool's* finger destinate to die,[17]

as if to raise the issue on the slightest of Habington's illustrations, Wordsworth rescues from its destined death even the small fly, in a poem which exhibits a curious kinship between these poets of seventeenth and late eighteenth centuries. Adapting Habington's fantastic address to Lucy, the countess of Carlisle—

> Should the cold *Muscovit,* whose fur and *stove*
> Can scarce prepare him *heat* enough for *love,*
> But view the wonder of your presence, he
> Would scorn his *winter's* sharpest injury. . . .
> As a *dull* Poet even he would say— [18]

Wordsworth prefers "the song of the kettle" to "languages German and Norse," "tongs and poker" to a metal stove in Goslar in 1800:

---

[17]Arber, p. 107. "Poor fool" was applied by Wordsworth to the "fly" of *Written in Germany* 6, 9.

[18] Arber, p. 91.

> Here's a Fly, . . . the *dull* treacherous *heat*
> Has seduced the poor fool from his *winter* retreat,
> And he creeps to the edge of my *stove.* . . .
> No brother, no Friend has he near him—while I
> Can draw *warmth* from the cheek of my *Love.*[19]

The "eye-sight and hearing" of the fly are lost; Lucy "neither hears nor sees," and there is neither sound nor sight to serve the parents of Lucy Gray for a guide; old Matthew's eyes are dim with childish tears; yet Wordsworth sustains them all through the refinement of his art. In terms of the Preface of 1800 he has traced the primary laws of our nature in a selection of language really used by men. In diction Wordsworth is concrete where Habington is abstract; in mood Wordsworth is joyful where Habington is plaintive; Wordsworth exhibits the fact in its proper relations while Habington often debases or overemphasizes or sentimentalizes it. And yet, in imagery and in reflective temper Habington and Wordsworth are strikingly akin. Moreover, to both of them poetry is an art developed out of personal experience; and in his lyric and elegiac poems Wordsworth scarcely less than Habington is a conscious artist working in a literary tradition no younger than the Psalms.

From this study of death in its domestic bearing Wordsworth went on to *A Poet's Epitaph.* Here he exhibited the kind of civic and professional death-in-life from which poetry could redeem unfeeling statesmanship and dishonest law, arrogance and self-indulgence in the military, academic, and ecclesiastical orders, and an egoistic and unsubstantial code of morals. With Wordsworth's poem we may profitably compare Habington's *Solum mihi superest sepulchrum* (Job).[20]

[19] The stanza directly following this in the editions from 1800 to 1815 may also be an answer to Habington. The warmth from the glance of the beloved is a familiar figure of *Castara.*

[20] Arber, pp. 121–122. Again, as a study of the simpler diction of Wordsworth, set the two poems side by side:

Habington's Poet welcomes the grave as a safe retreat; here equally soft lie slave, admiral, statist, and aged villager. Wordsworth's Poet welcomes to his grave fingering slave, soldier, statist, peasant. Taking his departure from Habington's own words "the poet's . . . epitaph," Wordsworth seems nevertheless to rebuke Habington's "fancy," which indites such "sad truth." He adapts and amplifies Habington's list of mortal func-

Habington	Wordsworth
Welcome, thou safe retreat!	(Welcome! 15)
Where th'injured man may fortify	(build thy house 60)
'Gainst the invasions of the great.	
Where the lean *slave, who th'oar doth ply*	(fingering slave . . . breaking wave 18, 58)
Soft as his *Admiral may lie*	(Soldier . . . this grave no cushion 14, 12)
Great Statist! 't is your doom	(Statist, in 1800–1 Statesman)
Though your *designs* swell high, and wide	(van of public business 1–2)
To be contracted in a tomb	(Shut close the door: press down the latch: 33)
And all your happy cares provide	(One that would peep and botanize
But for your heir authorized pride.	Upon his mother's grave? 19–20)
Nor shall your shade delight	
I' th' *pomp* of your *proud* obsequies	(man of gallant pride 13)
And should the present flattery write	
A glorious *Epitaph*, the wise	
Will say, "The *Poet's* wit here lies."	(A Poet's Epitaph)
How reconciled to fate	(lay thy sword aside,
Will grow *the aged Villager*	And lean upon a Peasant's staff 15–16)
When he shall see *your funeral state?*	(purple cheer 9)
Since death will him as *warm inter*	(Wrapt closely in thy sensual fleece 21)

tionaries, and in each case he deplores an exclusively sensual or an exclusively intellectual view of life, as does Habington. But to Habington's plea for virtue, humility, and faith, Wordsworth would add love and joy. And, mindful of the "humble zeal" of Habington, the poet, who cannot feel the sad truth he indites and so steals away from the dead—indeed, possibly recalling Habington's cry, "Who will remember, now I write"—Wordsworth in imagination brings another poet to the grave of such as Habington. Here, he represents the dead poet welcoming the living poet, strong or weak, and offering the grave as foundation for a new dwelling.

Wordsworth's scorn for the natural "philosopher," for the "sensual fleece," and for the "moralist" who is merely "a reasoning, self-sufficient thing," can be matched also with Habington's sneers at "that fool philosophy," "that beast dull sense," and "that bedlam reason," in *Deus deus meus* (David).[21] To Habington astrologers and physicians (astronomers and physicists)

Habington	Wordsworth
As you in your gay sepulchre	(rosy 10)
The great decree of *God*	(Himself . . . his own God 28)
Makes every path of mortals *lead*	(led . . . to this poor sod 26)
To this *dark* common *period*	(neither eyes nor ears . . . pin point of a soul 27, 24)
For *what by ways so ere* we tread	(Statist . . . Lawyer . . . Doctor . . . Soldier
	Peasant . . . Physician . . . Philosopher . . .
We end our journey 'mong the dead	Moralist . . .
	think upon the dead.)
Even I, while *humble zeal*	(modest looks 37)
Makes fancy a sad truth indite	(random truths . . . impart 50)
Insensible away do steale	(take . . . soul away 24)
And when I'm lost *in death's cold night*	(Sleep in . . . crust 34)
Who will remember, now I write?	(But who is He 37)

[21] Arber, p. 131.

seem jugglers, who by "slight of art the sight of faith delude"; [22]
to Wordsworth the man "all eyes" and the "fingering slave,"
physicist and philosopher, appear to have an "ever-dwindling
soul." To amend such ethical and civic flaws Habington draws
from his friend Talbot (third *Elegy*) a pattern of artistic life
for both moralist and statist:

> From thee, dear Talbot, *living* I did *learn*
> The arts of *life,* and by thy light discern
> The truth, which men dispute. But by thee *dead*
> I'm taught, upon the world's gay pride to tread:
> And that way sooner master it, than he
> To whom both th' Indies tributary be.[23]

"The dear Talbot," from whom, living, Habington learned before he learned from Talbot dead, may well be responsible for
Wordsworth's advice to the statist:

> First learn to love one living man;
> *Then* may'st thou think upon the dead.

The new poem finally erected by Wordsworth on Habington's elegiac version of Job's *Solum mihi superest sepulchrum* is
for its picture of the living poet indebted to Thomson, from
whom comes the phrase "russet brown," [24] and whose Philomelus is answer to the question, "Who is He, with modest
looks . . . ?" Was it not Philomelus who murmured near the
running brooks of the green isle of indolence a music sweeter
than their own? Was it not Philomelus "unpromising of mien"
who, when rightly judged, was "fair" of soul? [25] Thomson himself and the "easy bliss" of *The Castle of Indolence* may have
prompted Wordsworth to set forth also the reverse of the

---

[22] *Ibid.,* p. 119, *Paucitatem dierum meorum nuncia mihi* (David).
[23] *Ibid.,* p. 104.
[24] *The Castle of Indolence* II, 291; Lienemann (*op. cit.* p. 70) noted
the verbal debt.
[25] *Castle of Indolence,* I, 24–27; II, 293–299.

blazon of the poet; Thomson's "boyish plays . . . when each
thing joy supplied" becomes Wordsworth's

> But he is weak; both *Man* and *Boy*
> Hath been an idler in the land;
> Contented if he might *enjoy*
> The *things* which others understand.

Job, Habington, Thomson, Wordsworth: Job contributed the
"sepulchrum," Habington the elegiac pattern, Thomson the
"poet" in his strength and weakness, Wordsworth the poem,
with all that poetical rebirth implies.

Ruth and the Youth from Georgia's Shore

Still other poems added to the *Lyrical Ballads* in 1800 bear
witness to Wordsworth's elegiac experiments. Of these *Ruth* is
the most notable study of strength and weakness. With some
reservations as to the influence of books of travel on this poem,
and some memory of Waller's *The Battle of the Summer Is-
lands*,[26] we may contrast the setting chosen by Wordsworth for
his Youth from Georgia's shore with Habington's

> *Holy Shade*, where the chaste quire
> Of Muses doth the stubborn *Panther* awe,
> And give the wilderness of his nature law.[27]

Wordsworth's "green shade," his "happy rout . . . of girls
. . . with dance and shout," and "choral song," his "panther in
the wilderness" obviously belong to another century; and his
impetuous Georgian, misusing the "beauteous forms of nature"
to feed his own "voluptuous thoughts," is the antithesis of Habington's *Right Honourable Archibald Earl of Argyle*,[28] a char-

[26] E.g., Wordsworth's "dolphin" and the two whales of Waller;
Wordsworth's "strawberries" and "plants divine and strange, / That ev'ry
day their blossoms change" and Waller's "Palma Christi, and the fair
papá," and his "Ripe fruits and blossoms on the same trees live." Cf.
also Wordsworth's "panther in the wilderness" and the reference made
by Waller to Bacchus; Wordsworth's "happy rout . . . with dance and
shout" and Waller's "They sit, carowsing where their liquor grows."

[27] Arber, p. 19.   [28] *Ibid.*, pp. 86–87.

acter according to the classical pattern of the virtues. What is thereby implied about correspondent virtues and vices helps to explain the steps in the degeneration of the Youth from Georgia's shore. He is an illustration of the peril of exclusively natural modes of human conduct; contrasted with Archibald, in whom the Platonic ideal of justice prevails, the Youth from Georgia stands forth, even in his own phrase, as the result of "false thoughts, thoughts bold and vain." His confidence and pride and his fallacious idea of liberty make a paltry showing against that soul which is a "well-built city," rational, fearless, temperate, just. Nature may be comforting, glorious, beautiful, the cause of joy, pure hopes, and noble sentiment; she may be also tumultuous, irregular, languorous, and the cause of voluptuous thought, self-assertion, and lawlessness. Ethical responsibility lies in the mind of man.

Character itself is thus seen to be an elegiac theme—a theme to which we shall return in our discussion of *Peter Bell*. Ruth, who gives her name to the title of the poem, ill-fated when an unloved child and a deserted bride, mad, vagrant, "broken down and old," is the elegiac *persona* in simplest and least illuminated form. She is not Lucy; and there is no light in her, only sound and movement. "Sounds of winds and floods" made up the music she drew in childhood from her pastoral "pipe of straw." In her madness when deserted she caroused "her cup of wrong" "with many a doleful song / Made of wild words." At last, set free from madhouse to live "beneath the greenwood tree,"

> That oaten pipe of hers is mute,
> Or thrown away; but with a flute
> Her loneliness she cheers:
> This flute, made of a hemlock stalk,
> At evening in his homeward walk
> The Quantock woodman hears.

Did Wordsworth know elegy to have been originally flute song? It seems likely.

Farewell! And when thy days are told,
Ill-fated Ruth, in hallowed mould
Thy corpse shall buried be.
For thee a funeral bell shall ring,
And all the congregation sing
A Christian psalm for thee.

Thus, unobtrusively, Wordsworth submits character to disaster
and then derives salvation not from Nature but from character
itself. As early as 1799 his elegiac thoughts turn from pastoral
"hill and dale" and "airs that gently stir / The vernal leaves"
to "hallowed mould" and "funeral bell" and "Christian psalm."
Such an elegiac peripety composed in a Habingtonian stanza
would have been understood and commended by the writers of
the seventeenth century; and it is not without significance for
Wordsworth's literary biography. Henceforth he, too, will
more and more set aside his oaten pipe for a hemlock flute; and
we need not be surprised that still later his elegiac verse will
echo the psalmody of a Christian congregation.

CHAPTER V

Elegy and
Balladry

The Lucy Poems and *Ballads* of 1723

THE items in time that the chronicler assembles toward history
or the poet organizes as epic we call by their Latin name
"events." When these seem merely to occur, or when their
causes are hidden from us, we speak of them in our native English tongue as "happenings." Beyond elegy's association with the
flute, its skeptical procedure, its personal concern, and its use
of light from darkness as symbol of discovery, it has also a
strong if slender bond with temporal events or happenings. It
does not march in deferential sequence after the great exploits
of mankind as does heroic poetry nor will it be brought to account for its past as in drama. Rather, it challenges time, using
it as a springboard into the timeless.

The events of primary social or political importance in our
own day, events that as effects follow stratagems or, as causes,
precede debate, leave their voluminous record on the minutes
of assemblies and councils: they can be bandied about by the
press. As it were, they consume themselves in the collective di-
gestion of our mass media and call for no poet to interpret them.
It was before the days of radio and television that, when Na-

poleon threatened an invasion of England, a poet must interpret the danger with *Poems Dedicated to National Independence and Liberty*. A century and a half later on comparable occasions, poetry seems irrelevant; no contrived account of an event can so well symbolize man's profound concern as what our ears hear broadcast and our eyes see on the screen. Argumentative editorials there are and lyric cries of approval or disapproval, encyclopedic statistics; but there is no *Iliad*, no *Aeneid*, no *Paradise Lost*. The lofty bickering that accompanies mighty action is itself the poem.

Meanwhile, Lucy is in her grave and "oh! The difference to me." We may bungle in groups, but we suffer and die one by one. This is a fundamental distinction between experience as symbolized in epic and in elegiac ballad.

The best of the old ballads insisted that disaster was a happening whose causes were not to be controlled: storm during the changes of the moon (*Sir Patrick Spens*); the sudden tempest in the emotions of a son or lover (*Edward*); unforeseen misfortune in the adventures of the clan (*Chevy Chase*). If the strongest feelings were to be evoked—of fear or grief or dismay without a name—what had happened must not be blurred by alien images.

> Hame came his gude horse
> But never cam he!

Even as such disaster is known, it stirs us to the center; the bare recital of it is enough. We, too, have had that experience; our feelings, too, are aroused; something momentous has been shared; we are again made part of the human story.

The happening that affects us most deeply, death, is the one we least understand. Defeat, we apologize for or rationalize about; transience, we associate with growth and decay and thus are temporarily comforted; for death there is no balm but thought, and under the stroke of death rational thought is inadequate, almost irreverent. As a result the poetry in which death is the main temporal fact can ill afford vain ornament or impertinent meditation.

Recalling that in its origins elegy dealt, among its other concerns, with death, and that Greek elegiac style was spare and simple, we read the Matthew and Lucy ballads with a fresh awareness of their authenticity. Here is no elaborate discourse, no rhetoric, no lamentation: what dies merely provokes the consideration of what does not die. For instance, April is the recurring month that brings Matthew to his daughter's grave.

> "Six feet in earth my Emma lay;
> And yet I loved her more,
> For so it seemed, than till that day
> I e'er had loved before."

Turning from her grave, he met "a blooming Girl," hair dew besprinkled, brow "smooth and white," foot tripping free.

> "There came from me a sigh of pain
> Which I could ill confine;
> I looked at her and looked again:
> And did not wish her mine."

By dint of looking and looking again—an elegiac procedure—Matthew derives from sanctity of feeling the awareness of a unique relationship and the conviction of human identity—an elegiac *anagnorisis*. As Simonides, the Greek elegist whom Wordsworth admired, had written over two millennia before: "There is no greater touchstone [βάσανος] for any work than Time, who reveals the very heart [or soul, νόον] of a man within his breast."

Matthew's poet was heir not only of the sixth century B.C. but of the eighteenth Christian century, when Bishop Percy would apply the touchstone of time to the English ballad. What might Wordsworth in his turn take from or give to the elegiac balladry of his native land?

During the early years of the eighteenth century, when pastoral and moral writing was much in vogue and the authentic ballad tradition awaited the labors of the Bishop and his friend, William Shenstone, many spurious ballads, tales, and romances had crowded into print. Their attempt to dissipate the shock of death too often deprived it of its proper literary effect. Embellishments bequeathed from the funeral odes and encomiastic orations of a previous century and the *poésie larmoyante* of sentimentalists making the most of mortality stole from the direst of happenings its genuine character. There was a progressive leakage of feeling into images and concepts useless for either comfort or reassurance. We might say that when minstrelsy, however complicated with dance rhythms or folk song, surrendered its statements for protestation and adornment, the ballad suffered most of all.

Evidence of this is abundant in *A Collection of Old Ballads.* The title page continues: "Corrected from the best and most Ancient Copies Extant. With Introductions Historical, Critical, or Humorous, London: . . . MDCCXXIII." [1] The motto of Volume I is quoted from Rowe:

> *Let no nice Sir despise the hapless Dame*
> *Because Recording* BALLADS *chaunt her Name.*
> *Those Venerable Ancient Song-Enditers*
> *Soar'd many a Pitch above our Modern Writers.*
> *With rough Majestick Force they mov'd the Heart,*
> *And Strength and Nature make amends for Art.*

The title pages of Volumes II and III omit the words "or humorous." The motto of Volume II reads: "Celebrare Domestica facta." The motto of Volume III, which bears the date MDCCXXV, reads: "Omne malum cantu vinoq. levato. Hor."

To this *Collection* William Wordsworth probably refers in a marginal note in his copy of John Chetwind's *Anthologia Historica.*[2] Beside the anecdote of Stukely, an English Rebel, he

---

[1] See Francis James Child, ed., *The English and Scottish Popular Ballads* (5 vols.; Boston and New York, 1883–1898), V, 400, where the *Collection* is listed.

[2] See *Transactions of the Wordsworth Society*, VI, 202. The copy of Chetwind's *Anthologia Historica* here referred to is in the Wordsworth

has written: "There is a ballad upon this. See Ballads in 3 vols printed about 1727." On pages 188–194 of Volume I, the reader, as Wordsworth indicates, will indeed find a ballad entitled "The Life and Death of the famous *Thomas Stukely*, an *English* Gallant in the Time of Queen *Elizabeth*, who ended his Life in a Battle of three kings of Barbary." Moreover, on pages 221–226 of this same volume appears the ballad from which Wordsworth quoted memorably in The Preface of 1800: "The Children in the Wood: or, the *Norfolk* Gentleman's last Will and Testament."

If, then, we may assume that Wordsworth was familiar with the *Collection of Old Ballads*, when did it come into his possession or under his eye? [3] And, since there seems to be no proof external or internal of the influence of this *Collection* on *Lyrical Ballads* of 1798,[4] what is its relation to the elegiac *Ballads* of 1800, especially the so-called "Lucy poems"?

In the book of ballads to which he refers us Wordsworth's eye may have fallen upon "The *Suffolk* Miracle: Or, A Relation

---

Collection at Cornell University. Some 125 pages of the *Anthologia* are so marked and annotated that a reader infers the book to have been under the poet's hand during the years 1798–1800, or shortly thereafter. With one exception, the notes concern ballads; and the marks indicate passages suitable for balladry. After an extended survey of Wordsworth's handwriting I am reasonably certain that the book was annotated and marked by Wordsworth himself and, judging from the color of the ink and from the slant and vigor of the script, at one sitting.

[3] Wordsworth might have consulted these old ballads at Alfoxden, at Bristol, at London, or at Hamburg, where in October, 1798, he purchased Burger's poems and Percy's *Reliques*. From Hamburg he might have taken them for study to Goslar. In any case I believe the internal evidence strong to prove that he had carefully read Vol. I of the *Collection* before he wrote the Lucy poems.

[4] In his Advertisement to *Lyrical Ballads*, 1798, Wordsworth asserts that all the poems except the tale of Goody Blake and Harry Gill are "either absolute inventions of the author, or facts which took place within his personal observation or that of his friends." Note, however, that in the *Spectator Papers*, Nos. 70 and 74, familiar to Wordsworth, Addison discusses ballads; and in No. 85, *Two Children in the Wood*. The motto of No. 70 is: "Interdum vulgus rectum videt. Horace, *Ep.* 2.1.63."

of a Young Man, who a Month after his Death appear'd to his
Sweetheart, and carry'd her on Horseback behind him for forty
Miles in two Hours, and was never seen after but in his Grave"
(I, 266–269):

> A wonder stranger n'er was known
> Than what I now shall treat upon,
> In Suffolk there did lately dwell,
> A Farmer rich, and known full well.
>
> He had a Daughter fair and bright,
> On whom he placed his whole Delight;
> Her beauty was beyond compare,
> She was both Virtuous and Fair.
>
> There was a young Man living by,
> Who was so charmed with her Eye,
> That he could never be at rest,
> He was by Love so much possest:
>
> He made Address to her, and she
> Did grant him Love immediately;
> But when her Father came to hear,
> He parted her, and her poor Dear.

The maid was sent to reside with her uncle, forty miles distant. The young man grieved in vain.

> He mourn'd so much that Doctor's Art
> Could give no Ease unto his Heart,
> Which was so strangely terrified,
> That in short time for Love he dy'd.
>
> She that from him was sent away,
> Knew nothing of his Dying-day,
> But constant still she did remain,
> And lov'd the Dead, altho' in vain.

After he had been a month dead, the young man apparently came in the middle of the night to take the maid to her father's home, riding upon "her Father's Horse which well she knew." Her uncle permitted her to ride home with her lover; she mounted; they rode swiftly. His head was aching and she tied her handkerchief about it, promising that "When we come Home a Fire we'll have." Arrived at her home, he left her and went to put the horse in the stable. She called, and the frightened serving-man summoned the father, who now heard that the maid had ridden home with her lover—

> Which made his hair stare on his Head,
> As knowing well that he was dead.

They found the horse in a sweat, but the young man had disappeared. The maid then told of the handkerchief which she had tied about her lover's head. The men opened the young man's grave;

> And though he had a Month been dead,
> This Handkerchief was about his Head.

The maiden was told "the whole Truth" and thereat was so terrified and grieved "that she quickly died."

These are strange fits of passion indeed! much stranger than Wordsworth's simple elegiac ballad of the living lover riding a living horse beneath the real moon along actual paths to the actual cot of his beloved with fond and wayward thoughts in his head instead of a handkerchief bound around the skull of his corpse. The rhyme "head-dead" is insistent enough in the older ballad to have suggested or confirmed Wordsworth's last stanza with its imaginative conclusion "If Lucy should be dead!" The comparison illustrates Wordsworth's desire to keep his reader "in the company of flesh and blood." For an instance of elegy arising from the apprehension of death his change of such as "The Suffolk Miracle" into "Strange fits of passion" serves us well.

Upon the moon I fixed my eye,
All over the wide lea;
With quickening pace my horse drew nigh
Those paths so dear to me.

And now we reached the orchard plot;
And, as we climbed the hill,
The sinking moon to Lucy's cot
Came near, and nearer still.

In one of those sweet dreams I slept,
Kind Nature's gentlest boon!
And all the while my eyes I kept
On the descending moon.

My horse moved on; hoof after hoof
He raised, and never stopped:
When down behind the cottage roof,
At once, the bright moon dropped.

What fond and wayward thoughts will slide
Into a Lover's head!
"O mercy!" to myself I cried,
"If Lucy should be dead."

Nature's boon for a lover is sleep. In a gentle dream death has become a wayward thought. Only the moon has disappeared— to rise again tomorrow night in its properly natural lunar phase. Yet the springs of feeling have been opened and feeling itself emerges in a shape of remembered and imagined beauty.

Next but one to "The Children in the Wood" of the old *Collection* comes "The Bride's Burial," with which we may compare phrases in Wordsworth's Lucy poems, particularly those mourning the actual death of the beloved, the event out of which the elegiac form arises. Instead of the stiff fingers of the dead Bride, the face become like clay, the body as cold as stone, the beauty wasted like snow—all these gruesome details

insisted upon—Wordsworth enumerates the phenomena conces-
sively; and then, with a leap of the elegiac imagination, places
the beloved safe in the mind of the lover.

Old ballad	Lucy ballads
Her Beauty late so *bright*	When she I loved was strong and
Like Roses in their Prime,	gay
Is wasted like the Mountain's	*And like a rose in June.* . . .
Snow,	Her feet disperse the powdery
By force of Phoebus shine.	snow
	That rises up like smoke.
Her pretty Lilly Hands	She seemed a thing that could
With fingers long and small,	not feel
In Colour like the *earthly* Clay,	The *touch* of *earthly* years.
Yea, Cold and Stiff withal.	
When *as* the *Morning–Star*	Fair *as* a *star*, when only one
Her golden Gates had spread,	Is *shining* in the sky. . . .
And that the *glittering* Sun arose	Thy *mornings* showed, thy
Forth from fair Thetis Bed;	nights concealed
	The *bowers* where Lucy played.
Then did my Love awake,	Then Nature said, "A lovelier
Most like a Lilly-*flower*,	flower . . ."
And as the *lovely* Queen of	. . . evening moon . . . sinking
Heaven,	moon . . .
So shone she in her *Bower*. . . .	. . . descending moon . . .
	bright moon . . .
Down in a Swoon she fell	No motion has she now, no
In Colour like the earthly Clay	force;
As cold as any *Stone;* . . .	She neither hears nor sees;
	Rolled round in *earth's* diurnal
	course,
	With rocks, and *stones*, and
	trees.

In earth they laid her then,   But she is in her grave, and, oh,
For hungry worms a Prey;   The difference to me! . . .
So shall the *fairest Face* alive   But the *sweet face* of Lucy Gray
At length be brought to Clay.   Will never more be seen.

If this comparison of old ballads and Wordsworth ballads be justified, surely we gain a clearer understanding of the later poet's literary purposes and poetical method in 1800. Here, on the background of "The Bride's Burial," we have an instance of the Wordsworthian "coloring of the imagination," evidence for his belief that it is "the feeling developed" which "gives importance to the action and the situation." No assumption could be more encouraging to the elegist in any century or country or in regard to any event, simple or infinitely complex.

Only less grievous an event than death in human destiny is exile or banishment, the severance of a man from his native land. Let us note from the *Collection* (I, 120–127) the well-nigh authentic old version of "The Banishment of the Dukes of Herford and Norfolk, in the Time of King Richard the Second"; here the taste of the eighteenth century has less noticeably tampered with the ballad. Norfolk is speaking:

> Now take thy Leave, and last Adieu,
> Of this thy Country dear;
> Which never more thou must behold,
> Nor yet approach it near.
>
> Now happy should I count my self,
> If death my Heart had torn;
> That I might have my bones entomb'd,
> Where I was bred and born:
>
> Or that by Neptune's wrathful Rage,
> I might be forc'd to dye;
> Whilst that sweet England's pleasant Banks
> Did stand before mine Eye:
>
> How sweet a Scent hath English Ground
> Within my Senses now?

How fair unto my outward Sight
Seems ev'ry Branch and Bough?

The Fields and Flow'rs, the Streets and Stones,
Seem such unto my Mind,
That in all other Countries, sure,
The like I ne're shall find.

O that the Sun, with shining Face,
Would stay his Steeds by Strength;
That this same Day might stretched be
To twenty Years in Length! . . .

But Time, I see, with Eagle Wings
So swift doth fly away;
And dusky Clouds begin to dim
The Brightness of the Day.

The fatal Hour draweth on,
The Winds and Tides agree;
And now, sweet England over Sea,
I must depart from thee.

The old version has its proper ring; but how different in spite
of their likeness are the "orchard-plot," the "bowers," the
"green field," the "paths," the "shore," and the "descending
moon" in the poems of that occasional exile who wrote in 1799:

I traveled among unknown men,
In lands beyond the sea;
Nor, England! did I know till then
What love I bore to thee.

'Tis past, that melancholy dream!
Nor will I quit thy shore
A second time; for still I seem
To love thee more and more.

Among thy mountains did I feel
The joy of my desire;

> And she I cherished turned her wheel
> Beside an English fire.
>
> Thy mornings showed, thy nights concealed,
> The bowers where Lucy played;
> And thine too is the last green field
> That Lucy's eyes surveyed.

One's native mountains and the shore of one's country are lovely because they have been cherished by one's beloved. In the fatal hour of exile Norfolk has invoked the help of Neptune and Phoebus; Wordsworth's exile invokes only Lucy, turning her wheel beside an English fire. The pleasant banks, ground, branches and boughs, fields and flowers, streets and stones of the old ballad are in the elegy distinct from those in "all other countries" because they have been loved "more and more." Banishment as an event has become the way to self-knowledge. Sweet England has been recognized as an indestructible idea; and feeling for her is infinitely variable. On such a discovery—whatever the beloved, person or country or idea—the elegist may safely depend in our century as in Wordsworth's.

And Lucy, the catalyst of the poet's feeling? Directly following "The Children in the Wood" in the *Collection* (I, 228–229) comes "The Devonshire Nymph," the pertinent verses of which illustrate the mannerisms in the literary ancestry of Wordsworth's much simpler nymph.

> In the West of Devonshire,
> Liv'd a Maid of Beauty rare,
> Pretty Peggy was her Name:
> Every Creature lov'd her Nature,
> Peggy there had all the Fame. . . .
>
> Fame that oftentimes doth flatter,
> Told the Truth of all the Matter,
> To a young and Worthy Knight,

One lov'd Pleasure, more than Treasure,
Beauty was his sole Delight.

Strait in Love he was involved,
And to try he was resolved,
Whether Peggy would be kind;
But he did never meet with ever
Such a Face, and such a Mind.

When he first beheld the Creature,
All her Charms were lent by Nature,
Neither Spots nor Tower she wore,
But she was singing, and a spining [*sic*]
At her poor old Father's Door.

Burns had celebrated "my Peggy's face, my Peggy's form" in a poem written in 1787 possibly about Margaret Chalmers, but Wordsworth was more safely in the elegiac tradition with his Lucy who dwelt beside the springs of Dove, the Lucy whom there were none to praise and very few to love. That his maiden of the Lucy poems is represented at varying ages may arise from the description in the old ballad of Peggy as both beloved and daughter. The last stanza quoted from "The Devonshire Nymph," with the lines

But she was singing, and a spining
At her poor old Father's Door,

is illustrated in the *Collection* by an engraving (opposite I, 227). This fact, the rhyme on "door," and the change of emphasis from the relation of lover and beloved to that of father and daughter remind us of Lucy Gray, who was

The sweetest thing that ever grew
Beside a human door!

Peggy's "beauty" of "face" and "mind" was the "sole delight" of her knight; "beauty born of murmuring sound" shall pass into the "face" of Wordsworth's Lucy, and into her form "vital feelings of delight," and to Lucy shall be given not only beauty of face, but "thoughts." Peggy's knight resolved to try "whether Peggy would be *kind*," and he found that she was virtuous; Wordsworth's Lucy shall feel in Nature an overseeing power both "to *kindle* and restrain." Peggy sang and span; and the maid Lucy "turned her wheel beside an English fire." Nevertheless the poem Wordsworth began with the lines—

> Three years she grew in sun and shower,
> Then Nature said, "A lovelier flower
> On earth was never sown;
> This Child I to myself will take;
> She shall be mine and I will make
> A Lady of my own"—

depends upon a stanzaic form with tail-rhymes impressively akin to that of "The Devonshire Nymph" about a Peggy whose charms were also "lent by Nature." Did Peggy the Nymph suggest Lucy the Child of Nature?

Lucy died. But the event is not tampered with. There is no elaborate imagery, no ostentatious sorrow. The lover has his memories

> of what has been
> And nevermore will be.

To him has been bequeathed "heath" and a "calm and quiet scene." Although Lucy would now be without motion and force, hearing and sight, to him

> She seemed a thing that could not feel
> The touch of earthly years.

To him! This is the undeniable sign of elegiac writing. The difference is to the elegist.

Peter Bell and Chetwind's *Anthologia Historica*, 1674

Although Wordsworth's first publications were idylls, sketches whose prime reason for being was the peripatetic activity of the observer and whose main unity was spatial, in them are hints—witness the chamois-chaser of *Descriptive Sketches*—that mankind would soon emerge from this early work in a series of *characters*, studies of the elemental nature or humble calling of men and women important to each other and to themselves. The minstrel-bard-and-shepherd-swain of *The Vale of Esthwaite* and the pedestrian traveller of *An Evening Walk* and *Descriptive Sketches* are instances of a literary habit inherited chiefly from Beattie, Thomson, Gray, and Goldsmith, and appropriated by the young Wordsworth as a traditional garb for authorship. Soon, with his maturity, they made way for man more objectively viewed: not only the old beggar and discharged soldier, the guilt-stained sailor and sorrowful vagrant, victims of social injustice or disaster in whom the beginnings of personal responsibility are dimly evident, but also man at work, completely responsible, suffering now and then from his own lack of skill, sympathy, or foresight, and as often succeeding out of his own energy and sagacity.

This more objective view required from Wordsworth a powerful effort of the imagination as well as sharper scrutiny of his fellows and wider and deeper compassion with them. The actual shepherd resident on Westmorland hills and the potter and pedlar traversing them took on meaning and value not only for the author but for other agents in the poem. Thus his simple folks came to life in a web of external relationships. Thus, too, his poetry was brought into closer relation with popular lore, with ballad and folk tale. So many traits does it share with them that at the outset we must grant the relation to be probably collateral rather than surely lineal. Yet, we have some slight evidence of Wordsworth's reading in this literature as well.

His experiment to discover the value for poetic pleasure of poems written in the spirit and manner of ballads has been frequently discussed; but not much has been said about his actual knowledge of the tradition which he was to exalt and refine. Whereas in 1798 he used plots of his own invention or set forth

facts observed by himself or his friends, he went on in 1799 and
1800 to bring into the range of his observation the well-known
themes of elegy, legend, and romance, or facts documented as
historical. Although the ballads added to *Lyrical Ballads* in 1799,
and published in 1800, exhibit a more intimate knowledge of
the elegiac tradition, for that very reason we can the more
clearly detect the poet's own contribution to it. Also to the
"strange fits of passion" he found in balladry he gave a new
spiritual or imaginative character. And, in chief, what he learned
from his review of the fable of *Pilgrim's Progress* during his
own pilgrimage from the Wye to Goslar to Sockburn to Grasmere seems to have inclined him toward other old books of a
popular religious nature. Whether these were anecdotal or doc-
trinary, or both—as in the case of John Chetwind's *Anthologia
Historica*—they in their turn would yield fresh opportunity for
poetic adventure.

Again, the poet was exercising himself in problems of arrangement, poem with poem. As Bishop Percy had the counsel
of William Shenstone for the organization of those *Reliques* so
important to Wordsworth, writer of ballads, so Wordsworth
himself was not without help of a sort from Coleridge and,
possibly, from Southey, at work on his *Annual Anthology*. He
had gathered into a somewhat arbitrary series the poems of
Lyrical Ballads, not all of them ballads; but when the scope of
his characters and incidents was extended and he felt the need
of every good craftsman to exhibit his individual poems in their
right relation, he would more carefully observe whatever anthologies, collections, and miscellanies came within his view.
And there were many such current. Seventeenth-century anecdotes and eighteenth-century balladry and miscellany consti-
tuted a kind of literature for which his own two volumes published in 1807 were to serve as the most distinguished example.

In the rest of this chapter and the next, then, both of them
gathered together from sources not generally known and in
terms somewhat less worn than usual, let us follow him through

the anthologizing process. When he should come to unify the diverse materials of *The Prelude*, its rural and urban episodes and its tragic stories of revolution and reaction, his knowledge of the reading habits of a wide popular audience would help him to shape that yet unfinished poem for the convenience of humble readers of a later day. His own contribution to elegy and balladry, the spiritualization of character or event, is only less remarkable than his fusion of the experiences of boyhood and the meditations of youth into an autobiography. First, he added "spirits"; and, then, from his pantheon of "natural beings" he elicited an arch-being. The "Word" or λόγος of that arch-ballad *Peter Bell* is not unlike the "Nature" of *The Prelude;* both taught him how to organize himself in the light of an idea.

First, what of the poem begun on April 20, 1798, and read to Coleridge and Hazlitt in June of that year? Hazlitt says that when Wordsworth "announced the fate of his hero," Peter Bell the Potter, his tones were "prophetic" and "his face was as a book where men might read strange matters." [5] Since the earliest manuscript of *Peter Bell* is now a fragment, we can only infer the contents of that version of 1798. Except for Peter's oaths "by the devil's beard" and his suspicion of "witchcraft" in the resistance of the ass he was about to steal, there is little to distinguish its treatment from that of *Goody Blake and Harry Gill, The Thorn*, and *The Idiot Boy*, although the author who read it aloud must have been aware of its autobiographical implications and proud of its psychological and ethical truth.

With the revision into MS 2, in which Part III is separated from Parts I and II by matter written in 1800,[6] we find evidence, especially in Part III, of a piety not merely natural but strongly doctrinal; and for its literary ancestors we are compelled to look further along the shelves of Wordsworth's library, even into the disregarded corners of it.

[5] *My First Acquaintance with Poets*, first published, 1823, in Leigh Hunt's journal, *The Liberal.*

[6] *P. W.*, II, 528.

Here, in his copy of John Chetwind's *Anthologia Historica* (1674),[7] some 125 pages are marked and annotated in a way to suggest that the poet concerned himself with the book soon after his return from Germany in 1799. One marginal note refers to the first volume of Southey's *Anthology* (1799), which, according to Cottle,[8] Wordsworth came to know in 1799; a second marginal note mentions a ballad by Bürger, whose poems Wordsworth had bought October 1, 1798;[9] the remaining marginal notes give no useful evidence as to date. We must therefore assume 1799 as the prior date of the annotations. With one exception [10] the notes concern ballads, and the forty-nine marks

[7] See *Transactions of the Wordsworth Society*, VI, 202. The copy of the *Anthologia* referred to bears not only Wordsworth's signature, but in three places that of Samuel Bourn as well: "Sam: Bourn His Book"; "Sam: Bourn"; and, in a different hand, on lines ruled in copybook fashion, "Samuel Bourn's His incromprehensibilibus" [? incomprehensibilibus]. On the title page someone, possibly Wordsworth, has written of the author of the *Anthologia*, John Chetwind, Master of Arts, and Prebend of Bristol, "thro' sufferings conform'd." The motto runs: *Omne tulit punctum qui miscuit utile dulci.*

Samuel Bourn, the elder (1648–1719), was a dissenting clergyman, pastor at Calne in Wiltshire, a short distance from Bristol. In 1695 he went to Bolton, Lancashire, where his son Samuel, born at Calne, was educated. The latter settled at Crook, near Kendal, in 1711. A Samuel Bourn of the third generation was born at Crook in 1714; he is best known as the colleague of Taylor of Norwich, where he baptized Southey's friend, William Taylor (*DNB* VI, 24–28).

Which Samuel Bourn scrawled on the pages of the *Anthologia?* Might a book by a Bristol prebend have made its way five or ten years after its publication into the library of the older Bourn, a neighboring clergyman, to be used in the education of his son? And did Wordsworth come upon this book in the secondhand bookshops of Bristol during his stay at Alfoxden? Or did the book travel with the Bourns into Lancashire, and to Crook, to be picked up in Kendal or thereabouts by Wordsworth following his settlement at Grasmere?

[8] Joseph Cottle, *Early Recollections* . . . (London, 1837), II, 24.

[9] *Journals of Dorothy Wordsworth,* ed. E. de Selincourt (2 vols.; London, 1941), I, 31.

[10] Discussed in my article, "Wordsworth and William Fleetwood's Sermons," *Studies in Philology*, XXVI (October, 1929), 444–446.

call attention to passages suitable for balladry or elegy or of interest for a man speaking to men.

One of these marked passages reads as follows:

Luther adviseth *Erasmus Albert,* that when he preacht before the *Elector* of *Brandenburgh,* he should not order his *discourse* according to the *Elector,* but according to the *unlearned.* If I, saith he, should regard *Philip Melanchthon,* and other Learned *Doctors,* I should do but little *good,* I speak to the simple *plainly,* but when we Learned ones come together, we make it so *finical,* that God himself wonders at us.[11]

The argument of Luther agrees with Wordsworth's purposes as expressed in the Preface to *Lyrical Ballads,* 1800; also, Chetwind's address to his reader—Thou "wilt find more real and useful Content in perusing of six Leaves of these Miscellanies, than in sixscore of the most delightful Romances"—recalls the debate of that year as to *Peter Bell* versus *Christabel.* On July 31, 1800, Coleridge brought to Town-end the second volume of Southey's *Anthology;* poems were read and there was a long talk upon Loughrigg. On August 7 and 12 Wordsworth was composing and altering his poems; *Peter Bell* was read on August 23; a part of *Christabel* on August 31. On September 13 William was writing his Preface, and from September 30 to October 5 the Preface was copied, corrected and amplified. On October 6 it was determined not to print *Christabel* with the *Lyrical Ballads.* During that summer anthologies, the matter of poetry, the Preface, the contrasting methods of the elegiac *Peter Bell* and the romantic *Christabel* were often subjects of conversation. Although it was a little more than a year later, on February 17, 1802, that Dorothy copied the "second part" of *Peter Bell,* on the next day a "new part," two days later, the "first part," and, on February 21, a "second prologue" and a first

[11] Chetwind, *Anthologia,* p. 63. Italics are used as in the original, here and in following citations.

prologue," [12] some of what we have in MSS 2 and 3, as well
as the "new part," may be indebted to Chetwind's "fourteen
Centuries of Memorable Passages and Remarkable Occurrents,
Collected out of the English, Spanish, Imperial, and Jewish Histories, and several other Authors and Writers, London, Printed
by J. R. for P. C. 1674."

"What's in a Name?" asks Wordsworth in the motto to
Peter Bell; "Brutus will start a Spirit as soon as Caesar." In his
copy of Chetwind's *Anthologia* (pp. 12 and 43) he has marked
anecodotes of the magnanimity of Caesar; also one, from Boschier, of Alexander and the pirate who taunted the great con-
querer as follows:

I with one Ship seek my adventures, and therefore am called a
Pirate; thou with a great Army warrest against Nations, and therefore art called an Emperour. So that there is no difference between
us but in the name.

Indeed, while he prepared to revise the main situations of his
tale, the discovery of the corpse of a drowned man after the
attempted theft and the beating of a well-nigh human ass and
the effect on the guilty Peter of the sufferings of those whom he
was mistreating or had mistreated—situations in keeping with
the ballads of 1798—Wordsworth might well have read with
a judicious eye as he marked the following (pp. 71–72, 13, 19):

Luther relates this Law-case: A *Miller* had an *Ass,* which ran out of
his *Yard,* and came to a *River* side, where he went into a *Fisher-
mans Boat* that was in the *River,* and would *drink* thereout, but the
Boat being not tyed, swam away with the *Ass,* insomuch that the
Miller lost his *Ass,* and the *Fisher* his *Boat.* The *Miller* thereupon
complained of the *Fisher,* in that he neglected to tye his *Boat* fast,
the *Fisher* accuseth the *Miller* for not keeping his *Ass* at home, and
desired *satisfaction* for his *Boat.* Now the question is, what the *Law*
is? Who was in fault? Took the *Ass* the *Boat* away, or the *Boat* the
Ass? [Cf. the "river side" and the "tempest-shatter'd bark" of *Peter
Bell.*]

[12] *Journals,* I, 53–58, 61–64, 115–116.

Boschier relates of a man that when he went to confess himself would always beat his Wife, and being asked the reason of it, answered, That being to confess, he found himself very forgetful, so that he could not remember the one half of what he had done; but saith he, when I have beaten my Wife, she puts me in mind not only what I have done that year, but in all my life. [Cf. the reproachful look of the beaten ass in *Peter Bell*.]

Dr. *Boys* in his Postills [*Epistles*] relates a story of a Merchant that would never go to *Mass* but when he heard the *Saints* Bell, would say to his Wife, Pray thou for thee and me: And that this Merchant dreamed that he and his wife were dead and that when he knockt at Heaven gate for entrance St. *Peter* suffered his wife to enter but thrust him out, saying, Thy wife shall enter for her self and for thee. [Cf. Peter Bell's hallucination of his dead wife, who had been used to go to the kirk to pray, two long Scotch miles twice every Sabbath day.]

Those constituents of Wordsworth's revised narrative which exceed the range of the stark curse-ridden balladry of 1798— for instance, the obviously moral passages about the Babylonian harlot, the fervent Methodist, and the dread and potent Spirits of the Mind that play with soul and sense for gracious ends— may have taken color from Boschier's anecdotes of the "Boeotian Harlot" Phryne and the harlot converted by Paphnutius, both marked by the poet in the old anthology (pp. 14–15):

Paphnutius is reported to convert a *Harlot* by this means [:] pretending love he desired to be brought into the most private room she had, which she brought him into, but still he found fault and complained to her that he was afraid some Eye would see him; to which she answered, None can see thee here but only God. To which he replyed, And dost thou think that God sees thee, and yet wilt play the *Harlot?* Which he so enforced, that it prevailed upon her to a change. [Cf. the reproachful "shining hazel eye" of the "patient ass."]

Again, the "carousing crew" of whom a few hours ago Peter Bell would have been a jovial member may be related to the dice-playing Corinthians rebuked by Stubbs in his *Anatomy of Abuses* and marked by Wordsworth in Chetwind's *Anthologia* (pp. 427–428). And most notable among the passages from the moralists quoted by Chetwind and marked by Wordsworth are those which suggest curious hints for Peter's impious oaths, for the crimson stains caused by the blood dropping from the head of the wounded ass (p. 427), and for Peter's attempts to clear himself by blaming the devil (p. 1):

A young man dwelling in *Lincolnshire*, being a grievous *swearer* and his usual *oath* was, *Gods blood*, lying on his *death bed*, the people perceiving nigh his *end*, caused the *Bell* to be tolled for him, which he hearing, rusht up in his *Bed vehemently* saying, *Gods blood* he shall not have me yet. With that his *blood* gushed out, some at his *Toes end*, some at his *Wrist*, some at his *Nose* and *mouth*, some at one joynt of his *body*, some at another, never ceasing till all the *blood* of his *body* was strained forth. [Stubbs, *Anatomy of Abuses*.]

The Devil appeared to a dying man, and showed him a parchment very long, written on every side with the sins both of words, thoughts and deeds of the sick man, and said unto him: Behold thy vertues! see what thy examination shall be. To whom he answered, True Satan, but thou has not set all. Thou shouldst have added, The Blood of *Jesus Christ* cleanseth from all sin: and he that believeth and is baptised, shall be saved.

The redemptive wound and the ghostly word are powerful factors in Peter's conversion; might they be the Wordsworthian analogue of the following Lutheran doctrine (pp. 34–36)?

Luther relates of himself, that being at prayer, contemplating how *Christ* hung on the Cross and suffered for his Sins, there appeared suddenly on the wall . . . a glorious form of our *Saviour Christ*. . . . Now at the first sight, he thought it had bin some good *Revelation*, yet presently recollected himself and apprehended it some jugling of the Devil. For *Christ* appeareth unto us in his *word* and in a meaner and more humble form; like as he was humbled on the

Cross for us; Therefore said he, I spake to the *Vision* in this manner: Away thou confounded Devil, I know no other *Christ*, than
he that was Crucified, and who in his word is *pictured* and *preached*
to me; whereupon the Image vanished, which was the very *Devil*
himself. And in like manner said *Luther* further: A *Gentlewoman*,
a *Virgin* not far from my House at *Wittenburg*, lay very sick, to
whom also appeared a *Vision* after this sort. . . . I admonished her
seriously, that she should not suffer herself to be deluded by the
Devil; whereupon she raised up her self and spit upon the face of
the *Image*, and instantly the *Image* was changed into a great ugly
Snake, which slid to the *Gentlewomans* Bed, and bit her by the *Ear*,
so there stood drops of blood upon the *Ear* which trickled down,
and thereupon the *Snake* vanished. This I beheld with mine Eyes,
said *Luther*, with divers others that stood by.[13] [Cf. the repeated
mention of the ear of the ass.]

The chief redemptive agencies of Part III of *Peter Bell* are
the Spirits of the Mind and Peter's hallucinative memories of the
mother of his child Benoni; but Biblical exhortations assist, and
the whole action is prefaced by references to the gentle soul
reading the godly book. With this we may compare the anecdote Chetwind (p. 26) quotes from Luther concerning *"Al-
bertus Bishop of Mentz* reading by chance in the Bible." Again,

[13] Speaking of images, we recall from Part I the list of startling sights
which Peter Bell might have seen when he looked upon the face of the
dead man in the pool: "Is it the moon's distorted face? / The ghost-like
image of a cloud? . . . *a gallows* . . . *Is Peter of himself afraid?* . . . a
coffin . . . a shroud? / *A grisly idol hewn in stone?* / *Or imp from
witch's lap let fall?* . . . a ring of shining fairies? . . . *a fiend that to a
stake / Of fire his desperate self is tethering? / Or stubborn spirit doomed
to yell / In solitary ward or cell* . . . ?" I have added emphasis to the
items in this list which correspond to the following passages marked by
Wordsworth in the *Anthologia* (pp. 14, 52, 4, 39, 67, 26–27, 49): the
Milesian Virgins hang themselves; hunters lay looking-Glasses for the
Panthers; the Roman idol Janus and the Bavarian idol St. Leonard; the
Halberstadt Kilcrop (Changeling) in Saxony "who sucked the Mother
and five other Women dry"; Mathias de Vai and the Friar in Buda,
Hungary, offering to sit on two barrels of gunpowder to prove their
opposing doctrines true; the man in Milan, commanded never to go out
of its walls, who died of grief when denied his liberty.

when Peter recognized upon the ass the cross scored by the
Lord, who thus humbly deigned to ride into "the proud Jerusalem," he may have done so because his author took pains to
mark these pertinent words from Luther as quoted by Chetwind
(p. 34):

Christ lived three and thirty years, went every year thrice to *Jerusalem*, in all ninety nine times, and yet not withstanding *Jerusalem*
was destroyed. O what a bragging would the Pope have made, if
Christ had bin but once at *Rome?*

And, finally, noting that Peter's good works included comfort
given the widow and the fatherless, we recall that Peter's author
had marked such a function in the *Anthologia* (pp. 32–33):

One comforting a *widdow*, that had lately lost her *husband*, told
her that he was an *unthrift* and *unkind*. She answered, though he
were a bad *Husband*, yet he was an *Husband*.

When we consider the number and applicability of the anecdotes here quoted from what at first sight appears to be a
pseudohistorical junkheap and remember that all but one bear
Wordsworth's mark, we can scarcely deny their interest to an
elegist investigating the ways in which the mind of man is impaired and restored. And should the stanzas of *Peter Bell* here
concerned leave an original ballad intact, we might even further
trust our inference that Wordsworth was indebted to Chetwind's *Anthologia Historica* for the revision now to be read in
MSS 2 and 3, 1800.

Disregarding for the moment the passages that set forth the
list of possible horrors called up by the sight of the corpse in
the pool, certain markedly human traits in the demeanor of the
ass, the dropping of blood to make a "crimson stain," the gentle
Soul and the *Word*, the "Spirits of the Mind," the carousing
crew, the hallucination showing Peter Bell his wife, the fervent
Methodist and his promise of salvation upon repentance, the
Babylonian harlot, the "sweet tears of hope and tenderness,"
the journey on the ass into Jerusalem, Peter's attempt to com-

fort the widow, and especially the "subterraneous devil" of MS 2—most of these the major constituents of Part III—we still have a lucid and powerful ballad like its fellows written in 1798. This ballad would have brought under the influence of "Nature" the wild rude "Carl" to whom a primrose was only a yellow primrose and an ass only an ass; and it would have reunited Peter, the lawless husband of a dozen wedded wives, to the human heart as revealed by the widowed mother and the fatherless children. In treatment, too, the tale would seem more like the other ballads of 1798.

But when, more closely, we regard those passages of *Peter Bell* which have parallels marked in his copy of Chetwind's *Anthologia*, we find Wordsworth working toward a new procedure in the development of character. This procedure is consonant with the elegies written in 1799, also inspired by or indebted to writers of the seventeenth century. With him as with them ethical considerations depend on illumination. Their religious zest for revelation and conversion in the humblest not less than in the highest seems to give Wordsworth a new impetus and a new theme. On the title page of the *Anthologia* he has written of John Chetwind "thro' sufferings conform'd." This phrase points ahead to a literary future which, while it is concerned with what deeply matters to mankind, never loses its glimpse of the light ahead and above.

As late as October 22, 1831, Wordsworth wrote to Basil Montagu: "Traveling agrees with me wonderfully. I am as much Peter Bell as ever." So he had been since 1798 when his face as he uttered the original ballad of Peter Bell may well have seemed to Hazlitt "a book where men might read strange matters." The heartbroken mother of Benoni and the widowed mother of Rachel, like the widowed vagrant and the deserted women in *Guilt and Sorrow* and Margaret of *The Ruined Cottage*, must frequently in the writing and in the reading have recalled to the poet the destiny of Annette and Caroline. That problems of personal and domestic faith were uppermost in his mind also during this first thoroughgoing revision of *Peter Bell* these citations from Chetwind would indicate, even were other evidence of Wordsworth's patient study of his own responsibilities lacking. To the problem of regeneration he applied himself again and again; and in this one respect both the frankly autobiographical *Prelude* (Imagination How Impaired and Restored) and *The Excursion* (Despondency and Despondency Corrected) might seem to be reworkings of the tale of Peter Bell.

But our main concern here is not the problem of personal regeneration; to deal with this he had sterner and deeper messages from greater masters than Chetwind, the historical anthologist. We may note, rather, the mode of artistic transfiguration by which he shaped the homely anecdote, as it was told by such as Luther, Boschier, and Dr. Boys, into the elegiac form which permanently interests the mind. To transfigure the cheap earth of the moralist, the Poet as Potter (in a higher sense than his Peter is potter) skillfully substitutes dread Spirits of the Mind for devils and diabolism and turns the doctrine of the Blood into the conception of the illuminating Word, the λόγος. All this is in the direction of an ethics and psychology and poetics more "general and operative" than John Chetwind or his authorities had conceived. It is an authentic literary discovery, another "spot of time."

Like the lunar adventure and earthly return which constitute the first prologue of *Peter Bell* and like the *character* of the Potter himself drawn in the second prologue of the tale (both of which can be accounted for by Wordsworth's own experience and observations in 1798), the mystic "spots of time" in *The Prelude*, with its return to a bold treatment of substantial things and its careful delineation of Man and men on this green earth, are illustrations in a later period of the forthright poetry of 1798–1802.

In MS W,[14] however, the first which reveals his plan to study

[14] For a description of MS W see William Wordsworth, *The Prelude, or Growth of a Poet's Mind*, ed. Ernest de Selincourt (2d ed.; rev. by

the process of transfiguration or regeneration and the nature of
the imaginative faculty, Wordsworth fused the lunar adventure
and the return to earth by associating the Moon over Mount
Snowdon with the deep dark thoroughfare of the mist through
which the homeless voice of waters rose. Yet Nature working
"upon the outward face of things . . . by unhabitual influence
or abrupt," "that even the grossest minds must see and hear
and cannot chuse but feel," is Nature again at work on that
universal villain, Peter Bell, or William Wordsworth, or the
author and reader of this chapter. Even the horse of MS W

> that stood
> Alone upon a little breast of ground
> With a clear silver moonlight sky behind
> With one leg from the ground the creature stood
> Insensible and still . . .
> A Borderer dwelling betwixt life and death,
> A living Statue or a statued Life

is a rewriting of the stubborn animal true to his dead master,
just as the dead man, drowned in Esthwaite, imported into MS
W from MS JJ, is now to be substituted for the owner of the
ass. The "golden store of books," the "four large Volumes,"
and the "shrines": what are these but the "Word" of *Peter
Bell* in lay form? And, as when he revised *Peter Bell*, in MS W
Wordsworth has gone back to old books or historical anecdotes
for his stories of Columbus, Sir Humphrey Gilbert, Dampier,
and Mungo Park.

Most significant for our parallel, Wordsworth's "malady"
in MS W is the malady of Peter Bell; and Dorothy, like the
Widow of the ballad, helps to cure the sick man. Then, like
the regenerate Peter, who "became a good and honest man,"
the Poet of MS W stands again in Nature's presence "a meditative and creative soul." Along with its several other associations,
MS W of *The Prelude* is verily a *Peter Bell* in blank verse.

Helen Darbishire, Oxford, 1959), p. xxix. Unless otherwise indicated,
quotations from *The Prelude* are from the 1805 version in this edition.

The upshot of the tale of Peter Bell is that Peter emerges from a repeated series of shocks to become "a good and honest man." This brings him into accord with the earliest elegiac concern, the ἀνὴρ ἀγαθός and his ἀρετή. Solon and Xenophanes, says Sir Maurice Bowra, emphasized purity and holiness as the ethical norm for Greek manhood. Before his conversion, Peter had been an illustration rather of the baseness, blindness, and illusion which Solon had called ἄτη. That Wordsworth particularizes the process whereby his potter is enlightened gives his story fresh value in the tradition and foreshadows what would now be recognized as a forthright but more prosaic case study. So near is discourse to poetry.

In the dedicatory letter to Robert Southey, the author underlined his belief "that the Imagination does not require for its exercise the intervention of supernatural agency." The poem differs from many a seventeenth-century conversion primarily dependent on grace for enlightenment. Instead of invoking a miraculous "word" from a "godly book"—as Chetwind's authors would do—he bids the "Spirits of the Mind" to "try . . . / What may be done with Peter Bell"—an early version of psychoanalytic procedure. Peter is "turned adrift into the past": "self-involved," Peter makes no sign of life

> As if his mind were sinking deep
> Through years that have been long asleep.

Moreover, the lunar voyage of the Prologue helps us to span the elegiac gap between the highly calcined elegy of the seventeenth century and the elegiac writing of our own time, so grimly determined to actualize the moon. Between them Wordsworth offers us a humbly tinkered theory of poetry which has particular reference to the elegy. In his symbolic fabric the new romantic crescent moon has only temporarily taken the place of the old translunary sun as a vehicle for imaginative adventure. Although the poet curiously investigates the ten thousand stars, the zodiacal Crab, Scorpion, and Bull (mythic symbols), Mars (heroic), Saturn (georgic), Mercury (rhetoric), Jove (epic), none of these will serve the humble elegist:

> What are they to that tiny grain,
> That little Earth of ours?

He has "left [his] heart at home." Nor is he attracted by opportunities for romantic adventure "above Siberian snows" or "in the depth . . . of burning Africa"; his will be no "magic lore" of "Faery."

> Long have I loved what I behold,
> The night that calms, the day that cheers;
> The common growth of mother-earth
> Suffices me—her tears, her mirth,
> Her humblest mirth and tears.

More particularly invoking Sorrow, guilty Fear, Repentance, he will look homeward for such marvels as the mind finds in life's daily prospect, going on its way with sympathetic heart and lowly soul. This is the program of an elegist rather than an idyllist: calamity operates more effectively toward regeneration than nature; the bray of an ass conveys messages more telling than those from heavenly bodies, not even

> When the full moon was shining bright
> Upon the rapid river Swale.

"For the moon" Peter Bell and his author have not cared "a tittle." It is "in a deserted quarry" that both have come face to face with death in the form of a corse. The moonlight quivers not too helpfully upon the stream. An unintelligible cry is heard: plover? bittern? fox? night bird? wildcat? No, only a sorrowful child seeking a missing father. At every turn in the story, with a riddling suspensive procedure which clears the meaning only bit by bit, the elegist in proper psychoanalytical fashion takes Peter and us through the dolefulness of sound and the "sudden joy" of sight until he—and we—have a vision of errors we have long forgotten. Our guilt is made clear to us,

we are "smitten to the core / By strong compunction and remorse," and at last we may "Repent! Repent!" Peter has had
a psychologically valid vision, no mere "visionary gleam." His
story is indeed a new version of a very old miracle. This time
no taper's light spelling out a word on the sudden blackness of
a snow-white page and thus "disordering colour, form, and
stature" will serve the purpose of his elegiac affair. Good men
will rather feel the soul of nature; *"and see things as they are."*
Right feeling has been encouraged and regeneration has been
accomplished by a device we have come to know full well—
anagnorisis—although we have renamed it for our own satisfaction. When Peter sits quietly "self-involved,"

> As if his mind were sinking deep
> Through years that have been long asleep,

we associate with his cure not only the old comfort elegists
supplied mortals in centuries B.C. but the new relief psycho-
analysts afford them in the Christian centuries. "What's in a
name?" asks Wordsworth at the beginning of *Peter Bell*.

CHAPTER VI

Miscellany into
Autobiography

Poems in Two Volumes and Husbands' *Miscellany*, 1731

AT the other and more impressive end of the ethical scale from Wordsworth's Potter is his Pedlar: the former, powerful, intense, recklessly purposeful, is type of the Dionysiac in art; the latter, more deferential to other folks and other situations, man of counsel and affairs, endlessly patient, might illustrate our metaphor of heat and light as a son of Apollo. Both are elegiac persons studied in relation to weakness and strength of character and vicissitude in external circumstance; in both, energies are at the peak; and, in both, Wordsworth seemed to be exploring and balancing the two aspects of his own genius.

Just as the vagrant in him confessed himself a kind of Peter Bell, the philanthropist in him turned out to be a Pedlar with a somewhat "weary load," a "pack of rustic merchandise," singing "Scotch songs" and repeating

> Scotch poetry, old ballads, and old tales,
> *Love-Gregory*, *William Wallace* and *Rob Roy*.[1]

During his elaboration of this character to serve as interpreter of the sad tale of *The Ruined Cottage*, the future author of an

---

[1] MS B (1797) of *The Ruined Cottage;* verso of MS B, and MS D (1799); *Addendum* IV (1801–1802) to MS D. See *P. W.*, V, 380, 395, 404, 406, 413.

autobiographical poem was exercising himself in an assumed role just as surely as while he was composing and revising *Peter Bell*. Potter and Pedlar: in March of 1802, Dorothy wrote in her Journal, "William has been talking about publishing the York-shire Wolds poem [*Peter Bell*] with *The Pedlar*." [2] And in the Fenwick note to *The Excursion* Wordsworth states that, had he been deprived of "a liberal education,"

> it is not unlikely that . . . I should have taken to a way of life such as that in which my Pedlar passed the greater part of his days. At all events . . . the character I have represented in his person is chiefly an idea of what I fancied my own character might have become in his circumstances.[3]

For these reasons and also in view of the entanglement of *The Pedlar* with early blank verse destined to become part of *The Prelude*, we should inquire at this point what outstanding trait of this literary *persona* (whose boyhood was in its inner nature so like the boyhood of William Wordsworth) enabled James Patrick, the "intellectual Pedlar" of Kendal (alias the "Packman" of Hawkshead, alias "the venerable Armitage," alias "Patrick Drummond," Scotsman of Perthshire) to develop the imagination which in time would make him the highly effective Wanderer of *The Excursion* while the youth William was becoming the Poet of *The Prelude*.

We may infer the answer as we watch him fusing into one whole the disparate elements of his tale of Margaret of *The Ruined Cottage*. His "rustic merchandize" has become precious treasure of the spirit for salesmanship of a higher order; in his pack are now to be found the most interesting phenomena of Nature and Man both. His "words have consecrated many things"; he has "contemplated . . . forms in the relations which they bear to man." As one who contemplates and consecrates he is, of course, the elegist searching for light and human comfort from the diverse phenomena of life and death.

[2] *Journals*, I, 122.   [3] *P. W.*, V, 373.

The Bible had been the Pedlar's first book, which as "the written promise" he had learned to reverence when he was a shepherd communing with the living God on the high mountains under the sun and clouds, above the ocean and earth. Traditionary tales and legends "nourished Imagination in her growth":

Yet greedily he read and read again
Whate'er the rustic Vicar's shelf supplied,
The life and death of Martyrs [4] . . .
                                                    and here and there
A straggling volume torn and incomplete
Which left half-told the preternatural tale,
Romance of giants, chronicle of fiends
Profuse in garniture of wooden cuts
Strange and uncouth, dire faces, figures dire,
Sharp-kneed, sharp-elbowed, and lean-ankled too
With long and ghostly shanks, forms which once seen
Could never be forgotten.[5]

In short, books were the passion of the Pedlar, as Wordsworth tells us in his Fenwick note. The Bible, popular religious lore, Milton's poems bought with his earnings, mathematical books loaned by his schoolmaster, books of science explaining "the laws of light": these were the fare of the boy. And when come to man's estate he did not miss "the dead lore of schools," for he could repeat the songs of Burns. The Pedlar was mainly the product and interpreter of unsophisticated literature in the elegiac mode; and at the time this *character* was composed and recomposed, 1797–1802, its author must have been freshly aware of the influence of pietistic books, and of those miscellanies which aimed to popularize masterpieces by peddling their fragments.

Have we any hints of such contemporary interest or influence? Even if not the probable cause, might some "straggling

[4] Cf. Faithful in the Vanity Fair of *Pilgrim's Progress* and the Martyrs of Foxe.

[5] *P. W.*, V, 383, for the version in MS B of *The Ruined Cottage*.

volume" illustrate for Wordsworth, too, the traditional wares which must be transmuted into contemporary merchandise?

On April 15, 1802, returning home, via Gowbarrow Park and the daffodils, from a visit at Eusemere with the Clarksons, Dorothy and William took refuge from the rainy night at Dobson's inn, where after "a goodish supper" before "a bright fire" William amused himself with "a volume of Enfield's *Speaker*, another miscellany, and an odd volume of Congreve's plays." With the further help of "a glass of warm rum and water" brother and sister "enjoyed [themselves] and wished for Mary." [6]

Beyond the review of familiar poems, and the glance at its arrangement and manner of presentation, the *Speaker* would scarcely hold his attention; but that other "miscellany" tempts us to guess at its editorship and contents. In response to an inquiry the late Gordon Wordsworth wrote me as follows:

From my knowledge of Westmorland ways I should guess that what Dorothy calls (I expect ironically) the Library at Dobson's inn would be merely a heap of neglected books piled up in a corner of a window-seat. To this day it is the favourite receptacle for unwanted literature in the humbler houses, and after the lapse of a century and a quarter, and in view of the frequency with which houses of entertainment change hands in this district I am afraid any attempt at following up would be quite hopeless.

Quite hopeless. And yet that miscellany would have been one of a kind and might have been of a kind uniquely helpful to a

[6] *Journals*, I, 131–132. If Enfield's *Speaker* were the sixth European edition, which I have consulted in the first American edition (1799), its excerpts would have brought to mind well-known passages from Pope, Milton, Armstrong, Melmoth's *On Taste*, Shakespeare, Gray, Goldsmith, Mason, Warton, Collins, Thomson, Dryden, Sterne (on Negroes), Fordyce's *Character of the Virtuous Man* (an interesting analogue of Wordsworth's *Character of the Happy Warrior*); its quotation of the Spectator paper *On the Immortality of the Soul* would be a timely reminder for a poet composing an *Ode* on that theme; possibly its chief interest to Wordsworth would be its arrangement into Select Sentences, Narrative Pieces, Didactic Poems, Argumentative Pieces (including Odes, Elegies, Hymns, Characters), and Pathetic Pieces.

poet who was publishing a third edition of *Lyrical Ballads* [7] and composing a group of occasional poems—lyrics, idylls, *characters*, elegies, sonnets, and an ode—for which a fresh arrangement must soon be made: *Poems in Two Volumes, 1807.* Such a *Miscellany* by John Husbands [8] has been carefully reviewed by Professor Crane.[9] It was published in 1731 with a Preface "containing some remarks on the beauties of the Holy Scriptures"; and in this Preface certain phrases congenially foreshadowed the critical theory and poetic art of Wordsworth. Poetry is "the universal language of men"; the "sacred Authors" employed as images "sensible and familiar objects . . . with which those to whom [they] wrote were daily conversant." And for the great *Ode* in process during the spring of 1802, the following would be helpful in more ways than the establishment of a simple diction. The emphasis I have added:

Sometimes *Intimation* is stronger than Expression. The *Intimations of* God's Power in HOLY SCRIPTURE are so very strong that they surpass all the Force of Language. . . . Nature also is confederate with Providence: The Natural so corresponds to the Moral World, as if it was its Minister and Servants. The Mind is Here opened and enlarged to new Views, and more glorious Prospects: We are related to the Universe and the Family of Heaven and Earth become one. . . . Our hopes are raised and enliven'd and our Anxieties and Fears allay'd: We have a Mediator to intercede with God, who is God himself; the Courts of Heaven, and the thrones of Angels are the proposed Reward; this Corruptible shall put on Incorruption, and this mortal be cloathed with *Immortality.*

[7] These volumes arrived at Grasmere June 22, 1802 (*Journals*, I, 163).

[8] J. Husbands, A.M., Fellow of Pembroke-College, Oxon., *A Miscellany of Poems by Several Hands* (Oxford, 1731). There is a copy of this volume in the Newberry Library, Chicago.

[9] R. S. Crane, "An Early Eighteenth-Century Enthusiast for Primitive Poetry: John Husbands," *Modern Language Notes*, XXXVII (January, 1922), 27 ff. Professor Crane relates Husbands' preface to similar treatises of the time, notably those of Boyle (1663), Leclerc (1688), Nichols (1669), Jenkin (1700), *Spectator Papers* 327, 339, 453 (1712), Felton (1713), Gildon (1721), Fenelon (translated 1722), Calmet (1722–1724), and Blackwall (1725).

This is a clearer echo of seventeenth-century theology than harbinger of eighteenth-century metaphysics; and its "new views and more glorious prospects" illustrate even as they commend symbols and intimations rather than sententiae and doctrinal statements for the *anagnorises* of elegy.

There seems to be no record of the exact date in 1802 when the additions and Appendix to the Preface to *Lyrical Ballads* went to press; and there is likely only a coincidental relation between Wordsworth's famous adaptation of Aristotle—

Poetry is the most philosophic of all writing: . . . its object is truth, not individual and local, but general and operative; not standing upon external testimony, but carried alive into the heart by passion—

and the following from Husbands—

Fables of old were the Language of *Philosophy*. . . . Men will attend to Nothing so readily as to what flatters their Passions. . . . Pleasure . . . is the best vehicle to Precept. . . . The Foundation of all Beauty in Composition is Truth. . . . Yet pure truths . . . [here Husbands quotes Malebranche's *Recherche de la Vérité*] represented naked and as they are in Themselves, do not so forcibly affect the Mind as when they are convey'd to it under sensible Appearances. . . . Yet we must make use of such sensible Things as dazzle not too much, but such as make the Truth appear to Us in a charming and attractive dress. . . . The use of Fiction is . . . to animate the Thoughts and Affections, and to make them (as it were) breathe and live.

But the parallel is chastening for a criticism that overemphasizes the contribution of Wordsworth and Coleridge to English critical theory.

In the Appendix, Wordsworth (like Husbands) is particularly concerned with the language of passion and the way in which it has been wrested from its proper use. To illustrate this distortion he considers metrical paraphrases of passages in the Old and New Testaments to be inferior to their originals and, with

like judgment, refers to Pope's *Messiah*. Such biblical para-
phrases are important in the Table of Contents of Husbands'
Miscellany, along with Dr. Johnson's translation into Latin of
Pope's *Messiah*.

The *Miscellany* is not too loyal an illustration of Husbands'
prefatory argument; but the likeness of their theoretical positions places Wordsworth comfortably by the side of Husbands
with regard to the literary importance of biblical training. Sacred Scriptures, says Husbands in 1731, "fly all Dress, and
adventitious Ornament"; "Scripture-Comparisons" are never
used "but to cast some new Light upon the Thing to which they
are applied." Further, Husbands' Table of Contents approves
the juxtaposition of simple themes of diverse nature in poems of
various generic origin. He reminds us that "Palm-Trees, Cedars,
Lions, Eagles are common in Palestine" [10]—welcome encouragement for a poet in the Lake Country writing about daisies,
celandines, butterflies, glowworms, robins, cuckoos, green lin-
nets, sparrows, skylarks, and dogs, not to mention beggars,
tinkers, potters, and pedlars. In brief, Wordsworth would find
in Husbands' *Miscellany* an enabling pattern for his own *Poems
in Two Volumes*, 1807.

If from these two volumes of Wordsworth we set aside the
sonnets written after reading the sonnets of Milton, the poems
composed during his tour in Scotland in 1803, remnants of
balladry not assimilated in *Lyrical Ballads*, and a few other
local and temporal accounts of experiences to be found also in
Dorothy's *Journals*, there is a residuum of pieces effortful, almost pseudoliterary, as if deriving from models he was trying

---

[10] In the Fenwick note to his couplets *Suggested by a Picture of the
Bird of Paradise* Wordsworth would write almost in Husbands' phrase:

If it were not that we learn to talk and think of *the lion and the eagle,
the palm-tree and even the cedar* [my italics], from the impassioned
introduction of them so frequently into Holy Scripture and by great
poets and divines who write as poets, the spiritual part of our nature,
and therefore the higher part of it, would derive no benefit from such
intercourse with such objects.

to redeem or remake. Some of these are successful ("She was a Phantom of delight" and *Character of the Happy Warrior*); some still bear upon them the artifices of their possible models.

For instance, Wordsworth's nightingale of the "fiery heart," whose notes "pierce and pierce," singing "as if the God of wine / Had helped [him] to a Valentine," recalls the "Anacreontick" from the Greek of Julian, Cupid caught and steept in wine, which the Lover quaffs, "wine and God together," only to suffer from "tingling Veins" and "thrilling Smart." [11] Wordsworth contrasts the song of such a nightingale with the homely tale of the stock dove, which suits him better. This kind of literary exercise is in the vein of another old Anacreontic, *A Night Piece to Eliza:*

> Arise my Fair, Arise my Dove,
> With Me along the Meadows rove,
> Beside the Stream, within the grove.
> The fragrant, cool, and silent Hour,
> The pleasing Walk, the woodbine Bow'r,
> The mild Approach of peaceful Night,
> Ten thousand lovely Scenes invite,
> The smiling Meads, the gentle Air,
> The Streams and Groves invite my Fair. . . .
> *Sweet Musick warbles on thy Tongue,*
> *Sweeter than Philomela's Song.*[12]

Enough of Eliza, dove though she be. Let the reader now review Wordsworth's *Louisa*, and he will be grateful for Louisa's rocks and rivulets, moorland and waterfalls, and better understand why Wordsworth was proud to include her in his miscellany of 1807.

And when we investigate further the Anacreontics of the *Miscellany* with their echoes of Anacreon and Theocritus and Julian, Cupid hunting "Butterflies with painted Wings," plucking "from Wasps their forky Stings," gathering posies

---

[11] *Miscellany*, pp. 153–154. See also *On Valentine's Day* in the volume.
[12] *Ibid.*, pp. 126–150.

> Where silver-circled Daisies rise,
> Where knots of snow-white Lillies grow,
> And scarlet-tinctur'd Roses glow,[13]

we prefer Wordsworthian butterflies and daisies even while we recognize their formal association with the idyllic trifles and love elegies of a century before. Did not Wordsworth write of the daisy's "silver-shield with boss of Gold"?

We note, also, that when, a fortnight after the visit at Dobson's, Wordsworth praised the celandine visited by the "curious Bee," again he was in the elegiac tradition of the *Miscellany*—

> With wanton Flight the curious Bee
> From Flower roves to Flower free,
>   And where each Blossom blows
> Extracts the Juice of all He meets,
> But for the Quintessence of Sweets
>   He ravishes the Rose.[14]

"Poets . . . are wanton wooers," he says, agreeing with the retort of the mistress Rose to her apologetic lover:

> The faithless, fickle, wav'ring Loon,
> That changes oft'ner than the Moon,
>   Courts each new Face he meets;
> Smells ev'ry fragrant Flow'r that blows,
> Yet slily calls the blushing Rose
>   The quintessence of Sweets.[15]

Within a fortnight after the inspection of the "miscellany" at Dobson's, Wordsworth was correcting his Chaucer translations; Husbands' *Miscellany* has two Imitations of Chaucer. Within three weeks after the inspection of the "miscellany" at Dobson's, Dorothy was reading *Il Penseroso* to her brother; Husbands' *Miscellany* has an *Il Penseroso* on the theme of solitude taken as a text from Milton's *Il Penseroso*. The *Miscellany*

---

[13] *Ibid.*, p. 151.
[14] *Ibid.*, pp. 56–57, *To his Jealous Mistress, an Ode.*
[15] *Ibid.*, p. 71.

includes also a search into "the stupendous Miracles of Nature's daedal Hand" [16] by means of an "optick Tube," reminding us of the "Telescope" of *Star-gazers,* a less well-known item in Wordsworth's miscellany of 1807. Similarly Wordsworth's *Power of Music,* another tour de force in the volumes of 1807:

> An Orpheus! an Orpheus! yes, Faith may grow bold,
> And take to herself all the wonders of old;—
> Near the stately Pantheon you'll meet with the same
> In the street that from Oxford hath borrowed its name—

gains a new value as a simplification of the *Orphic Fragments* paraphrased in the stately *Miscellany* of John Husbands, Oxon. If the "miscellany" at Dobson's had been that of Husbands, what strong and lasting impressions from it would have been made upon the sensitive mind of the anthologist warm from fire on the hearth and rum-and-water in the glass after the wet journey of April 15, 1802!

It is from the paraphrase of Psalm 104 and a poem entitled *The Country* in the *Miscellany* of 1731 that the diverse items later gathered together in 1807 find their amplest license; but even without Husbands' volume, Psalm 104 is one source for all the wonders in Wordsworth's *Ode* with its manifold expression of praise. Only less revealing is a comparison of *On Happiness* of the *Miscellany* with its more optimistic successors, Wordsworth's *Happy Warrior* and *Ode to Duty;* the long life of the beatitude is no accident. I have added the emphasis to what the contributor of 1731 says:

> Distant our Prospects beautiful appear,
> Beheld thro' Fancy's magnifying Glass,
> But th' unsubstantial *Phantoms, brought too near,*
> Like any *Ghosts* elude our fond embrace.
> What . . . the *Virgin's* Beauty, and the Lover's Sigh?

---

[16] *Ibid.,* p. 164. Wordsworth's one use of "daedal" occurs in his *Sequel* (1817) to *The Beggars* (1802).

In answer we have only to quote the lines about Mary Wordsworth:

> She was a *Phantom of delight*
> When first she gleamed upon my sight. . . .
> I saw her *upon nearer view,*
> A *Spirit,* yet a Woman too. . . .
> Her household motions light and free,
> And steps of *virgin*-liberty;
> A creature not too bright or good
> For human nature's daily food.

Although the contributor of the *Miscellany* found felicity

> in Him alone. . . .
> Here Happiness immortal does reside
> With full Contentment, perfect Love, and
> Wisdom by her side,

instead of concepts and abstractions and symbols Wordsworth
offers us a happy Man and a happy Woman.

In 1802, however, Wordsworth was not only recording
moods of his own mind but meditating on the story of his own
career. Although we must not assert any genetic influence between an hypothetical miscellany and an actual poem, there
is a profitable discovery awaiting us when we place Husbands'
Miscellany at the side of Wordsworth's *Prelude.* How completely the autobiography has absorbed the poetic themes of its
century! How successfully the autobiographer has fused the
diverse literary interests of the anthologist!

For instance, those three Epistles from Oxford should be
compared with the account of Wordsworth's college life at Cambridge; and that catalogue of rural delights, *The Country,* with
his sketches for Summer Vacation. The literary Imitations and
Paraphrases run parallel to his Book on Books. *Reflections* on
the pastorals of Solomon and Virgil in the *Miscellany* fore-
shadow the large illustration of artificial pastoral in Book VIII
of *The Prelude.* Elegiac verse in the *Miscellany* is akin to the

elegies in *The Prelude*, especially the passages on the Maid of
Buttermere and Raisley Calvert. Fables from Phaedrus and an
address to a favorite Horse in the *Miscellany* inhabit the same
literary barnyard with the Parent Hen, the Mountain Terrier,
the Lamb and the Lamb's Mother, the Lost Sheep, the Shepherd's Cur, and the Heifer of the Hunger-bitten Girl of *The
Prelude* whose Horse, indeed, had been excised from MS W.
An address "to the Reverend Mr. Rodd, School-Master in
Hereford," would make way for Wordsworth's address to his
schoolmaster William Taylor; both addresses are in close prox-
imity to noble hymns. Dreams and Rhapsodies and Morning
Hymns, Chansons and Evening Hymns, Odes and Palinodes
aplenty need only to be related to the autobiography of a Poet
to gain fresh interest for their matter and form.

Chiefly in the epic passages of *The Prelude* we find echoes
of the loftier items in Husbands' *Miscellany*. Prophecies from
Isaiah 60 sound the key for Wordsworth's prophetic passages.
Beatitudes for obedience and curses for disobedience from
Deuteronomy 28 anticipate his severity in the treatment of
personal error and national injustice. Psalm 137, of the Babylonian captivity, sets the fashion for his later record of actual and
spiritual exile and nostalgia. Ezekiel 34 with its reproof of the
shepherds is an earlier instance of the literary denunciation
heard again in Wordsworth's rebuke to British shepherds, states-
men, during the French Revolution. Job (3) with his curses for
the day of his birth prefigures Wordsworth's bitterness against
his fatherland. And was Habakkuk (3) not one of those "ancient Prophets" denouncing

> On Towns and Cities, wallowing in the abyss
> Of their offences, punishment to come?

Again, we must say that, if a miscellany like that of Husbands
pointed out to Wordsworth the ample circuit of literary genera
possible in one volume, it would have been welcome to the
author of an unfinished poem. With his energies heightened and

his imagination refreshed on that actual evening at Dobson's, Wordsworth would in one reading of that other "miscellany" have discovered what it needed. Instead of such an aggregate of many miscellaneous poems he would write the autobiography of one poet, fusing the items of peddled poesy into merchandise of rare new value.

How such fusion takes place in the mind he himself has told us in a letter of May 21, 1807, to Lady Beaumont. He is speaking of his own miscellany, the *Poems in Two Volumes*, of 1807:

Who is there that has not felt that the mind can have no rest among a multitude of objects, of which it either cannot make one whole, or from which it cannot single out one individual, whereupon may be concentrated the attention divided among or distracted by a multitude? [He describes a particular instance.] My mind may be supposed to float up and down among them in a kind of dreamy indifference with respect either to this or that one, only in a pleasurable state of feeling with respect to the whole prospect. . . . This continued till that feeling may be supposed to have passed away, and a kind of comparative listlessness or apathy to have succeeded. . . . All at once, while I am in this state, comes forth an object, an individual, and my mind, sleepy and unfixed, is awakened and fastened in a moment. . . . The mind being once fixed and rouzed, all the rest comes from itself.[17]

But it is high time for us to return—as did the poet of Peter Bell—from all these monstrous zodiacal constellations to the green earth of literary fact. What in the structure of *The Prelude* bears out our study of Wordsworth as an elegiac poet?

The Elegiac Form of *The Prelude*

The various themes and the constituent literary forms of *The Prelude* have been discussed elsewhere; in chief, its structure as an epic or monodrama has been detailed.[18] Recalling

[17] *The Letters of William and Dorothy Wordsworth: The Middle Years*, ed. E. de Selincourt (2 vols.; Oxford, 1937), I, 128–129.
[18] E.g., in Potts, *Wordsworth's Prelude*.

Aristotle's preference for an involved plot, in which *anagnorisis* accompanies *peripeteia*, we may note that in this modern action, too, the Poet's discovery of the nature of his selfhood precedes and justifies his final dedication.

Here let us consider Wordsworth's autobiography as an extended elegy, a series of revelatory moments for their own sake; furthermore, let us view it as a love elegy in the traditional Latin sense, a persistent inquiry into the soul of the shining beloved and on a mightier scale than was possible in the Lucy poems. Indeed, now that Nature's Child, Lucy, is dead, it is his maturing love for Nature herself that the Poet celebrates. As devotedly as Propertius ever with Cynthia or the Black Knight with Blanche his Duchess or Habington with Castara, William will consider himself married to that "external world" of Nature and Man for whom he proposed to

> chant, in lonely peace, the spousal verse
> Of [a] great consummation.

Especially when *The Prelude* by-passed *The Recluse* and the external world was personalized in Nature the Beloved, did the spousal symbol fit his purpose; it presides over a love elegy told in as mellifluous a blank verse as was ever substituted for flute song.

No more than in the autobiographical series of Propertius or the various Propertian love series of our modern world—those of Pound, Yeats, and Lawrence, for instance—can we disregard the exploratory nature of the writing. Wordsworth's, like theirs, is no mere aggregation of memories leading to generalizations; its episodes are speculative tools to release and channel feeling toward what Husbands would call "more glorious prospects." The tissue of the very first paragraph of *The Prelude* is interrogative, seeking out the Poet's destination and his "course." When the "gleams of light / Flash[ing] often from the East" disappear to mock him "with a sky that ripens not / Into a steady morning," or "the meditative mind" of the

Poet has "goadings on / That drive [him] as in trouble through the groves," he is the veriest poetical tyro or freshman in need of what is now called "orientation." No curriculum of themes from heroic legend, no song of Truth fitted to the Orphean lyre, contents him; nothing but a lofty Song of Love will do.

He thinks of Nature first as a *docta puella*, a schoolmistress opening up the clouds for his comfort or employing "severer interventions" for his discipline. All her lessons end in revelation. Her influence enlarges the threatening mountain under the stars and the grey sky when he has stolen the skiff from the shores of Patterdale; here the *anagnorisis* reveals unfamiliar Forms, huge and mighty, threatening, chastening. The more familiar image of a star gleaming upon the ice as he skates over Esthwaite is one of the "beauteous forms or grand" with which she delights him, as is the "spectacle" of the "rising moon" over the Sands of Westmorland, the Creek and Bays of Cumbria's rocky limits. When a child, then, he has felt "gleams like the flashing of a shield"; or in a more personal way he has begun to think of the "face of Nature" as having "substantial lineaments" both "visible" to the eye and "depicted" on the brain. Therefore his "recollected hours" have for him "the charm of visionary things" that

> almost make our Infancy itself
> A visible scene, on which the sun is shining.

This discovery of another being is an early stage in the process of self-discovery and as in much older elegiac writing—before the chthonian gods were to take over—it is symbolized by sunshine. Sun and moon both assist in the enlargement of the boy's sympathies, the sun

> as a pledge
> And surety of our earthly life, a light
> Which while we view we feel we are alive . . .
>   . . . . .

And from like feelings, humble though intense,
To patriotic and domestic love
Analogous, the moon to me was dear.

When Nature "at length was sought / For her own sake" and his "mind lay open" to her "finer influxes," his moments with her "appear'd like something in [him]self, a dream / A prospect in [his] mind." He would walk with her in the "spirit of religious love"; and she for her part would defer to him:

An auxiliar light
Came from my mind which on the setting sun
Bestow'd new splendor. . . .
And the midnight storm
Grew darker in the presence of my eye.

Thus, giving where he has received, he acknowledges that, like a good spouse, Nature has fed his "lofty speculations." The *anagnorisis* of Book II is spousal: he "saw one life, and felt that it was joy."

But, as in other unions, there were tasks ahead and further and more confusing experiences. When he became a student at Cambridge, that "motley spectacle," he was at first "dazzled by the novel show" and retreated. With a hidden reference to Narcissus, he turned

the mind in upon itself,
Pored, watch'd, expected, listen'd; spread [his] thoughts
And spread them with a wider creeping.

He was still idly pleased with whatever "Nature's daily face put on"; yet, as he associated with his unthinking fellows, "easy minds / And pillowy," and noted that academic manners "collaterally" portrayed "the limbs of the great world," he remained content with superficial likenesses; his deeper probings were suspended. "Imagination slept." Book III has no major *anagnorisis;* he saw "but darkly."

> The memory languidly revolv'd, the heart
> Repos'd in noontide rest; the inner pulse
> Of contemplation almost fail'd to beat.

At his return to Hawkshead and the sight of what he had earlier loved, little by little in a climax of recognitions his vision cleared until there was a moment of complete revelation: again he looked upon the Beloved.

>   Magnificent
> The morning was, a memorable pomp,
> More glorious than I ever had beheld.
>   .   .   .   .   .
>
> My heart was full; I made no vows, but vows
> Were then made for me; bond unknown to me
> Was given, that I should be, else sinning greatly,
> A dedicated Spirit.

In no other passage of the poem is the close association of the *anagnorisis* with *praxis* and a possible *peripeteia* better illustrated.

The Dream of the Arab in Book V ("Books") has a more visionary than speculative function; it furnishes one of those discoveries of likeness mentioned earlier as characteristic of the observant rather than the theoretic or skeptical eye. It is, however, appropriate to the activity of the student of times and places, for whom

>   images, and sentiments, and words,
> And every thing with which we had to do
> In that delicious world of poesy,
> Kept holiday; a never-ending show.

Thereupon the delighted spectator of the show addresses the poetic "dreamers" as those whom

>   Time
> And Seasons serve; all Faculties; to whom
> Earth crouches, th' elements are potter's clay,

> Space like a Heaven fill'd up with Northern lights;
> Here, nowhere, there, and everywhere at once.

There are corollary lessons from "the shining streams / Of Fairy Land, the Forests of Romance," sights of death otherwise shocking but now to be hallowed

> With decoration and ideal grace;
> A dignity, a smoothness, like the works
> Of Grecian Art, and purest Poesy.

For the most part, however, this poet celebrates verse

> dedicate to Nature's self,
> And things that teach as Nature teaches.

Finally, from "the great Nature" that exists in "works of mighty Poets" he acknowledges "enduring touches of deep joy." The Book on Books ends with an apocalypse:

> Visionary Power
> Attends upon the motions of the winds
> Embodied in the mystery of words.
> There darkness makes abode, and all the host
> Of shadowy things do work their changes there,
> As in a mansion like their proper home:
> Even forms and substances are circumfused
> By what transparent veil with light divine;
> And through the turnings intricate of Verse,
> Present themselves as objects recognis'd,
> In flashes, and with a glory scarce their own.

During his later college residence and his vacations at home and abroad he advanced by way of Spenserian "tranquil visions . . . of human Forms with superhuman Powers" or inquiries into "geometric science" to what was the most profound discovery of his young manhood. Trudging along the alpine valleys and up a lofty mountain he found that he had "cross'd the Alps."

> I was lost as in a cloud,
> Halted, without a struggle to break through.

And now recovering, to my Soul I say
I *recognize* thy glory; in such strength
Of usurpation, in such visitings
Of awful promise, when the light of sense
Goes out in flashes that have shewn to us
The invisible world, doth Greatness make abode.
There harbours; whether we be young or old,
Our destiny, our nature, and our home
Is with infinitude, and only there;
With hope it is, hope that can never die,
Effort, and expectation, and desire,
And something evermore about to be.

At last the restless Lover, speculative in the actual as in the imaginative realm, has achieved a proper *recognitio* of himself as a Poet, an imaginative soul: this is I.

Many times thereafter his loyalties were to be tested not alone in the declivities of the actual Alps but in deeper valleys of great cities and great revolutions. Baudelaire's Paris must always face comparison with Wordsworth's London (*Prelude* VII) and Hardy's *The Dynasts* with Wordsworth's Residence in France (*Prelude* IX, X). Wordsworth's moments of vision come clearer out of the gloom of disillusionment and despair than do the visions of these other speculative writers; yet with him, too, there are ironic glimpses of likeness and unlikeness shading what has been anticipated, and deeper shadows now and again becloud what should be fair. Spectacles outdoors and "within doors," exhibitions and theatrical entertainments, performances of lawyer, orator, or preacher are particulars preparing for the revelation of a theoretic city of some sort. Yes, here it comes at the end of Book VII: the Fair of St. Bartholomew:

Oh, blank confusion! and a type not false
Of what the mighty City is itself.

Meanwhile, Nature has been waiting at home and in retrospect the wandering Lover goes back from his experience of urban life to fresh views of remembered beauty. These departures and returns are an old trait of classical love elegy, too, where the Propertian hero is often tempted into personal inconstancy or wavers between a private and a professional career, whether to write of love or to celebrate the glory of the state. Wordsworth is here decidedly original. He asks rather: can love of Nature lead him to love of Man? Thus he grasps the whole range of human life, all its vicissitudes, and appropriates, as neither Baudelaire nor Hardy could seem to do, the comfort as well as the threats of human existence.

There follows a series of Arcadian, pastoral, and Paradisal sketches revealing the primal destiny—as D. H. Lawrence in our day was to seek it so unremittingly. The Lawrencean Pan's pipe is also heard prophetically in *The Prelude*,

> thrilling the rocks
> With tutelary music, from all harm
> The Fold protecting;

yet it was not Pan or the Virgilian *pastor* but the Westmorland Shepherd who gave Wordsworth his profoundest sight of the Nature of Man. That this was so, that he first looked at Man "through objects that were great or fair," bears witness again to his skeptical vision as an elegist. Again we have an *anagnorisis*, this time in dialectical mode, a Miltonic spectacle with its "deep shade in counterview," "its gloom / Of opposition" yielding to what Adam saw in Paradise:

> Darkness ere day's mid course, and morning light
> More orient in the western cloud, that drew
> O'er the blue firmament a radiant white,
> Descending slow with something heavenly fraught.

Thereafter the Poet would undergo an ordeal related rather to the monodramatic than to the elegiac structure of his autobiographical poem; but without his skeptical eye the *peripeteia* would have lacked its complete revelatory value. For the story of his residence in France during the French Revolution is one of "mistakes" that led to "false conclusions of the intellect"; "scrupulous and microscopic views" furnished "materials for a work / Of false imagination, placed beyond / The limits of experience and of truth." As a skeptic he

> took the knife in hand
> And stopping not at parts less sensitive,
> Endeavoured with my best of skill to probe
> The living body of society
> Even to the heart.

"Demanding proof" in matters not susceptible of proof, he lost all feeling of conviction and yielded up moral questions in despair. There was an "eclipse," he says. This is a notable instance in modern elegiac literature of Aristotle's fifth form of discovery, unintentional fallacy, and it constitutes the darkest shadow of elegiac questing. When first set forth to public view in 1850, at the middle of a century that should have paid Wordsworth better heed, it anticipated by seven years what would be written in France and by a half-century—with a naiveté hard to understand—what would be gloomily accepted by some as the norm of human life and to that date the ultimate accomplishment of English poetry, Hardy's *The Dynasts*.

But there abides in the spousal figure the constant hope of renewal: in times of storm and disaster Nature's self, by human love assisted, has preserved the feelings of earlier life:

> in Nature still
> Glorying, I found a counterpoise in her,
> Which, when the spirit of evil was at height
> Maintain'd for me a secret happiness;
> Her I resorted to, and lov'd so much
> I seem'd to love as much as heretofore.

And hence the final *anagnorisis* of this elegiac autobiography leads to no cheap hope or shallow regret. There were "visionary dreariness" and "midnight darkness," dripping mist, fog, damp, storm, and rain; but, come free of these, Wordsworth, climbing

Snowdon effortfully "with forehead bent Earthward," was rewarded by a light flashing upon the turf

> and lo!
> The Moon stood naked in the Heavens.

The poet has indeed kept his date with his Spouse. This is no
mere gratuitous vision. Nor is it merely ecstatic reunion. Meditating on the "universal spectacle" of Nature's domination, he
recognizes in her power an image of the poetical power of the
mightiest minds of mankind. She has pointed him from love of
herself to love of Man. Such is the consummate *anagnorisis* of
this modern Love Elegy.

CHAPTER VII

Gnomes of Liberty and Odes of Thanksgiving

IN the decade from 1804–1805, when the first version of Wordsworth's autobiographical poem, *The Prelude,* had been completed, to 1814–1815, when *The Excursion* and the first collected edition of his poems were published, the inner form of his poetry became ever more profoundly thoughtful and its discoveries more explicit. As we move ahead to a consideration of his sonnet series on National Independence and Liberty and his dialectic blank verse on Despondency and Despondency Corrected, we shall not forget that in Greek literature, too, the elegiac imagination came temporarily to rest in gnomes and epigrams on its way to speculative dialogue. With classical patterns in view we may be able to bridge what is too often considered a lapse in Wordsworth's creative power or a gap in his poetical development; and, thus, we can more justly estimate his gift to the cultural habit of the nineteenth century and his example still available for writers in our own time.

For of all poets the elegist is most easily tempted into maxims. To capitalize on his discoveries he must invest what he has experienced or learned in a convenient statement. Indeed, a proposition may be itself a discovery in the sense of Aristotle's fourth kind, discovery by inference.[1] Especially when the skeptical mind is exercised on political and religious problems, must it make its report in the formalities of statecraft and ritual: definite phrases, conventional images, well-known rhythms and meters.

Such stylistic economy is apparent in the use by Solon of Athens and Theognis of Megara of elegiac distichs for their ethical gnomes; and so it was that Wordsworth fitted his meditations on civic matters into the traditional sonnet form. This form proved highly flexible for his purpose. As his varied patterns of search and his ingenious modes of riddling and challenge took shape, he became, with the possible exception of Shakespeare, the most skillful sonneteer in English letters. Not only are his individual sonnets models of thoughtful expression; in his several series of sonnets one leads on to another with notable ease of transition and progression, as if his discoveries must be tested again and again from still other angles and by still other logical procedures. With their resulting continuity they have what we miss in Milton's spurts of invective or approbation, courage or dismay. Moreover, they also make manifest human gallantry in facing what is bitter or doubtful as well as in accepting comforts and certainties—thus carrying on the habit of ethical reference in the sonnets of both Shakespeare and Milton.

This habit we remember was the distinguishing trait of Greek elegy as it came into full vigor. The main theme of Solon [2] had been liberty with justice, and his main concern the servitude arising from unrighteousness. Good rule, εὐνομία, makes all things orderly and fit. As would be true of Wordsworth, too, Solon located εὐνομία in the mind and believed that ill rule

[1] *Aristotle on the Art of Poetry*, ed. Lane Cooper (New York, 1913), p. 55.

[2] For the fragments of Solon see *Elegy and Iambus*, I, 104–155. An admirable edition of text and translation, with pertinent bibliographical and biographical information, is that by Ivan M. Linforth, *Solon the Athenian* (Berkeley, 1919).

would follow upon ignorance and greed: "It is because of their ignorance that the common folk (δῆμος) is enslaved by the tyrant"; Athenians "for the sake of lucre (χρήμασι πειθόμενοι) are ruining their great city." Solon's formula for justice was to fit "might and right together," ὁμοῦ βίαν τε καὶ δίκην συναρμόσας, he tells us in his *iambi,* and to deal righteously by each man good or bad, ὁμοίως τῷ κακῷ τε κἀγαθῷ.

"Virtuous Liberty," says Wordsworth in his turn, is "the scope" of his song. The word "scope" (σκοπεῖν = to peer) reminds us that he is looking deeply and widely into civic responsibility for freedom or tyranny. The warnings and maxims that announce themselves in the *Poems Dedicated to National Independence and Liberty* frequently bear the stamp of their classical origin. "Ye men of prostrate mind . . . / Shame on you, feeble Heads, to slavery prone!" The classical hatred of the tyrant is most clear in the sonnets concerned with Frenchmen under Napoleon—"a Nation who, henceforth, must wear / Their fetters in their souls." Like the Athenian Solon the English Wordsworth is sure that "ennobling thoughts depart / When men change swords for ledgers, and desert / The student's bower for gold."

It would be idle to assume that this agreement in theme and doctrine arises from any special study of Solon's elegies in 1802 by a young poet who had been bred on classical literature and was reviewing the sonnets of Milton. In Part I of Wordsworth's series, sonnets i–xi, xiii–xxiii, xxvi–xxvii, dealing with patriotic action at that time of frightening crisis when Napoleon was in the ascendant and threatened invasion, reflect a temper long familiar in the theoretical statesmanship, if not always the practice, of his native England.

But the form of these sonnets is meditative in a new English way which is a very old Greek way. When we set side by side not only the convictions but the patterns of the elegies of the sixth century B.C. and the sonnets of the nineteenth century, we see that Wordsworth's poems are classical in the formal sense, too. While advancing toward his revelatory gnomes Solon had exhorted, threatened, and prayed, thus flinging his message into the future toward desirable action. Exhorting, he had counseled a kinsman, the golden-haired Critias, "to listen to his father; for if so, he will have a guide of unerring counsel." Threatening, he had told the men of the great city of Athena that their follies would bring ruin upon it. He had rebuked the unjust mind of their leaders, ἡγεμόνων ἄδικος νόος, their pride, their prosperity inviting arrogance in men whose mind is unfit, μὴ νόος ἄρτιος ᾖ. He had prayed for good leaders. All these threats and prayers can be paralleled in Wordsworth's longing for counsel from Milton, Sidney, Marvel, Harrington, young Vane, because

> These moralists could act and comprehend;
> They knew how genuine glory was put on.

His diagnosis of civic peril echoes that of Solon:

> Milton! thou shouldst be living at this hour:
> England hath need of thee: she is a fen
> Of stagnant waters: altar, sword, and pen,
> Fireside, the heroic wealth of hall and bower,
> Have forfeited their ancient English dower
> Of inward happiness. We are selfish men;
> Oh! raise us up, return to us again;
> And give us manners, virtue, freedom, power.

Solon's warning against despotism had placed the responsibility for slavery on the shoulders of the citizens themselves: "do not blame the gods for it." And in a characteristic disclosure he had told why they were deceived in their leaders: they believed what was said and disregarded what was done. This is more than gnomic generalization; it is imperative and looks toward rhetoric. In *November, 1806,* Wordsworth likewise advances from doctrine to prophecy:

> from this day forward we shall know
> That in ourselves our safety must be sought;

> That by our own right hands it must be wrought;
> That we must stand unpropped, or be laid low;

and in a sonnet as yet undated (I, xxiv) he calls the "foreign hordes" "Slaves, vile as ever were befooled by words."

Warning and invective, however, are useless without the benignities of profounder thought and hence more luminous revelation. Wordsworth goes on to probe to the heart of Wisdom, true Power, true Sway (I, v), laying bare the conditions for civic happiness, what Solon would have called εὐνομία.

> Happy is he who, caring not for Pope,
> Consul, or King, can sound himself to know
> The destiny of Man, and live in hope.

He declares that virtuous action is the result of right thinking (I, vii), what Solon called σεμνὰ θέμεθλα Δίκης, the awesome basis of Justice. For instance,

> the illustratious Swede hath done
> The thing which ought to be; is raised *above*
> All consequences.

Part I ends with an Ode in which France appears as a Dragon "Whose panoply is not a thing put on / But the live scales of a portentous nature"; thus Spenser's romantic image of unholiness enters the classical argument. Moreover, Spenser's Redcrosse Knight will appear in *Ode 1814* near the end of Part II: the poet of George III agrees with the poet of Gloriana that the real problem of civic life is ethical and beyond expediency. Then, having made his point in the idea, as it were, Wordsworth proceeds from allegory to fact: human error is a real and substantial monster. Similarly, Solon's Pallas Athene, holding her hands over Athens, ὕπερθεν, found her adversary to be the vanity of men, albeit men who walk with the steps of a fox.

Careful readers may note that except for one verse—"The great events with which old story rings"—there is in Part I no explicit mention of ancient history or classical literature. But

at its very beginning Part II summons Antiquity for a reference
to the Isthmian Games, where in 196 B.C. a Roman general, Ti-
tus Quinctius Flamininus, "proclaims THE LIBERTY OF GREECE"
for degenerate sons of the heroes of Marathon. At this, the disaffected Aetolians suggested that in so doing Flamininus had un-
fettered the feet of the Greeks and bound them by the neck.[3]
When associated with such instances from "Antique ages,"
events of a later age in Spain, Germany, Switzerland, and Russia
gain significance; the operations of a tyrant and the unconquer-
able power of civic justice are both illuminated. Poetically, too,
the base of the elegiac process is broadened, and the fierce energy aroused to expression by the contemporary crisis in Europe
can be refined only *sub specie eternitatis.*

Classical allusions abound. The "fair Star of evening" which
initiated Part I and determined its metaphorical quality has in
Part II become the vividly mirrored "repetition of the stars" in
Grasmere Lake: "Jove, Venus, and the ruddy crest of Mars."
Dodona's oak and its divine voice are the sounding board for
the Oak of Guernica under which meet the "Guardians of Bis-
cay's ancient liberty." Tyrolean Liberty is another nymph like
Echo. Napoleon follows the lead of Fortuna, the "blind Goddess." The Tower of Babel in Mesopotamia, the pyramids on
the Nile, the boast of a Pharaoh, the audacities of a Nimrod [4]
bear witness to "the rash Spirit" of early times. To resist tyranny the name of Arminius is invoked for Germany, of Wilhelm
Tell for the Tyrol, of Virathus for the Lusitanians, of Sertorius
for the Romans.

The stage for noble resistance is represented to be not only in
early historical times but also early in cultural time, beginning
with the primal pattern of Nature herself. Her "wild blasts"
prophesy "bright calms that shall succeed." With a classical

---

[3] The story may be read in Plutarch's Life of Flamininus. Wordsworth
owned the North translation of Plutarch's *Lives.*

[4] In *The Statesman's Manual* and elsewhere Coleridge also mentions
Nimrod the Hunter.

metaphor reflecting the signal fires in the *Agamemnon* of
Aeschylus, Liberty, the "dread Power," is sped

> Through hanging clouds, from craggy height to height,
> Through the green vales and through the herdsman's bower—
> That all the Alps may gladden in [her] might,
> Here, there, and in all places at one hour.

It is humble folk like herdsmen with their "few strong instincts"
and their "few plain rules," their "old songs, the precious music
of the heart," in their "rude untutored Dales," who bear the
brunt of the struggle to maintain or regain ancient freedom. In
another classical image the poet describes the power of "a brave
People" combating

> whether on the wing
> Like the strong wind, or sleeping like the wind
> Within its awful caves.

And, finally, even as Wordsworth discovers Tell's "great Spirit"
reborn in the Swiss Hofer, who

> comes like Phoebus through the gates of morn
> When dreary darkness is discomfited,

he is reflecting elegiac form as Solon had understood it in his
references to the sun—

> λάμπει δ'ἠελίοιο μένος κατὰ πίονα γαῖαν
> καλόν, ἀτὰρ νεφέων οὐδὲν ἔτ' ἔστιν ἰδεῖν—

and to Apollo, ἄναξ ἑκάεργος, the Far-shooting Lord who makes
some men seers. This is the characteristic image of Greek elegy.

Dorothy had been reading "one or two of Plutarch's lives" [5]
in 1806; and on July 7, 1808, she wrote to De Quincey that her
brother wanted books, "any of the elder Histories—translations
from the Classics chiefly historical—Plutarch's Lives—Thucydides, Tacitus . . . (by the bye, he *has* a translation of Herodo-

[5] *Letters: Middle Years*, I, 19, in a footnote added to a letter of De
Quincey dated April 6, 1806, and forwarded to William.

tus)." [6] Since William already owned North's Plutarch, might this request have brought the more recent translation of the Langhornes with its voluminous notes? [7]

Undeniably the poet was reviewing his Greek, and not alone for the sonnet. While he composed the Iberian and Tyrolean poems of Part II of *National Independence and Liberty* (to be published in *The Friend*, 1809, and in the first collective edition of the poems, 1815) he was at work also on his tract, *The Convention of Cintra*. Many of his classical references and elegiac devices in the verse can profitably be compared with similar allusions, turns of thought, or images in the prose. Thanks to Plutarch, the events ended by the Convention of Cintra were judged by Wordsworth in the light of the "principles of justice" of Phocion and Philopoemen.[8]

Furthermore, the revelatory image that we have discovered common to classical elegy and the sonnets of Part II is used as a rhetorical device in *The Convention of Cintra*—so much alike are meditative verse and meditative prose. "These are times . . . of deep-searching visitation," says Wordsworth in his tract. "I have drawn out to open day the truth from its recesses in the minds of my countrymen." "As to the fact—it appears, and sheds from its own body, like the sun in heaven, the light by which it is seen." A tree in "the forest of Freedom" "must have power to toss its branches in the wind and lift a bold forehead to the sun." The main discovery of the tract, its supreme *anagnorisis*, is, in Wordsworth's phrase, "a revelation of the state of being that admits not of decay or change"—this time no mere proposition but a moment in experience, a spot of time. Such revelation was, he says, accompanied by

the returning sense . . . of inward liberty and choice, which gratified our moral yearnings, inasmuch as it would give henceforth to

[6] *Ibid.*, I, 233–234.
[7] See Senex, *Notes and Queries*, CLXXVII (November 18, 1939), 366–367.
[8] To be read conveniently in *The Political Tracts of Wordsworth, Coleridge, and Shelley*, ed. R. J. White (Cambridge, 1955).

our actions as a people, an origination and direction unquestionably moral—as it was free—as it was manifestly in sympathy with the species—as it admitted therefore of fluctuations of generous feeling —of approbation and of complacency. We were intellectualized also in proportion; we looked backward upon the records of the human race with pride, and, instead of being afraid, we delighted to look forward into futurity.[9]

Indeed, such a revelation, such a sense of liberty to choose, is never out of date. In our own seemingly regimented age, as in the years when Napoleon threatened Britain, the individual is still the center of all the freedoms. The power of moral choice Wordsworth's sonnets assert and illustrate again and again. For instance, at the Isthmian Games the Aetolians tell the sons of those who fought at Marathon that liberty cannot be given but must be earned (I, i, ii). It is their "moral end" that justifies patriots, even in defeat (II, ix, x, xi, xv). Throughout the series about the Tyrolese Wordsworth dwells on the courage of simple folk to resist and overcome tyranny by their proper choices.

And in a further meditative reach he discovers that when fear and pain usurp on "hope and steadfast promise," it is not only "among rude untutored dales . . . that the heart is true" nor "by rocks and woods that man prevails." Like the tranquillity in the realm of "great Pan" himself there dwells

> O'er the wide earth, on mountain and on plain, . . .
> A Godhead, like the universal Pan;
> But more exalted, with a brighter train.

Arrived at by instance after instance, the nature of what men call freedom is persistently clarified:

> though Nature's dread protection fails,
> There is a bulwark in the soul.
> We know the arduous strife, the eternal laws
> To which the triumph of all good is given,
> High sacrifice, and labour without pause,

[9] *The Convention of Cintra*, ed. White, pp. 128–129, 141, 150–151, 163, 182.

> Even to the death:—else wherefore should the eye
> Of man converse with immortality.

Thus, the elegiac procedure carries us from natural experience to spiritual conviction, from classical Pan to a "Godhead" not yet distinctly Christian but—to quote a phrase from the tract—"intellectualized in proportion to fluctuations of generous feeling."

Only with Part II, sonnet xxxviii (composed in November, 1813, the year following the deaths of Wordsworth's children, Catherine and Thomas) is the dread "King of Kings" of Christendom invoked, for "grace" upon the forlorn condition of an earthly king, George III. In 1810 (II, xxvii) "piety towards God" had been mentioned as a native growth of England and Spain "(Thanks to high God)," and in this same year "the uplifted cross / Of Jesus" and "Christian faith" (II, xxv) pointed the way to the more traditionally mediaeval terms and images often quoted by critics of the poet to illustrate a suppositious anticlimax in his poetical career.

After the Battle of Waterloo (II, xlii), moreover, Wordsworth acknowledged the need for a Bard who could recognize "one Almighty sway," a poet

> whose experienced eye [could] pierce the array
> Of past events; to whom in vision clear
> The aspiring heads of future things appear,
> Like mountain tops whose mists have rolled away

This Wordsworthian Bard is scarcely Christian; rather, a modern version of Solon's μάντις, the seer, who knows the evil coming from afar, κακὸν τηλόθεν ἐρχόμενον. Moreover, in the Odes with which the series on National Independence and Liberty ends, the classical element is so particularized as to suggest that the poet was familiar with one of the most astutely elegiac sequences in Greek, Solon's distichs beginning

Μνημοσύνης καὶ Ζηνὸς Ὀλυμπίου ἀγλαὰ τέκνα,
Μοῦσαι Πιερίδες.[10]

Calling upon these Pierian Muses, Solon begs his deserts from the gods and a good name from men. Then he considers the nature of unrighteousness and the vengeance of Zeus, who foresees the outcome of all things, πάντων ἐφορᾷ τέλος. Whereas human purposes vary, σπεύδει δ' ἄλλοθεν ἄλλος, and each man, good or bad, has his own way of deceiving himself, it is Fate, Μοῖρα, who brings good or ill; and when the gifts granted by the immortals to mortals prove ruinous now to one, now to another, ἄλλοτε ἄλλος ἔχει, it is Zeus who has sent retribution.

In the Greek elegy Solon's (1) invocation to the Pierides, (2) his epic simile for retribution and epiphany, and (3) his impressive catalogue of human activities can be paralleled by the invocation, imagery, and catalogue of the elegiac passages which Wordsworth composed early in 1816 during the Napoleonic crisis to celebrate the overthrow of a great modern tyranny.[11] This exalted poem, lifting itself from meditation to joy, can now be read in four parts as *Ode* (at the end of Part I), and *Ode 1814, Ode 1815,* and *Ode: The Morning of the Day Appointed for a General Thanksgiving, January 18, 1816* (at the end of Part II). It was, as Wordsworth wrote to Southey, neither a hymn nor, "strictly speaking," an ode; it uttered "the sentiments of an individual" upon a certain occasion and might be called "a *dramatised ejaculation*" (Wordsworth's italics).[12] We may add that, despite their irregular meter, in their intense fervor, their revelatory procedure, their solar imagery, and their dignified sentiments these "ejaculations" are elegiac as Solon understood the elegy. Let us, then, set the Thanksgiving poem

[10] In a prefatory note Wordsworth refers to the Pierides of Horace.
[11] Now included in *Poems Dedicated to National Independence and Liberty,* they were "first published in the volume entitled *Thanksgiving Ode, January 18, 1816, with other short pieces, chiefly referring to recent public events,* 1816" (*P. W.,* IV, 461).
[12] Letter to Robert Southey (*Middle Years,* I, 717).

of Wordsworth beside the elegy of Solon. First, the invocation. Solon: Glorious children of Mnemosyne and Olympian Zeus, Pierian Muses, listen to me praying; Wordsworth: And ye, Pierian Sisters, sprung from Jove / And sage Mnemosyne.

Second, Solon compared the retribution of Zeus to the natural scene when the wind scatters the clouds in spring, stirs the depths of the many-billowed unharvested sea, lays waste the lovely fields of the wheat-bearing earth, and brings clear into view the sky—those heavens where sit the gods—until the strong sun shines again over a fruitful land and no more cloud can be seen. This is an early instance of epiphany in elegiac literature, revealing the quasi-divine power of the sun to orient man actually in life as well as metaphorically in letters.

Solon's classical scene and those gods whom Wordsworth in *Ode 1814* calls "Olympian . . . Deities" have made way for the "august . . . landscape" of Britain and in *Ode 1815* for the "Just God of christianised Humanity." But even this "God of peace and love" will not disapprove "martial service" if it be necessary to chasten the unrighteous—and in ways comparable with those of Solon's Zeus. Wordsworth's God, too, "darkens the sun," consumes "the region that in hope was ploughed," summons "the fierce Tornado," "and navies perish in their ports."

Meanwhile, to permit the beneficent entrance of St. George, the champion of Britain, in the second of Wordsworth's four "dramatised ejaculations" (*Ode 1814*), "the sun's triumphant eye" has—again like Solon's sun—opened a portal in the sky "Brighter than the brightest loop-hole in a storm"; and in the last ejaculation (*Ode . . . 1816*) the "impartial Sun," hailed as "orient Conqueror of gloomy Night," climbs the sky

> In naked splendour, clear from mist or haze,
> Or cloud approaching to divert [his] rays,
>
> . . . . .
>
> —Divinest Object which the uplifted eye
> Of mortal man is suffered to behold,

> And for thy bounty wert not unadored
> By pious men of old.

Like the first Athenian poet, one of those pious men of old, the English poet leaves us in no doubt as to his cosmic discovery and his elegiac inference: "How dreadful is the dominion of the impure!" Neither his elaborate solar metaphor nor his bare gnomic statements are novel to us; but we do well to note how faithfully through the centuries both devices have served the elegiac poet who writes of civic matters.

That Wordsworth is aware of his classical antecedents we may be sure. He says explicitly that "the deed of Marathon arrayed . . . upon Athenian walls" in Solon's city encourages "victorious England" to celebrate her achievement at Waterloo with

> Records on which, for pleasure of all eyes,
>   The morning sun may shine
> With gratulation thoroughly benign.

Third, "Man," says Wordsworth in *Ode 1815*, "is God's most awful instrument, / In working out a pure intent." And in a striking parallel to Solon's reminder that divine favor is incalculable he acknowledges that "the God of peace and love" is also a "tremendous God of battles":

> Thou cloth'st the wicked in their dazzling mail,
> And for Thy righteous purpose they prevail.

Heads must be bowed before Him; His name must be magnified; and, in *Ode . . . 1816*, thanksgiving itself arises out of "dust and ashes":

> The very humblest are too proud of heart;
> And one brief day is rightly set apart
> For Him who lifteth up and layeth low;
> For that Almighty God to whom we owe,
> Say not that we have vanquished—but that we survive.

Wordsworth's Almighty God sounds more and more like Solon's Zeus. Although the man with a sinful heart—or his children—in the end suffers sure retribution from Zeus, Solon observes that good and evil alike, ἀγαθός τε κακός τε, are only wise in part, whatever their ways of life.

At this point in his elegy Solon introduces the catalogue of human crafts that was to reappear so often in literature: σπεύδει δ' ἄλλοθεν ἄλλος: one seeks gain on the sea in ships, another ploughs, some are craftsmen of Athena and Hephaestus, working with their hands, others—gifted by the Muses—know the dimensions, μέτρον, of charming works of art, ἱμερτῆς σοφίης, still others as physicians labor endlessly but with varying success toward life and health, and the man whom Lord Apollo makes a seer, μάντιν, can foresee although not prevent mischief coming from afar.

In Wordsworth's imagination this diversity of human functions will be elaborated or applied as follows: "navies perish in their ports"; "the upturned soil receives the hopeful seed"; craftsmen will erect "a new Temple . . . / High on the shore of silver Thames; . . . there meet / Dependence infinite, proportion just"; painters and sculptors and architects will "reflect" England's "high achievements"; songs will be sung

> For them who bravely stood unhurt, or bled
> With medicable wounds, or found their graves
> Upon the battlefield, or under ocean's waves;
> Or were conducted home in single state,
> And long procession—there to lie,
> Where their sons' sons, and all posterity,
> Unheard by them, their deeds shall celebrate!

Here, the children or children's children of such as Solon's men with an evil heart are spared rather to celebrate brave deeds than to pay for evil ones. With "religious eloquence," "visual pomp," "sweet and threatening harmony," solemn rites shall be performed, "commemoration holy" within Westminster Abbey, where "Kings, warriors, high-souled poets, saint-like sages" are laid. And, finally, "some . . . favoured Bard" will with "rapt ear" catch songs sung by the "celestial maids" of Greece and thus reiterate a "mighty theme from age to age." Wordsworth is that humble bard, reiterating Solon's themes in his later day.

Mankind is catalogued by Wordsworth geographically as well. The joyful announcement of victory—"*Lo, Justice triumphs! Earth is freed!*"—will be carried wherever "the Sun rules." Thus, the English poet preserves the metaphor of the Athenian elegist and maintains his expansive view of human affairs.

Although the Pierian Muses are first invoked, the final prayer of Wordsworth's "ejaculations" is to the Holy One. All men who "simply feel and purely meditate" will offer their prayers "before the throne of Grace." Their meditations spell out the elegiac themes for any century:

> warnings—from the unprecedented might
> Which in our time the impious have disclosed;
> And of more arduous duties thence imposed
> Upon the future advocates of right;
> Of mysteries revealed
> And judgments unrepealed,
> Of earthly revolution
> And final retribution.

Solon's final words, too, are ἄτη . . . ἦν ὁπότε Ζεὺς / πέμψῃ τεισομένην—retribution.[13]

---

[13] Where might Wordsworth have read the Greek elegies of Solon? At Allan Bank, where Coleridge and De Quincey, both classical scholars, took up their residence in 1808? As far back as 1794 Coleridge had recommended R. F. P. Brunck's *Analecta veterum poetarum Graecorum* in a letter to Francis Wraugham (*Collected Letters of Samuel Taylor Coleridge*, ed. E. L. Griggs, I [Oxford, 1956], 121). Volume I of these Analects, which I have consulted in Butler Library, Columbia University, contains the elegiac distichs of Solon and Simonides side by side. To Simonides Wordsworth refers in his *Essay on Epitaphs*, written 1808–1809 "for Mr. Coleridge's periodical work, *The Friend*." This was the year when the two friends, so soon to be estranged, were still helpful to each other and together dedicated to the service of mankind. Words-

What is terrible—"wide-wasted regions—cities wrapt in flame," "agonies" and "ghastly sights"—is to be humbly referred to the "sovereign penetration" of Him

> Before whom all things are, that were,
> All judgments that have been, or e'er shall be;
> Links in the chain of [His] tranquillity.

The retributive justice of the Pagan Zeus is not forgotten in the Christian paean of victory. On the other hand, there is a finer than Pagan quality in the phrases "Forgiveness from God's mercy-seat," and "gratitude / For Thy protecting care," and in the lines:

> For to a few collected in His name,
>   Their heavenly Father will incline an ear
> Gracious to service hallowed by its aim.

And that leads us to still another element in the Odes of National Independence and Liberty. A half-millennium before Xenophanes and Solon were using elegiac couplets for their speculations about the nature of the Greek gods, in another corner of the ancient world David had sung wonderingly if reverently about the God of the Hebrews. Whether named Zeus or Jehovah, the presiding power of the early eastern Mediterranean peoples was an awesome enigma, whose worshippers were puzzled by the prosperity of the wicked and the incalculable ways of retribution. From the familiar Psalms even more pertinently than from Greek elegy Wordsworth could draw inspiration and formal help for his version of the Napoleonic crisis; the God of Israel would dignify both his peripety and his revelation.

There is only one clear echo of the Psalms in the *Ode* ending Part I of the series: "How long shall vengeance sleep? Ye patient Heavens, how long?" We think of the refrain in Psalm 13:

---

worth's hypothetical familiarity with Solon's argument suggests that host and guest might have been reconsidering the elegiac literature of Greece in the light of the current crisis.

"How long shall mine enemy be exalted over me?" And the main device of *Ode 1814* comes from *The Faerie Queene* rather than the Psalter: a triumphant dream paralleling ceremonies in the last canto of Spenser's Book of Holiness, where an allegorical dragon has been slain by an heroic Redcrosse Knight.

> But garlands wither; festal shows depart,
> Like dreams themselves.

To get to the heart of the matter Wordsworth thinks back to the actual "deed of Marathon" as depicted "upon Athenian walls": it may be that painting, sculpture, and architecture will furnish a better record of Britain's courage in resisting the tyrant. Or let "the Pierian Sisters" be invoked to help a British bard sing of Britain's acts in the British tongue. In *Ode 1814* all is of romantic or classical origin.

In *Ode 1815*, however, with the mention of snakes and lions and locusts and the address to the "Lord of Hosts," we are aware that allegorical romance and Greek myth alone will not serve to reveal the whole truth of Britain in a civic emergency. The poet must not forget the Psalms of David in his picture of an angry Jehovah:

> He guides the Pestilence—the cloud
> Of locusts travels on his breath;
> The region that in hope was ploughed
> His drought consumes, his mildew taints with death;
> He springs the hushed Volcano's mine,
> He puts the Earthquake on her still design,
> Darkens the sun, hath made the forest sink
> And, drinking towns and cities, still can drink
> Cities and towns—'t is Thou—the work is Thine!—
> The fierce Tornado sleeps within Thy courts—
> He hears the word—he flies—
> And navies perish in their ports;
> For Thou art angry with Thine enemies!
> For these, and mourning for our errors
> And sins, that point their terrors,

> We bow our heads before Thee and we laud
> And magnify Thy name, Almighty God!

Such a passage is in a great tradition; witness Psalm 107 and verses 43–58 of Psalm 78:

> He turneth rivers into a wilderness,
> And water springs into a thirsty ground;
> A fruitful land into a salt desert,
> For the wickedness of them that dwell therein.
>
>   . . . . .
>
> [He] turned their rivers into blood,
> And their streams, that they could not drink,
> He sent among them swarms of flies, which devoured them;
> And frogs, which destroyed them.
> He gave also their increase unto the caterpillar,
> And their labour unto the locust.
> He destroyed their vines with hail,
> And their sycomore trees with frost.
> He gave over their cattle also to the hail,
> And their flocks to hot thunderbolts. . . .
> He spared not their soul from death,
> But gave their life over to the pestilence.[14]

Although David's Jehovah had been more violent in wrath than Solon's Zeus, the vengeance of the latter, Ζηνὸς . . . τίσις, was as sure. He never forgot the man with a wicked heart, ὅστις ἀλιτρὸν θυμὸν ἔχῃ; he foresaw the end of every matter, πάντων ἐφορᾷ τέλος; and none could escape the fate sent from Heaven, θεῶν μοῖρα.

After the defeat of Napoleon by the British at Waterloo, over countries north, south, east, and west fly the "ministers of Fame" with the announcement of triumphant justice and an earth freed from tyranny. The good news speeds like an "unwearied arrow" in whose "sparkling progress" all may read "of virtue crowned with glory's deathless meed." We are reminded not

[14] Passages from the Psalms are quoted from *The Modern Reader's Bible*, ed. Richard G. Moulton (New York, 1915).

only of the classical Fama but more vividly of the arrow of the Lord in Psalms 7, 64, and more particularly 77:

> The skies sent out a sound:
> Thine arrows also went abroad;
> The voice of thy thunder was in the whirlwind,
> Thy lightnings lightened the world,
> The earth trembled and shook.
> Thy way was in the sea,
> And thy paths in the great waters.

Wordsworth traces the arrow of the Lord across the Andes, the vast Pacific, the Lakes of Asia, and the Arabian desert: did he have in mind Psalm 83 with its Edom, the Ishmaelites, Moab, the Hagarenes, Gebal, Ammon, Amalek, Philistia, Tyre, Assyria? From biblical lands, however, "where snakes and lions breed," he returns to the Thames and Westminster. "Within the circuit of those Gothic walls" we are to hear "solemn rites,"

> Commemoration holy that unites
> The living generations with the dead.

The transition in this *Ode 1815* from section IV to section V, from "the tremendous God of battles" to the "just God of christianised Humanity" recapitulates the shift from Old to New Testament both in the history of human experience and in Wordsworth's own religious development. This is a signal passage. Might it not be that the scope and weight of national calamity rather than his advancing years inclined the poet to more traditional patterns of thought and diction? What some consider the flat or lifeless phrasing characteristic of his later years will be recognized by readers familiar with the Psalter as the noble language of the Psalms themselves, evoking the profoundest of memorial feelings.

Yet the real problems of tyranny and justice have not yet been probed in this mighty meditation: what is the secret of thanksgiving for victory? Remembering that Jehovah had been to his people as a sun and a shield (Psalm 84) and the heavens as a tabernacle for the sun (Psalm 19), and that the Lord "giveth snow like wool; He scattereth the hoar frost like ashes" (Psalm 147), Wordsworth looked out over the "frosty plains" and "snow-clad heights" of Grasmere on the glorious winter morning of January 18, 1816, and wrote a Thanksgiving for Victory which drew its strength mainly from Psalms 5 and 145–150. *Ode . . . 1816* opens with an address to the sun in all the beauty of biblical and classical imagery. Although the matins are first addressed to the "Divinest Object which the uplifted eye" of man beholds, the poet goes on to acknowledge that "the quickening spark of this day's sacrifice" comes "from a holier altar . . . / Than aught dependent on the fickle skies." What in Grasmere is "simply [felt]" and "purely meditate[d]" recalls the morning "meditation" of Psalm 5. Especially in Wordsworth's section X, "*O enter now his temple gate!*" can we hear the psalmist singing "In thy fear will I worship toward thy holy temple."

The terrible conflict of the early nineteenth century has taken on an archetypal character. When in section V "the bold Archdespot" reappears,

> As springs the lion from his den,
> As from a forest-brake
> Upstarts a glistening snake,

we seem to witness again the violent man of Psalm 140 "sharpening [the] tongue like a serpent" with "adders' poison . . . under [the lips]." And when Napoleon is overthrown, Psalm 91 furnishes the appropriate words:

> Thou shalt tread upon the lion and adder:
> The young lion and the serpent shalt thou trample under feet.

Victory belongs to the Lord.

And why has the "exterminating sword" been given to Britain?—She has labored "with an eye / Of circumspect humanity"; firm, rapid, fierce, she has fulfilled "all martial duties"; she has conquered "by dint of Magnanimity." Nevertheless, true glory comes only to those "who through the abyss of weakness dive": "Say not that we have vanquished—but that we survive." When Wordsworth praises the Lord

> for tyranny subdued,
> And for the sway of equity renewed,
> For liberty confirmed and peace restored,

he is rephrasing the new song of Psalms 97–100, where much is said of equity and righteousness: He shall judge the peoples with equity; He shall judge the world with righteousness. And when the Ode speaks of the "more arduous duties . . . imposed / Upon the future advocates of right" and urges "internal conquests made by each"—"the labor of the Soul"—his exhortations repeat the code of Old Testament ethics. Those laws of the Lord that are still for Englishmen "a solid refuge for distress" can be read in Psalm 94:

> the Lord hath been my high tower;
> And my God the rock of my refuge.

Finally, it is with Psalms 145–150, their choruses of praise and their characterization of Jehovah, that the Thanksgiving Ode most resonantly chimes. Like Solon's Zeus, Jehovah is a just God, a God of statutes and judgments and decrees, who "bringeth the wicked down to the ground" and protects the righteous. When the psalmist exhorts—

> Let them ever shout for joy, because thou defendest them,
> Let them also that love thy name be joyful in thee—

Wordsworth sings obediently:

> The banner of our joy we will erect,
> And strength of love our souls shall elevate.

The worshippers entreat forgiveness and pray that the memory of divine favor may be preserved in their hearts

        as the power of light
   Lives inexhaustibly in precious gems
   Fixed on the front of Eastern diadems.

Precious gems on Eastern diadems? In this magnificent series of
elegiac odes indebted to Spenser, Solon, and David, Wordsworth has explored tyranny and victorious war back to their
judgment seat at "the throne of Grace."

CHAPTER VIII

Solar Dialectic
in *The Excursion*

THE literary themes of a maturing writer appear to follow each other in a typical sequence; and this characteristic is true of his literary forms as well. Indeed, similar thematic and formal behavior may be observed in the history of all literary cultures as these advance from dynamic youth to meditative age. In the books of the Bible fable and chronicle and code precede prophecy; psalm precedes proverb; biography and epistle precede admonitory revelation. Whatever were the constituents of Greek heroic poetry, the *Iliad* and the *Odyssey* anticipated Greek elegy and Greek drama and the Dialogues of Plato, and in that order. At Alexandria, elegy itself, modified in the scholarly experience of its foremost librarian, Callimachus, finally took on the form of αἴτια, poetry interpreting social and civic origins. And in the empire of Augustus, Virgil advanced from eclogues and georgics to an epic celebrating Roman military prowess and the Roman ancestral hero, while—not less characteristically— the Latin elegist Ovid, as a young man concerned with amorous love and lovers, moved forward through epistles and epistolary dialogues to legendary metamorphoses and then to the *Fasti*, the

register of Roman ceremonial.[1] Callimachus had been acknowledged by Propertius and Ovid in Rome; Simonides and Theo-
phrastus in Sicily had set a pattern for Horace and Virgil; in 73
B.C. the elegist Parthenius of Nicaea, brought as a prisoner to
Italy, became the teacher of the Latin elegist Gallus. This cultural story is always one of books and teachers, of weightier
responsibilities evoking profounder poems. A new cycle is initiated whenever poets enter a higher sphere; and this means
question and debate. Dialectic is the last resort of elegy as *dia-
noia* is the last stage of drama and, indeed, as dialogue is the
ultimate vehicle of all speculative thought. For their discoveries,
thinkers and poets must unshackle their ankles, twist their necks,
challenge their fellows, and thus struggle up out of Plato's Cave
toward the light.

Again, if we may lift our own eyes from the Corinnas, Delias,
and Cynthias of pagan elegy to the Beatrice of the greatest
Christian poet, from Rome, the eternal city, to the Eternal City
Itself, we observe that Dante's imaginations or visions of his
beloved in the sonnets and *canzoni* of *La Vita Nuova* [2] merely
prefigured the luminous epiphany he would experience when he
climbed still further through the spiritual cosmos out of Inferno
up the Purgatorial Mount into Paradise. In England, too, there
would always be, somewhere ahead or somewhere above, a
pilgrimage to Canterbury or to the Court of a Faerie Queene, a
Paradise Regained or a New Jerusalem, whether of Bunyan or
Blake or another. Most surely, the outcries of Romeo and the
grievances of Hamlet would be superseded in the dramatic art
of Shakespeare by the imperial themes of *Macbeth* and *Antony
and Cleopatra*, by the elegiac probing of *King Lear* and the
fierce dialectic of *Coriolanus*.

[1] Edward Kennard Rand says: "Ovid, like a true Roman, has a relish
for liturgy," and "all Roman poets are liturgical" (*Ovid and His Influence*, Boston, 1925, pp. 16, 80).

[2] Charles S. Singleton, *An Essay on the Vita Nuova* (Harvard University Press, 1949), p. 74: "The *Vita Nuova* is . . . *theory* in a first
sense of the word: a *beholding* of how certain things may be."

Examples of such cultural progression can be multiplied from the country and century nearest to our own. In the decades just before and just after the publication of *The Excursion* Wordsworth greatly increased the scope of his meditation upon human affairs; and Coleridge, on his way from *The Friend* (1809–1810) to *The Statesman's Manual* (1816) and *Biographia Literaria* (1817) had transformed his poetical fervor into critical power of the highest order—thanks, we may say, to his "shaping spirit of Imagination." Their contemporaries, too, were assuming the sober duties of scholarship and thoughtful comment: by his study of Elizabethan literature Lamb was prepared for his *Essays* (1820–1825); Southey, by his histories and biographies for his *Book of the Church* (1824); Cary was translating the *Divina Commedia* from 1805 to 1814. The Reviews were establishing themselves and at once fostered a serious attitude: *Edinburgh* (1802); *Quarterly* and *Examiner* (1808); *Blackwood's* (1817). Although Byron, Keats, and Shelley would die young, already they were advancing from lyric and romance to speculative poetry, from Hebrew melodies and Greek love songs and Mediterranean adventures to the ironic comment of a Don Juan on ugly war and ugly peace, from *belles dames sans merci* with wild eyes to lunar goddesses and solar gods—Apollo shrieked at the end of *Hyperion*—and from a Queen Mab in a magic car to a chorus of real Greek women. Greece was in the news: young poets defended her repute even as they appropriated her mythology. The last volume of Mitford's *History of Greece* was published in 1818; Shelley's *Hellas* would appear in 1822, the very year of Wordsworth's *Ecclesiastical Sonnets*.

Moreover, as the century wore on, itself growing old, its writers in prose and verse came to depend increasingly on elegiac themes and a dialectical procedure. Carlyle wrote in the sun and shade of the everlasting yea and the everlasting nay; Ruskin's critical temper and sermonizing style provoked the dissent that he seemed to invite. Browning's dramatic actions were clogged by reflection and entangled in controversy, as witness the debate between Gigadibs and Bishop Blougram; Tennyson's *Two Voices*, Arnold's "dialogue of the mind with itself," and Clough's *Dipsychus*, of the man with a split soul, translated social schism into personal tension. Editors, historians, biographers were eager to take issue; scientists quarreled with their ancestry and invalidated their heritage; and the family dissensions of the theologians grew monstrous. Everyone was on the wrangling road to Utopia or the slippery path to the Kingdom of Heaven on Earth.

Would the century, uneasily poised between old faith and new science, become neopagan or neo-Christian? Or was there another way, a kind of Third Empire, asked Ibsen in his *Emperor and Galilean*. Swinburne's paganism, Rossetti's mediaevalism, and Morris' revival of Northern barbarism all proved culturally unproductive. Pater's Marius was sensitive and curious but not ready for conversion. And the *Fleurs du Mal*, 1857, of the passionate and skeptical Baudelaire encouraged writers in Britain as in France to report all things out of traditional focus, alluringly askew or shockingly upside down. However objectively scientists viewed assumptions inherited from Antiquity or Christendom, however subjectively the poets dealt with classical or mediaeval themes, the message of faith, hope, and love bequeathed by early Christians suffered violent attack again and yet again from the disciples of late paganism. The elegist, trained in the debates of two millennia, was again called on to preside over the warring arguments of a later age. Out of the conflict there would emerge a dialectical drama in Shaw's Britain as already in Ibsen's Norway; but at the turn of the century, when from satires of circumstance Hardy arrived at a melancholy record of dynastic error, relentlessly probed for an apocalypse of disaster, the ironies and the pities must perforce take over. Within its huge arc of speculative thought the nineteenth was surely the elegiac century.

Because of the Napoleonic crisis threatening the West at the beginning of the century and the imperial tendencies already in precarious balance at its end, matters of dispute had been raised from eighteenth-century metaphysics and theology into something of intense personal and religious concern; witness, first of all, Wordsworth's *Excursion*, 1814, Books III and IV, Despondency and Despondency Corrected. Those who have watched George Bernard Shaw's unresting drive from feebly censorious plays, pleasant or unpleasant, through the representation of Platonic justice in *Caesar and Cleopatra* and Christian imagination in *St. Joan* and thence to the befuddled alcoholic Mariner piloting the disintegrating ship of state in *Heartbreak House* will need no reminder of the literary difficulties to be surmounted when an author must transform his personal irritations into spare action and then, more shrewdly, parcel out his queries among the various dramatic agents inhabiting the England of 1914 at the outbreak of World War I. Those who have watched Mr. Eliot's progress from a plaintive literary wasteland toward harmonies above space and time and then homeward to share his disquisitions with the several *personae* surrounding a confidential clerk or an elder statesman still in the grip of World War II will be quick to recognize Wordsworth's comparable problems in his effort to deal with the spiritual ravages of Napoleonic war and uncertain Georgian peace. The Pastor whom in 1814 the Poet summoned as umpire for the debate between the unbelieving Solitary and the religious Wanderer knew his business—the business that the willfully self-indulgent Mariner of 1914 may have known but surely had forgotten—the very same business that, with a new set of terms, the Psychoanalyst of *The Cocktail Party* was painfully learning, only yesterday.

Might it not be advantageous to review the career of William Wordsworth as paradigm of an elegiac poet in an elegiac century? Going on from his ballads of Lucy and Matthew and his Intimations of Immortality and those idylls which would seem trifling were they not so powerfully imagined, he had probed his own mind in a representative autobiography and, thereafter, under impetus from Milton had written a noble sonnet series.

Now, during the second decade of the century and at the very crisis of his thought, he would enter the debate on ultimate questions. Dividing himself, the author, into the two *personae* of a dialogue or even into a cast of *personae* for a dramatic conversation, he would attempt the most difficult metamorphosis of elegy on its way toward the spiritual action that underlies liturgy. When the sage and pious Wanderer started out with the Poet to redeem the disheartened Solitary—a task scarcely to be accomplished even by the rhetoric of the Pastor—*The Excursion* became, we may suggest, the enabling pattern according to which future poets would attempt, now from one angle, now from another, to reveal the central issue of the life of modern man. It became, also, the next thematic and formal step in Wordsworth's progress as a poet. Along with his study of the cardinal virtue of justice (and righteousness), to which Greek (and Hebrew) models had helped him in the *Poems Dedicated to National Independence and Liberty*, he was investigating the long record of Christian adventure. Was this myth of faith, hope, and love memorialized in the life of one person a true revelation? A genuine sun rising over the "region" of man's mind? In what appropriate elegiac form might it be tested?

If he were to answer such queries, he must go on from Plutarch's Lives of the Greeks and Romans to the Lives of the Greek Fathers. There is no passage of his blank verse more delightful than that in *The Tuft of Primroses* (1808) where he centers his thought on St. Basil and St. Gregory Nazianzen,[3]

---

[3] *P. W.*, V, 354–359, 483–485. At the entreaty of his sister Macrina, Basil had left the "vain felicities of Athens," had "abandon'd Alexandria's splendid Halls, Antioch and Cesarea" for "his delicious Pontic solitude," an "enduring Paradise . . . of Contemplation." That later he "went forth"

> To a station of authority and power
> Upon an urgent summons, and resigned,
> Ah, not without regret, the heavenly Mount,
> The sheltering valley, and his lov'd Compeers,

has a bearing on Wordsworth's shift from a reclusive way of life and

Bishop of Amphilochius, and the monastery near Anneci in Pontus. This winsome use of example to enforce doctrine—the device of Jesus in his parables and, as Curtius notes, of Dante with highly original force in his *Commedia*—would be helpful to Wordsworth not only in *The Excursion* but in the *Ecclesiastical Sonnets* of 1821–1822. The search for a mode of expression proper to traditional patterns required a stretch of imagination not to be accomplished by a mere literary senescent. Like the sonnet series on Liberty, *The Excursion* is an effort to investigate for his own time—and under circumstances of war or peace— the truth about man, nature, and especially, the truth about society.

Wordsworth's original plan for his "literary Work that might live" had been just that: A philosophical poem, containing "views" or "pictures of Man, Nature, and Society";

and to be entitled *The Recluse*, as having for its principal subject the sensations and opinions of a poet living in retirement . . . the first and third parts of [which] will consist chiefly of meditations in the Author's own person; and in the intermediate part [*The Excursion*] . . . something of a dramatic form [will be] adopted [by the intervention of characters speaking].

This is to say that elegiac meditation and speculative conversation would be the generic mode of *The Recluse*.

In the Prospectus to this poem at the end of the single book of Part I to be finished ("Home at Grasmere"), the poet had represented himself as musing, perceiving, feeling, weighing and— important for the speculative elegist—*looking into* the Mind of Man. Furthermore, almost like a sedate and exalted echo in the upper air over Latin love elegy, he had considered his poem a spousal verse to be chanted, a proclamation of the blended might of "the external World" and "the individual Mind." Upon "madding passions mutually inflamed"—here we recall Proper-

---

thought to the consideration of social and ecclesiastical matters of wide and profound human concern.

tius and Cynthia—"solitary anguish, and the fierce confederate storm / Of sorrow, barricaded evermore / Within the walls of cities"—the Athens of Solon and the Rome of Ovid and the London of Milton—he would furnish "authentic comment." These, surely, are elegiac themes and an elegiac procedure. He had begged "a gift of genuine insight"—the elegiac tool—that his "Song," true to the heavenly metaphors of elegy,

> With star-like virtue in its place [might] shine,
> Shedding benignant influence.

In what he had contemplated he had hoped to see a "Vision"— sorting with the revelation at the end of an elegiac investigation; and he had prayed that he himself might express an "image,"

> the image of a better time,
> More wise desires and simpler manners.

He would be, it seems, a true descendant of the ἀνὴρ ἀγαθός of Solon.

A poem of "views," a "vision," and an "image," although its discoveries might now and again remind us of idyllic poetry, would be, thanks to its "genuine insight" and its "authentic comment," prevailingly elegiac. As thus intended by Wordsworth, however, *The Recluse* did not become the "first genuinely philosophic poem" hoped for by his fond but mistaken friend Coleridge, the visionary. Coleridge yearned for systems and was a notable interpreter of them in prose; the less systematic Wordsworth would penetrate experience rather than philosophize about it. His prayer was first to Urania; but alas! Parts I and III of *The Recluse* were never constellated; rather, his elegiac debate in Part II of *The Excursion* became not only the consummate echo of eighteenth-century meditative poetry but itself the influential forerunner of all the tentative and skeptical writing of the nineteenth century, in verse and even more notably in prose. *The Excursion* is not an anticlimax.

Of those who had probed most deeply into human destiny

and universal life in the century of Wordsworth's birth, Swift and Newton, Swift had elegiac as well as satiric power but seemed not to be deeply involved in the salvation of those he satirized; and Newton, "voyaging through strange seas of thought alone," was a dispassionate seeker for light in a dispassionate universe. The immediate influential prototypes of *The Excursion* may rather be found in the meditative or dialectical poems of James Thomson, David Mallet, Dr. Mark Akenside, John Armstrong, Dr. Edward Young, William Cowper, Richard Savage, Bishop George Berkeley, and John Thelwell.[4] Except for the *Night Thoughts* of Young, these poems also lack the self-involvement of elegy. *The Seasons, Pleasures of [the] Imagination, Alciphron,* and *The Task,* like Pope's detached contemplations on man, the jest and riddle of the world, would hurry poets rather into gnomic or idyllic writing than into elegy proper. As Professor Carl L. Becker has indicated,[5] the Ultimate City had become too easy of access in the complacent eighteenth century to arouse deep anxiety in its metaphysicians and theologians. Nevertheless, Young's excursive talks with Lorenzo in the Christian Triumph, Relapse, and Infidel Reclaimed prefigured Wordsworth's Sage on his excursion to reclaim his Skeptic. It is the night sky that helps Young to his discoveries, whereas Wordsworth's imagination works in the sunshine; Young's celestial panorama is used in the main for decoration, Wordsworth's, less ostentatiously, to show the structure of his thought; but both writers display the intense concern we have found to be characteristic of elegy down the centuries.

[4] Whatever is said here about the generic ancestors of speculative conversation is a kind of footnote to the judicious chapter on the English sources and analogues of *The Excursion* in Professor Judson Stanley Lyon's study of that poem (New Haven, 1950). Professor Lyon relates Wordsworth's composition to the didactic blank-verse poems of the eighteenth century and to its philosophical dialogues, to its short stories of humble life, "separate or in framework," and to its funeral elegies. Throughout, his argument is clearly and substantially illustrated.

[5] *The Heavenly City of the Eighteenth-Century Philosophers* (New Haven, 1932).

Too sentimental and pretentious for our taste, Young, nevertheless, pleased several generations of thoughtful readers; and many of his passages, stripped of their verbiage, will be found not only to impart doctrine but to urge meditation. His concern is always for real people whom he will exhort or persuade into heaven; and he peers valiantly into the vast phenomena half-hiding and half-revealing the mysterious inner truth of cosmic life.

One other English poet may be mentioned in this connection. Beside Young wrestling with Lorenzo and Wordsworth's Sage trying to persuade his Skeptic, Blake has presented for our spiritual eye in pictorial light and darkness his memorable sketch of Michael and Lucifer. And when Blake's graphic *Jerusalem* and Wordsworth's argumentative *Excursion* face Darwin's century together, even with their awkwardness upon them, succeeding elegists more cautious and formally more exquisite are hard put to improve upon them. The only appeal is to Plato— Platonic justice and Platonic dialectic—and here, too, Wordsworth's Sage has anticipated them. His setting, his devices, his method are all Socratic. His symbols are often Greek, and his explicit references to Greek myth allow us to place his excursive poem in the shadow of those investigations of truth made on the banks of the Ilissus or thereabouts by the peripatetic sage of classical Antiquity.

It is as significant as it is undeniable that a poem predominantly Christian in its final books has been initiated in the mode of Socratic dialogue. *The Excursion,* therefore, is an attempt to reveal in a particular place and at a particular time the secret of a western world reluctant to surrender either its skeptical thought or its dedicated faith. This fact may account for the mixture of approval and disapproval in the contemporary reviews of the poem and in the usual scholarly estimate of its assets and liabilities. Asking why *The Excursion* pleased that lover of Greek Antiquity, John Keats, we guess that in it he found fruitful hints for his pseudoclassical struggle between

Titanic twilight and Olympian sunrise. Asking why the poem
so displeased Shelley, we may assume that in his single-minded
dedication to a new faith at variance with both Socratic methods
and Christian principles he could approve neither the dialectic
of the argument nor the tenor of the doctrine.

If in our day, however, we should consent to value the formal
structure of the poem more justly, we might be helped to detect
and identify the generic nature of our own prose and verse.
Granted the diversity of modes and meters in today's ingenuous
speculations, our symbols, antinomies, discoveries—or near-discoveries or riddling non-discoveries—bear a strong family resemblance to those of dialectical elegy, in a tradition of which
The Excursion is an important example.

For *The Excursion* is a solar myth, a poem of orientation
from its first line—" 'Twas summer and the sun had mounted
high"—to the sunset of lines 590–608 in its last book and the
vesper service that concludes the poem. Furthermore there may
be an elegiac prophecy in the farewell words of the Solitary.

> "Another sun,"
> Said he, "shall shine upon us, ere we part;
> Another sun, and peradventure more."

Sunrise and sunset and, meanwhile, an observant stroll over the
human countryside among the many scenes of diurnal life and
death—not for idyllic reasons, rather for evidence in a mighty
argument. Let us study it, then, as a modern solar myth, an *"excursive"* adventure toward a dependable revelation. We shall be
justified in our analysis of its formal organization if we can reveal its mastery of solar metaphor as a device for elegy become
dialectic. In it, straight from the symbolic sun, there are energies
still beneficent for the imagination of poets who a century later
conceive of great spheres in a celestial orbit or plunge into
chthonian depths in search of dark suns.

Although the opening scene of Book I is not obviously mythical, its "shadows flung / From brooding clouds" and its "steady

beams / Of bright and pleasant sunshine," and chiefly its dreamer in "some huge cave" looking upon the landscape "with side-long eye" remind us of Plato's Myth of the Cave. The idea comes to us that, like Plato's pupils, we readers of *The Excursion* are in search of the Form of Good, that we, too, shall be led "to observe and contemplate the nature of the sun, not as it *appears*, . . . but as it is." [6]

On this mythic background, yet in an actual "grove" on an open moorland, the Poet meets again with an old "comrade," a "Man of reverend age" whose mind is filled "with inward light." Sage and Poet plan an excursion, the symbol of an excursive jaunt of two minds in communion. Thus the reader is prepared for an elegiac poem leading toward the revelation of truth; and if he be familiar with the dialectic of Socrates, he will expect similar devices in the conversation of the peripatetic Sage and his young companion.

We are then told of the training of the Sage, of his successive discoveries made as a boy, as a youth, as a man. He had spent "many an hour in caves forlorn, / And 'mid the depths of naked crags," where he learned "to fasten images / Upon his brain": images of the hills growing larger in the darkness and, above them, images of the stars. Hills and stars lay upon his mind like substances. As his earliest memory of joy, however, in youth "he beheld the sun / Rise up, and bathe the world in light." Observing that this luminous power gave life to ocean's liquid mass and the solid frame of earth, he was able to commune with the living God; he "[felt] his faith." Now "how beautiful, how bright" appeared Holy Writ. Now all things "breathed immortality"; the least of them seemed "infinite." This was, indeed, an effort up out of the Cave.

With his scanty earnings he bought and gazed upon "that

[6] I quote from the Davies and Vaughan translation of *The Republic* (London, 1920) at the beginning of Book VII. Pages 235–243 should be read by any interpreter of *The Excursion* who wishes to discover the secret of the Sage's education.

mighty orb of song, / The divine Milton"—note the celestial
metaphor. From his schoolmaster he borrowed

> books that explain
> The purer elements of truth involved
> In lines and numbers;

but, thanks to Nature, mathematics, geometry, and surveying
did not wean him from the stars. Moreover,

> he scanned the laws of light
> Amid the roar of torrents, where they send
> From hollow clefts up to the clearer air
> A cloud of mist, that smitten by the sun
> Varies its rainbow hues.

How often during the century that rainbow would reappear to
assert its primacy among domes of many-coloured glass and
jewelled bows! [7]—Until in our day the last line of Robert Lowell's *The Quaker Graveyard in Nantucket* reads "The Lord
survives the rainbow of His will."

Thus enlightened in a life of experiences still available for
good teachers of tomorrow's wise men, the Youth became a
Teacher, a wandering Pedlar, a Sage acquiring the wisdom
"which works thro' patience," dispensing fraternal sympathy
out of his best experience. "He could *afford* to suffer / With
those whom he saw suffer." The note of personal concern and
of compassion is strong, stronger than in a merely Platonic curriculum.

How will such a one reveal the meaning of human life? By a
Platonic myth? A Christian parable? A mediaeval *exemplum?*
A modern symbol?

In a functional analogy with all four he recounts the tale of

[7] Cf. Shelley's *Adonais*, LII; and Browning's *Deaf and Dumb*, 1-4, as
discussed by William O. Raymond in " 'The Jewelled Bow': A Study
in Browning's Imagery and Humanism," *PMLA*, LXX (March, 1955),
115-131. The verse by Robert Lowell is quoted from "The Quaker
Graveyard in Nantucket" in *Poems 1938-1949* (London, 1950); quoted
by permission of Faber and Faber Ltd.

Margaret of the Ruined Cottage not so much for its own sake
as in evidence toward an elegiac discovery.

> The Poets, in their elegies and songs
> Lamenting the departed, call the groves,
> They call upon the hills and streams to mourn,
> And senseless rocks; nor idly; for they speak,
> In these their invocations, with a voice
> Obedient to the strong creative power
> Of human passions. Sympathies there are
> More tranquil, yet perhaps of kindred birth,
> That steal upon the meditative mind,
> And grow with thought.

His tale told, he reveals his doctrine:

>   consolation springs
> From sources deeper far than deepest pain,
> For the meek Sufferer. Why then should we read
> The forms of things with an unworthy eye?

And again we hear Platonic echoes:

>   All the grief
> That passing shows of Being leave behind,
> Appeared an idle dream, that could maintain,
> Nowhere, dominion o'er the enlightened spirit
> Whose meditative sympathies repose
> Upon the breast of Faith.

Thus Book I ends with the Sage turning to face the light even
as the declining sun shoots "a slant and mellow radiance" upon
the persons in the elegy.

For the Poet the Sage has become "a light unfailing"; but before the debate proper can be joined a deuteragonist must be
presented—a Skeptic darkening from fallacy to fallacy. Of this
man's irresolute and hopeless ways the Sage tells a second tale.
He had been a military chaplain, living and roaming "where
Fortune led." It was Fortune that brought him his bride; it was

Fortune that deprived him of wife and children. Then across
his "anguish" and "apathy" appeared as by chance

> A glorious opening, the unlooked-for dawn
> That promised everlasting joy to France!

And again impelled by chance,

> from the pulpit, [he] zealously maintained
> The cause of Christ and civil liberty,
> As one, and moving to one glorious end.

Wordsworth is at some pains to present him as a person out of
relation, a cultural opportunist. How will he fare in debate with
the Socratic Sage?

From his "intoxicating service" toward as yet untested glory
there arose in the adventuresome Chaplain "A proud and most
presumptuous confidence / In the transcendent wisdom of the
age." Untrammeled by the past, he broke faith with his loved
ones, and

> An infidel contempt of holy writ
> Stole by degrees upon his mind.

Fallaciously he inferred that it was the part of wisdom to disregard "known restraints"; "hopeful prognostications" were
drawn

> from a creed
> That, in the light of false philosophy,
> Spread like a halo round a misty moon,
> Widening its circle as the storms advance.[8]
>
> . . . . .
>
> The glory of the times fading away—
> The splendour, which had given a festal air
> To self-importance, hallowed it, and veiled
> From his own sight—this gone, he forfeited
> All joy in human nature.

[8] In the next chapter we shall refer to Coleridge's lunar images in
Dejection.

The debate, then, would take place between a joyful Sage and a joyless Skeptic.

When the Sage and the Poet seek out this joyless man, they are met by a "funeral dirge"; and Book II continues as an elegy in its restricted sense of death-initiated feeling and thought. Putting to rest their fear that the dirge is for himself, the Skeptic soon comes to meet them, "all fire": "vivid was the light / That flashed and sparkled from his eyes." The image is of sudden and impermanent energy; and this is borne out when he bids them into his attic cell, a "small apartment dark and low," a "wreck" of scattered

> books, maps, fossils, withered plants and flowers,
> And tufts of mountain moss. Mechanic tools
> Lay intermixed with scraps of paper, some
> Scribbled with verse: a broken angling-rod
> And shattered telescope, together linked
> By cobwebs, . . . within a dusty nook;
> And instruments of music, some half-made,
> Some in disgrace.

This aggregation of elegiac symbols is to be contrasted with the treasures of the wandering Sage:

> Birds and beasts,
> And the mute fish that glances in the stream,
> And harmless reptile coiling in the sun,
> And gorgeous insect hovering in the air,
> The fowl domestic, and the household dog—
> In his capacious mind, he loved them all.

The pastoral banquet served by the host was, however, and is, a reminder of natural bounty: oaten bread, curd, cheese, and cream;

> And cakes of butter curiously embossed,
> Butter that had imbibed from meadow-flowers
> A golden hue, delicate as their own
> Faintly reflected in a lingering stream.
> Nor lacked, for more delight on that warm day,

> Our table, small parade of garden fruits,
> And whortle-berries from the mountain side.

We are not allowed to forget the hot sun. And from the window can be seen two huge peaks:

> the clouds,
> The mist, the shadows, light of golden suns,
> Motions of moonlight; . . . there the sun himself
> At the calm close of summer's longest day,
> Rests his substantial orb;—between those heights,
> And on the top of either pinnacle,
> More keenly than elsewhere in night's blue vault,
> Sparkle the stars.

Only out of the Skeptic's window, then, is there prospect of restoration.

The story of the death of the "homeless Pensioner," which in Book II balances the tale of Margaret in Book I, contrasts the "anger and resentment" of the Skeptic with the serenity of the Sage. It also gives occasion for an idyllic passage of brilliant although deceptive vision. In his "dolorous tale" the Skeptic tells us that during the search for the missing Pensioner he had seen emerge from "the dull mist," the "blind vapour" of the storm, a fantastic and "unimaginable sight." [9] This "appearance," "sinking into splendour,"

> wrought
> Upon the dark materials of the storm
> Now pacified,

ends Book II. Its effect is unreal, as of a discovery not quite genuine. The Sage says courteously: "Now let us forth into the sun."

"Anon," as Book III begins "beneath the concave of a blue / And cloudless sky," the three elegiac *personae*, probing deeper into a rocky countryside, hope to follow a streamlet to its source, where

[9] Reminiscent of Bunyan's vision of the Ultimate City.

> The mountain infant to the sun comes forth
> Like human life from darkness;

but instead they find themselves barred by water

> Descending, disembodied, and diffused
> O'er the smooth surface of an ample crag.

They have come to a nook furnished with mossy shapes of rock,
and the Sage has some "shadowy intimations" that in these
"shows" of nature "a chronicle survives / Of purposes akin to
those of Man," a record "of power intelligent," of "design not
wholly worn away." He is, of course, reasoning by analogy, but
his analogy introduces the elegiac argument—"Hail Contemplation." To him the Skeptic replies: These shapes are rather to
"be deemed / The sport of Nature aided by blind Chance."
Design versus chance: the issue is made clear. But he, too, anal-
ogizes: fancifully he calls one rock Pompey's pillar, another his
Theban obelisk, still another a Druid cromlech. Such freaks of
Nature "and her blind helper Chance" feed his "pity and scorn,
and melancholy pride"—as do also Stonehenge, the Egyptian
pyramids, and Baalbec on Syria's desert "in the light / Of sun
and moon." He is depressed by the very same evidence that
exalts the Sage. Better to be a curious but unspeculative Herbal-
ist or Geologist, he says.

> Ah! What avails imagination high
> Or question deep

"through time or space," if no "words of assurance can be
heard"? He is asking for an Aristotelian discovery by arbitrary
statement rather than a discovery by inference or out of the
nature of the incidents of human life. He would prefer to "decline"

> All act of inquisition whence we rise,
> And what, when breath hath ceased, we may become.

Here and now we are in "a bright and breathing world": so
much he acknowledges. Let us with the Athenians choose grass-

hoppers as our ancestors or with the Hindoos derive our stream from seats of divine power like the Ganges from its skyey fount, sinking engulfed in sands and darkness like the Niger; meanwhile, we may enjoy "the vital beams / Of present sunshine." We think ahead to Pater's gemlike flame, to the aesthetes as a group, to art for art's sake, or to aught else divorcing human happiness from the human story—and hence meriting Shaw's rebuke to Clive Bell in their debate of 1922.[10]

When the Skeptic scornfully pities Myth and Poesy, the Poet intervenes to challenge Philosophy—Epicurean? Stoic? But the Skeptic continues to approve rather the effort toward

> confirmed tranquillity,
> Inward and outward; . . .
> The life where hope and memory are as one.

His own brief joy has been no more solid than "the gilded clouds of heaven." He rehearses the story of his domestic losses, not for itself but as self-urged evidence for his hopelessness. The Fall of the Bastille had interrupted his profitless "inquisition" of life even as "a flash / Of lightning" startles a thoughtful shepherd "in a gloomy cave." The deuteragonist is still facing the wall in the Platonic Cave.

Assuming that "the Saturnian rule" had returned, he had been one of those who forced liberty to an unscrupulous licence. Barely avoiding infamous deeds, for safety he must fly over the Atlantic Main to a foreign shore. But under the "bright" sun of the Western World primeval Man, "free as the sun, and lonely as the sun," was discovered—desperate discovery!—to be no "pure archetype of human greatness" but a creature squalid, vengeful, impure, remorseless, superstitious, and abjectly slothful. Here, with the American Indian, the Skeptic rests his case.

Against such despair what can the Sage retort? Only faith, hope, and love. As the Skeptic has pointed to himself in evidence, the Sage also personalizes his argument. He refers to his

[10] *The New Republic,* XXIX (February 22, 1922), 361–362.

own search for repose, repose among eternal things: duty, the forms of an abstract intelligence "where time and space are not"; and God operating in all the events of a daily life "glorious! because the shadow of [His] might." Asserting that happiness arises from humble exploration and understanding of "all natures," that knowledge is a "delight [breeding] love," the Sage illustrates the placidity of the lesser creatures with a reference to the Phoenix, a traditional elegiac symbol, later to be used by both Yeats and Lawrence:

> Ambition reigns
> In the waste wilderness: the Soul ascends
> Drawn toward her native firmament of heaven,
> When the fresh eagle, in the month of May,
> Upborne, at evening, on replenished wing,
> This shaded valley leaves; and leaves the dark
> Empurpled hills, conspicuously renewing
> A proud communication with the sun
> Low sunk beneath the horizon.

Another elegiac symbol, "the rainbow, smiling on the faded storm," is added to support his argument, in company with

> The gilded summer flies that mix and weave
> Their sports together in the solar beam;

and the argument is clinched by

> The mild assemblage of the starry heavens;
> And the great sun, earth's universal Lord.

When the Skeptic distinguishes the light of reason from the light of imagination and finds the latter suspect (IV, 771–773), the Sage places against the exhausted shell of a world analysed to death by the unfeeling philosopher, the living universe of solar, lunar, and stellar beauty as it was conceived in early times in Sion, Persia, Babylonia, Chaldea, and Greece: a youthful Phoebus Apollo filling "the illumined groves with ravishment"; Phoebe, who bestowed "timely light" on the hunter;

Oreads on the mountains, "sunbeams . . . with shadows in their train." Looking back at Newton and as if ahead to Darwin, he asks (IV, 941–978):

> shall our great Discoverers . . . obtain
> From sense or reason less than these obtained
> Though far misled? Shall men for whom our age
> Unbaffled powers of vision hath prepared,
> To explore the world without and world within,
> Be joyless as the blind?
>
>   . . . . .
>
>   And if . . . there be
> An all-pervading Spirit, upon whom
> Our dark foundations rest, could he design
> That this magnificent effect of power,
> The earth we tread, the sky that we behold
> By day, and all the pomp that night reveals;
> That these—and that superior mystery
> Our vital frame, so fearfully devised,
> And the dread soul within it—should exist
> Only to be examined, pondered, searched,
> Probed, vexed, and criticised?

This is the critical challenge of the elegist. The answer, "No," is the elegiac discovery. Uninspired research is a "gloom" when the heart

> On its own axis restlessly revolving,
> Seeks, yet can nowhere find, the light of truth.

A third traditional image in elegiac writing is the sundial, here carved by the Westmorland Shepherd-boy to remind him of his daily duties and pleasures. It provides him conveniently,

> Within himself, a measure and a rule,
> Which to the sun of truth he can apply.

The main pragmatic discovery of Book IV, however, is the joyful effect of truth. When the light of love does not fail and when sense is made auxiliary to divine purpose (IV, 1251–1263),

> Science then
> Shall be a precious visitant; and then,
> And only then, be worthy of her name:
> For then her heart shall kindle; her dull eye,
> Dull and inanimate, no more shall hang
> Chained to its object in brute slavery;
> But taught with patient interest to watch
> The processes of things, and serve the cause
> Of order and distinctness, not for this
> Shall it forget that its most noble use,
> Its most illustrious province, must be found
> In furnishing clear guidance, a support
> Not treacherous, to the mind's *excursive* power.

Science as a vital part of the revelatory process becomes a necessary constituent of elegiac poetry. With such a message the sun goes down on Book IV, Despondency Corrected.

In Book V, the central book of the poem, the scene shifts at high noon to the village churchyard, "where sun and shade [are] intermixed." Moreover, there is a formal change, from the dialectic of the two Scotsmen to the idylls and *characters* of the English Pastor. When the latter enters, he is besought to give "solid facts" for "abstractions" and "plain pictures" for "disputes." "Instances" will "epitomise the life"; "authentic epitaphs" are to be pronounced, what the Greek had called ἐγκώμια. That these followed each other through Books V, VI, and VII in a revelatory series suggesting transformation would remind the classically educated reader of Ovid's metamorphoses; and the student of the New Testament would bethink him of the parables of Jesus. *Idyllia* and *epyllia*, little sketches and little stories or fables, had added light to the revelations of classical elegy and played a vivid part in mediaeval doctrine and homily; and, indeed, a similar pattern had amused the world in many another framework throughout literary history.[11] But how sim-

[11] Professor Haight has set forth instances of *epyllia* in the writing of the Latin elegiac poets Catullus, Tibullus, Propertius, and Ovid. Ovid's *Metamorphoses* had been a stand-by down the ages not alone

ply Wordsworth adapts the device to the curious mind of the nineteenth century, without the dusty echoes of didactic poetry or memories of the windy homilist.

What the Pastor says is wrought into an answer to the Skeptic's challenge: Is ".Religion [with] its [stately] retinue, / Faith, Hope, and Charity," ever triumphant? Has not "profession mock[ed] performance" in all Christian lands "from age to age"? To elicit the Pastor's comment the old elegiac questions already debated in Books II–IV are again posed: "Is Man / A child of hope?" "Do generations press / On generations, without progress made?" "Are we a creature in whom good / Preponderates, or evil?" "Doth the will acknowledge reason's law?" Is virtue "a living power," or only a name? Can the Pastor through his experience—not by his arguments, be it noted—"dispel this gloom"?

Before answering, the Pastor reminds his listeners that for imperfect man the "cogitations" of an "inquest," "knowledge" itself, or "reason, best reason" are only an effort and an aim. Since the good and evil we judge are "our own" and our very feelings prevent indifferent judgment, we cannot attain the "speculative height" of angelic vision.

> Thus comprehension fails, and truth is missed;
> Thus darkness and delusion round our path
> Spread, from disease, whose subtle injury lurks
> Within the very faculty of sight.

These are chastening words for the elegist, too. His tentative discoveries are doomed to become ever more engaging puzzles, ever more baffling riddles.

For one such elegiac riddle, death, the Pastor's symbol is the

---

for writers of fables but for those who detected in the metamorphosis theme itself the mainspring of all poetry, whether of action or vision. That Wordsworth spent two books of his excursive poem in the churchyard looks back beyond the Graveyard School to Ovid, as it looks ahead to Edgar Lee Masters and Thornton Wilder.

grave-mound under an April snow. Viewed from the "sullen north" the mound is

> An unillumined, blank, and dreary plain,
> With more than wintry cheerlessness and gloom
> Saddening the heart. Go forward, and look back;
> Look, from the quarter whence the lord of light,
> Of life, of love, and gladness doth dispense
> His beams, . . .
> *Then* will a vernal prospect greet your eye
> All fresh and beautiful, and green and bright,
> Hopeful and cheerful.
>
> . . . . .
>
> —This contrast, not unsuitable to life,
> Is to that other state more apposite,
> Death and its two-fold aspect! wintry—one,
> Cold, sullen, blank, from hope and joy shut out;
> The other, which the ray divine hath touched,
> Replete with vivid promise, bright as spring.

The Holy Man gives one picture of faith, hope, and love from the living before he turns to stories of the dead. In it "a wedded pair in childless solitude" live and work, she at her hearth, he in a quarry where the ground is stony and barren, yet

> Bright as a sunbeam sleeping till a shower
> Brush it away, or cloud pass over it.

During the winter, when the husband "quits / His door in darkness, nor till dusk returns," the sunshine must be concentrated into the wife's "lantern" for guidance and her "bright fire" for comfort. And for added assurance

> each evening hath its shining star,
> And every sabbath-day its golden sun.

The symbolic nature of these references is undeniable; and our thoughts are again turned sunward when we come to the final discovery of Book V, expressed in terms of the solar rhythm:

> Life, I repeat, is energy of love
> Divine or human; exercised in pain,
> In strife, in tribulation; and ordained,
> If so approved and sanctified, to pass
> Through shades and silent rest, to endless joy.

In Book VI the revelatory "instances" elicited from the Pastor's experience for the most part take form in abstract nouns. The botanist illustrates "faithful love"; the miner, "temperance"; "flaming Jacobite / And sullen Hanoverian" are reconciled in the inscription promising "peace" on the sundial erected to take the place of a mouldering yew seat, the scene of their earlier contentions.

And what of unhealthy curiosity about evil men and wretched situations? "I pass them by," says the Pastor, "loth to disturb what Heaven hath hushed in peace." But, urges the Skeptic,

>   if the thing we seek
> Be genuine knowledge, bear we then in mind
> How, from his lofty throne, the sun can fling
> Colours as bright on exhalations bred
> By weedy pool or pestilential swamp,
> As by the rivulet sparkling where it runs,
> Or the pellucid lake.

He, too, it seems, acknowledges the transforming power of a higher and greater energy.

Confining his "narratives" in Books VI and VII to subjects exciting "feelings" accordant with "love, esteem, / And admiration," the Pastor introduces "a sunbeam . . . among hearts / Retired and covert." Nevertheless, he does not leave "wholly untraced a more forbidding way": it is not unprofitable to discover "truth every day exemplified" even "in the perverseness of a selfish course." Elegy, we note, can lend its aid to the poetry of ethical action: parsimonious Matron invoking the planet Jupiter; unwed Mother Ellen with her Babe like "the first pale speck serene / Of day-spring in the gloomy east"; Wilfred Armathwaite, who could find

> No quiet in the darkness of the night,
> No pleasure in the beauty of the day;

bright sisterhood of motherless daughters, revealed to the sight of passerby "through the blazing window" of their tidy, well-loved home; frolic priest of "flashing eye" and "burning palm" with "inward hoard / Of unsunned griefs," likened

> to the setting sun
> As seen not seldom on some gusty day,
> Struggling and bold, and shining from the west
> With an inconstant and unmellowed light;

deaf Dalesman for whom "dark winter night" and "stormy day" were "silent as a picture," yet who had as resource songs and tales or "word of Holy Writ"; blind Dalesman whose

> eye-balls rolled,
> Beneath his ample brow, in darkness paired,—
> But each instinct with spirit; and the frame
> Of the whole countenance alive with thought,
> Fancy, and understanding,

giving to the imagination

> A type and shadow of an awful truth;
> How, likewise, under sufferance divine,
> Darkness is banished from the realms of death,
> By man's imperishable spirit quelled.

All of these "instances" owe to Wordsworth's solar metaphor not only touches of idyllic clarity but, in chief, their part in the revelatory structure of the poem.

To represent the apparently flawless innocence of infancy and worth of youth the Pastor tells the tales of little Margaret Green on Gold-rill side and young Oswald like "Apollo veiled in human form"—

> In him revealed a scholar's genius shone; . . .
> In him the spirit of a hero walked.

And when the talk shifts from young heroes to those "Oppressors of the world" who evoke heroism,

> Like cedars on the top of Lebanon
> Darkening the sun,

the Pastor has riddling words of comfort:

> So Providence is served;
> The forkèd weapon of the skies can send
> Illumination into deep, dark holds,
> Which the mild sunbeam hath not power to pierce.

Finally, the ruins of time itself appear in the fortunes of Eliza's Knight, Sir Alfred Irthing, whose mansion arose like a "bright star" and now "is gone." So, too, other "stars of human glory are cast down." The "bright order" of knighthood fades; old religious houses are overthrown; "Human-kind rejoices in the might / Of mutability." In the churchyard among the mountains all the evidence tends

> to patience when affliction strikes;
> To hope and love; to confident repose
> In God; and reverence for the dust of Man.

Here it is the abstract words, truth, patience, hope, love, repose in God [? faith], reverence, into which the revelatory accomplishment is channeled.

For the most part, however, the Pastor has given "for abstractions facts" and "plain pictures for disputes." Instead of the mythologies, philosophies, and theologies in the dialectic of Books III and IV, he has driven the thought of his listeners home to what is actual, to matters of fact—always a favorite procedure of Wordsworth. That is why we have in Book VI the address to the State of England and "the spiritual fabric of her Church" as witnessed by her churchyards, steeples, spires, and ancient minsters and by her priests, scholars, and martyrs.

Here, then, is no question of Anglican propaganda on Wordsworth's part, or of an old man's surrender to a tradition, or
undue deference to ceremony or rite. Rather, we must ask
whether or no the elegiac disputation has uncovered its own
truest answer, not in schemes and dreams but in truth.

So it is, also, with the probing of what goes wrong in Church
and State and hence the imperative demands for universal education, improvement in the condition of industrial workers,
refinement in taste. Do such ethical and political revelations not
justify *The Excursion* as an elegy rather than cramp it into a
Tract for the Times? Carlyle and Kingsley and Maurice, and
other pamphleteers, critics, and reformers without number, would
soon turn these elegiac *anagnorises* into discursive writing and
speaking; but the revelations themselves were first of all poetical,
literary symbols of a slowly enlightened humanity.

And there exists no stronger argument for a universal system
of education than Wordsworth's Book VIII. Light, albeit an
"unnatural light," still shines as unremittingly in the factories
where the master idol Gain is served as tapers shone on the
"dim altars" of an earlier age vowed to God under "the punctual
stars." In a world of time and space elegiac *anagnorisis* of necessity leads on to ethical action. The uncouth savages and torpid
churls and pallid boys of the farm and cotton mill had to be
recognized as such before anything could be done about or for
them.

In Book IX, therefore, once the unhappy situation has been
revealed, the lines are laid for action. If the age is to achieve
"fresh power to commune with the invisible world," childhood
must be "fairly dealt with."

> O for the coming of that glorious time
> When, prizing knowledge as her noblest wealth
> And best protection, this imperial Realm,
> While she exacts allegiance, shall admit
> An obligation, on her part, to *teach*
> Them who are born to serve her and obey;

Binding herself by statute to secure
For all the children whom her soil maintains
The rudiments of letters, and inform
The mind with moral and religious truth,
Both understood and practised,—so that none,
However destitute, be left to droop
By timely culture unsustained; or run
Into a wild disorder; or be forced
To drudge through a weary life without the help
Of intellectual implements and tools;
A savage horde among the civilized,
A servile band among the lordly free!

Thus Wordsworth throws down the poetical gauntlet to the nineteenth century.

The lakeland picnic with which this excursive poem ends has many sunny touches, although its fire sinks into ashes. When its sun sets in "a refulgent spectacle, diffused / Through earth, sky, water, and all visible space," amid this reflected light,

> this local transitory type
> Of [His] paternal splendours,

the Eternal Spirit is besought for "further grace." Rarely in such a long poem—Dante's *Commedia* is an exception—has light been made so pervading and consistent a symbol for truth to be revealed. This surely is elegiac writing at its mightiest. Nor has the light of common day ever before—not excepting even Dante—shone so revealingly on the life of every day and its abiding elegiac questions, "Life, Death, Eternity! momentous themes."

This partial analysis of *The Excursion* in terms of its discoveries and its symbol of light does not completely mirror the worth and beauty of the poem; rather, as if the text were a daguerreotype belonging to the same quarter-century, we have tipped it toward the sunshine at an angle proper to reveal what there is in it true to form as well as true to life. Doing this has helped us to speak of *The Excursion* as a single poem and as an elegy.

Moreover, aware as we are of the dialectic form of this elegy, whose themes are investigated by two *personae*, then by three, by four, and finally in the series of metamorphic "instances," each shedding light of its own upon the point at issue, we may with more explicit justification speak of Wordsworth's influence on the century to come. In *The Excursion* was already evident the pattern of controversy for many valiant battles down the years.[12] Sage and Skeptic could be heard again not only in the ambivalent yearnings of Tennyson, Arnold, and Clough and in their dialectic patterns[13] but in the imaginary dilemmas of writers great and small at the end of the century, not least among them William Butler Yeats before he achieved his *Vision*.[14] The century did not produce these oppositions, but it intensified them. Bishop versus agnostic, optimist versus pessimist, would strain at the old issues less temperately and much more verbosely than the disputants of Wordsworth's churchyard in the mountains.

Finally, in the ethical and social realm the activists—Carlyle, the Kingsleys, Henley, and the founders of settlement houses, of which Arnold's niece, Mary Augusta Ward, was one—could not do better than rest their case on the initial passage of Book

---

[12] In the words of Jerome Hamilton Buckley (*The Victorian Temper: A Study in Literary Criticism*, Cambridge, Mass., 1951, p. 6), "Almost every Victorian thesis produced its own antithesis, as a ceaseless dialectic worked out its designs."

[13] All three were students of Wordsworth's poetry. Certain paragraphs of Clough's Lecture on Wordsworth can be read conveniently in Walter E. Houghton, "A Checklist and Calendar, with Some Unpublished Passages [from] The Prose Works of Arthur Hugh Clough" in the *Bulletin of the New York Public Library*, LXIV (July, 1960), 386.

[14] Thomas R. Whitaker ("W. B. Yeats: History and the Shaping Joy," in *Edwardians and Late Victorians, English Institute Essays*, New York, 1959, p. 81) speaks of Yeats's "great Work as a dialectical progress of the soul through the opposites toward ever greater completeness."

IX, where the Sage discovers an *"active* Principle" in "every Form of being":

> howe'er removed
> From sense and observation, it subsists
> In all things, in all natures; in the stars
> Of azure heaven, the unenduring clouds,
> In flower and tree, in every pebbly stone
> That paves the brooks, the stationary rocks,
> The moving waters, and the invisible air.
> Whate'er exists hath properties that spread
> Beyond itself, communicating good,
> A simple blessing, or with evil mixed;
> Spirit that knows no insulated spot,
> No chasm, no solitude; from link to link
> It circulates, the Soul of all the worlds.
> This is the freedom of the universe;
> Unfolded still the more, more visible,
> The more we know; and yet is reverenced least,
> And least respected in the human Mind,
> Its most apparent home. The food of hope
> Is meditated action; robbed of this
> Her sole support, she languishes and dies.
> We perish also; for we live by hope
> And by desire; we see by the glad light
> And breathe the sweet air of futurity;
> And so we live, or else we have no life.

Here was a passage that might have reconciled theologian and scientist, positivist and humanist, had they been willing to listen; but the many escapists, of whom, later in the century, John Davidson was one of the most gifted, chose rather to echo with ever more plaintive exasperation the feeble rejoinders of the excursive Skeptic.

Then, too, many such writers were dissuaded by the exhausting business of "reform," although Wordsworth preferred "to speak of improvement, and the correction of abuses." Ten years before the Benthamites became vocal in *The Westminster Review*, 1824,[15] and the grounds and procedures of reform began to arouse dissension, Wordsworth's Sage had recommended a system of government-supported education for all British children, and called for humane conditions of work. Nor could the revelatory principle for social dealing, man with man, be anywhere in the decades to come more clearly stated than in the words of the venerable Sage of 1814 (IX, 113–119):

> Our life is turned
> Out of her course, wherever man is made
> An offering, or a sacrifice, a tool
> Or implement, a passive thing employed
> As a brute mean, without acknowledgment
> Of common right or interest in the end;
> Used or abused, as selfishness may prompt.

How such words ring out over all other socio-economic discussions between Wordsworth's day and ours!

The passage of the Reform Bill in 1832, the year of Bentham's death, provoked from Wordsworth still further meditations, penetratingly set forth "in plain prose" in the Postscript of 1835. To this main social action of the century Thomas Hood, Elizabeth Barrett Browning, and Charles Dickens also would give support in their own time and manner by sentimental anecdote and the delineation of exaggerated *characters*. Frederick Maurice, with his code of the Christian Socialist and his Working Men's Colleges in 1854, would help to keep theory and practice together. Yet the very circumstances of the century were unfavorable for cultural fusion, as Mrs. Gaskell reported in her study of industrial and agrarian life, still opposed in 1855, *North and South*. And social fusion must wait upon religious harmony, and religious harmony must wait upon a cultural, even a theological, agreement about the nature of "life, death, and eternity." The elegiac probe must go on.

[15] Buckley, p. 23.

Meanwhile, as we regretfully trace the squabbles of the century—Ruskin disapproving of Whistler's Nocturnes with the ensuing action at law, Philistines and Parnassians at odds, schools of the spirit vying with fleshly schools—we could wish for services as helpful in reconciling tensions and differences as the Wordsworthian Pastor had furnished in 1814. Unfortunately, the Man of God no longer stood above the fray. Wordsworth had memorably phrased the shift in authority when he wrote in the Postscript: "Latitudinarianism is the parhelion of liberty of conscience, and will ever successfully lay claim to a divided worship."

What has all this to do with elegy? Each man had become his own elegist, busily seeking for his own revelation. The parhelion itself had come to earth in the diffracting spectroscope of 1814, the very year of *The Excursion.* Newton's prism, it seemed, would win out over Wordsworth's sunshine and rainbow. Like the spectrum out of sunlight, meditation was more widely and variously shared; symbolic thought had started its adventure into the thrillingly new patterns on the colorful light charts of the physicist or the deceptively glamorous iridescence of the aesthete. Through the fitfully flaring decades we peer into a chiaroscuro to be terminated only by the kaleidoscopic artificiality of *fin de siècle* and the glare of two world wars.

Now the kaleidoscope was an invention of 1816. In 1821 Shelley had described life itself to be

> like a dome of many-coloured glass,
> Stain[ing] the white radiance of eternity.

Some years later, in Browning's jewelled rainbow,[16]

> Only the prism's obstruction shows aright
> The secret of a sunbeam, breaks its light
> Into the jewelled bow from blankest white;
> So may a glory from defect arise.

[16] *Deaf and Dumb,* 1-4.

About the same time Clough's schismatic and satirical Spirit
was tempting Dipsychus with a *siccum lumen* of common sense,
reconstituted out of those dreams of saint, sage, and poet that
"divide the light in coloured streams." [17] For such association of
diffracted light with stain, defect, and decay there had been
some encouragement in *The Ancient Mariner*, where "the very
deep did rot" and "slimy things did crawl with legs / Upon
the slimy sea," where the very water "burnt green, and blue
and white." But a fairer estimate of the symbolic multicolor of
the "decadence" will assume it to be an elegiac phenomenon:
through all possible channels of thought, fancy, feeling, and
sense, all kinds of persistent elegists were seeking each his own
particular light of truth, even in all kinds and qualities of morbid experience. The elegiac investigation had been wrested from
Sage, Poet, Skeptic, Pastor in a mountain churchyard to be
continued rather in hospitals, gas-lit cafés, barracks, brothels,
even unto John Davidson's Houndsditch. Revelation had been
democratized. Small wonder that, as truth appeared in all its
diversity, many a will-o'-the-wisp was mistaken for a beacon.
Wanderers came to the lighthouse late and even now must peer
across St. John Perse's purifying sea-marks and into the teeth
of his freshening winds.

[17] Martha Hale Shackford, *Studies of Certain Nineteenth Century
Poets* (Natick, Mass., 1946), section on Clough's *Dipsychus*, p. 55.

ELEGY IN OUR TIME

CHAPTER IX

The Elegiac Century
(1801-1900): Its Symbols

NOT only by dialectics did the nineteenth century pursue its search for truth. Logicians were busy with what they called heuristic, their new name for the "Art of Discovery" [1] by way of those ideas of reason that enabled them to ask questions. Scientists were patiently assembling data to substantiate their hypotheses. What can be said of the procedures and accomplishments of the elegist in this most curious of centuries? Would literary *anagnorisis*,[2] the recognition of truth in human affairs through the speculations of the poet, continue to symbolize itself in metaphors of light and darkness? [3]

In such an investigation we must avoid the "isms" with which a generation of imprecise critics has blanketed the minute particulars of the poetry and art of the century. Instead, we may now concentrate on the veriest of particulars and relate what we learn to a theory of poetry rather than to a history of philosophy.

[1] So William Whewell in 1860.

[2] Although in the *Poetics* of Aristotle, *anagnorisis* is recognition leading to the dénouement of a dramatic action, its Aristotelian definition as "a transition from ignorance to knowledge" makes it an appropriate term also for elegiac discovery, as explained in Chap. II above.

[3] Or what of Lucy in the nineteenth century?

With that purpose in mind let us exemplify the three kinds of discovery made possible by the three modes of vision as denoted by the three Greek verbs for look or see: ἰδεῖν, θεωρεῖν, σκοπεῖν.

The lily on the brow of Keats's Belle Dame sans Merci and the fading roses on her cheek, for instance, or, in his *Ode on Melancholy*, the peerless eyes, like food, of his mistress, or Autumn, the "bosom friend of the maturing sun," can illustrate idyllic or perceptive vision, leading to the discovery of likeness or unlikeness. This phenomenon is like or unlike that phenomenon, actual or imagined: *res vero pro rebus*.[4] Out of such comparable items arises the fabric of correspondences and differences furnishing a young poet's metaphors.

Theoretic vision reveals concepts within the world of particulars. Such discoveries, often richly freighted or clearly pointed, are embodied in abstract nouns chiefly: temperance, justice, constancy, faith, hope, love. They promote the general statements or sententiae of the gnomic writer. However initiated, abstraction is characteristic of Shelley:

> Rome's azure sky,
> Flowers, ruins, statues, music, words, are weak
> The glory they transfuse with fitting truth to speak.

Skeptical vision proceeds to discover identity and community: this is this and none other, with all its pertinent associations in and out of space and time. Witness, from Shelley's *Epipsychidion* (341–344):

> I . . . felt the dawn of my long night
> Was penetrating me with living light:

[4] Professor Richard Hamilton Green quotes this convenient Latin phrase from Colluccio Salutati's *De laboribus Herculis* ("Classical Fable and English Poetry in the Fourteenth Century," *Critical Approaches to Mediaeval Literature*, Selected Papers from the English Institute, 1958–1959, ed. Dorothy Bethurum, New York, 1960, p. 118). Quotations from Keats are from *The Poetical Works of John Keats*, ed. H. W. Garrod (2d ed.; Oxford University Press, 1958); quoted by permission of The Clarendon Press, Oxford.

I knew it was the vision veiled from me
So many years—that it was Emily.

Witness also, from Arnold's *Terrace at Berne* (13–16):

Ah! shall I see thee, while a flush
Of startled pleasure floods thy brow,
Quick through the oleander's brush,
And clap thy hands, and cry: *'Tis thou!*

For the elegist the importance of this kind of identification needs
only to be hinted. It rewards his speculations, gives form to his
search, and suggests the proper mood and the fitting symbols.
Moreover, it conserves and enhances the particulars it seeks
to challenge and question; these do not surrender to other particulars or give up their identity to an abstract idea.

Under the name of realism, discoveries of identity and matter
of fact took on new vigor when scientists also were seeking
truth by way of particulars. John Keats's *Song About Myself*
gives a humorous turn to the search. The restless naughty boy
who ran away to Scotland found

That the ground
Was as hard,
That a yard
Was as long,
That a song
Was as merry,
That a cherry
Was as red—
That lead
Was as weighty,
That fourscore
Was as eighty,
That a door
Was as wooden
As in England—
So he stood in his shoes
And he wonder'd,
He wonder'd.

He stood in his shoes
And he wonder'd.

Now the distinct identity of a particular is best seen in its organic relationships, its membership in a community. From the discovery that something or someone is itself or himself arises the awareness that it or he is part of a whole—not this time merely one of a sort. And hence, in great literature—beyond self-discovery and the identification of one's kindred—we come upon the prevailing symbols of the state, the pantheon or church, the cosmos; and with them, often, the corollary inference that the admirable patterns of the past and the desirable patterns of the future must be reconciled. Shelley's Hellas, the Athens of Swinburne, the Rome of Newman, the Paris and London of the *fin de siècle*—not to mention Camelot and Valhalla and their like—all manoeuvre in the mind of the poet for first place as ultimate fatherland of the spirit. In this regard a speculative poet, an elegist, is one who is trying to find his way home; and his arrival is a *recognitio*.

For such kind of speculation none is more ready than Wordsworth. With the advance of his thought he recognizes his place in the natural world, in the family of mankind, in the government of his country, in the guild of poets, and, at last, in the spiritual tradition of Christianity. This would seem to be no anticlimax but rather the normal development of the elegiac imagination. Little by little the elegist is content to belong in a dependency of his own choice.

Wordsworth's contemporaries did not, of course, write poetry primarily to illustrate old generic schemata or to interpret or apply new doctrinal systems; and, like theirs, Wordsworth's minor poems accord with the literary habit of his time,[5] its various ballads, tales, songs, inscriptions, *characters*, and sonnets.

[5] Robert Mayo, "The Contemporaneity of the *Lyrical* Ballads," *PMLA*, LXIX (June, 1954), 486–522.

Also the terms "elegy" and "elegiac" were used by him and by other writers of the nineteenth century as they would be most easily understood by the generality of their readers, to refer to meditation about death and personal loss, transience, and unfortunate love. In our study of elegy as a form depending on discovery for its main device let us review the better known elegies of the century, beginning with several written by Wordsworth. Thence advancing, we may traverse later decades starred by *Adonais, In Memoriam, Thyrsis,* and *The Wreck of the Deutschland.* When clouds or storms arise to blot out the sunshine and the fickle moon has disturbed the waters of the sea, by what kindly light shall the elegist be guided amid the encircling gloom?

Wordsworth's "elegiac pieces," [6] most of them written under the immediate pressure of loss and sorrow, are less obviously artful than the elegies of Shelley, Tennyson, Arnold, and Hopkins; but they share with their successors traits that bring the genre into clearer focus. Although he was not the only source of Victorian elegy, we shall be rewarded if we follow with care his speculations in the "elegiac stanzas": *Peele Castle in a Storm* (painted by Sir George Beaumont), *To a Daisy,* and *In Memory of My Brother,* John Wordsworth, lost in the shipwreck of the "Earl of Abergavenny," February 6, 1805. Shipwreck for the poets of Britain as for the poets of Antiquity —notably Simonides and Propertius—would be a recurrent anxiety and therefore a revealing symbol.

As a young man Wordsworth during four summer weeks

[6] Here we may disregard the *Epitaphs* he translated from Chiabrera and a few instances of lapidary verse the nature of which he himself has discussed in his *Essays on Epitaphs.* We may note briefly that the pieces in blank verse are *characters* rather than elegiac meditations. The amplified ballad stanzas of the extempore effusion upon the death of James Hogg, reverberating sorrow at the loss also of Scott, Coleridge, Lamb, Crabbe, and Hemans, is more lyrical than elegiac—
How fast has brother followed brother,
From sunshine to the sunless land.

had watched the "Form" of Peele Castle sleeping peacefully "on a glassy sea." Had he been himself a painter then, he says,

> I would have planted thee, thou hoary Pile . . .
> Beside a sea that could not cease to smile;
> On tranquil land, beneath a sky of bliss.

Such a picture, as he now knows, would have been deceptive. His brother's death in a storm at sea has taught him to commend rather the painting of a "sea in anger, and [the] dismal shore." The poet's recent experience of loss is revelatory; it makes possible a new attitude, and it asks a new choice.

> Farewell, farewell the heart that lives alone,
> Housed in a dream, at distance from the Kind!

In his sorrow the soul of the poet has been "humanised"; he has submitted "to a new control." Moreover, the elegy as a poem has moved from an illusory "gleam,"

> The light that never was, on sea or land,
> The consecration, and the Poet's dream,

to

> frequent sights of what is to be borne!
> Such sights, or worse, as are before me here.

Peele Castle was a new referent for elegiac feeling; the poet's renovated vision was a new kind of elegiac discovery; the "new control" was an augury of appropriate action. Such a symbol, discovery, and peripety were to be characteristic not only of Tennyson and Arnold but of Henley later on and of the activist tendencies of the century as a whole. As Dr. John Brown in *Rab and His Friends* said of the medical students crowding noisily into the operating room where lay the little Scotswoman awaiting surgery without anaesthesia: "With them pity had ceased to be an emotion; it had become a motive."

Has it been noticed, further, that Hopkins' *Wreck of the Deutschland*, Part II, recapitulates in theme and, now and again, in formal device Wordsworth's verses in tailed rhyme on the wreck of his brother's ship, the "Earl of Abergavenny"? Wordsworth's diction is spare, understanding both the situation and the sorrow it has caused. Set by the side of Hopkins' richly annotated shipwreck, the account of the "Abergavenny" lacks both color and outline, both intensity and poetic value. The two elegies, however, have much in common. Wordsworth and Hopkins both contrast the scene of the shipwreck with the landlocked sorrow of the mourners: Wordsworth contemplating the "bright daisy Flowers" sleeping and waking upon John's "senseless grave" in the "neighbourhood of grove and field," and Hopkins

> Away in the lovable west,
> On a pastoral forehead of Wales.

Both use as hero (heroine) a dedicated representative of a time-hallowed social pattern: the commander of a ship, and an exiled nun. Both concentrate the experience of shipwreck into a single intense cry: "Silence" followed by a death shriek; and "O Christ, Christ, come quickly." Wordsworth sees survive a few "upon the tall mast's height"; unavailingly Hopkins' crew took "to the shrouds," to "the tops and the tackle." It was beyond Wordsworth's habit and skill to "christen [the] wild worst Best," as Hopkins would do. He could, however, as he writes in *Elegiac Verses,*

> With calmness suffer and believe,
> And grieve, and know that [he] must grieve.[7]

Hopkins may have been familiar not only with the structure of *To a Daisy* but with the stormy details of *Peele Castle,* too.

[7] We think back to the dirges of Simonides, for instance: "Being a mortal man, never say what tomorrow will bring; nor, seeing a man prosperous, how long he will remain so." "Shortly God turns all things upside down." (*Lyra Graeca*, II, 290, 298.) After John's death by drowning William would recall with special interest the story of Simonides saved from shipwreck by the ghost of one for whom he had performed burial rites. The verses from the *Wreck of the Deutschland* are quoted from *Poems of Gerard Manley Hopkins* (3d ed.; London, 1956); quoted by permission of Oxford University Press.

The "sea in anger, and that dismal shore," "the lightning, the fierce wind, and trampling waves" of Wordsworth,

> That Hulk which labours in the deadly swell,
> This rueful sky, this pageantry of fear,

will become with Hopkins a "flint-flake" sea, "black-backed," "combs of a smother of sand," "hurling and horrible airs," "sea-romp" of "swirling and brawling" waves, "wind's burly and beat of endragonèd seas"—"rueful a day." Wordsworth's is a hopeful sorrow rather than a "blind" happiness; but his "fortitude and patient cheer" lack the refulgence of Hopkins' "Orion of light" above, nor would he refer in 1805 as Hopkins did in 1875 to "Jesu" as "heart's light." Yet when we observe that the "mid-numbered He in three of the thunder-throne" was "not a dooms-day dazzle in his coming," "not a lightning of fire hard-hurled"; when we read Hopkins' gorgeously phrased version of Wordsworth's "new control"—

> Let him easter in us, be a dayspring to the dimness of us,
>   be a crimson-cresseted east,
> More brightening her, rare-dear Britain, as his reign rolls,
>   Pride, rose, prince, hero of us, high-priest,
> Our hearts' charity's hearth's fire, our thoughts' chivalry's throng's
>   Lord—

behind the "dazzle" surrendered for "our heart's charity's hearth's fire" we recognize the familiar Wordsworthian shift from "the light that never was" to "frequent sights of what is to be borne."

Along with traditional symbols of elegiac feeling—the finger of God, the hourglass, "the beacon of light"—Hopkins represents the humanizing, spiritualizing process by a vivid image of the "lush-kept, plush-capped sloe . . . mouthed to flesh-burst, [gushing, flushing] the man . . . brim . . . full"—a notable elaboration toward religious fervor of John Keats's percipiently "strenuous tongue . . . [bursting] Joy's grape against his palate fine." Moreover, for his telling metaphors of fear and sorrow

Hopkins may have appropriated imagery set aside by Keats when he excised the first paragraph of the *Ode on Melancholy* —a stanza made public by Lord Houghton from Keats's original manuscript:

> Though you should build a bark of dead men's bones,
>   And rear a platform gibbet for a mast,
> Stitch shrouds together for a sail, with groans
>   To fill it out, blood-stained and aghast;
> Although your rudder be a dragon's tail [8]
>   Long sever'd, yet still hard with agony,
>   Your cordage large uprootings from the skull
> Of bald Medusa, certes you would fail
>   To find the Melancholy—whether she
>   Dreameth in any isle of Lethe dull.

Keats was an idyllist before he became an elegist; and in the particulars of this discarded stanza we can study the means by which, out of the wealth of his percipience, he began to elicit thought toward vision.

Similarly, despite his invertebrate argument in the lunar myth *Endymion*, he has dreamed through elaborately perceived situations toward a cumulative revelation. At last, "spiritualized," he can see his beloved. With *Hyperion*, on the other hand, the beginnings of a more rigorous dialectic are evident. Oceanus, we note, is the sophist and sage, trained in "no Athenian grove, / But cogitation in his watery shades." He will bring comforting "proof" that the Titans have fallen "by course of Nature's law." His account of the origin of light and his warning—

> So on our heel a fresh perfection treads,
> A power more strong in beauty, born of us
> And fated to excel us, as we pass
> In glory that old Darkness—

are in the elegiac pattern; and he clinches his case with the elegiac formula: "Receive the truth, and let it be your balm."

Although Keats thought of *The Excursion* as one of the

---

[8] Compare Hopkins' term "endragoned."

"three things to rejoice at in this age," [9] would be sensitive to the solar metaphors throughout its argument, and could not fail to note the sketch of Apollo as seen and heard by the lonely shepherd, whose fancy fetched (IV, 858–860)

> Even from the blazing chariot of the sun,
> A beardless Youth, who touched a golden lute,
> And filled the illumined groves with ravishment,

it would be idle to assert a clear genetic relationship between Wordsworth's dialectics and *Hyperion*. Yet, the plight of Titans overthrown by upcoming Olympians and the discouragement and bitterness of the followers of Saturn echo the situation and mood of Wordsworth's Book III, Despondency. It may be that Keats foresaw his poem as a kind of Despondency Corrected: what else would have been possible to him? And when Mnemosyne cradles Apollo into meditation and thence into the series of mighty elegiac questions with which the fragment ends—"What are the stars?" "Where is power?"—and, then, when "knowledge enormous" as if he has drunk a "bright elixir peerless" "pour[s] into the wide hollows" of the young God's brain, this, we may say, is elegy as the most variously perceptive poet of the early part of the century was constrained to produce it.

Throughout his speculations the many and minute particulars of the later Keats identify themselves rather than betoken other things. They are rarely metaphors; they are rarely abstractions; they are living instances, spots of existence and value in space and time. This distinctive trait of Keats's elegiac workmanship Shelley has detected and set forth in *Adonais* (XIV, XLII):

> All he had loved, and moulded into thought,
> From shape, and hue, and odour, and sweet sound,
> Lamented Adonais.
>   .   .   .   .   .
> He is made one with Nature: there is heard
> His voice in all her music, from the moan

[9] Keats to B. R. Haydon, January 10, 1818.

Of thunder, to the song of night's sweet bird;
He is a presence to be felt and known
In darkness and in light, from herb and stone,
Spreading itself where'er that Power may move
Which has withdrawn his being to its own.

If Keats revealed truth by way of concrete appearances, Shelley unveiled mystery in a series of abstractions enhanced, as they were, by all the charms of color and light. His "forms," whether concealing or revealing, are gnomic or idyllic more often than elegiac. Keats induced his effects almost as a scientist assembles his data; Shelley's ideal hypotheses were deductively applied—we might almost say appliquéd—to the matter in hand. He caresses those abstract words that he has already idolized— Splendours, Desires, Adorations, Persuasions, veiled Destinies, Glooms, Incarnations, Fantasies, Sorrow, Pleasure, Remorse, Self-contempt, Shame, Life, Death, Desolation, Time, or (LIV)

That Light whose smile kindles the Universe,
That Beauty in which all things work and move, . . .
                     that sustaining Love
Which through the web of being blindly wove
By man and beast and earth and air and sea,
Burns bright or dim, as each are mirrors of
The fire for which all thirst; now beams on me,
Consuming the last clouds of cold mortality.

The fate and fame of Adonais are "a light into eternity," a preconceived rather than a participated eternity. There is little progression in Shelley's thought: we get from here and now to his Platonic realm by a leap of the imagination upward. Neither in *Adonais* nor in *Hellas* does he tell us anything about the steps whereby "the unborn hour" is "unveil[ed]" (*Hellas* 752–754). Nevertheless, the elegiac questions tentatively shaped by the Keatsian Apollo are driven home with high authority by the author of *Adonais* (XXI):

Whence are we, and why are we? Of what scene
The actors or spectators?

And, finally, in its advance from grief to speculation, and from speculation to revelation Shelley's poem maintains the familiar metaphorical pattern of elegy: the soul of Adonais, "burning through the inmost veil of Heaven" beacons "like a star."

Wordsworth may have recalled or reread *Adonais* when, on Christmas eve of 1845, he learned that his five-year-old grandson had been laid to rest in Rome. Two sonnets on this occasion, written in January 1846, reflect even as they simplify Shelleyan images and queries, words and rhymes: these need not be detailed here.[10] Yet, it would be pleasant to think that the words of Shelley, almost a quarter-century dead, had been of some comfort to the aged Wordsworth.

For Wordsworth had been helpful to Shelley in 1814–1815, as we know from the quotation of lines 500–502 from Book I of *The Excursion* at the end of the Preface to *Alastor:*

> The good die first,
> And they whose hearts are dry as summer dust
> Burn to the socket.[11]

[10] *P. W.*, IV, 19, 266, 456. Cf. also the final stanzas of *Lines* composed September, 1806, when the death of Fox "was hourly expected" (*ibid.*, IV, 266–267).

[11] This and other parallels between *Alastor* and Wordsworth's *Tintern Abbey, Intimations of Immortality,* and *The Excursion* were set forth by Paul Mueschke and Earl L. Griggs, "Wordsworth as the Prototype of the Poet in Shelley's *Alastor*," *PMLA*, XLIX (March, 1934), 229–245. The hypothesis of the writers, although debatable, will not be debated here; nor that other hypothesis, that Shelley's Poet is a self-portrait, advanced by John Harrington Smith in *PMLA*, LIV (September, 1939), 785–815. Instead, let us keep to literary judgments: the Shelleyan Poet appears to be a reduced sketch of Wordsworth's two main *personae* in Books I–III of *The Excursion.* It was possibly the older poet's implied criticism of a perfervid, impractical, and disillusioned revolutionary in a time of political unrest that alienated Shelley and prompted Mary Shelley to write in her Journal of 1814: "Shelley . . . brings home Wordsworth's *Excursion,* of which we read a part, much disappointed. He is a slave." (*Mary Shelley's Journal*, ed. Frederick L. Jones, University of Oklahoma Press, 1947, p. 15.) Nevertheless, Shelley has made use not alone of the blank verse, images, and sententious passages of Wordsworth's poem but of the ethical traits of the Skeptic and Sage and of

Following close upon references to "Poets, in their elegies and songs / Lamenting the departed" (475–476), these lines of Wordsworth were originally part of the tale of Margaret of the Ruined Cottage. Margaret had come to grief because she was "self-occupied"; Alastor's "self-centred seclusion," as it is called in the Shelleyan Preface, "was avenged by the furies of an irresistible passion pursuing him to speedy ruin." Both for "luminaries" and "meaner spirits" the cure is to "love . . . [one's] fellow-beings." Again, we hear the Wordsworthian refrain: love of Nature should lead to love of Man.

In this prime *anagnorisis* of the century Shelley does not forget the differing natures, education, and pursuits of the Sage and Skeptic of *The Excursion;* and closer study of *Alastor* in conjunction with *The Excursion*, Book III, Despondency, and Book IV, Despondency Corrected, furnishes many parallels. When the wife of the Skeptic had "melted from his arms," he "called on dreams and visions, . . . conjured Eternity" to no avail (III, 678–688). Bereft of his loved ones, deceived by his false hopes of the French Revolution, he took ship and sailed over the Atlantic Main toward the new Western World and archetypal man, only to be again deceived. Similarly, when the Shelleyan Poet lost the "veilèd maid of Cashmir" who had seduced him in a "vision," a "dream" of happiness, he, too, embarked, on a "little Shallop," for a precarious trip down the stream of life to a death wished for and accomplished in the strictest sense of natural—not human—piety.

That it is the unsocial and fugitive Skeptic in a retreat somewhat like the valley of Blea Tarn in the Lake Country, hoping to "live and die forgotten"—rather than Wordsworth or Shelley himself—who served as model for the moribund Poet of *Alastor*

---

the structural outline of their debate. Unfortunately, when *The Prelude*, published in 1850, revealed the story of Wordsworth's own revolutionary experience, Shelley had been over a quarter-century dead and could not modify his snap judgment of his predecessor as one who had deserted truth and liberty.

is further indicated by a comparison of their common lack of energy. The Skeptic "languidly looked upon the visible fabric of the world"; the Poet looked upon "an empty scene" with "wan eyes." Together they initiated a long line of emotional invalids.

Shelley must have realized that he was constituting his elegiac *character* of a poetical weakling out of the "self-indulging spleen" (II, 311) of Wordsworth's disillusioned revolutionary. The scenic traits of the green recess where the Poet laid him down to die reflect the green recess of the lowly vale of Blea Tarn. Into "children of the autumnal whirlwind" bearing "bright leaves" later becoming "damp leaves" he transformed the children playing in the Skeptic's retreat with the "damp" "leaves" of Voltaire's *Candide* (II, 440, 469). And, as previously noted by Professors Mueschke and Griggs, the address to the stream imaging the life of the Poet (*Alastor* 502–514) may have taken its form from the final passage of Despondency, the plaintive self-portrait of Wordsworth's escapist.

Imagery of "mountain brook," "abrupt / Precipitations," "untoward straits" is not the exclusive property of Wordsworth and his Solitary or Shelley and his Poet, or of the nineteenth century. Nevertheless, revolutionary disillusionment as expressed by the Solitary and poetical frustration as set forth in *Alastor* are seen to be increasingly morbid. The Solitary's hope that his "particular current" would soon reach "the unfathomable gulf, where all is still" was granted in another scene to the Shelleyan Poet; yet, lacking a Wordsworthian Sage to correct his despondency, the Poet never discovered that without love of human kind there would be no vision of truth to reward meditation or encourage action. *Alastor* is an elegy manquée: it is without new light or new life. Shelley himself was speculating but had not advanced beyond a vague literary melancholia, an indistinct idyll of social failure. His somewhat less than credible Poet he saved from shipwreck on romantic seas only to bid him die passively in a "silent nook" far from mankind. "[The] last sight [of the Poet] was the great moon"—the moon that had warned Coleridge of shipwreck, the moon that was to blanch the land and sea of Arnold and mislead Yeats into his monstrous lunar vision, the moon that masters the tides and presides over the storms but is itself lifeless and cannot create life.

What, we may next ask, is the relation of Shelley's "little Shallop" for elegiac adventure and the "little Boat" repudiated by Wordsworth in the Prologue to *Peter Bell?*

The Wordsworthian "little Boat" dates from April 20, 1798, when, according to Dorothy's *Journal*, "The moon [was] crescent" and "*Peter Bell* [was] begun," suggesting the lines:

> But through the clouds I'll never float
> Until I have a little Boat
> Shaped like the crescent-moon.
>
> And now I *have* a little Boat,
> In shape a very crescent-moon.

After a preliminary voyage, however, Wordsworth dismissed his "adventurous Skiff" and returned to "the dear, green Earth." Now, since *Peter Bell* was not published until 1819, the Shelleyan "little Shallop" could not have been patterned on Wordsworth's "little boat." Therefore it is with some reason that Shelley might have considered Wordsworth's poem an intended slight on the shallop of *Alastor* (1816), and Wordsworth's disavowed wanderings among the Zodiac, sportings over Andes, Alps, Libya's sands, and "Siberian snows" as an uncomplimentary cross reference to the itinerary of the Shelleyan Poet. At once he composed a tasteless and ungenerous satire on what he called Peter's "ultra-legitimate dullness." *Peter Bell the Third*, intended for anonymous publication, was acknowledged as his in 1839 by Mary Shelley. Enough of *Peter Bell the Third*.

But in 1820 in prefatory verses for his "visionary rhyme," *The Witch of Atlas*, Shelley told Mary and tells us that he considered the author of *Peter Bell* an "over-busy" gardener and his nineteen-year revision of the tale mere "blundering"

toil. He seems to insist on his own "lovely lady"—"not so sweet
a creature / As Ruth or Lucy" but a match for Peter. He seems
also to insist on his own procedure: the "little Shallop" of
Alastor has become

> the lightest boat
> Which ever upon mortal stream did float.

Yet there was an elegiac change. Although hers was not a
"mortal boat," in it the Witch revisited the "works of man"
and "the peopled haunts of humankind" and humankind itself:
princes, priests, peasants, sailors. Over all of them she had transforming power: she revealed them as they ought to be, their
"inner form most bright and fair." This is the elegiac revelation
lacking in *Alastor*. And she gave to each the power to dream
himself true, the elegiac peripety lacking in *Alastor*.

Might Wordsworth's Sage have assisted Shelley from *Alastor*
to *The Witch of Atlas;* or even—perish the thought!—might
his Potter, Peter Bell, have helped to direct the vagrant Shallop
of *Alastor* back to the "cities / Of mortal men"? At least we
are able to associate in time a group of elegiac *personae:* the Sage
and Skeptic of *The Excursion*, the Poet of *Alastor*, and—along
with Lucy, Ruth, and Peter—the Witch of Atlas. So doing, we
may observe the wide range of treatment of elegiac themes in
the early nineteenth century. Moreover, beneath the diverse
styles of Wordsworth and Shelley we detect a growing conviction that the discoveries of the elegist can be activated by the
storyteller, the playwright, and the social reformer—a task to
which later poets and humanitarians of the century will apply
themselves with renewed vigor.

Whereas the Witch of 1820 is still only a *persona*, a goddess
in a little boat, Prometheus of *Prometheus Unbound*, 1818–
1819, has become a thoroughgoing dramatic agent, his ordeal
bringing to pass a peripety from hate to love and the revelation
of an earth cleared of evil. Act IV with its orbs and wheels and
"cancelled cycles" is lyrical and visionary; to match the con-

trived ugliness of Act I, Act III turns into an idyll of contrived beauty; but between them in Act II, scene iv, there occurs what might be called the mainspring of the drama, the colloquy between Asia and Demogorgon, that "veilèd form" sitting on an ebon throne in a cave symbolic of the mind of man. To this image of the cave the rock of Prometheus' unshakable will and the empyrean wherein lovely concepts graciously flit and sing are subordinate. The colloquy itself, with its dialectic approach to truth, its searching questions and persistent drive through myth and legend, and its acknowledgment that Prometheus is "henceforth the sun of this rejoicing world" is an elegiac argument without which the poem would be as featureless as Demogorgon itself. Here, Asia by asking when the destined hour shall arrive brings on, even if she does not cause, the release of Prometheus. Here, the solar references are many and proper to the speculative passages. In scene v, finally, Asia's presence is "unveiled" to be

> love, like the atmosphere
> Of the sun's fire filling the living world.

She it is who illuminates Earth and Heaven.

The *anagnorisis* of the drama is a discovery of personified ideas, abstractions; these we reconceive as Shelley has preconceived them. What still remains for the action is a melodious echo, a picturesque afterimage. But when the loathsome mask has fallen from the features of humanity, we observe that it is for his elegiac power that Man is to be celebrated:

> And the Abyss shouts from her depth laid bare,
> Heaven, hast thou secrets? Man unveils me; I have none.

Again, we recognize Shelley's fascination with the process of "unveiling" the form to get at the Form; and, again, in his final stanza we observe that as an elegist his abiding interest is in unveiled or explicit concepts or ideas—Hope, Death, Power, Goodness, Life, Joy, Empire, and Victory. Yet it may with reason be urged that his revelations are disclosures of his own conceits, not valid discoveries arrived at through the processes of thoughtful experience.

The symbol of unveiling was given its full connotation in *Epipsychidion*, 1821. Emily,[12]

> Veiling beneath that radiant form of Woman
> All that is insupportable . . .
> Of light, and love, and immortality!

Emily, "veiled Glory of this lampless Universe," "Moon beyond the clouds," "Star above the Storm," "an image of some bright Eternity," was "the veiled Divinity" within the Chaos of the self as Keats's Psyche had been shrined in the untrodden region of the Poet's own mind. She must, therefore, be sought nearby in the "many mortal forms" that the lover as elegist probes to find

> one form resembling hers
> In which she might have masked herself from [him].

At length "the Vision veiled from [him] / So many years" comes to him as "living light"—"Emily!" This is a signal instance of discovery of identity, recognition proper.

The "ship floating in the harbour" of *Epipsychidion* is a somewhat more substantial vessel than the "little Shallop" of *Alastor* or the "pinnace" of *The Witch of Atlas;* and the desirable "Ionian" isle to which Emily and her lover will flee, the "Elysian" people native there, bear some resemblance to actuality. Nevertheless the

> clear exhalations, soft and bright
> Veil after veil, each hiding some delight,

can scarcely content the two loving souls "ever still / Burning, yet ever inconsumable." The cadence of *Epipsychidion* is a

[12] For pertinent discussion of Wordsworth's Emily see the edition of *The White Doe of Rylstone* by Alice Pattee Comparetti (Cornell University Press, 1940).

pathetic one; as in *Alastor* the elegist has been frustrated; Truth, Beauty, and Goodness are yet to seek.

> Woe is me!
> The wingèd words on which my soul would pierce
> Into the height of Love's rare Universe,
> Are chains of lead around its flight of fire—
> I pant, I sink, I tremble, I expire!

The choice between hopeful and hopeless feeling, between resolute action and plaintive surrender, is the conspicuous dilemma of the nineteenth and twentieth centuries. In ethical and social conduct and in poetical habit—and not least in elegiac writing—it is easy for the poet to tip the scales toward despair even as he deceives himself with half-truths or cloudy visions. Moreover, he is often tempted into enigmatic diction when confronted by old queries for which there are no tidy answers. Now and again he seems to be sentimentally, if not maliciously, obfuscating the issue, taking a juvenile delight in what makes trivial matters momentous, clear evidence foggy, or precious values cheap.

Such a one was not Alfred, Lord Tennyson. With him—and it is one main reason for his just repute—the intensity and single-mindedness of the greater elegists were illustrated anew. In what temper and with what glimpses of truth would he end his speculations?

The year 1850, middle year of the elegiac century, saw brought to late publication two deeply meditative autobiographical poems, *The Prelude* and *In Memoriam*, both conceived and written much earlier. Neither could have had any genetic influence on the other, although the clarity and comfort of Wordsworth's poetry already published was influential in Tennyson's series of thoughtful lyrics. Like Shelley, who in *Alastor* quoted "too deep for tears" from *Intimations of Immortality*,

Tennyson seems to have had this Ode by heart.[13] His *In Memoriam* is very close to it: in tender mood, in range of allusion to nature and man, in giving timely utterance to thoughts of grief, in assumptions of a life above, before, and after earthly life, in "obstinate questionings / Of sense and outward things," and in "high instincts," "first affections," "shadowy recollections," and "primal sympathy"—these great phrases of Wordsworth served to inspirit Tennyson even as they rebuke all that is spiritless and nerveless in the decades to come.

Wordsworth's Ode fitted Tennyson's experience; moreover, its "celestial light" and "visionary gleam" fitted Tennyson's poetical eye. Interpreters of *In Memoriam* have noted the importance of light and darkness in the structure of the poem: [14] human "systems" are seen as "broken lights" of an unseen Immortal Love, and Knowledge as "a beam in darkness"; Sorrow whispers that the stars run "blindly" and that the sun is "dying." In the "dark house" so much like that of Chaucer's Criseyde— modernised by Wordsworth as "O Palace whilom day that now art night"—when Tennyson cannot find Hallam at home "all the magic light / Dies off at once."

Many of Wordsworth's elegiac devices are borrowed and modified by Tennyson. Wordsworth's Babe leaping up on his Mother's arm "while the sun shines warm" becomes Tennyson's

[13] Alfred Domett says that Tennyson told him "in 1883 that he sometimes thought of writing an ode on the same subject as Wordsworth's 'Intimations' ode" (Jerome Hamilton Buckley, in *Tennyson: Growth of a Poet*, Harvard University Press, 1960, p. 286, n. 24).

[14] For instance, Jerome Hamilton Buckley (*ibid.*, pp. 110–111): "Throughout the poem 'dark' appears as the most frequent connotative epithet; and the light-dark antithesis provides a ready though still compelling tension of opposites—which are the correlatives of life and death, assent and denial—until at last, as in the climactic ninety-fifth lyric, the polarities may be reconciled in a mystic half-light, where

> East and West, without a breath,
> Mixt their dim lights, like life and death,
> To broaden into boundless day."

"infant crying in the night," "an infant crying for the light"
(LIV). When Tennyson prays (XXX)

> O Father, touch the east, and light
> The light that shone when Hope was born,

he is such a one as Wordsworth's anxious Youth daily traveling
"farther from the east" (71). The cataract of the Ode (25) is
heard again in the cataract of the elegy (LXXI);[15] its tabor
(21, 174) and pipe (176) resound in Tennyson's elegiac pipes
(XXI); its "philosophic mind" echoes in Tennyson's "many an
old philosophy" (XXIII); the "season of calm weather" encourages Tennyson's repetition of "calm" (XI), possibly by
way of Byron's device with the adjective "sweet" in *Don Juan*
(I, cxxii–cxxvii). The pansy at Wordsworth's feet (54) is literary kin of, may even have suggested, the violet to be made
from Hallam's ashes (XVIII), a violet annually blooming "by
ashen roots" to symbolize the regret budding and blossoming in
Tennyson's breast whenever spring awakens there (CXV); the
Tennysonian violet harks back also to Wordsworth's "meanest flower that blows," giving thoughts that do often lie too deep
for tears (206–207). It is not their ornamental value but their
thought-provoking power that allows natural phenomena an
affecting part in the meditations of man: pansy and violet both
"speak of something that is gone" (53). Most memorably,
Wordsworth's "Tree, of many, one" (51), first appearing in

---

[15] This cataract is probably British and Wordsworthian, although
W. D. Paden (*Tennyson in Egypt*, Kansas University Humanistic
Studies, No. 27, Kansas University Press, 1942, pp. 24–25) refers us to
The Hundred Wonders of the World, by the Rev. C. C. Clarke [Sir
Richard Phillips], for the young Tennyson's use in his *Ode on Sublimity*
of cascades, lochs, whirlwinds, Niagara, Cave of Winds, Fingal's Cave,
etc. Also accessible in the library at Somersby were the *Works* of Sir
William Jones, with valuable comment on sun and moon worship; and
Tennyson was familiar with Savary's *Letters on Egypt* (Paden, p. 34).
That his elegy is not so obtrusively symbolic as are many of his early
poems may be due in part to his study of Wordsworth's elegiac writing,
where Nature is allowed to speak for herself, naturally.

In Memoriam as an allegorical yew, "sullen tree" whose "stubborn hardihood" sickened the bereft poet (II), and whose gloom (XXXIX)

> is kindled at the tips
> And passes into gloom again,

is later particularized as a "towering sycamore" (LXXXIX) associated with Arthur Hallam, who found its shadows fair.

Upon such identifiable particulars in Nature are pivoted the memories and hopes of the "human heart." As Shelley had heard Keats's voice in all Nature's music, felt his presence "in darkness and in light, from herb and stone" (*Adonais* XLII), so Tennyson has heard Hallam's voice "on the rolling air," feels him to be "some diffusive power" "in star and flower" (CXXX). Whether it be youth past, a friend lost, a hope surrendered, an ideal blurred, Man refers to Nature to identify his experience: "the woodspurge," Rossetti notes in his deep sorrow, "has a cup of three." Furthermore, there are man-made tokens that serve the same purpose. The revelation of identity that comes to Tennyson as in a trance when he reads again the noble letters of the dead Hallam is no mere abstraction; it is an experience, the deepest and clearest possible to Man (XCV):

> So word by word, and line by line,
> The dead man touch'd me from the past,
> And all at once it seem'd at last
> The living soul was flash'd on mine,
>
> And mine in this was wound, and whirl'd
> About empyreal heights of thought,
> And came on that which is, and caught
> The deep pulsations of the world.

His revelatory trance ended, the poet observes that a breeze is trembling over "the large leaves of the sycamore," rocking "the full-foliaged elms," swinging the rose and flinging the lilies to and fro.

After so climactic a revelation of identity, Tennyson—like his predecessors, notably Wordsworth—goes on to the elegiac peripety (CVIII): "I will not shut me from my kind." It is to this resolve that we owe the last score of poems in the series; by way of Hallam's social sympathies Tennyson binds himself also to "a life in civic action warm" even as he probes "Wisdom heavenly of the soul" (CXIII–CXIV); and the series ends with a spousal verse.

Tennyson's dreams are not all clear discoveries of identity; some, for instance in CIII, are enigmatic and recall *The Pearl* of the mediaeval tradition and riddling Blakean visions. Such picturing of his sorrow and hard-won joy is a kind of diaphany,[16] an inclusive discovery by metaphor. Moreover, his times were busy with freshly induced generalizations, and abstract nouns had been bequeathed to him in great number: from Wordsworth's "We live by admiration, hope, and love" to Shelley's frequent slogans, personifications as of intellectual beauty, or glorious words like Liberty, Hope, Love, Gentleness, Virtue, Wisdom, Endurance, and Victory. We are not surprised, then, at Tennyson's "Immortal Love," although it is a belief rather than a proof, or at his "Faith," an hypothesis rather than a surety; yet these are arrived at by one always serviceable elegiac device, the elimination of alternatives; and hence they are much more than the verbalization of woe.

It may have been the Aristotelian wisdom of Wordsworth that helped Tennyson give concrete shape to what was in Shelley's poetry a Platonic or neo-Platonic idea of form, inviting a plethora of abstract nouns. "The Form remains, the Function never dies" had been the central discovery and the final assertion of the Duddon sonnets, to be read again in Tennyson's "faith thro' form" (XXXIII), his confidence that (XLVII)

> Eternal form shall still divide
> The eternal soul from all beside,

[16] Father Pierre Teilhard de Chardin uses the word "diaphany" (*The Divine Milieu*): "The Divine Diaphany, the Divine Heart shining in the very heart of matter."

his corollary belief that "in that deep dawn behind the tomb" "the eternal landscape of the past" shall bloom "clear from marge to marge" (XLVI). This is the particularity of authentic elegy as over its generality.

The Tennysonian elegy advances by association rather than logical penetration: images and events crowd into the argument, which thereby gains richly in substance for what it loses in outline. Nevertheless, the skeptical traits of elegy, challenging further speculation and directing the ultimate probe, are helpful to Tennyson in his day. "Is this the end? Is this the end?" (XII) Or (LVI):

> shall . . . Man . . .
> Be blown about the desert dust,
> Or seal'd within the iron hills?

No more?

> What hope of answer, or redress?
> Behind the veil, behind the veil?

Tennyson, like Shelley, must pull aside the veil, reveal the living truth. Now we "see in part" (CXXVIII)

> That all, as in some piece of art,
> Is toil coöperant to an end;

Hallam will be finally discovered standing "in the rising sun," or fair "in the setting sun"; and Tennyson will advance "to meet and greet a whiter sun." The dim lights of East and West, "like life and death" will broaden "into endless day." [17]

Matthew Arnold and his friend Arthur Hugh Clough were both students of and commentators on Wordsworth's poetry.[18]

[17] In *Critical Essays on the Poetry of Tennyson,* ed. John Killham (New York, 1960), Arthur J. Carr (pp. 61 ff.) discusses some traditional elegiac devices of *In Memoriam*: the formal invocation, the description of the funeral procession, the mourning of nature, the sober and noble themes.

[18] For the concluding paragraphs of Clough's lecture on Wordsworth, see Houghton's checklist, *Bulletin of the New York Public Library,*

There is no need here to argue his influence upon them; but we should not forget that in the skeptical Solitary of *The Excursion* earlier than in the sulky heroes of Byron and closer at hand than in the Obermann of Senancour, there existed the prototypical despondent of the century and its honest doubter as well, already subject to the inner conflicts and dialectical habits of modern literary *personae*. Readers familiar with the biographies of Wordsworth and Arnold will think of analogies between Annette and Marguerite [19] and the efforts of each poet to establish his life and work in a more mature relationship and more serene domestic surroundings; they will note that personal tensions in the friendship of Arnold and Clough resemble difficulties that estranged Wordsworth and his friend Coleridge. Such analogies are incidental, and yet they tell us something about the typical development of an elegist. That the careers of Wordsworth and Arnold reveal a similar transformation of youthful energy and feelings into ever more shapely ethical form parallels the structure of elegy itself, the advance of the argument from what is powerful and obscure to what is effective and clear. Moreover, in this stylistic growth of the elegist we may observe with special relevance many of the devices whereby elegiac themes—youth, love, friendship, transience, disillusionment, personal or social or civic loss, death—must be directed toward explicit or implicit discovery. The suffering or mental ordeal, the queries, the debates, the negations and asseverations, the metamorphoses intermediate between the original and final self, the will-o'-the-wisp or *ignis fatuus*, the glimpses of truth on the way to the ultimate revelation: these are at the very center of the

---

LXIV (July, 1960), 385–386. Arnold's essay on Wordsworth was published as preface to the poems of Wordsworth in The Golden Treasury Series, 1879. Under the heading, Reflective and Elegiac Poems, he groups a wide selection of characteristic titles, the themes of which vary from death to the "great Apocalypse" on the Simplon Pass. Arnold's poems are quoted from the *Poetical Works of Matthew Arnold* (London, 1929).

[19] Ruth Zabriskie Temple (*The Critic's Alchemy*, New York, 1953, p. 30) asks: "Is there not one of the many parallels between Arnold and Wordsworth in the love of each for a fair 'daughter of France'?"

actual art of growing up and they constitute the logical art of speculative thought and the formal art of elegiac poetry.

Wordsworth had lost "the visionary gleam"; for Coleridge earth was no longer enveloped in "a fair luminous mist." Whereas Wordsworth resolutely pressed on with his sunny poems into the light of common day and Coleridge out of his dejection became the voluminous critic, seeing rather than feeling how beautiful are the clouds, the stars, the moon, man himself with his waxing and waning purposes—and whereas Tennyson turned from grief to allegorize the present into romantic discoveries of the past—Matthew Arnold confronted the puzzles and problems of his age directly, bringing the past to bear upon the present for the sake of the future. That in so doing he must renounce verse for prose and take upon himself the humblest duties of the teacher was not an anticlimax. His adaptation of literary criticism into ethical and social exhortation made him no less an elegist. Short of action, his was the development of elegiac form into didactic form. Its discoveries were in widest commonalty spread.

Our present concern, however, is with Arnold's elegiac poetry, with the literary symbols in which his dubious thought was expressed, and with the peculiar nature of his discoveries. His search, we notice, takes him from the uplands to the seashore, from what is stable to what is mobile, from the dependable recurrence of stars and sun, the comfort of mountains and vegetation, to a less calculable moon-blanched land and sea, to an incalculable outer and inner world of storms and flux. He mediates between what has been sure and what is to be uncertain: he is both traditional and contemporary.

First, then, let us think of his monody, *Thyrsis*, as successor in some part to the elegiac Odes of Coleridge and Wordsworth, with their theme of disillusionment and their celestial imagery—sun, moon, stars, clouds, and winds—to symbolize aspects of joy and despair in terms of light and darkness.

Intimations of Immortality is a solar poem. The "celestial light" of yore, the "visionary gleam," the "clouds of glory," have faded into "the light of common day"—ordinary sunshine. Although the sun of a sweet May morning continues to "shine warm" upon flowers, cataracts, young lambs, babies, and shepherd boys, thoughts of grief weaken the poet, who regrets the inevitable yoke destined for the child growing to manhood:

> Full soon thy Soul shall have her earthly freight,
> And custom lie upon thee with a weight,
> Heavy as frost, and deep almost as life.

Wordsworth's frosty, deep, and heavy weight on the "Soul" suggests diminished heat from the sun, a trope emphasized by the welcome discovery of "something that doth live" "in our embers."

Dejection is a lunar poem. Through a long evening Coleridge has been drearily gazing on the yellow-green western sky at sunset, on the stars gliding between thin clouds, and on the crescent moon. The appearance of the moon, "with swimming phantom light o'erspread," reminds him of a stanza from the *Ballad of Sir Patrick Spence:*

> Late, late yestreen I saw the new Moon,
> With the old Moon in her arms;
> And I fear, I fear, my Master dear!
> We shall have a deadly storm.[20]

He, too, discovers in the lap of the bright new moon the calamitous old moon. Thereupon the lunar phantom light becomes for him symbol of the "beauty-making power," Joy; Joy is the light, the glory, the "fair luminous mist" issuing from the "soul

[20] In a poem of 1826–1827 (*P. W.*, IV, 163–164) Wordsworth wrote an explicit answer to *Dejection* with the same quotation from *Sir Patrick Spence* and the same lunar metaphor:
> No faculty yet given me to espy
> The dusky Shape within her arms imbound.
The poem, "Once I could hail (howe'er serene the sky)," repays study; it is most skillfully phrased and its structure is at once spare and vertebrate.

itself." And by the old moon in the lap of the new moon he symbolizes the "smothering weight" upon his breast, his

> grief without a pang, void, dark, and drear,
> A stifled, drowsy, unimpassioned grief.

He is "wan"; like the moon he has waned from the time when joy could dally with distress. "Now," under afflictions, he has lost his mirth and his shaping spirit of Imagination; "reality" has become a "dark dream." In the predicted storm he welcomes a possible release of his feelings from the "abstruse research" infecting his soul and the "viper thoughts" coiling around his mind. The lunatic Wind, raving as if it were a tragic Actor or a frenzied Poet, speaks for him: first in screams of agony, telling of the groans of men and their "tremulous shudderings," and then—"hush!—with sounds less deep and loud." The Wind as a "mad Lutanist" is obviously under the influence of the moon; but at midnight, when the storm subsides, the stars are invoked to hang bright over the "gentle Sleep" of the "friend devoutest of [the poet's] choice." In spite of the sunset at its beginning and the stars at its ending, *Dejection* follows the destiny of the moon, its revelatory light dimmed by the waning of "genial spirits" and the stormy weather interposed between earth and heaven.

Wordsworth related his solar catastrophe to imperishable truths,

> Which neither listlessness, nor mad endeavour, . . .
> Nor all that is at enmity with joy,
> Can utterly abolish or destroy—

here he seems to cross-refer us to the "wan" poet of *Dejection* and his "mad Lutanist." How might these truths be revealed? Coleridge had done it with a symbolic storm, clearing to show the stars; Wordsworth does it with a reference to "our life's Star," "the Soul that rises with us," coming from afar. Above lunar changes and solar rhythms, our stellar destiny allows us those shadowy recollections that are the "fountain-light of all our day," "the master-light of all our seeing." *Who* will discover these truths? Wordsworth's Actor is no raving, mad, tragic lunatic but a busy little Child, an "Eye among the blind," a "Seer blest" for those lost in darkness, "the darkness of the grave." *What* does this Seer discover? He beholds the light as flowing "from God, who is our home." Upon him Immortality broods "like the Day"; and when as a Man he has watched over human mortality, his eye can still color soberly "the Clouds that gather round the setting sun." [21]

Difficult and unnecessary as it would be to distinguish the Wordsworthian and Coleridgean influence in Arnold's *Thyrsis*, we may observe that all three make use of a tree: Wordsworth's "Tree, of many, one"; Coleridge's green-tasseled larch, excised from *Dejection;* Arnold's signal-elm. The larch was an idyllic tree; but the trees of Wordsworth and Arnold are properly elegiac, speaking of "something that is gone," as do the witch-elms and the sycamore of *In Memoriam,* its "hoary knoll of ash and haw." Thanks to this device associating feeling with particular things, the elegist is enabled to discover by identification the unique quality in his experience and recall vanished glory with a resolute faith that it is not lost. Arnold's spirit is lifted by his discovery: he bids us "see,"

> Back'd by the sunset, which doth glorify
> The orange and pale violet evening-sky,
> Bare on its lonely ridge, the Tree! the Tree!

And he hears as if whispered by the voice of his dead friend, Clough:

> *The light we sought is shining still.*
> *Dost thou ask proof? Our tree yet crowns the hill.*

This tree is not any tree; it is not a generalized or ideal tree; it does not serve as metaphor for something; it is not an ornament.

---

[21] One origin of this luminous imagery I have studied more fully in "The Spenserian and Miltonic Influence in Wordsworth's 'Ode' and 'Rainbow,'" *Studies in Philology,* XXIX (October, 1932), 607–616.

It identifies itself and so gives identity to those for whom it is unique. Furthermore, on its background of sunset, it bears witness to the luminous purposes of the friends thus identified.

Coming back to Oxford without Clough, who died at Florence in 1861, Arnold further identified him for us in terms of the local circumstances of their college friendship. Tentatively, while the elegist's feet stray along a familiar path, his elegiac eye seeks familiar sights. Where is the girl . . . ? Where are the mowers . . . ? All are gone, "and thou art gone as well?" Across these echoes of *ubi sunt*—"hush!"—come the hunters "as in old days," another instance binding past and present together. Memories of the Scholar-Gipsy, the mythic companion of Arnold and Clough on their rambles, symbolize not only Clough but all those who down the centuries leave the academe to seek " a fugitive and gracious light"—Tennyson had spoken of following the gleam. "Out of the heed of mortals" they fare, "by their own heart[s] inspired." Human recurrence is never more potent than in an academic frame, where the generations come and go in a rhythm scarcely less strict than that of the sun and moon; and although Arnold is left "sole" in these fields of Oxford, he will not despair.

> Despair I will not, while I yet descry
> 'Neath the mild canopy of English air
> That lovely tree against the western sky.

In *Thyrsis* as in *The Scholar-Gipsy* Arnold had hit upon a stanzaic pattern allowing full opportunity for the pastoral idyll as well as the elegiac meditation. Some of the imagery is decorative rather than symbolic; but the landscape comes alive more variously and immediately than in most modern pastorals, thanks to Wordsworth's elegiac "Tree, of many, one," with its power to identify a uniquely valid experience. Thanks also to Wordsworth's Child, Arnold's Scholar-Gipsy is "a truant boy / Nursing [his] project in unclouded joy," outliving both Thyrsis and Corydon. The yearning for joy, the fear of "infection [from]" our mental strife" and the flight "to where the Atlantic raves" are more particularly echoes of themes and patterns in Coleridge's *Dejection*. When the piping of Thyrsis

> took a troubled sound
> Of storms that rage outside our happy ground,

Arnold was remembering S.T.C. as well as Arthur Hugh Clough.

Neither in *Thyrsis* nor in the great Odes of which it is a not unworthy successor is regret quite transformed: "many a dingle . . . / Hath . . . put by / The coronals of that forgotten time." Similarly with Wordsworth: however keenly he shared the fullness of the bliss of the child of Joy on that May-morning in 1802, his head no longer wore "its coronal." Around Coleridge no longer hope grew "like the twining vine." So persistently is meditation tinged with regret in Arnold's poetry that he is remembered as the elegist of the century in the restricted meaning of the word. And there is more than a hint that out of his classical scholarship he was aware of the literary distinction he had earned. Many of his symbols, metaphors, and melodies revive the elegiac tradition as Wordsworth and Coleridge had reinterpreted it. The dead Matthew of Wordsworth "with a bough / Of wilding in his hand" recalled the dead Cynthia of Propertius with twining tendrils of ivy binding her delicate bones; Arnold's Obermann with "a mountain-flower . . . in his hand" is an afterimage of Matthew. The "light-house top," "the hill," and the kirk in "mine own countree," to which Coleridge's Old Sailor returned from his guilty and sobering adventures at sea, anticipated "the peak of Jaman" and "the domed Velan" of the Swiss Alps to which Arnold returns from the "shipwreck in [his] own weak heart." Through Obermann's tale of cultural change, when

> Blocks of the past, like icebergs high
> Float on a rolling sea,

we glimpse more than accidental similarities to the mist and snow and wondrous cold of *The Ancient Mariner*, when "ice,

mast-high, came floating by." From the shipwrecks of John
Wordsworth and Coleridge's Old Sailor Arnold has gone on to
envision the threatened wreck of the Ship of Human State and
the problems of political seamanship; and when Obermann sends
Arnold back to the world's work and prophesies

> *One common wave of thought and joy*
> *Lifting mankind amain,*

it is as a mariner to a world in flux that the poet returns. The
sea of *The Ancient Mariner* had been a romantic sea, but the
sea of the classical scholar Arnold is an elegiac sea, serving as
symbol for the tides and storms of meditative feeling, its crests
and troughs, its perils and shipwrecks. Had not the waves around
Melos washed over the gunwales when Theognis feared lest his
ship be swallowed, μή πως ναῦν κατὰ κῦμα πίῃ? Was not his city
under worthless leaders like a ship out of her course, running
too near the shore? [22] And from the few surviving fragments of
Mimnermus had not Arnold been reminded of Jason's misad-
ventures at sea in his quest for the Golden Fleece? And did he
not know the *Odyssey* by heart?

Wordsworth had been concerned with the functional, even
the institutional, life of those he mourned. The deaths of the
Schoolmaster (Matthew), the Painter (Sir George Beaumont),
the Commander (John Wordsworth), the Statesman (Charles
James Fox), the Poet (Charles Lamb, James Hogg), the Beggar,
and the Farmer and Hermit not less than the Martyr and
Churchman (Wickliffe and Cranmer) were events of communal
importance. Loss of representative man poses problems inviting
sternest thought. Arnold, too, made an effort to probe the mean-

[22] *Elegy and Iambus*, I, 310–311, 330–331. Arnold was familiar with
Greek elegy, at least with those of Theognis and Mimnermus (Lionel
Trilling, *Matthew Arnold*, New York, 1939, p. 138). Witness also his
note on lists of poems to compose: "8. Shelley-Spezzia—ah an eternal
grief. The Alexandrian pessimism" (*The Poetry of Matthew Arnold:
A Commentary*, ed. Tinker and Lowry, Oxford University Press, 1940,
p. 12). It is a reasonable assumption that he knew also the elegies of
Solon in their ethical and political frame of reference.

ing and enhance the value of our social nature, turning his attention from the romantic and escapist Scholar-Gipsy to the actual Poet (Goethe, Byron, Wordsworth, Heine), the Public Servant (William Arnold), the Novelist (Brontë), and the Schoolmaster (Thomas Arnold), the chief of those

> whom a thirst
> Ardent, unquenchable, fires,
> Not with the crowd to be spent,
> Not without aim to go round
> In an eddy of purposeless dust,
> Effort unmeaning and vain . . .
> Not without action to die
> Fruitless, but something to snatch
> From dull oblivion, nor all
> Glut the devouring grave.

These "helpers and friends of mankind," appearing "like angels . . . / Radiant with ardor divine," help to explain the Arnolds, father and son; and they illustrate the representative dimension of elegy. Similarly, the *Stanzas from the Grande Chartreuse* include nature and man in their scope, children and the dead and dying, action and passion, soldiers and hunters and recluses, even "two worlds, one dead, / The other powerless to be born." And in the poems remembering Obermann, ideas of fidelity and honest doubt are universalized still further in the direction of the brotherhood of men and the common destiny of mankind.

Again, Arnold links the elegist with the problems of his time; the persons of his elegies, like those of Wordsworth's poems, fall into mutually dependent relation, testing and fulfilling each other—master and pupil, mentor and disciple, lover and beloved —until both voices [23] are unified in the one voice of oracle. This, as has been pointed out in the last chapter, is the Socratic tend-

---

[23] W. Stacy Johnson (*The Voices of Matthew Arnold: An Essay in Criticism*, Yale University Press, 1961) discusses the formal result in his poetry of the ambivalence of Arnold's thought.

ency in most elegiac discourse: finally, all the listeners side with
the oracle and perforce the skeptic is silenced. The phrase
Scholar-Gipsy, coming from Glanvill's *Vanity of Dogmatizing*,
resounds also from the Sage-Skeptic or Wanderer-Solitary of
Wordsworth's *Excursion;* it hyphenates even as it distinguishes
the two sides of the poetic character. And in the Obermann
poems of Arnold not infrequently we hear again Wordsworth's
arguments in "Despondency Corrected" for faith, hope, and love.
The scene is also similar: instead of the Langdale Pikes, the
poet breathes "virgin mountain-air" under the Peak of Jaman
and the dome of Velan. From Wordsworth's "sweet calm" and
Goethe's "wide / And luminous view," however, the poet of the
"harass'd" mid-century turned for sympathetic counsel rather to
their contemporary,[24] Étienne de Senancour, author of *Ober-*
mann. In the Swiss letters of Obermann he gained comfort for
his own tensions:

> Ah! two desires toss about
> The poet's feverish blood,
> One drives him to the world without,
> And one to solitude.

And again we experience—although in briefer and tidier form—
the matter and mood of the remarks of the Solitary and Sage of
"Despondency Corrected," this time without benefit of clergy.

Although Arnold's are not often the speculations that resist-
lessly probe into the greater mysteries but are rather those that
eternize the lesser woes, his own final discovery was of the possible dignity and beauty of the active life and the poetical nature
of dialectic and discursive writing. May it not have been these
tendencies in elegy itself that tipped Arnold's scales from verse
toward prose? We can say of his flute song what he said of the
poetry of Arthur Hugh Clough: "What though . . . too soon"
the music of his rustic flute "learnt a stormy note" and "failed,"
"yet [had he] alway visions of [the] light." "What though . . .
yet": to bring the concessive clause into the sentence structure

[24] Wordsworth, Goethe, and Senancour were all born in 1770.

of meditation without loss of feeling was Arnold's distinction in the later as it had been Wordsworth's in the earlier years of the elegiac century.

If, moreover, we are to understand Arnold's position as a link between the elegiac century and our own we must speak further of those symbols of flux, into which the more decorous patterns of stellar and solar energy were modified by way of the moon and her influence over the sea. Water, Arnold declared, was the Mediator between the inanimate and man.[25] And in the increasing cultural *mal de mer* of the century his master symbol of waters on their way to "the infinite sea" outdoes Wordsworth's Duddon and Holy River; it approaches the surging element in Swinburne's poetry and allies itself with the scenic frame of Melville's *Moby Dick* and the essential force of St. John Perse's *Sea Marks*—yet to come.

The evidence for this leads us, with new awareness of Arnold's skill, from his Shakespeare, who knew both the stars and sunbeams, and his Mycerinus, who reckoned his six years in the rising of suns and the waning of moons, on to his image of Time as a current in *A Memory Picture*. Boat music enters the plaint of *A Modern Sappho* and in *Requiescat* "peace laps [the lady] round." The boat of *A Dream* "hung poised" only a moment before it was received by the sea. The sirens of Ulysses,

> who on shores and sea-washed places
> Scoop the shelves, and fret the storms,

give a marine background to those *New Sirens* for whom "the slow tide sets one way," toward death. An unforgotten voice beats upon the poet's ear like the glances of the bright moon "at the sleepless waters / Of a lonely mere" or "the bright waves that fall . . . / On the lifeless margin of the sparkling Ocean." Youth's passions "for ever ebb and flow" in "thwarting currents of desire." In *Stagyrus* "Love is half mistrust, / Hungry, and barren, and sharp as the sea." Usually human life is imaged as

[25] Tinker and Lowry, *op. cit.*, p. 81.

a voyage on an "incognizable sea" with an "inly-written chart"
to steer by; its chief trait appears as

> the foaming swath
> Of torn-up water, on the main,
> [Falling] away with long-drawn roar
> On either side the black deep-furrow'd path
> Cut by an onward-labouring vessel's prore.

And, to show mankind at home in himself and his world,
terrestrial and celestial images are fused in a remarkable poem
published in 1849 with the Ulyssean *Strayed Reveller* and entitled *Resignation*. Brother and sister coming to the shore from
the upland farms gleefully bathe their hands "in the wide-glim-
mering sea"; and each moment is discovered to be a "quiet
watershed / Whence, equally, the seas of life and death are fed."

The *personae* of Arnold's narrative verse are often met on the
sea or the seashore, as in the address *To a Gipsy Child* near the
"swinging waters," where Earth and Ocean labor on "not idly";
nor idly do the sea birds hover near. In the old Northern myth
Frea sends Hoder down to Ocean's strand, "Ocean, whose
watery ring enfolds the world"; in the Christian fable, floating
past St. Brandan on the northern main come

> an iceberg white,
> And on it—Christ!—a living form;

and in those legends of Neckan, singing his "plaintive song"
along the Baltic Sea, and that Margaret who has deserted her
Merman for the blessed light of the holy sun but still looks long-
ingly over the sand toward the unholy sea: in all these, the verse
is swung into marine rhythms dependent on the moon.

It is on the seashore that Tristram and the two Iseults identify
themselves. Iseult of Brittany, that "snowdrop by the Atlantic
sea," Iseult of Ireland and Tristram in the moonlight, and
Tristram's children sleeping in "the moon's ray" share the lunar
regret of elegy; and the Huntsman on the arras looks beyond the
"kneeling lady fair" and the "pale knight," beyond

> The castle-court all wet with rain,
> The drawbridge and the moat . . .
> And then the beach, and, mark'd with spray,
> The sunken reefs, and far away
> The unquiet bright Atlantic plain.

The infinitude that Wordsworth had discovered in the mountains Arnold found on the infinite moonlit sea.

Notably in the more extended fables, the waters help the movement of the poem. Sohrab compares men to swimmers in the sea,

> Poised on the top of a huge wave of fate,
> Which hangs uncertain to which side to fall.
> And whether it will heave us up to land,
> Or whether it will roll us out to sea,
> Back out to sea, to the deep waves of death,
> We know not, and no search will make us know;
> Only the event will teach us in its hour.

Rustum's grief when he has slain his son is likened to "the vast tide / Of the bright rocking Ocean" when it "sets to shore / At the full moon." And for the end of the story Oxus strains along "under the solitary moon"

> Through beds of sand and matted rushy isles
>   . . . till at last
> The long'd-for dash of waves is heard, and wide
> His luminous home of waters opens, bright
> And tranquil, from whose floor the new-bathed stars
> Emerge, and shine upon the Aral Sea.

Finally, although Marguerite lived in Switzerland, there her poet discovered "vast seas of snow"; there "a sea [rolled] between them"; they were

> Like driftwood spars which meet and pass
> Upon the boundless ocean-plain.

With fateful power a God had ruled their severance

> And bade betwixt their shores to be
> The unplumb'd, salt, estranging sea.

Yet, "enisled" as they were in the sea of life, now and again by moonlight they might believe themselves "parts of a single continent." Tentative comfort this, for the stronger rhythm prevails on the shore at Dover, "where the sea meets the moon-blanch'd land," where "with tremulous cadence slow" the pebbles are drawn back and flung up the high strand and we hear the "melancholy long withdrawing roar" of the Sea of Faith

> down the vast edges drear
> And naked shingles of the world.

Thus Arnold in and for his day illustrated what, being a classical scholar, he would recognize as "Alexandrian pessimism."

Whatever peripety from pessimism into faith, hope, and love exists in Arnold's poetry can best be indicated when we turn his pages from *Dover Beach* to *Obermann Once More*. Although the passage reviewing the plight of world culture (82–324) shows a relaxation of doctrinal positions and aesthetic rhythms from the historical review made by the Sage in Wordsworth's "Despondency Corrected" (*The Excursion*, IV, 631–887), another cultural morning does "break"

> Across the glimmering lake
> High in the Valais-depth profound.

The elegist returns to his work in the world. Thenceforth his career as critic and teacher will become his poem.

"See! the sun is risen!" says Arnold's Obermann,

> "He breaks the winter of the past;
> A green, new earth appears.
> Millions, whose life in ice lay fast,
> Have thoughts, and smiles, and tears.
>
> "What though there still need effort, strife?
> Though much be still unwon?
> Yet warm it mounts, the hour of life!
> Death's frozen hour is done!

"The world's great order dawns in sheen,
After long darkness rude,
Divinelier imaged, clearer seen,
With happier zeal pursued."

This is the recurrent discovery of the elegiac century. Almost fifty years earlier Shelley had written in *Hellas* similar stanzas to the same rhythmic effect:

The world's great age begins anew,
    The golden years return,
The earth doth like a snake renew
    Her winter weeds outworn:
Heaven smiles, and faiths and empires gleam
Like wrecks of a dissolving dream.

A brighter Hellas rears its mountains
    From waves serener far;
A new Peneus rolls his fountains
    Against the morning star.
Where fairer Tempes bloom, there sleep
Young Cyclads on a sunnier deep. . . .

Another Athens shall arise,
    And to remoter time
Bequeath, like sunset to the skies,
    The splendour of its prime;
And leave, if nought so bright may live,
All earth can take or Heaven can give.

And in the same vein in the same year of 1821–1822 Wordsworth had brought his Holy River to rest:

The living Waters, less and less by guilt
Stained and polluted, brighten as they roll,
Till they have reached the eternal City—built
For the perfected Spirits of the just!

As the century wore on, which symbols for elegiac feeling would prevail: sun, moon, and stars to reveal? steadfast upright tree or flooding and ebbing waters? battered hulk or ship of state? crumbling ruin or eternal city? Rereading the poems of Algernon Charles Swinburne, who resembles his own Thalassius, born of the sea nymph Cymothoe and "the live sun's very God," [26] we anticipate certain flux along with possible sunshine. Many of his titles show him prepossessed by the sights and rhythms of the sea: *A Swimmer's Dream, The Seaboard, A Sea Mask, In the Water, By the North Sea, On the Southcoast, The Sea-Mew, Neap-tide.* He knew the salt marshes at Dunwich, and in his dedicatory epistle to Watts-Dunton (1904) spoke of "the joyful and fateful beauty of the seas off Bamborough and the seas about Sark and Guernsey." In *Laus Veneris* it was the "great elder-tree" up on "the Horsel" under which he recognized his beloved; in *The Triumph of Time*

> The loves and hours of the life of a man,
> They are swift and sad, being born of the sea.
>
> · · · · ·
>
> It is not much that a man can save
> On the sands of life, in the straits of time,
> Who swims in sight of the great third wave
> That never a swimmer shall cross or climb;

nevertheless, the poet will go back to "the great sweet mother" whose "sweet hard kisses are strong like wine" and whose "large embraces are keen like pain." He is

> A pulse of the life of [her] straits and bays,
> A vein in the heart of the streams of the sea.[27]

His discovery of the identity of the sea—"from the first thou wert; in the end thou art"—leads to the discovery of his own identical nature—"As I have been, I know I shall surely be."

Swinburne's sea is not that on which John Wordsworth had

[26] In the first few paragraphs of his *Swinburne* (Boston, 1929) Professor Samuel C. Chew presents *Thalassius* as an autobiographical picture of the poet himself.

[27] Swinburne's poems are quoted from the edition in six volumes, fifth impression (London, 1912).

been shipwrecked, nor that of Hopkins' *Wreck of the Deutsch-land*. It is a mightier inner sea, with an undertow even more dismaying for the humankind it has invaded, as Arnold realized when he confronted it on the "naked shingles of the world." Sharing its nature, man, too, is in flux. There is the merest hint of stability in the Swinburne *Hymn to Proserpine*—

Fate is a sea without shore, and the soul is a rock that abides;
But her ears are vexed with the roar and her face with the foam
    of the tides.

The imagination of the poet does not abide with the rock; rather it follows the "foam of the present," sweeping far out "to the surf of the past" "beyond the extreme sea-wall" where "waste water washes, and tall ships founder, and deep death wails." Whereas Arnold, son of a schoolmaster, had been content to stay his steps on Dover Beach, Swinburne, son of an admiral, weighed anchor and set sail. Riding the literary billows he would develop those mounting anapestic rhythms that none has mastered so well as he: "the words of the spell of the sea / Mine."

A lyrist in command of all the measures, burdens, and refrains of song, Swinburne had made his first notable, if shocking, effect with the poetry of feeling. Faustine must hear her name again and again, punctuating his grim vignettes of unholiness. The burden of fair women as the "end of every man's desire" repeats this phrase for its expressions of grief and shame and fear and regret. "O mystic and sombre Dolores" becomes with gruesome lyrical insistence, *Our Lady of Pain*. Might this lyrist ever become an elegist?

In his confessional poem, *On the Downs*, he tells us:

> By footless ways and sterile event
> My thought unsatisfied, and bent
>   With blank unspeculative eyes
> On the untracked sands of discontent
>   Where, watched of helpless skies,
>   Life hopeless lies.

When his soul asked the old elegiac questions—

> Then "Where is God? and where is aid?
> Or what good end of these?" she said;
> "Is there no God or end at all,
> Nor reason with unreason weighed,
> Nor force to disenthrall
> Weak feet that fall?"—

the answer that he heard from the evolutionary doctrine of his own day, and in a 4–4–4–4–3–2 diminuendo echoing the elegiac cadence, was the merest beginning of patient thought:

> A multitudinous monotone
> Of dust and flower and seed and stone,
> In the deep sea-rock's mid-sea sloth,
> In the live water's trembling zone,
> In all men love and loathe,
> One God at growth.

Moreover, although Swinburne's power of recognition was swift and his insight keen, at first he had little taste for speculation, was content to labor riddling themes in quibbling phrases. Witness *Hertha:* "Find thou but thyself," says Hertha to the poet; "Thou art I." And the final revelation of such doctrinal exercise is another quibble: "Man, equal and one with me, man that is made of me, man that is I." For Hertha, the "mother," Swinburne by-passes God as Shelley had by-passed Jupiter for Asia. *Hertha* is, however, a *Song before Sunrise;* the poet was himself "at growth" into a more vertebrate stage. The "multitudinous monotone" would become complex music of a higher order.

For Thalassius was also "seed of Apollo," who had given his son "visions truer than truth." And had Tiresias not prophesied of "sun-light, who [was] blind"? Was Shakespeare not "sun-like"? Walt Whitman was bidden to "send but a song oversea" "out of the sun beyond sunset"; Giuseppe Mazzini was "the sunlike man"; and, unless it were Walter Savage Landor,

> none of all that search the heavens, and try
> The sun, may match the sovereign eagle's eye—

so he wrote of Browning, poet of "the strong and sunlight sense." Landor himself was "strong like the sun, and like the sunlight kind." Thanks in some part to Landor, to Victor Hugo, and to Mazzini, Swinburne came back to metaphorical land from the surging waters of his prepossession, was anchored for a time on the shore of the eternal city, and shared its concern for human liberty, a struggle in which he joined all the greatest of his predecessors. As Shelley had found his footing in Hellas, Swinburne reached a haven in Athens. His *Athens, an Ode,* celebrating in trochaic rhythm "Children all we sea-fold of the Salaminian seamen," ends with a reference to "the sun that crowns the sea."

> Through the fights of old, your battle-cry was healing,
>   And the Saviour that ye called on was the Sun:
> Dawn by dawn behold in heaven your God, revealing
>   Light from darkness as when Marathon was won.

"Watchman, what of the night?" he had asked in a challenging appeal to his fellows: Prophet, Mourners, Dead Men, Statesman, Warrior, Exile, Captive, Christian, High Priest, Princes, Martyrs, England, France, Italy, Germany, Europe, Liberty! He was widening the circle of his sympathy for various classes of men; and although his deification of humanity in the *Hymn to Man* was not a profound discovery, he considered the poem "the birthsong of spiritual renascence," as the *Hymn to Proserpine* had been "the deathsong of spiritual decadence." With another resonant refrain—"Couldst thou not watch with me?"— he announced his Apollonian origin and destiny (*A Wasted Vigil*):

> Lo, far in heaven the web of night undone,
> And on the sudden sea the gradual sun;
> Wave to wave answers, tree responds to tree;
>   Couldst thou not watch with me?

Sunbeam by sunbeam creeps from line to line,
Foam by foam quickens on the brightening brine;
Sail by sail passes, flower by flower gets free;
    Couldst thou not watch with me?

The problems of cosmic order and universal relationship had
been posed in *Genesis*, where he came to recognize

The immortal war of mortal things, that is
Labour and life and growth and good and ill,
The mild antiphonies that melt and kiss,
The violent symphonies that meet and kill.

Tentatively, at least for purposes of argument, he was consider-
ing God "the shade cast by the soul of man." Not until Chthonia,
daughter of Erechtheus, would give her "poor girl's blood to
build again [her] city" did the idea of redemption open vistas
upon a gentler kind of divinity in a firmer and more hopeful
world.

Erechtheus, 1876, is surely one of the noblest poems of the
century. Briefly stated, its action is the "strife / 'Twixt God and
God," Poseidon and Athena, for the citadel of Man's mind.
Poseidon,

the lord
Whose wheels make lightnings of the foam-flowered sea
    Here on this rock, whose height brow-bound with dawn
    Is head and heart of Athens,

is in competition with Athena. Once, twice, and

Now this third time his wind of wrath has blown
Right on this people a mightier wave of war.

The herald of Eumolpus, son of Poseidon, challenges Erectheus,
"one . . . in the sun's sight born," to "join hands in battle grip
for death / With them whose seed and strength is of the sea."
Thus "land-wind and sea-wind . . . gird them to battle." This
attack upon "the south sea-line" is repulsed, and the battle is
won for the sons of Athens not only by the sacrifice of the

maiden Chthonia, whose "heart as a citadel strong . . . guards the heart of the city" so that, "unbreached of warring waters, Athens like a searock stands," but also by her father, Erechtheus, "steersman" of the Ship of State, "fallen with tiller in hand" and now for ever to be seen at the "ship's helm." Seamanship thus justified, there is reconciliation:

> And the sons of [the] earth shall have help of the
> Waves that made war on their morning,
> And friendship and fame of the sea.

Finally, in her supreme speech Praxithea, the mother of the sacrificed maiden, recognizes Athena as the crown of "the whole world's crowning city"; praise of her shall fulfil Athens for ever

> As the sun's eye fulfils and crowns with sight
> The circling crown of heaven. There is no grief
> Great as the joy to be made one in will
> With him that is the heart and rule of life
> And thee, God born of God.

This is the *anagnorisis* of Swinburne's tragic myth: the thoroughly Greek discovery of the divine nature of wisdom to control the divine energy of passion.

He called *Erectheus* a tragedy; but, in spite of its Aeschylean models,[28] it is not tragedy in the Greek sense, lacking as it does the involvement of erring agents in a self-initiated action: all three of its main persons are flawless, and its foreordained peripety does not necessarily follow the course of precedent events. Most germane to our argument here is the symbol of light that makes possible the *anagnorisis*. The blind sea to which earlier the poet had thoughtlessly and arrogantly surrendered himself has now been studied, mastered in terms of itself, and is "in fierce recoil" under the eyes of those two luminaries, Athena

[28] See Marion Clyde Wier, *The Influence of Aeschylus and Euripides on the Structure and Content of Swinburne's "Atalanta in Calydon" and "Erechtheus"* (Ann Arbor, 1920).

and Phoebus Apollo. In the address to the sun in the first Chorus, in the revelatory moment when Chthonia lifts up her eyes

> from the skirts of the shadow,
> From the border of death to the limits of light,

and in the final invocation to the "fair God of the morning," the poem is more than a marine symbol; it is also a solar myth, an elegiac action not unworthy of Wordsworth and Keats. The son of Cymothoe and Apollo is not now merely singing the tides of wayward passion; he is meditating upon them, symbolically using their varied patterns as tools in his speculation upon the vast correspondences and multitudinous relationships between luminous power, fluent power, and stable power, between sun and sea and earthly citadel, between Phoebus Apollo and Poseidon and Athena. By wise seamanship shipwreck may be avoided.[29]

Our chapter that began in shipwreck and continued through perilous metaphorical travels by sailing vessel, "bark of dead man's bones," "driftwood spars," shallop and pinnace, or "great ship [with] shining sides," bearing the beloved friend

> toward a crimson cloud
> That landlike slept along the deep,

may now pause with some assurance of a successful voyage. Whether it be Peele Castle in storm, the rock of the Shelleyan Prometheus, the "towering sycamore" of Tennyson or the "signal-elm" of Arnold, the "tall nun," "Tarpeian-fast," of Hopkins' *Deutschland,* or the "rock" of Athens so reverently crowned by Swinburne, something steadfast down the decades has permitted the elegist his many discoveries of identity in a world of growth and flux under the rule of sun and moon and stars.

[29] This will be Shaw's thesis in *Heartbreak House,* 1914.

CHAPTER X

The Elegiac Century:
Its Rhythms

IN September, 1819, Wordsworth looked upon departing summer in an elegiac mood, and, using the expanded ballad measure,
tailed rhyme, rejoiced in the deathless powers of verse, for

> they like Demi-gods are strong
> On whom the Muses smile

Recalling "the spirit-stirring note" of Alcaeus and Sappho's
"touch of passion," he longed also for

> One precious, tender-hearted, scroll
> Of pure Simonides.[1]

[1] *Upon the Same Occasion* ("Departing summer hath assumed," *P.W.*,
IV, 99–101). Wordsworth may have been thinking of the scroll in which
Simonides quoted Homer: Οἵη περ φύλλων γενεή, τοιήδε καὶ ἀνδρῶν, "Even
such as the leaves on the tree are the generations of men" (*Lyra Graeca*,
II, 338), for he is aware that his own "leaf is sere / And yellow on the
bough." The Simonidean elegy (Fr. 97) should be read entire for the
better enjoyment of Wordsworth's poem, the fourth stanza of which
reflects Simonides' ἄνθος . . . πολυήρατον ἥβης, much loved flower of
youth, in contrast to the inescapable illness of age:

> Yet will I temperately rejoice;
> Wide is the range, and free the choice
> Of undiscordant themes;
> Which, haply, kindred souls may prize

With the "lyre" of Alcaeus and the "lute" of Sappho the elegy
should have specified the flute of Simonides, on whose "scrolls"
along with hymns, paeans, prayers, dithyrambs, eulogies, dirges,
and victory-songs would have appeared also elegiacs.

From Coleridge and Wordsworth—and Walter Savage Landor, that confirmed Greek and Latin scholar—to A. E. Housman, the enthusiasm of educated Englishmen for the formal
beauty of classical rhythms and meters was more than a reflection of the subjective or "romantic" hellenism [2] of the eighteenth
century. The influence of Winckelmann, Lessing, and Goethe
in Germany and in England Fuseli and Sir William Jones had
been and would continue to be tempered or rectified by the
persistent editing of texts and a shrewd study of originals. R. F.
P. Brunck's *Analects of the Old Greek Poets* was known to
Coleridge and Wrangham as early as 1794, and in 1797 Coleridge reviewed Bishop Horsley's tract on prosody.[3] Wordsworth's reading of neoclassical English authors, detailed elsewhere,[4] would be supplemented in the second decade of the
nineteenth century by his firsthand review of classical writers.
Little by little classical scholarship became the mainstay of
poets and aesthetes in their competition with theologians, soci-
ologists, and scientists for the eyes, ears, and minds of modern
man; and as a result there was an increasingly better understanding of form as function and a marked improvement in literary
taste.

When John Keats thumbed the classical dictionary, he was
qualifying rather as an able student than as a learned scholar;
he would observe myths, legends, and antiquities and invest
these with his own bounty, not least with suggestions of kinaesthetic form and tonal quality. Daring "to stammer where old

----

Not less than vernal ecstasies,
And passion's feverish dreams.

[2] Harry Levin, *The Broken Column: A Study in Romantic Hellenism*
(Cambridge, Massachusetts, 1931); Bernard Herbert Stern, *The Rise of
Romantic Hellenism in English Literature 1732–1786* (Menasha, Wiscon-
sin, 1940).

[3] See Ch. I, n. 21.   [4] E.g., in Potts, *Wordsworth's Prelude.*

Chaucer used to sing," he conceived "a shrilly mellow sound / With ebon-tipped flutes" to introduce Endymion. In that "very pretty piece of paganism" recited to Wordsworth in December 1817, *The Hymn to Pan*, he represented the god hearkening "the dreary melody of bedded reeds" and considered him an elegist indeed,

> the unimaginable lodge
> For solitary thinkings; such as dodge
> Conception to the very bourne of heaven,
> Then leave the naked brain.

And when in the Third Book of *Hyperion* Keats paid fealty to Apollo, "the Father of all verse," and begged the Muse to "touch the Delphic Harp," he insisted that

> not a wind of heaven but will breathe
> In aid soft warble from the Dorian flute.[5]

Shelley, reading Greek epic, drama, and lyric as an expert, was better provided to capture for his own rhythms the audible cadences of classical poetry. As a youth he composed two elegiac distichs and put the Epitaph of Gray's *Elegy* into Latin verse. His translations from the Greek of Bion and Moschus, published posthumously except for one in sonnet form with *Alastor* in 1816, are experiments with the pentametrical line and move laboriously. Four epigrams, two from the Greek of Plato, are somewhat more skillful.[6] But Shelley's early predilection for elaborate stanzaic patterns, his habitual unwillingness to shorten the alternate lines of his quatrains, and his recourse to stanzas of five-beat lines diminished the probability of flutelike rhythms in his verse. *The Cloud*, mostly in tetrameter and trimeter, is delicately but thoughtlessly anapestic as befits its theme; but in *The Pine Forest of the Cascine near Pisa* the poet seems almost to stumble upon the common measure with some advantage in

[5] *The Poetical Works of John Keats*, ed. H. W. Garrod (2d ed.; Oxford University Press, 1958).

[6] *The Poetical Works of Percy Bysshe Shelley*, ed. Thomas Hutchinson (Oxford University Press, 1908), pp. 830, 712–715.

speeding up the discovery of the poem at its end. What might
have been accomplished with a swifter rhythm, however, can
be seen in an address to Emilia Viviani, "I fear thy kisses, gentle
maiden" (1820), and the trochaic song, "Rarely, rarely comest
thou / Spirit of Delight" (1821). Indeed, when Shelley's verse
is not lyric or idyllic, it is more often a gorgeously ornamented
rhetoric than a spirited elegy: it advances in a leisurely way
from presumptions, positive or negative; not often does it urge
its speculations toward a new vision.

Lord Byron,[7] so we are told, was a flutist; but in his translations from the classics he chose to celebrate the lyre rather than
the flute: "my quivering lyre," "my wayward lyre";

> Love, love alone, my lyre shall claim
> In songs of bliss and sighs of flame

It is "the braying trumpet and the hoarser drum" that ring
through the decasyllabic quatrains of the elegy on Newstead
Abbey; "hush'd is the harp, unstrung the warlike lyre" until
in gentler time "the horns proclaim a mellow note"; but there is
no flute. Nor does the flute inspire the Hebrew Melodies; nor
are there any indications in *English Bards and Scotch Reviewers*
that the bardic instrument is other than a lyre; in *Hints from
Horace* "lute"—not "flute"—rhymes with "fruit." In *The Adieu*
it is the Aeolian lyre from which come the "dying strains," and
in *The Farewell to the Muse* the apprehensive young poet says
goodby to the "themes of [his] rude flowing lyre." There is,
however, a stirring anecdote in common measure written during
a thunderstorm under the Pindus mountains (1809), and the
couplets of the familiar *Maid of Athens* (1810) with their trochaic lilt, their refrain, and their hortatory temper could have
been sung to the flute; also the war song, Δεῦτε παῖδες τῶν
Ἑλλήνων, is fittingly translated:

> Sparta, Sparta, why in slumbers
> Lethargic dost thou lie?

[7] *The Poetical Works of Lord Byron* (Oxford University Press, 1909).

So might have spoken Tyrtaeus. But in Byron's early poems the rhythms are for the most part pedestrian, and we look in vain for that drive of the inquiring mind and that reach of the soul toward revelatory experience that distinguish the elegist singing to his flute. Moreover, Byron was to go on from romance into satire, which feeds on romantic preconceptions, not into elegy, which hungers for what is real and true.

During the twenties, thirties, and forties essays, tracts, and imaginary conversations offered a prosaic escape for the less profound meditations of a large group of thoughtful writers: those were the years of Lamb's *Elia*, of Coleridge and his *Table Talk* and *Aids to Reflection*, of Hazlitt and De Quincey, and of Carlyle and Newman. All were dedicated to truth and skillful in the arts of speculation and discovery; but not before Tennyson and Arnold at mid-century would anyone restore the vigorous pulse to vertebrate thinking—none except possibly the older Wordsworth, many of whose late poems profit by the use of the ballad stanza so effective for Lucy and Matthew. Too frequently disregarded by critics of our day, several of these ballad-like elegies rang authoritatively in the ears of a generation that sang its hymns in common measure and craved a simple comfort for never-lessening woes. Wordsworth is rarely banal, and his sparest lines reveal the temperance and wisdom lacking in much of the so-called religious or antireligious verse with which the century was flooded.[8]

Let us briefly refer to two of these late poems in a search for elegiac rhythms. In *The Primrose of the Rock*, 1831, he invested with a web of delicate imagery one bold naturalist prepossession of his day, the great chain of being:

> What hideous warfare hath been waged,
>   What kingdoms overthrown,
> Since first I spied that primrose-tuft

[8] See Hoxie Neale Fairchild, *Religious Trends in English Literature*, IV (Columbia University Press, 1957); Alfred Henry Miles, *The Poets and Poetry of the Nineteenth Century*, X (London, [1892–1897]).

And marked it for my own;
A lasting link in Nature's chain
From highest heaven let down!

The flowers, still faithful to the stems,
    Their fellowship renew;
The stems are faithful to the root,
    That worketh out of view;
And to the rock the root adheres
    In every fibre true.

Close clings to earth the living rock,
    Though threatening still to fall;
The earth is constant to her sphere;
    And God upholds them all:
So blooms this lonely Plant, nor dreads
    Her annual funeral.

In the familiar measures of balladry, minstrelsy, and hymnody
again and again he tried to make important truths clear to the
simple-minded and humble-hearted. He knew what his harassed
century needed to hear and he tempered language and rhythms
to the shorn lambs he was addressing. He may have been an
elegist turned preacher, but no theological controversy, theo-
sophical vacillation, scientific discovery, or aesthetic sophistication can impugn words like the following (1833):

If this great world of joy and pain
    Revolve in one sure track;
If freedom, set, will rise again,
    And virtue, flown, come back;
Woe to the purblind crew who fill
    The heart with each day's care;
Nor gain, from past or future, skill
    To bear and to forbear!

Walter Savage Landor (1775–1864) was a contemporary of
the minstrel Scott (1771–1832) and the ballad-writers Words-

worth (1770–1850), Coleridge (1772–1834), Southey (1774–1843), Thomas Campbell (1777–1844), and Tom Moore (1779–1852); but he survived them all well-nigh into the lifetime of William Butler Yeats (1865–1939). Thus his career as a classical scholar and English metrist was central to the fortunes of flute song in the nineteenth century; none of the poets who knew and admired him was better able than he to maintain appropriate rhythms for elegiac writing. One of his first book purchases had been a "tiny edition of Catullus, Tibullus, and Propertius, which as an old man he presented to Pen Browning"; [9] and he is reputed to have praised most highly among the ancients Lucretius, Catullus, and Tibullus.[10] Of the various meters in the Poems on Books and Writers, there is *rime couée* for Catullus, and he is translated into octosyllabic couplets; and in one instance the distichs of Tibullus approximate English elegiacs—

> May I gaze upon thee when my latest hour is come!
> May I hold thy hand when mine faileth me.[11]

In 1806 the *Simonidea* of twenty-five English poems was named for its elegies, this being "a species of composition in which Simonides excelled."

Although Landor fancied he

> had strength to climb
> A loftier station at no distant time
> And might securely from intrusion doze
> Upon the flowers thro' which Ilissus flows,

[9] R. H. Super, *Walter Savage Landor: A Biography* (New York University Press, 1954), pp. 7, 512. The volume of elegies was Item 558 in the auction catalogue of Sotheby, Wilkinson, and Hodge, *The Browning Collections*.

[10] *Ibid.*, p. 26. Tibullus was the favorite of Tom Moore, too.

[11] By 1808 Landor had written thirty-four verses of Latin elegiacs, which he then translated into long meter (Super, *op. cit.*, p. 81); yet the pattern of a four-four beat seems not to give his rhythm quite the impetus *pour mieux sauter* of elegiac verse and thus diminishes its drive forward or inward.

he was in fact not less metrically simple than his predecessors
who had

> loiter'd in green lanes
> Content to catch the ballads of the plains.

As an expert in classical elegiacs he well knew where to find
the most appealing equivalent of the rise and fall of elegiac
verse, its authentic cadence. He is the author of *Rose Aylmer*
and many another memorial in common measure. The revised
stanzas for Rose have the quality of flute song at its best, challenging comparison with those for her contemporary, Lucy:

> Ah what avails the sceptred race,
>   Ah what the form divine!
> What, every virtue, every grace!
>   Rose Aylmer, all were thine.
>
> .   .   .   .   .
>
> Rose Aylmer, whom these wakeful eyes
>   May weep, but never see,
> A night of memories and of sighs
>   I consecrate to thee.[12]

Landor's references to flute and pipe attest above all his love
for the elegiac strain in ancient and modern letters. For instance,
when Apollo saw the lovers Enallos and Cymodameia "in the
calm depth" of the sea, they were surrounded by an orchestra
of nymphs whose instruments could be nicely distinguished
(*Hellenics* I):

> One blew aloud
> The spiral shell; one drew bright chords across
> Shell more expansive; tenderly a third

[12] Published originally in *Simonidea* for 1806 but, since Rose died in
1800, likely written soon after Wordsworth mourned Lucy. The last
two lines originally read: "A night of sorrows and of sighs / I conse-
crate to thee." The verses of Landor are quoted from *The Complete
Works of Walter Savage Landor*, Vols. XIII–XVI, ed. Stephen Wheeler
(London, 1933–1936); quoted by permission of Associated Book Publishers Ltd.

With cowering [? covering] lip hung o'er the flute and stopt
At will its dulcet sob, or waked to joy;
A fourth took up the lyre and pincht the strings,
Invisible by trembling; many raised
Clear voices.

When Landor wrote to Southey "we have had too much of the lute and of the lyre. We forget that there are louder, graver, more impressive tones," [13] he was praising *Gebama* but he was also pointing ahead to his own long preoccupation with heroic poetry. And he was reminding himself of the possibilities of flute or reed as well as of trumpet and clarion; for, with some help from Keats, Shelley, and especially Elizabeth Barrett Browning, it was Landor who resuscitated for his own time the Great God Pan.[14] Pan had been bereaved of his beloved Pitys, slain by the jealous Boreas with a rock (*Pan and Pitys* in *Hellenics* II, 26–27, 163 ff.):

> Ever since, beneath
> That rock sits Pan: her name he calls; he waits
> Listening, to hear the rock repeat it; wipes
> The frequent tear from his hoarse reed, and wears
> Henceforth the pine, her pine, upon his brow.

In *Pan Speaks to Walter Savage Landor* (12–15) this service of the elegist is acknowledged by the god himself:

[13] Super, *op. cit.*, p. 81.

[14] While this chapter was in process, W. R. Irwin's "The Survival of Pan" appeared in *PMLA*, LXXVI (June, 1961), 159–167. His excellent article is easily accessible and furnishes evidence from a wide circle of writers for the validity of the myth in modern times: Pan "dead, ever-living, or revived." From the evidence Professor Irwin represents Pan as a power-god with a terrestrial vigor, a resistless will, and sometimes a kind heart; and he sets forth the character of this mythic figure in literature since 1890, especially in the works of D. H. Lawrence and E. M. Forster. After this chapter and my chapter on Lawrence were written, Professor Carl Woodring called my attention to a recent Harvard dissertation on the myth of Pan in Western literature by Patricia Merivale.

> Though others had loud lyres and struck them well,
> Few could bring any harmony from reeds
> By me held high, and higher since thou hast breath'd
> Thy gentle breath o'er Pitys and her Pan.

Because flute and the pastoral pipe both derive from Pan's reed, their part in poetry was further identified and enhanced when Landor wrote as *A Friend to Theocritus in Egypt* (24 ff.):

> Take thou, meanwhile, these two papyrus-leaves,
> Recording, one the loves and one the woes
> Of Pan and Pitys, heretofore unsung.
> Aside our rivers and within our groves
> The pastoral pipe hath dropt its mellow lay,
> And shepherds in their contests only try
> Who best can puzzle.
>   Come, Theocritus,
> Come let us lend a shoulder to the wheel
> And help to lift it from this depth of sand.

Landor could not know how very puzzling and sandy poetry might become after him. Although like Theocritus he appears in the speculations of his age somewhat less of an elegist than an idyllist, and although his own impatience and illogic—was he not already right?—marred his personal and literary career, he expressed admiration for the temperance of the Greeks:

> Their muses were sedate,
> Never obstreperous: you heard no breath
> Outside the flute; each sound rang clear.

In a letter to Browning November 10, 1845, this somewhat obstreperous poet wrote: "In prose I found more room [than in verse]." [15] Surely in his *Imaginary Conversations* and his *Heroica Idyllia* he *took* more room; he must study situations to understand and record them or to applaud or rebuke the men and women conversing or debating; he must actualize these in their several situations by reaching backwards to their motives and antecedents. Not often did he drive his *personae* forward by

---

[15] Super, *op. cit.*, p. 355.

way of choice and ordeal to a discovery or a peripety. Being a
patriot, however, he wrote laments and addresses in great number; being a critic, he displayed uncanny awareness of the poetic
assets and liabilities of his predecessors and contemporaries; but
he was too self-involved a poet to construct plots for the theatre [16] or to examine the mysteries of the study.

Notwithstanding his unreflective nature, throughout his valuable contribution to letters he was faithful to Greece and Rome
and could appreciate the purposes and skill of the classical elegists from Tyrtaeus to Callimachus,[17] from Catullus to Tibullus
and Ovid. On the eve of his final trip to Italy in 1858 to avoid
trial in a libel suit, he discussed with Dickens the character of
Catullus, Tibullus, and other Latin poets.[18] And, whether or not
we agree with his judgments, he thought he had a touchstone
for what is classical. Why should he not?

> Goldsmith was classical, and Gray almost.
> Cowper had more variety, more strength,
> Gentlest of bards! still pitied, still beloved.
>
> . . . . .
>
> Wordsworth, in sonnet, is a classick too,
>
> . . . . .
>
> Classic in every feature was my friend
> The genial Southey.

What was it in the poetry of Robert Southey, only a year
his senior, that made Landor call him "classic in every feature"?
Possibly the ability to conduct an action. The precision of the
fable in his ballads, the clarity into which well-known legends
were brought by means simpler and yet more artful than at first

[16] Yet Browning dedicated the final number of *Bells and Pomegranates*
"to a Great *Dramatic Poet* . . . Walter Savage Landor," as Super notes
(p. 357).

[17] In his *Song for the Centenary of Walter Savage Landor*, stanza 15,
Swinburne represents Simonides himself as hailing Landor "his one
brother mateless else of peers." And in a letter to Forster, *c.* January
5, 1847, Landor allies himself with "the great and glorious Callimachus"
(Super, *op. cit.*, pp. 377, 585).

[18] Super, *op. cit.*, p. 456.

appears, might be considered "classic." The unobtrusiveness of
the author, who is content to let his poems speak for him, is
another "feature," as is the refusal of dim views and spurious
feeling. The Advertisement for Ballads and Metrical Tales II,[19]
announces that they were "written with . . . facility and glee,"
a probable reason for their vogue. Southey's was not a speculative mind; his ballads are not elegiac. He did, however, preserve
in the affections of those who recited *The Battle of Blenheim*
(1798) and *King Henry V and the Hermit of Dreux* (1798) the
rhythms of the common measure; and the *Annual Anthology*,
1799–1800, to which he contributed largely, maintained the
melancholic tinge of poems elegiac in the more restricted sense.
Like Landor he was to go on into heroic poetry.

But popular rather than heroic meters impressed upon the
century the rhythm nearest in English to flute song in Greek
and Latin. With true Irish plangency Tom Moore wrote his
elegiac songs in ballad form: to the tune of Gramachree,

> The harp that once through Tara's halls
> The soul of music shed,
> Now hangs as mute on Tara's walls,
> As if that soul were fled;

or, with equal regret, in *The Ruined Isle*,

> Weep on, weep on, your hour is past
> Your days of pride are o'er;
> The fatal chain is round you cast,
> And ye are men no more;

or, most memorable of plaints, this one in anapests:

> Believe me, if all those endearing young charms,
> Which I gaze on so fondly to-day,
> Were to change by to-morrow, and fleet in my arms,
> Like fairy-gifts fading away.[20]

[19] *Poems of Robert Southey* . . . , ed. Maurice H. Fitzgerald (Oxford University Press, 1909).
[20] *The Poetical Works of Thomas Moore, Collected by Himself* (10
vols.; London, 1840–1841).

Moore was a classical scholar, had translated the Odes of
Anacreon in 1800 and later adapted passages from Propertius
and Catullus. He thought (Preface to Little's poems) that "Ovid
made love like a rake, and Propertius like a schoolmaster"; he
preferred Tibullus for his "genuine feeling." That is to say,
his tendencies were more lyrical than elegiac. In his "elegiac
stanzas" he used the octosyllabic quatrain and seems concerned
rather for his music than his theme; but he well knew what
fitted the ear and pulse of his contemporaries. Generally, his
stanzas and songs of love to Julia are to be sung in long or
common measure; and his National Airs—

> Oft in the stilly night
> Ere slumber's chain has bound me,
> Fond memory brings the light
> Of other days around me—

and his Sacred Songs, not very profound either of them, in-
gratiated themselves with contemporary readers.

Another lyrist, Thomas Campbell,[21] translated Tyrtaeus, but
into heroic couplets. For his tales in verse—*Lord Ullin's Daughter*, *Gilderoy*, and *The Ritter Bann*, for instance—he found
ballad meters appropriate. There is a meditative quality in
Hohenlinden, although the lines *To the Rainbow* disclaim
thought:

> Triumphal arch, that fill'st the sky
> When storms prepare to part,
> I ask not proud Philosophy
> To teach me what thou art.
>
> . . . . .
>
> When Science from Creation's face
> Enchantment's veil withdraws,
> What lovely visions yield their place
> To cold material laws!

[21] *Complete Poetical Works of Thomas Campbell*, ed. J. L. Robert-
son (Oxford University Press, 1907).

> And yet, fair bow, no fabling dreams,
>   But words of the Most High,
> Have told why first thy robe of dreams
>   Was woven in the sky.

His verses *To the United States of America* are in the spirit of
Tyrtaeus and they still sting:

> United States, your banner wears
>   Two emblems—one of fame;
> Alas, the other that it bears
>   Reminds us of your shame.
>
> Your standard's constellation types
>   White freedom by its stars;
> But what's the meaning of the stripes?
>   They mean your negroes' scars.

Of the elegists of the century Elizabeth Barrett Browning
was one of the truest to type; no poet would better profit by a
generic study. One of the four or five distinguished classical
scholars who wrote verse, even more than Landor and Swinburne and fully as much as Arnold and Clough she maintained
the elegiac tone of Victorian poetry. Writing elegies in the
narrow sense of the term and in the classical sense, too, she
associated her poems with a wide range of elegiac themes. She
understood the possibilities of flute song, and none has more
deftly employed the common measure and kindred rhythms
toward speculative discovery.[22] Like Wordsworth she knew
the costly workings of principle and the dangers of myopic
vision. Whereas Landor's assumptions took shape in the ethos
of contentious, sometimes disagreeable *personae*, and Swinburne's ingenuous thought was suffused with irritated or rebellious feeling, like Arnold Mrs. Browning remained com-

[22] In her *Book of the Poets* Mrs. Browning calls the ballad "a form
epitomical of the epic and dramatic and often vocal when no other
music is astir."

passionate, even when curious and skeptical; and she was always temperately artful—in this like Arthur Hugh Clough, whose precision of phrase she often approximates. Her discoveries or revelations are not arbitrary as with Landor or capricious as with Swinburne; they are justly earned out of the nature of her imaginings. Finally, whenever we are tempted to think of her religious language as too explicit or rhetorical,[23] we should remember that she came to Christianity by way of the Greek Fathers and the Greek Christian poets;[24] her terms were not thoughtlessly borrowed or tritely used but fraught with rich cultural associations.

Her elegy for Byron was written, appropriately, in the metrical and stanzaic form of *Childe Harold's Pilgrimage;* but in *Stanzas* about him she reverted past the Spenserian pattern to balladry: in the words of the old Roumeliot,

> His arm was in the foremost rank,
> Where embattled thousands roll—
> His name was in the lore of Greece,
> And his spell was on her soul.

In her early verses she had not, of course, probed very deep, not even in *The Poet's Vow,*[25] *The Exile's Return,* and *Cowper's Grave.* What is noteworthy, however, is her choice of

[23] In the Preface to her Poems published in 1844 she answered criticism of her introduction of "the divine Saviour" in *Drama of Exile* and the frequent recurrence of "a Great Name." After appealing to Milton's practice, she wrote: "As if life were not a continual sacrament to man, since Christ broke the daily bread of it in His hands! . . . As if the word God were not, everywhere in His creation, and at every moment in His Eternity, an appropriate word!" (*The Poetical Works of Elizabeth Barrett Browning,* ed. Frederick G. Kenyon, New York, 1903).

[24] In translating some of Gregory Nazianzen's 30,000 elegiac verses Mrs. Browning observes the contenting effect on the ear of "the sequence of pentameter to hexameter."

[25] The sinful poet, forswearing "man's sympathies," was to be unhappily realized again and again before the century closed. E.B.B.'s *Vision of Poets* is also dismayingly prophetic.

eights-and-sixes as the right vehicle for the advance and recoil
of speculation; and in *Wine of Cyprus* trochaic eights-and-
sevens are skillfully adapted to a classical theme:

> And I think of those long mornings
>   Which my thought goes far to seek,
> When, betwixt the folio's turnings,
>   Solemn flowed the rhythmic Greek—

the Greek of Aeschylus, Sophocles, Euripides, Pindar, Theocritus, Bion, Plato, and the "noble Christian bishops." Thanks to
Hugh Boyd, Elizabeth's knowledge of the classics was more
than a series of lessons.

Meanwhile, she is sure that reeds still grow by the river to
be turned into musical instruments by lesser deities with goat-
like hoofs and horns who drop their mouths to a hole in the reed
and blow:

> What was he doing, the great god Pan
>   Down in the reeds by the river?
> Spreading ruin and scattering ban,
> Splashing and paddling with hoofs of a goat,
> And breaking the golden lilies afloat
>   With dragon-fly on the river.

> Sweet, sweet, sweet, O Pan!
>   Piercing sweet by the river!
>   Blinding sweet, O great god Pan!
> The sun on the hill forgot to die,
> And the lilies revived, and the dragon-fly
>   Came back to dream on the river.

> Yet half a beast is the great god Pan,
>   To laugh as he sits by the river,
> Making a poet out of a man:
> The true gods sigh for the cost and pain,—
> For the reed which grows nevermore again
>   As a reed with the reeds in the river.

The reeds of Pan can be heard in many another later and as delicately modulated elegy of this accomplished metrist, who played death, love, and transience all as flute song:

> I am no trumpet, but a reed—
> A broken reed, the wind indeed
>   Left flat upon a dismal shore;
> Yet if a little maid or child
> Should sigh within it, earnest-mild,
>   This reed will answer evermore.

No one was more highly qualified to analogize the flute in music and the elegiac tone in poetry than E. B. B.'s fellow poet, Robert Browning: [26] witness his *Flute-Music, with an Accompaniment*. This dialogue between the man ("He") and the woman ("She") reminds us of passages between Propertius and his Cynthia. The man is an aesthete seeking the perfect moment, disdaining as pedantry the "mere repetition," "practise-pother," of the tireless technician. When at the song of "birdlike fluting," "bullfinch-bubblings," "He" exclaims

> Fine-pearled notes that surely
>   Gather, dewdrop-fashion
> Deep-down in some heart which purely
>   Secretes globuled passion—
> Passion insuppressive—

"She," astute and critical, finds "stale thrush-songs tiresome":

> Songs, Spring thought perfection,
>   Summer criticises:
> What in May escaped detection,
>   August, past surprises,
> Notes and names each blunder.

When "He" praises the flutist who pipes for him "Gounod's / Bits of passionate imploring," "She" shivers at "tootings" that "vitiate / Romeo's serenading." Then, more shrewdly, "He"

[26] *The Complete Poetic and Dramatic Works of Robert Browning* (Boston, 1895), *passim*, especially pp. 999–1001, 916–918, 987.

asks whether in her view the love of a woman may not also be "so many juggles, / Tricks tried—oh, so often!" Whether, when noon has "expanded / Rathe pink to raw redness," even distance can brighten "stuff fast fading." This is a stock theme with the Latin elegists. No. "He" prefers rather to dream than to analyze, to

> conjecture,
> From one phrase trilled deftly,
> All the piece. So, end your lecture.

"All [Browning's] piece" is an elegy in the classical mode with nineteenth-century psychological accompaniment. Its rhythm not less than its theme modernizes the erotic flute song of Propertius, Tibullus, and Ovid. What had been Latin dactyls and spondees have become English trochees and spondees in a twelve-line stanza of three quatrains; each quatrain has the alternation of a twelve-syllabled unit with a fourteener: Poulter's measure. Behind the twelve-syllabled unit, however, we hear an echo of the elegiac pentameter (with feminine ending), and behind the fourteener we hear the ballad measure, both akin to flute song. Witness:

> Ah, the bird-like fluting
> Through the ash-tops yonder—
> Bull-finch bubblings, soft sounds suiting
> What sweet thoughts I wonder?

Browning's dramatic monologue *Ixion* is more elaborately discursive than elegiac, but it comes to us in an accentual measure the exact counterpart in English of the classical elegiac distich. No better instance could be found to show why our dactylic hexameter fails to accomplish the flutelike effect of ancient meditation in this mode. The weight of nineteenth-century skeptical thinking as Browning thought it is too heavy to be supported by any but a near-dramatic action in blank verse; we have, therefore, an adventure in dramatic prose marked off with an old elegiac measuring rod. When we read of Browning's Man "Tartaros-doomed to the wheel,"

Whirling forever in torment, flesh once mortal immortal
Made—for a purpose of hate—able to die and revive,

we turn with relief from such "tears, sweat, blood" back to
Wordsworth's Lucy, who in simple ballad measure "could not
feel / The touch of earthly years."

Although "the rush of the wheel ordained [Ixion's] place of
reposing," his "torment [was] bridged by a rainbow." This
lift of the imagination from dark and cyclic suffering to hopeful
light we have found to be characteristic of elegy. Long ago in
a memorable hexameter Xenophanes had said: "She whom they
call Iris, she too is a cloud, purple and red and yellow to
view." [27] Xenophanes was also, as Browning would be, concerned with debunking the Pantheon. His statement—"There's
one God greatest among Gods and men, who is like to mortals
neither in form nor mind" [28]—chimes with the "Purity all-
unobstructed" of *Ixion*. Characteristic of the skeptical poets of
his own time, Browning resembles the Greek elegists in pointing the way toward that form of discursive meditation that becomes dramatic action in one phase and ethical criticism in
another.

Ixion may be Browning's most exact replica of the classical
distich; it is not, of course, his only attempt at elegiac music.
The beat of the ballad measure, disguised somewhat with
trochees and anapests, can be detected in *Cristina* and in *The
Lost Mistress;* and the common measure with an octosyllabic
second line gives elegiac quality to *Memorabilia.* Of the Dramatic Romances, within *Incident of the French Camp* and *A
Light Woman* we hear the familiar rhythm; but *Christmas-Eve
and Easter-Day*, using octosyllabic couplets, misses the drive
which septenaries might have afforded. In *Men and Women* the
poet is well on his way toward dramatic blank verse. He had
reverted to simpler rhythms, however, in *Dramatis Personae*,
for instance: *Along the Beach, Gold Hair, Confessions.* And
finally, in the Prologue to *Asolando*, published on the day of
his death, he seems to elegize himself in the simplest of rhythms:

[27] *Elegy and Iambus*, I, 210–211.   [28] *Ibid.*, I, 207.

"The Poet's age is sad: for why?
  In youth, the natural world could show
No common object but his eye
  At once involved with alien glow—
  His own soul's iris-bow.

And now a flower is just a flower:
  Man, bird, beast are but beast, bird, man—
Simply themselves, uncinct [?untinct] by dower
  Of dyes which, when life's day began,
  Round each in glory ran."

At last in the discovery of identity—the greatest discovery of the century's literature, art, or science—Browning, too, with single vision, could see "the naked very thing."

In the best known elegy of the mid-century, Tennyson recalled that Hallam and he had studied Greek together—

And many an old philosophy
  On Argive heights divinely sang,
  And round us all the thicket rang
To many a flute of Arcady.

Indeed, his *Leonine Elegiacs* indicate that he knew well the classical pattern of flute song, only to deviate from it in quatrains reminding us of the stanzas of Gray—without Gray's extra foot of dissyllabic adjectives. Like the earlier *Elegy*, *In Memoriam* is slow-moving, regretful and possibly better fitted to dwell on feeling and conserve images than to advance speculation toward discovery. People and scenes had crowded into his first poems, needing to be described and revealed. The Lady of Shalott must linger to look at reflected pictures; *The Palace of Art* must be hung with pictures; *A Dream of Fair Women* would be revelatory but not meditative. *Edward Gray* and *Lady Clare* give us a distant echo of flute song as Coleridge and Wordsworth had sung it; but the common measure of *The Talking Oak* is monotonously iambic, and *Saint Agnes Eve* has too few spondees to recall the lilt of *The Ancient Mariner*, its rhythmic poise and its room to manoeuvre both thought and feeling. The lyrics of *The Princess* carry feeling rather than thought; but the swiftly advancing common measure of *The Brook* shows what Tennyson might have accomplished with the balladry of speculation if he had been an authentic elegist; and the skeptical argument of the young man in *The Ancient Sage*, when set against the blank verse of the Sage himself, shows that the author realized the propriety of eights-and-sixes for challenge and debate. The repute of *In Memoriam*, however, rests rather upon his considerable gifts as verbalist, lyrist, and idyllist. He seems not to have had the inner ear for flute song; rather, for the lute and lyre.

Humorous poems may—indeed, must—depend upon critical and speculative thought for their motive power; and the chastening discoveries to which they invite us are usually recognitions of identity. Such and such are ourselves. The humorist of the mid-century was Thomas Hood, according to Chesterton—who had not yet read Joyce—"the last great man who really employed the pun in a tradition that includes Homer and Shakespeare." [29] In the poems he wrote to tease and please his readers, laughter and tears were closely allied; but today we find his jokes less thought-provoking than his elegiac verses barbed for the Philistines who took misery for granted: witness his often quoted lines about those women

> Sewing at once with a double thread
> A shroud as well as a shirt—
>
> . . . . .
>
> Oh God, that bread should be so dear
> And flesh and blood so cheap!

For the humorist, too, the common measure served well; as it came from the pen of a wide variety of jokers, it fitted the ear

[29] *The Victorian Age* (New York, 1913), pp. 28-29. The humor of the century can be reviewed in Miles, *op. cit.*, Vol. IX.

and pulse and tongue of a wide variety of readers and speakers.

On the other end of the scale leading from informal verse to formally versified dogma [30] we note that what passes for religious poetry among unspeculative worshippers ingratiates itself most often by approximating the rhythms of balladry, its common and long meter. Yet versified dogma, however singable, is gnomic or didactic rather than elegiac poetry. From it we turn to those poems in which poets verging toward or away from doctrinal conviction set down their skeptical experience as probers toward central truth, seekers for reality. For a valid *anagnorisis*, the revelation must be earned, not previously dictated by church or priest, metaphysician or theologian. In this sense the more memorable poets of the century are of necessity skeptics, eager to participate in spiritual life, curious about its very nature, and intent upon widening its scope.

There is, however, one vehicle of spiritual discovery—even of liturgical experience as distinguished from theological doctrine —through which intense feeling raises verse into lyrical beauty: hymnody.[31] In the writing and singing of hymns from Isaac Watts,[32] the Wesleys, Newton, and Cowper to Heber, Newman, Keble, Faber, students of the elegiac imagination will find among personal lyrics and heavenly idylls many a search by way of particular discoveries toward the divine epiphany. Such elegies use feeling not as an end in itself, nor fair scenes for themselves alone, but, in Newman's distinctively tentative mode,

[30] See instances and arguments in Hoxie Neale Fairchild's *Religious Trends in English Poetry*, Vol. IV. Professor Fairchild's monumental work, and especially his volume dealing with Christianity and Romanticism in the Victorian era, seems primarily concerned to distinguish in the matter of English poetry its authentic from its spurious Christian doctrine.

[31] There is an excellent compendious study of this subject by Jeremiah Bascom Reeves, *The Hymn As Literature* (New York and London, 1924).

[32] Watts affected later poetry generally. Professor Martha England reminds me that the poems of Watts influenced the poetry of Emily Dickinson.

"one step" at a time, "O'er moor and fen, o'er crag and torrent, 'till / The night is gone." It is this gradual progression of an elegiac poem, step by step toward an outlook, that accelerates "Nearer, my God, to Thee," by Sarah Flower Adams, whose wanderer in the darkness after sundown at Beth-el dreams of a ladder—climax—and sees his way as "steps unto heaven," and in his "waking thoughts" flies upward "on joyful wing,"

> Cleaving the sky,
> Sun, moon, and stars forgot

for a superior illumination.

Not all of the eights-and-sixes of the Christian poets Newman, Faber, Keble, Caswell, Hawker, de Vere, are in the hymnal; but with each other and with elegists generally they share the elegiac preference for swift pulsing measures; witness the ballad swing of the choirs of angelicals in Newman's *Dream of Gerontius*. Also they share the effort toward epiphany.

But the study of Greek texts kept up apace with the singing of Christian hymns. Whether the renewal of the century be called neo-Catholicism or neo-Hellenism, in either case it was thanks to scholars that poetry held its head up in the floods and tides of a newly discovered world and the flotsam and jetsam deposited by natural scientists on the shore at Dover Beach and elsewhere.

Although his be a *lumen siccum* rather than a "kindly light," the classical scholar Arthur Hugh Clough is one of the most skillful prosodists of the middle years. No couplets measured by Greek and Latin rule can be found in English as true to the emphases of the Latin elegiac poets as those at the beginnings and ends of his Cantos in *Amours de Voyage:* [33]

Ah, that I were, far away from the crowd and the streets of the city,
Under the vine-trees laid, O my beloved, with thee!

[33] *Poems of Arthur Hugh Clough*, ed. H. F. Lowry, A. L. P. Norrington, F. L. Mulhauser (Oxford, 1951); quoted by permission of The Clarendon Press, Oxford.

Eastward, or Northward, or West? I wander and ask as I wander,
Weary, yet eager and sure, where shall I come to my love?

Expert as he was also in transforming classical hexameters into
the accentual hexameters of the stories in his *Bothie of Tober-
na-Vuolich,* when Clough sharpened his inner eye to probe
into the mysteries of personal life, as in the *Ambarvalia,* his
interrogative cries come to us in exquisitely phrased eights-and-
sixes:

> Ah, what is love, our love, she said,
>   Ah, what is human love?
> A fire of earthly fuel fed,
>   Full fain to soar above.
>
> With lambent flame the void it lips,
>   And of the impassive air
> Would frame for its ambitious steps
>   A heaven-attaining stair.
>
> It wrestles and it climbs— Ah me,
>   Go look in little space,
> White ash on blackened earth will be
>   Sole record of its place.
>
>   . . . . .
>
> Ah love, high love, she said and sighed,
>   She said, the Poet's love!
> A star upon a turbid tide,
>   Reflected from above.
> A marvel here, a glory there,
>   But clouds will intervene,
> And garish earthly noon outglare
>   The purity serene.

This is a kind of obverted revelation; but from his intensity, his
use of question and answer, the strong effort and quiet surrender of his meditation, and his celestial and terrestrial symbols
can be illustrated the elegiac machinery of many centuries. The
"questioning spirit" of the lovers—

> Oh, ask not what is love, she said,
>   Or ask it not of me;
> Or of the heart, or of the head,
>   Or if at all it be—

is contented only by what they find in themselves. Man is to "wait out" the divine epiphany (*When Israel Came Out of Egypt*), although "God, unidentified, [be] thought of still" (*Blank Misgivings of a Creature moving about in Worlds not realized*).

Clough's last important, although unfinished, poem is a collection of stories in heroic couplets, entitled *Mari Magno*. Scarcely less than his friend Arnold, he was prepossessed by the sea and its tides, its tributaries, and its ships becalmed or faring forth. His marine lore, however, never furnished an answer to his elegiac queries:

> O end to which our currents tend,
>   Inevitable sea,
> To which we flow, what do we know,
>   What shall we guess of thee?

Over this sea the sun and stars can scarcely be discerned.

> Where lies the land to which the ship would go?
> Far, far ahead, is all her seamen know.
> And where the land she travels from? Away,
> Far, far behind, is all that they can say.

Granted that Clough failed to furnish his seamen with compasses, not since Wordsworth's Matthew poems had a poet revealed the plight of modern man so humbly and so simply; furthermore, when Clough's despair becomes a hope, it is with the revelatory sunshine of Wordsworth that his dry light is most cheerfully fused ("Say not the struggle nought availeth"):

> And not by eastern windows only,
>   When daylight comes, comes in the light,
> In front the sun climbs slow, how slowly,
>   But westward, look, the land is bright.

In such a deft adaptation of long meter Clough's elegiac balladry is best remembered.

Meanwhile Clough's friend, Matthew Arnold, another connoisseur of Greek elegiac verse, was also working toward an
English rhythm akin to flute song. It was the thoughtful and
regretful Swiss lyrics rather than the stanzas of *Thyrsis* that
gave him his most suitable medium for poetical speculation and
that "pleasing melancholy" which was the basis of his nature—
and of his poetics.[34] While he recapitulated Wordsworth's search
to find the right meter for memorial poems, his octosyllabic
couplets remembering Wordsworth, and the frequently trochaic
short lines, unrhymed, of *Haworth Churchyard*, *Rugby Chapel*,
and *Heine's Grave* proved not so appealing as his quatrains and
ballad-like stanzas for William Arnold, his brother, even his
ballad stanzas for Edward Quillinan. Especially in the common
measure of the Obermann poems [35] did Arnold come very close
to the melodies of the Old Sailor of Coleridge and the Old
Teacher, Matthew, of Wordsworth, echoing a half-century
later the flutings of these greater melodists of 1797–1799.

Thought is swift, as Hamlet was not the first to remark, and
for the poetry of thought, whether in verse or in prose, Arnold
did not always follow his own "rigorous line" to the center; [36]
but, in spite of his illogic and vacillation, for the urgent questionings of a new time there was no swifter vehicle than these
eights-and-sixes, nor is it probable that any writer to come will
risk so much so simply.

Now and again there had been Victorian quests over a difficult ethical or aesthetic terrain, allegorical idylls or fables rather

[34] *The Poetry of Matthew Arnold: A Commentary*, by C. B. Tinker
and H. F. Lowry (Oxford University Press, 1940), p. 146, quoting a
letter to Clough.

[35] *Ibid.*, p. 269: "Obermann was reread along with Propertius and
Tibullus."

[36] As has been pointed out by D. G. James in *Matthew Arnold and
the Decline of English Romanticism* (Oxford, 1961).

than elegies proper, with discoveries foreordained and artificial: for instance, George Macdonald's "Tell me" [37] from the *Parables, Songs, and Ballads—*

> "Traveller, what lies over the hill?
> Traveller, tell to me:
> Tiptoe-high on the window-sill,
> Over I cannot see."

The answers are spare and forthright. As explicit, and more violent, is *The Naked Thinker* by Ebenezer Jones; but much more delicately imaginative is the uncanonical *Goblin Market* (1862) of Christina Rossetti, to which the swing of balladry here and there lends its sure elegiac effect:

> "We must not look at goblin men,
> We must not buy their fruits:
> Who knows upon what soil they fed
> Their hungry thirsty roots?"

In this meter also were composed several of the *Songs of a Worker* of Arthur O'Shaughnessy; [38] and the septenaries of Joseph Skipsey's *Carols from the Coal-fields* recall ballad rhythms: [39]

> The stars are twinkling in the sky
> As to the pit I go;
> I think not of the sheen on high,
> But of the gloom below.

Roden Noel's *Lament* for his son in *A Little Child's Monument* (1881) [40] is elegiac in the restricted sense:

> A monarch had a little son,
> A child of five years old,
> The loveliest earth ere looked upon;
> And he is lying cold.

[37] Miles, *op. cit.*, V, 232–234.

[38] Arthur O'Shaughnessy, *Poems*, ed. William Alexander Percy (Yale University Press, 1923).

[39] Miles, *op. cit.*, V, 522.   [40] *Ibid.*, VI, 105, 113.

The intensity of Noel's elegies somewhat atones for their lack of thought; yet there is in the generous spread of his compassion also a lift of the mind toward discovery (*That They All May Be One*):

> Whene'er there comes a little child,
> My darling comes with him.

No rereading of elegies of the second half of the nineteenth century may omit those of its most able metrist, Algernon Charles Swinburne, of whom Tennyson said: "He is a reed through which all things blow into music." [41] That Swinburne was always aware of the musical associations of verse is apparent in his poems on the flute-player, Pan, and in his lines from the seventeenth stanza of his *Song for the Centenary of Walter Savage Landor:* [42]

> And through the trumpet of a child of Rome
> Rang the pure music of the flutes of Greece.

With Greek flute song in the original elegiac meter Swinburne was himself amazingly skillful: again in affection for Landor, he wrote a series of distichs in Greek; and his Greek elegiacs prefixed to *Atalanta in Calydon* reveal "the extent of [his] early assimilation of the diction and phraseology of that language." [43] What, then, was his metrical habit in writing English elegies?

His *Ave atque Vale* for that "sweet strange elder singer," Charles Baudelaire, was sung in pentametrical stanzas with final trimeter—

> For whom all winds are quiet as the sun,
> All waters as the shore.

For his memorial of Théophile Gautier he used blank verse and

[41] *Memoirs*, II, 285.

[42] Swinburne's verses are quoted from *The Poems of Algernon Charles Swinburne* (6 vols.; London, 1904).

[43] Marion Clyde Wier, *The Influence of Aeschylus and Euripides on the Structure and Content of Swinburne's "Atalanta in Calydon" and "Erectheus"* (Ann Arbor, 1920), p. 2.

for Rossetti pentameter; for Browning a series of sonnets; for Burns, eights-and-fours; for the poem to Walt Whitman in America, hexameter. Yet of the *Poems and Ballads*, Second Series (1878), Professor Chew says: "[in place of] the tambourines, cymbals, kettledrums, timbrels, and taborets of 1866 and the trumpet tones of 'Songs [before] Sunrise' there sounds a new music, as of a flute, not less melodious but tenderer"; [44] and in the Third Series of *Poems and Ballads* (1889) eights-and-sixes are noticeably more frequent, or eights-and-fours as in his verses on Florence and Landor:

> So shall thy lovers, come from far,
>   Mix with thy name
> As morning-star with evening-star
>   His faultless fame.

Many of Swinburne's poems are idylls of feeling, not properly lyric or elegiac. Where he utters only to describe but does not participate, his invective and praise alike seem ostentatious, at times artificial; he is not a patient or vertebrate thinker. Nevertheless throughout his career he experimented with verse of a swifter and more logically articulate nature: *The Brothers*—

> There were two brethren fell on strife;
>   Sweet fruits are sair to gather—

and *The Jacobite's Farewell* and *A Jacobite's Exile*—

> The Wansbeck sings with all her springs,
>   The bents and braes give ear:
> But the woods that rings wi' the song she sings
>   I may not see nor hear;
> For far and far thae blithe burns are,
>   And strange is a' thing near—

these are in the strain of flute song. Their revelatory passages indicate high powers for elegiac balladry; and with the *Tale of*

[44] Samuel C. Chew, *Algernon Charles Swinburne* (Boston, 1929), pp. 141–142.

Balen he gave undeniable evidence not only of his interest in "the old and unrivalled model of the English ballad," [45] but of his skill in enhancing it [46] for purposes that looked beyond his own *May Janet, the Witch Mother,* and *The Bride's Tragedy* toward the ballads of Hardy and Yeats and Chesterton, of Stevenson, Henley, and Housman.

Before we advance into a discussion of the major transformation of elegiac poetry at the turn of the century we may pause briefly to notice the growing habit of elegy to depend on its old friend, the epyll,[47] for assistance in what threatened to be a perilous exhaustion of its skeptical power; in a century so prevailingly meditative and dialectic as the nineteenth, thought tends to wear itself out. There were, of course, many instances of wearily negative poetry: dissident in belief, perverse in feeling, merely "different" in technique. Many minor writers were saying "no" just for the pleasure gained from contradiction; some of the greater ones were seduced by the Black Mass. Negativism is the easiest of all the "-isms"; it has only to veto what abler minds have already wrought with courage and ingenuity. We are, therefore, reassured to find the more gifted poets maintaining or regaining balance by practising the necessary economies of a poetry of action, articulating their thoughts along the joints of a vigorous plot.[48] John Stuart Blackie, the Greek

[45] Dedicatory Epistle to Theodore Watts-Dunton; *Border Ballads,* printed for the Bibliophile Society (Boston, 1912).

[46] See Chew, *op. cit.,* pp. 40–41: "Rossetti once said that Swinburne knew more about folk ballads than all the specialists . . . for the language and lilt of Northumberland were native to him."

[47] See Elizabeth Hazelton Haight, *Romance in the Latin Elegiac Poets* (New York, 1932).

[48] In a much needed anthology of the ballads of the late nineteenth century the following would surely find a significant place: 1857, Charles Kingsley, *The Last Buccaneer;* 1869, *The Soldan's Daughter,* by the classical scholar, George Augustus Simcox (a romance of conversion rather than an elegy of discovery, in a stirring ballad rhythm); 1870, *Bisclaveret,* by Arthur O'Shaughnessy (an allegory of emotional

scholar of Edinburgh University and author of *Lays and Legends of Ancient Greece* (1857), had translated the *Iliad* in ballad measure in 1866; and in 1876 William Morris had issued *The Aeneids of Virgil done into English Verse:* that verse was the septenarius which, to quote Professor Frye, is "the meter which Chapman had used to reproduce the rhythm of the *Iliad*, the meter of the ballads and of historical and didactic epics down to Warner's *Albion's England*." [49]

Morris' original verse, too, often reflects what his daughter reported as his love for the music of the people.[50] Common measure varied into three-beat lines appears in *Shameful Death*, and ballad rhythms often give a swing to the songs in *The House of the Wolfings* (1888); its tales make good use of four-teeners. And may it not have been unfortunate that the first draft of the Prologue of *The Earthly Paradise*, in a four-line stanza, and an early draft of *The Man Born to Be King*, in tetrametrical couplets, were set aside for massive heroic couplets? The fragment, says his daughter, "calls up . . . the picture of a wandering minstrel reciting his tale to a few chords on his vielle as he stands by the market-cross on a feast-day." [51] Morris, however, would not—could not—renounce his opulent designs in space and time for the rigors of non-spatial and non-temporal adventure: his affinity was with the graphic arts.

---

and ethical adventure); 1872, *The Ballad of May Margaret,* by John Payne (with a peripety but no discovery); 1886, *The Cruise of the Rover,* by Edmund Gosse (with a final revelation when "their lives rose before them in crystalline completeness"); 1888, *Mad Madge o' Cree,* by William Sharp; 1890, *Daniel Periton,* by H. D. Rawnsley; 1890, Robert Louis Stevenson, *Christmas at Sea* (with its poignant discovery)—

But all that I could think of, in the darkness and the cold,
Was just that I was leaving home and my folks were growing old.

[49] Northrop Frye, *Fearful Symmetry: A Study of William Blake* (Princeton University Press, 1947), p. 185.

[50] *Collected Works of William Morris,* with Introductions by his Daughter, May Morris (London, 1911), XII, ix.

[51] *Ibid.,* III, xiii, xvi.

Along with his effort to discover truth, the elegist is often tempted to separate meditative soliloquy from the epyll or legend he adopts. In such wise the interludes of Morris' *Earthly Paradise* revived the tradition of *chante-fable*. Rossetti,[52] too, in *The White Ship, Sister Helen,* and *The Blessed Damozel* furnished his stories with tag ends of personal comment: a gnomic or lyrical refrain, an invocation, or a parenthesis. Especially in *The King's Tragedy* he was experimenting with the relation of thought to action. Should the tale be retarded by apostrophes, queries, maxims? Although the discoveries in his extended ballad—a pathetic, not a tragic ballad—are showy rather than revelatory, the use of Kate Barlass as witness and narrator allows the poet to shape the series of events into a symbolic representation of kingly valor and courtly love. The wraiths appearing in climactical form to the "woman tattered and old," the moonlight cast through heraldic glass upon the floor of the King's chamber, and the ultimate discovery of the King slain—

> O God! and now did a bell boom forth,
>   And the murderers turned and fled;—
> Too late, too late, O God, did it sound!—
> And I heard the true men mustering round,
>   And the cries and the coming tread.
>
> But ere they came, to the black death-gap
>   Somewise did I creep and steal;
> And lo! or ever I swooned away,
> Through the dusk I saw where the white face lay
>   In the Pit of Fortune's Wheel—

all this imbues the poem with the intense concern of the person using its episodes as steps toward the royal epiphany.

A third singer of British renown, Rudyard Kipling, writes

[52] *The Collected Works of Dante Gabriel Rossetti,* ed. William M. Rossetti (2 vols., London, 1888), I, 66–74, 137–175, 232–236. The same editor issued a "Revised and Enlarged Edition" of D. G. Rossetti's *Works* (London, 1911).

verses in common measure linking the stories of *Puck of Pook's Hill* in order to probe the nature of England's greatness—

> She is not any common Earth,
>   Water or wood or air,
> But Merlin's Isle of Gramarye,
>   Where you and I will fare—

or in order to make the discovery of earth's renewal in English terms:

> And we bring you news by word of mouth—
>   Good news for cattle and corn—
> Now is the Sun come up from the South,
>   With Oak, and Ash, and Thorn! [53]

Less well known and less skillful instances of the fusion of meditation and action are two ballads by Rossetti's adversary, Robert Buchanan. *The Lights of Leith*—

> O Robin, Robin . . . they doom'd her to burn . . .
>   Doon yonner upon the quay . . .
> This was the night . . . See the light! See the light
>   How it burns by the side o' the sea!

This and the *Ballad of Judas Iscariot* are not mere ballads of events: violent and terrible as they seem, lacking in a reasonable *catharsis*, they seek out *anagnorises*. As on that sea shore when the old witch mother is burned to death, so in the Court of the Bridegroom who welcomes the soul of Judas Iscariot there are "lights," in each case illuminating the nature of love, human or divine.

Somewhat later Chesterton,[54] at the furthest reach of his power, will be redeemed from his parodies and captious para-

---

[53] Lines from "Puck's Song" and from "A Tree Song," from *Rudyard Kipling's Verse: Definitive Edition* (New York, 1940); reprinted by permission of Mrs. George Bambridge, Doubleday & Co., Inc., and Macmillan & Co., Ltd.

[54] *The Collected Poems of Gilbert Keith Chesterton* (New York, 1956).

doxes by *The Ballad of St. Barbara* and *The Ballad of the White Horse*, a poem challenging comparison with Coleridge's *Rime*. Balladry such as this differs from the stories of Southey's Wicked Bishop and Macaulay's Horatius in that it makes event the occasion for thought; and it differs from the romantic poetry of Morris and Rossetti in that picturization is less an aim than meditation. Finally, it differs from the ballads of Swinburne because its feeling has been associated with lofty and significant patterns of thought suggesting dedicated action. In this regard, Chesterton and Kipling are comparable: larger issues are at stake than any precious assurances, however craved by individuals. Again, as with Wordsworth at the beginning of the century, the elegist will become, in the best sense of the term, a man of the world. And flute song may possibly regain the ascendancy it enjoyed in Greek letters in the seventh and sixth centuries B.C.

Meanwhile the steadying influence of Greek and Latin symbols and meters had continued, even among the minor writers of the century,[55] whose chief claim to remembrance is often their association with the classics. So, for instance, William Johnson Cory's *Ionica* in 1858 included *Mimnermus in Church*:

> Forsooth the present we must give
>   To that which cannot pass away;
> All beauteous things for which we live
>   By laws of time and space decay.
> But oh, the very reason why
> I clasp them, is because they die.

His *Heraclitus*, in thirteeners and fourteeners, recalls both Greek distich and English ballad line:

> And now that thou art lying, my dear old Carian guest,
> A handful of grey ashes, long, long ago at rest,
> Still are thy pleasant voices, thy nightingales, awake;
> For Death, he taketh all away, but them he cannot take.

[55] Buchanan, Cory, Noel, Ingelow, Lee-Hamilton, and their contemporaries can be conveniently reviewed in Miles, *op. cit.*, V, VI, VII, VIII.

And Eugene Lee-Hamilton, an avowed neo-Hellenist, wrote elegiacs in the classical rhythm:

> Nature for me has most charm in what is her moment elegiac,
> When she brings home to the mind, all that is fleeting and fair.

From Jean Ingelow in the sixties to Edmund Gosse in the seventies and Roden Noel and Eugene Lee-Hamilton in the eighties flute and lyre were debated as the proper instrument for poetry. Jean Ingelow's Scholar had been shamed out of playing the flute of Ganymede,

> Dropped from his heedless hand when, dazed and mute,
> He sailed upon an eagle's quivering wing.

This Scholar's hunt for himself becomes another Victorian elegy;

> And still for ever yaws before our eyes
> An UTMOST—that is veiled.[56]

And in the last quarter of the century Edmund Gosse, in *The Gifts of the Muses* (1879), retailed at some length the peripety of one young flutist, Daphnis. Gosse's Daphnis, whose "rustic round" was gilded by "song and the flute's bright sound," had been tricked by the "serene and stately" Muses as he lay sleeping with his loved Lycoris. She was given an opal instead of her mother's ring and became a peerless queen, the bride of a conquering king; and Daphnis, "past his whole desire," was given "a massive ivory lyre / Gold-strung and meet to hymn a king's delight." As years went by Daphnis became "the deftest minstrel under coronals" and reached the court of that conquering king, where he was praised for his singing and given a bowl of wine from the hand of the queen. When their eyes met, the one-time shepherd and shepherdess had their moment of mutual discovery:

[56] *The Poetical Works of Jean Ingelow* (Chicago and New York, 1886), pp. 21–26.

So memory stirred in each
As, o'er a tideless beach,
Some wandering wind may ape the loud sea-wave;
Then, in a moment's space,
Faded from either face
The shade of shades that dim remembrance gave.
She was a queen, erect and fair and cold,
And he a singer to be fee'd with gold.

The poem supplies not only a mutual discovery but an epiphany as well: "the radiant Pythian came" to grant the aging poet his heart's desire and—yes, we have guessed it:

"Give back the homely flute,
Now long disused and mute,
The sovereign Muses stole to make me great."

When at last the ancient bard lay dead, "the lyre they found not," but his fingers were closed upon a flute of "beech-wood tight." [57]

It would be unkind to break this delicate pastoral elegy of such high ancestry on the wheel of our pedantic argument; but the scholar Gosse evidently knew where the strength of the fading century lay. Moreover, he remembered the sixth and tenth *Eclogues* of Virgil, whose friend Gallus is the classical model for the nineteenth-century Daphnis. Gallus' elegiac sequence, *Lycoris*, has been lost; but the Virgilian pastorals furnished Gosse with an epyll and names for his elegy and an instance of the elegiac queries, the epiphany of Apollo and Pan, and a final reference to the evening star, Vesper or Hesperus, all to be celebrated on an Arcadian *fistula*, reed or flute.[58]

Gosse's poem has been quoted at some length because the discovery identifying the lover with his characteristic instrument is highly appropriate for the century, too. What its elegiac poetry needed for structural support was *epyllia*, a procedural method, an interrogative technique, and revelatory devices.

[57] Miles, *op. cit.*, VIII, 309, 314–323.   [58] Haight, *op. cit.*, pp. 33–37.

Lee-Hamilton was also preoccupied by the rivalry between Apollo and Marsyas (1884), seeming to favor flute against lyre; but in Roden Noel's *Modern Faust* (1888) with its Christian epiphany it is Pan who surrenders: [59]

> Sun, and Moon, and Earth, and Stars,
> Serene behind our cloudy bars,
> With the Magi from the East
> Yield glad homage to the Least,
> Offer myrrh, and gold, and gem
> Before the Babe of Bethlehem,
>   Now Pan is dead.

Whether or not Pan was quite, quite dead is debatable; surely without the reedy tone of his flute the late century would be at a serious loss, as Lord de Tabley had indicated in *An Ocean Grave*

> The passion of the wave is mute
>   No sound or ocean shock:
> No music save the trilling flute
>   That marks the curlew flock.
>
>   .   .   .   .   .
>
> There's nothing in the world to me
>   So dear as my regret.

These various Greek and Latin scholars well knew the difference between poetry of the lyre, lyric, and poetry of the flute, elegy. Arnold, too, had kept an eye on generic distinctions when he spoke of Tennyson as following Theocritus in adding the "elegiac, or the poetry of reflection and sentiment to the little epic fusion of lyric, epic, and dramatic." In the 1879 Preface to the Poems of Wordsworth in the Golden Treasury Series, although Arnold objected to Wordsworth's own categories as ingenious and farfetched in the definition of them by their supposed unity of mental origin, he went on to approve "the [Greek] categories of epic, dramatic, lyric . . . elegiac." "The

[59] Miles, *op. cit.*, IV, 143.

ballad kind," he says without defining his terms, "is a lower
kind; the didactic kind, still more, is a lower kind." His arrangement of Wordsworth's poetry by kinds gives us a helpful picture of generic assumptions as the last quarter-century started
on its way.[60]

Such distinctions were also familiar to Swinburne when, in
his Dedicatory Epistle to Theodore Watts-Dunton, he referred
to his "first volume of miscellaneous verse, lyrical and dramatic
and elegiac and generally heterogeneous." And he commended
the division of poems "after the old Roman fashion into sections
and classes: . . . their lyrical and elegiac works ranged and regi-
stered apart, each kind in a class of its own, such as is usually re-
served, I know not why, for sonnets only." Against these various
classical tendencies toward order there was arrayed the aesthetic
rebellion of a group of individualizing writers less prepossessed
by the forms of Greek and Latin poetry. And it was left for
George Saintsbury to disvalue generic study when he argued
"that [a] multiple, atomic, myrioramic style of poetry is in-
trinsically superior to the old substantive or structural kind." [61]

Had Saintsbury wished to trace generic development across
the end of the century—and who was better furnished to do

---

[60] Under the title "Reflective and Elegiac Poems," along with "Wis-
dom and Spirit of the Universe," "There was a Boy," *Tintern Abbey*,
Yew-Trees, *The French Revolution* (from *The Prelude*), *The Simplon
Pass* (from *The Prelude*) with its "great Apocalypse," the Prayer to
Urania at the beginning of *The Recluse* and that to "the dread power /
Whose gracious favour is the primal source of all illumination," he
included *Matthew*, *The Two April Mornings*, *September*, *1819*, *The
Primrose of the Rock*, the three poems on Yarrow, and certain episodes
and idyllic sketches or inscriptions suffused with thought and hence
akin to elegy but scarcely leading to momentous discoveries. Not quite
aware of any functional distinction between elegiac and idyllic poetry,
he calls *Lucy Gray* "a beautiful success," *The Sailor's Mother* "a failure."
And he makes the mistake of contrasting drama and epic with "a collection of short pieces"—i.e., contrasting poetry as generic with poetry as
quantitative.
[61] *The Later Nineteenth Century* (Edinburgh and London, 1907),
pp. 10–12.

this?—he would have found his clearest evidence for continuity in the ballad, the form that without ever surrendering its audience developed its traditional action toward elegiac vision. It is true that modern poetry is a myriorama; but its atoms did not, do not lack association or control. However variously the poems of the last quarter of the century have been labeled—songs, chants, odes, lyrics, sonnets, verse tales, ballads (and ballades), legends, dramas, and elegies [62]—all offer evidence of the contemporary desire to probe the feelings and thoughts of modern man, and most of them furnish revelations, superficial or profound, of his nature and destiny. Prose had its novelists in the vein of Dickens and its dramatists in the style of Scribe; poetry must depend on its elegists to qualify what was sentimental in the lyric and fanciful in the idyll. That elegists chose balladry as the best vehicle for their speculative thinking was a latter-day justification for Aristotle's hint as to the importance of plot. Moreover, there may have been in the vogue for ballads a prudent concern for a popular audience demanding poems fit to be spoken orally or sung. Says Miles:

What the ballads owe to the reciter, the songs owe to the singer; and while elocutionists may be said to have declaimed the ballads of Mr. Clement Scott and Mr. George Sims from almost every platform of the kingdom, vocalists, it may with equal truth be affirmed, have rendered the songs of Mr. [A. P.] Graves and Mr. Weatherly in almost every concert-hall and drawing-room in the land.[63]

Yet poets more withdrawn, speaking to more fastidious audiences, did their part, too, and often with a metrical variety and verbal finesse too little acknowledged. In Robert Louis Steven-

[62] Or, as Richard Le Gallienne phrases it in his notice of Mrs. Graham R. Thomson (Miles, *op. cit.*, VIII, 617): "weird Scots ballads after the manner just then revived by Mr. Swinburne, imitations of the Greek anthology, poems on pictures, bookish poems, *vers de société* in Mr. Dobson's metres, reminiscences of Herrick, ballads, rondeaus and villanelles, folk-songs, 'marches,' translations from Provençal poets."

[63] *Ibid.*, VIII, 690.

son's *Underwoods* (1887),[64] *A Song of the Road* placed ultimate discovery well on the distant horizon and proceeded toward it in octosyllabic couplets:

> The gauger walked with willing foot,
> And aye the gauger played the flute;
> And what should Master Gauger play
> But *Over the hills and far away?*

With equal rhythmic assurance Stevenson wrote for a Gaelic
air, *Over the Sea to Skye:*

> Sing me a song of a lad that is gone,
>   Say, could that lad be I?
> Merry of soul he sailed on a day
>   Over the sea to Skye.

> Mull was astern, Rum on the port,
>   Egg on the starboard bow;
> Glory of youth glowed in his soul:
>   Where is that glory now?

Further, we may quote *Youth and Love* (I) from *Songs of
Travel* for still other queries and discoveries in the identification
of self:

> The untented Kosmos my abode,
>   I pass, a wilful stranger:
> My mistress still the open road
>   And the bright eyes of danger.

> Come ill or well, the cross, the crown,
>   The rainbow or the thunder,
> I fling my soul and body down
>   For God to plough them under.

Moreover, to Stevenson's metrical skill we owe not only the
deceptively simple verses for children and the Scots ballads, but

[64] Robert Louis Stevenson, *Poems and Ballads* (New York, 1896).

what has become the best loved *Requiem* (1887) of the late
century in a rhythm of undeniable antiquity yet fresh power:

> Under the wide and starry sky,
>   Dig the grave and let me lie.
> Glad did I live and gladly die,
>   And I laid me down with a will.
>
> This be the verse you grave for me:
> *Here he lies where he longed to be;*
> *Home is the sailor, home from sea,*
>   *And the hunter home from the hill.*

Finally, to his friend, William Ernest Henley, Stevenson had
written in blank verse:

> But O thou!
> Uprise and take thy pipe.
>
>   .   .   .   .   .
>
> Small the pipe; but O! do thou,
> Peak-faced and suffering piper, blow therein
> The dirge of heroes dead; and to these sick,
> These dying, sound the triumph over death.

No poet of the time felt himself to be more surely on the right
track in his speculations than Henley; [65] none was a more per-
severing prober of pain and loss, especially in his self-revelatory
sketches *In Hospital:*

> Out of the night that covers me,
>   Black as the pit from pole to pole,
> I thank whatever gods may be
>   For my unconquerable soul.

And, indeed, none had greater occasion for courage in personal
life, for vigor and sanity as a citizen. As if he were another
Tyrtaeus or Solon, he devoted the energies of his later career

[65] Jerome Hamilton Buckley, *William Ernest Henley* (Princeton
University Press, 1945). Henley's poetry is quoted from *Poems* by
W. E. Henley (New York, 1898).

to health and probity in the cultural and political affairs of his
country:

> Sound, Sea of England, sound and shine,
>   Blow, English Wind, amain,
> Till in this old gray heart of mine
>   The Spring need wake again.

Both Stevenson and Henley were writers to content the
greater elegists of the earlier years of the century. With these
R. L. S. had arrayed himself ethically and technically in his
poem *To the Muse:*

> Resign the rhapsody, the dream,
>   To men of larger reach;
> Be ours the quest of a plain theme,
>   The piety of speech.

To this effect, also, the art and criticism of Henley were dedicated (*Echoes,* 1875):

> The nightingale has a lyre of gold,
>   The lark's is a clarion call,
> And the blackbird plays but a boxwood flute,
>   But I love him best of all.

CHAPTER XI

Thomas Hardy
as Elegist

FROM the elegiac balladry of Wordsworth and Coleridge to that of Stevenson and Chesterton, the concern of poets of the nineteenth century with love, transience, disillusionment, death, and kindred puzzling and challenging themes needs no further illustration; on the evidence here presented their notable success seems to have been the preservation and development of a vehicle proper for flute song. Not even the stabilizing quatrains of Tennyson could long retard the skeptical imagination in its advance toward a metrical form recalling the Elegeia of Ovid, in verses now long, now short, alternate, *pes illi longior alter erat.* Yet before we finally assess the value of our evidence we should consider the superior gift to elegiac poetry of those two skillful writers of yesterday, Thomas Hardy and William Butler Yeats. What, we may ask, was the nature of their discovery? In what symbols was it set forth? And what rhythms did they employ for their curious probing?

Thomas Hardy, the colossus whose writing spans our former and present centuries, is the elegiac heir of Wordsworth, as not a few references in his prose [1] and echoes in his verse will in-

[1] For instance, in the Apology for *Late Lyrics and Earlier,* 1922, where he makes good use of Wordsworth's phrases, "obstinate ques-

dicate. His attention to what Wordsworth called "humble and rustic life" is a signal instance and, as was true of the earlier poet, throughout his maturity his sympathetic inquiries extended to all mankind, especially in its plight during the Napoleonic Wars. Like Wordsworth he was a student of the classics and of the balladry of his native land. And—in this most surely an elegist among elegists—he never abandoned his study of the relation between Man and Nature: Wordsworth's concern, too, but with Hardy an overriding prepossession. Had not Man been orphaned of a Father in Heaven? Was he not sure only of his brotherhood with "creeping things," with sod and clod?

Such doctrinal assumptions have a technical bearing. A hundred years earlier, because Wordsworth had conceived of Man and Nature as distinct but wedded "in love and holy passion," he might symbolize their trysting with images culled from the natural English countryside under the not less natural sun, moon, and stars and the eye of a beneficent supernatural God. When that holy tryst was over, an apprehensive Arnold on the verge of a moon-blanched land and a contentious Swinburne on the tides of a moon-driven sea somehow missed the comfort of an anthropomorphic Nature as they had renounced the belief in an anthropomorphic Deity. Indeed, the more industriously the versifiers, scientists, and philosophers of the late century pecked at the cosmic shell for life beyond life, light beyond light, the lonelier Man became, without an authoritative ancestry, genial companionship, a creditable progeny—and without authentic symbols. Now that Nature was acknowledged to be an ignoble and Man a scarcely more noble part of an impersonal "All," whither should poets turn for their wingèd words?

Hardy gave an ironic answer. By using men and women as symbols of their own frustrate tendencies he would clarify the merely natural destiny of those whom a Divine Father could no longer redeem through a Divine Son. Like Plato in search of justice, Hardy in search of humanity would scour Man of all

tionings" and "blank misgivings," *Collected Poems of Thomas Hardy* (New York, 1952), p. 526.

sentimental or ideal relationships and all favoring circumstances. Furthermore, lest acquired characteristics or the intellectual accomplishments of individual men and women might falsify the evidence, he would deprive mankind of both foresight and insight. When Providence Majuscule went out, out went providence minuscule.

But rather than blanket his elegiac art with such imprecise and unliterary "-isms" as "fatalism," "pessimism," or even the term in which he himself begged the question, "evolutionary meliorism," let us place him squarely in the elegiac tradition, heir of its continuing technical problems. To that end we may adduce his poem on the early Greek elegist, Xenophanes of Colophon. Xenophanes is represented speaking to his "Great Dumb," the Immanent Will, "It":

> "Are You groping Your way?
> Do You do it unknowing?—
> Or mark Your wind blowing?
> Night tell You from day,
> O Mover? Come say!

Here are the age-old questions of the skeptical poet; and here they are asked of Something made new in his own skeptical image.

> "I mean, querying so,
> Do You do it aware,
> Or by rote, like a player,
> Or in ignorance, nor care
> Whether doing or no?"

Hardy's Xenophanes, attempting to "plumb [the] depths of his 'All,' " conceived a unity easier for philosophers to explicate than for poets to symbolize; the monist hypothesis of "All in One" puts a very severe strain on the writer needing to substitute a modern polarity [2] for the ancient Platonic opposition

[2] This word is here used in its general sense and not with the particular connotation D. H. Lawrence was to give it in 1922 (*Fantasia of the Unconscious*, New York, pp. 94 ff.).

between the phenomenon and the noumenon, the actual and the ideal, and the venerable Christian distinctions between body and soul, Man and God. And the "It" to which Hardy gave its bleak neutral name "three thousand years" after Xenophanes addressed it discouraged any but a vaguely monotonous treatment; its chief opposition is the before and after of Time in the obvious pagan routine of the seasons and hours. That is why Hardy's poems are for the most part poems of past and present; and that is why, also, they are so dependent on local scenery and petty similes and so scant of lofty symbols.[3] Whenever they hazard "a clue / To this riddle immense" of Time and Space, they disregard the Word Spoken, ὁ λόγος, with its inference of a Divine Speaker, for the word heard by "the listening Years"; and hence they subordinate the Deed-to-be-Done to mere "doings":

> "Yea, on, near the end,
> Its doings may mend;
> Aye, when you're forgotten,
> And old cults are rotten,
> And bulky codes shotten,
>   Xenophanes!"[4]

Xenophanes is now indeed forgotten, and speculation has a new cult, a new code, and a new vocabulary, mathematical and hence even less humane; but for every physicist making a scientific discovery there will doubtless be an elegist needing literary tropes in which to symbolize his feelings about it. Balked of both superhuman and subhuman scales of metaphorical value— lacking both a pantheon and a bestiary—Hardy fell back on the ironic treatment of Man Himself. Reluctant to acknowledge

[3] For an admirable recent discussion of metaphors and symbols see Philip Wheelwright, *Metaphor and Reality* (Indiana University Press, 1962).

[4] Quotations of Hardy's poetry are from *The Collected Poems of Thomas Hardy* (New York, 1926) and *The Dynasts* (London, 1923; Vol. II of *Poetical Works*); quoted by permission of St. Martin's Press, Inc., Macmillan & Co., Ltd., and the Trustees of the Hardy Estate.

living ideas within which particulars might be subsumed and hence similitude established, he was betrayed into mere contrast and opposition, at times even into saying a blank "no." Or, when faced with scientific facts and historical events, for the usual sort of theoretical induction he substituted on the one hand verbal abstracts, "purblind" Time, Fate, Casualty, or, on the other, an instinctive, subrational kind of experience shared by Man in his labyrinthine nervous system with the rat in his maze. His most characteristic discovery is the apperception and recognition of identity: "this is this" and "this is this again." As he tells us in the first year of the twentieth century, "unadjusted impressions have their value, and the road to true philosophy of life seems to lie in humbly recording diverse readings of its phenomena as they are forced upon us by chance and change." [5]

This justifies us in humbly recording as evidence the particulars of his poetry; but we need not rest satisfied with a merely impressionistic estimate of its value. He minimized his endowment: what he translated from Plato's *Ion* in 1897 as inspiration, not technicality, θεῖον καὶ μὴ τεχνικόν, was his in generous share. He was a graphic genius; and he was also a master of ethical design. When we have acknowledged the monotony of his temporal sequences, the forbidding effect of his irony, and the discomfort of his revelation of natural doom, his persons remain to confute his assumptions. They are not "it's" but "he's" and "she's"; they are men and women with light in their eyes. To adopt his own adjective, his poetry is "personative." [6]

Not often are these persons "characters" as the idyllist observes them, lively but insignificant; they are not "agents" as employed by the dramatist to advance his "action"; instead they serve as counters to provide evidence for the *anagnorises* of an elegist. They furnish the recognition of personal identity by all possible varieties of recognitive device: by such tokens as voice

[5] Preface to *Poems of the Past and Present*, 1901 (*Collected Poems*, p. 75).
[6] *Collected Poems*, Preface (1898).

or physical mark or habit, by inference, by outright statement, and by memory with the display of identifying emotion; and very often—to continue with Aristotle's category—by the discovery of what is not true, through unintentional fallacy or sophistical deception. Since Hardy scarcely believes in universals, his persons are not educable and the disclosure of fact often outweighs or overbears the recognition of their likeness to or unlikeness from their common humanity. Within the necessitous lapse of time there is little room for pleasant hypothesis or imaginative escape. Nevertheless, Hardy's supreme elegiac accomplishment is the recognition of a man as himself, a woman as herself: οὗτος ἐκεῖνος, this is the very one.

It follows, therefore, that light from human eyes or man-made candle, torch, hearthfire, or beacon will best serve him in his attempt to pierce terrestrial and celestial darkness. Sun, moon, and constellated stars, the dim luminescence of the will-o'-the-wisp over the marshes, or the twilight states of earthly dawn too soon becoming earthly eve exist to disappear before the burning glance of dubious man.[7]

With deferential regard for Hardy's own procedure, at this point let us cease generalization and particularize in roughly temporal sequence his symbols for such discoveries as he almost fears or regrets that he has verified. The "onward earth-track" of this honestly ironic writer would never be quite "transcended," as he foresaw in the initial poem of his collected verse, *The Temporary the All;* but his effort to widen his scope and raise his sights from what was temporal in Time and terrestrial in Space sharpened his objective vision as his "Years" went by. In the *Wessex Poems* his "God-curst sun" is subjective, but his "sunless church," "old earth's glooms" and "mirage-mists" help only to furnish a scene. Gradually, as *A Sign-seeker* tells, he became more eager to "mark the months," "the noontides,"

---

[7] James Granville Southworth (*The Poetry of Thomas Hardy*, Columbia University Press, 1947, Chap. VII) gives a compendious analysis of Hardy's imagery.

"nightfall shades," "evening bonfires of the sun," "the lightning-blade," "the leaping star."

> I learn to prophesy the hid eclipse,
> The coming of eccentric orbs;
> To mete the dust the sky absorbs,
> To weigh the sun, and fix the hour each planet dips.
>
> . . . . .
>
> —There are who, rapt to heights of trancelike trust, . . .
> Read radiant hints of times to be.

"Such scope" was not yet, not ever, granted to Hardy; there were no "whisperings" "to open out [his] limitings"; and, although "in vision [he] roamed the flashing Firmament," his natural symbols like his natural settings are generally lacklustre or gloom-burdened. *To Outer Nature* reflects Wordsworth's Immortality Ode without its hard-won assurance; instead, we have an elegiac query that dims rather than enhances the light:

> Why not sempiternal,
> Thou and I? Our vernal brightness keeping,
> Time outleaping;
> Passed the hodiernal.

Yeats would outleap lunar time into a Great Sphere; for Hardy

> such re-adorning
> Time forbids with scorning.

Instead, light from the eyes of a daughter (*San Sebastian*) or sounds from street-fiddling or tavern gaiety (*Leipsig* and *The Dance at the Phoenix*) or bird auguries (*The Alarm*) evoke memories that bring on disclosures of personal feeling and hence human identity. The smile on the face of the dying woman in *Her Death and After* as she suggests the advantageous lie to the man who has loved her, and the "liquor-fired face" of *My Cicely*, driving her lover to his specious denial that she is indeed she, tell us as much about the persons soliloquizing as does the outright confession of guilt in *The Peasant's Questioning*. Frank avowals become possible as a result of the "wild rainy eyes," "great gallied eyes," of Barbree in *The Bride-night Fire;* and when Tim Twink brought news to Mistress Damon that her goodman John had been gored to death by a bull, the eyes with which she "gazed and gazed" upon him and then "scanned far Egdon-side" reveal the depths of her shock and sorrow far more truly than does her concern to put her house in order.

Hardy evidently admired Wordsworth's elegiac balladry; there are frequent echoes of the Lucy and Matthew poems of a century ago, as for instance in *Her Immortality:*

> I lay and thought; and in a trance
> She came and stood thereby—
> The same, even to the marvellous ray
> That used to light her eye.

Hardy's trance here, like Wordsworth's trance in "Strange fits of passion," allows the elegist a kind of stereoscopic vision long familiar in dream literature and sometimes leading to a love of apparitions for their own sake. Hardy has some such phantoms helping to bind the present to the past, but for the most part the *personae* of his early ballads have no vision except of actual images. When they cannot focus two disparate images in terms of a visual idea, they are tempted to deny one or the other and are "illuded," like the lover of *My Cicely:*

> Far better
> To dream than to own the debasement
> Of sweet Cicely.

Or, like the Wife of Froom Valley, they pine "in a slow decay." Since they are nearsighted, their discoveries are necessarily fallacious, with mistaken behavior to follow. Their author has not endowed them with the resolute insight of the little Maid of Wordsworth's *We Are Seven* or with Matthew's power to identify his daughter Emma, dead, but as his still loved more intensely than any living girl, however "fair."

Nevertheless, to compensate for the gentler irony made possible by Wordsworth's wider and higher scope, Hardy's insistence on unaccommodated, defective, or feeble vision often arouses in his reader well-nigh tragic feelings of pity and terror. His blindness to the sights others see is not willful, not the tragic *hamartia*, but it is, as he acknowledges in *The Impercipient*, a "shortcoming."

> Why always I must feel as blind
>   To sights my brethren see,
> Why joys they've found I cannot find,
>   Abides a mystery.
>
>   . . . . .
>
> I am like a gazer who should mark
>   An inland company
> Standing upfingered, with, "Hark! Hark!
>   The glorious distant sea!"
> And feel, "Alas, 'tis but yon dark
>   And wind-swept pine to me!"

At the ending of the nineteenth and beginning of the twentieth century there is no body of verse that reaches so far back into the one and so prophetically ahead into the other as Hardy's *Poems of the Past and the Present*, published in August, 1901, a few months after the death of Victoria. In it appeared a remarkable collection of war sonnets and elegies written in 1899 on the occasion of the Boer War, poems that deserve to be set beside Wordsworth's series, *National Independence and Liberty*, with the observation that Hardy is as full of queries as Wordsworth of gnomes. We notice, also, that Hardy has profited by Tennyson's modification of national doctrine in the direction of Parliaments of the World. Witness *The Sick Battle-God:* "new light spread"; "modern meditation broke his spell";

> Yea, seeds of crescent sympathy
> Were sown by those more excellent than he,
>   Long known, though long contemned till then—
>   The gods of men in amity.

There is reminiscence of Swinburne in *The Souls of the Slain*
with its "criss-crossing tides" and its "sea-mutterings"; and in
Drummer Hodge, young Hodge, dead on a kopje-crest of the
veldt, anticipates the fallen British soldier of Rupert Brooke.

> Yet portion of that unknown plain
>   Will Hodge for ever be;
> His homely Northern breast and brain
>   Grow to some Southern tree,
> And strange-eyed constellations reign
>   His stars eternally.

It must be confessed that in the ballads of *Past and Present*
Hardy's epylls or brief tales have a drive and impact lending
to their discoveries a power to shock that Wordsworth neither
desired nor achieved.[8] Here often we are reminded of Byron,
and again of Swinburne's "fresh-fluted notes" in the *Poems and
Ballads* that Hardy read enthusiastically in 1866. Although *The
Well-Beloved—*

> I went by star and planet shine
>   Towards the dear one's home
> At Kingsbere, there to make her mine
>   When the next sun upclomb—

starts out like another "Strange fits of passion have I known,"
it ends, not in the imagination, but in the grimly ironic sight of
the physical eyes:

> —When I arrived and met my bride,
>   Her look was pinched and thin,
> As if her soul had shrunk and died,
>   And left a waste within.

And the *anagnorisis?* A blank disclosure: "Brides are not what
they seem." Hardy appears less unwilling to generalize toward

---

[8] Hardy's knowledge of Greek tragedy, studied as a youth, furnished
him rather with its shocking changes of fortune than with its *anagnorises*
and true peripeties.

despair than toward hope. So, in *The Widow Betrothed, The Dame of Athelhall,* and *The Supplanter,* preoccupation is seen to harden a "sweet face"; a penitent wife returning from an intended elopement overhears her husband say, to his new beloved, "her going is good"; a lover at the grave of his dead sweetheart from whom he has been temporarily distracted to father the living child of a living woman, cries out to the living one: "I know you not!"

> "Nor know your child. I knew this maid
>   But she's in Paradise!"
> And he has vanished in the shade
>   From her beseeching eyes.

The most grotesque of these elegiac ballads are *The Tree* and *The Church-builder:* in the former a woman's confession of involvement in a murder that sent one lover to "wive . . . the gibbet tree" sends a second lover wandering. The woman herself goes "distraught":

> —Under that oak of heretofore
> Sat Sweetheart mine with me no more.
>
>   . . . . .
>
> Its roots are bristling in the air
> Like some mad Earth-god's spiny hair;
> The loud south-wester's swell and yell
> Smote it at midnight and it fell.
>   Thus ends the tree
>   Where Some One sat with me.

Distorted memory, this, of the Wordsworthian "tree, of many, one" and the Tennysonian sycamore; and there is an even greater distortion of the elegiac tree in *The Church-builder,* whose titular person hangs himself "midway 'twixt Cross and truss" because the sneers and smirks of "the deeper thinkers" and the rebellious curses of his sons have dimmed his faith:

> Well: Here at morn they'll light on one
>   Dangling in mockery

> Of what he spent his substance on
> Blindly and uselessly! . . .
>   "He might," they'll say,
>   "Have built, some way,
>   A cheaper gallows-tree."

As did Wordsworth in his travels, early and late, Hardy extended his study of Time from personal to civic events. The coin of Constantine in the hand of a child of Fiesole "flashed home . . . / The power, the pride, the reach of perished Rome." Such coins might be found also in "English loam"—a discovery by token. A Strauss melody played in "Time's central city" near the dissolving pile of Caligula blended with the ruins "Till Time seemed fiction, Past and Present one"—a Wordsworthian "spot of time." And when the inconstant lover of each of the Muses sat in the Sala delle Muse of the Vatican, still another Muse, "essence of all the Nine"—was it possibly Ovid's Elegeia?—appeared walking "with tentative foot . . . / A pensive smile on her sweet, small, marvelous face," saying:

> I am projected from thee,
> One that out of thy brain and heart thou causest to be—
> Extern to thee nothing.

Whether or not Elegeia, this pensive Muse was projected from the poet's brain and heart through a consistently nearsighted eye. No better instance of ironic revelation can be found than his account of the Genoese Mediterranean, whose "face first flash[ed] on [him]" across a wash-line of "high-hung smocks, / Crome handkerchiefs, scarlet hose, darned underfrocks"— "squalid undress."

Beyond elegiac balladry and the ironies of pilgrimage in *Poems of Past and Present* there exists a quizzical challenge to Dame Nature herself. Time tells the poet that the Mother's eyes are sightless (*The Lacking Sense*); "unlit with sight is she" (*Doom and She*). She laments "such insight in Earthland" as has been developed by "Man's mountings of mindsight" (*The Mother*

Mourns). She rues that she "did rashly / Man's vision unrein." A series of questions to her in *The Sleep-worker* begins with "When wilt thou wake, O Mother, wake and see?" She is mated with Doom or an unknowing God or a blundering Lord who says to Time (*By the Earth's Corpse*):

> "As when, in Noë's days,
> I whelmed the plains with sea,
> So at this last, when flesh
> And herbs but fossils be,
> And, all extinct, their piteous dust
> Revolves obliviously,
> That I made Earth, and life, and man,
> It still repenteth me!"

Nevertheless, there is also in the 1901 collection a strong indication that Hardy wishes to relate personal destiny rather with personal responsibility than with either Nature, Time, or an ineffectual Creator. Thus, he will disengage Man from the monistic All. The seven-beat lines of *In Tenebris II* discover that "what is the matter is I, I say." With this we may compare the discovery in *Tess's Lament:* "And it was I who did it all." Such convictions will be to the advantage of Hardy's personative writing through the years to come.

In 1909 under the general title, *Time's Laughingstocks*, there appeared along with love lyrics and country songs and occasional pieces a series of elegiac ballads in which personal destiny was taken further out of the hands of Nature, Time, and God, and character was more clearly revealed to be a personal matter, an asset or liability inviting some effort toward personal strength or dignity—the beginnings of an ethical action. The effort may be frustrated, as when in *The Revisitation* the feeble lover— "Alas, what greyhead perseveres!"—does not live up to his discovery that his beloved has "a nobler soul than [his]." Repentance may be delayed: the Trampwoman of *The Trampwoman's Tragedy* has deceived her lover into thinking that their child to come is not his, whereupon he slays his supposed rival and

is hanged; his baby is born dead. Then, when the true father's
ghost haunts the twice wretchedly bereaved woman,

> O doubt not but I told him then,
>   I told him then,
> That I had kept me from all men
>   Since we joined lips and swore.
> Whereat he smiled and thinned away
> As the wind stirred to call up day . . .
> —'Tis past! And here alone I stray
> Haunting the Western Moor.[9]

The mother of *A Sunday Morning Tragedy* is responsible for
the use of an ill-advised "brew" to prevent the birth of a child
to her daughter—"physic for untimely fruit." The daughter is
found dying just as her lover agrees to wed her. In a properly
tragic reversal, the mother says:

> I kissed her colding face and hair,
> I kissed her corpse—the bride to be!—
> My punishment I cannot bear,
> But pray God *not* to pity me.

The Flirt's Tragedy is a texture of false and true discoveries in-
volving murder and suicide. "Time," however, "unveils sorrows
and secrets":

> By inches the curtain was twitched at,
>   And slowly undrew.

In the recognition and acknowledgment of his mistakes the
protagonist pays the elegiac penalty, re-enacting dumbly the
whole weird drama,

> Each scene, sight, and circumstance passing
>   In spectral review.

[9] "Hardy considered this, upon the whole, his most successful poem."
It was first published in November, 1903, in the *North American Re-
view* (*The Later Years of Thomas Hardy*, by Florence Emily Hardy,
New York, 1930, pp. 92–93, 101–102).

As yet Hardy was inclined to record natural men and women as their own unenlightened or disillusioned selves, shiftless, fickle, jealous, suffering, without will or means to transmute the day's circumstances. However skillful he had become in many forms of *anagnorisis*, his changes of fortune lacked the true catharsis dependent upon the recognition and confession of guilt and the comfort of penitence; and for guilt and penitence he would need a frame of reference assuming in mankind an ethical and spiritual, and hence a religious nature. If his poems were not to be an increasingly monotonous echo of the *ubi sunt* laments of traditional lyric and the harsh disclosures and violent disasters of unreflective balladry, he must find a new pattern allowing analogy and ambivalence; for weightier themes both stronger contrast and higher tension were imperative.

Such an effort we discover at work in the use of an adversative structure for his ironic graphs of circumstantially delimited selves. His persons become ever more deeply involved in the struggle expressed by "but" and "yet": witness *The Curate's Kindness*, putting man and wife in the same poorhouse.

> I thought they'd be strangers aroun' me,
>> But she's to be there!
> Let me jump out o' waggon and go back and drown me
>> At Pummery or Ten-Hatches Weir.

The old woman of Autumn in *King's Hintock Park* resolves her ponderings on the deceitfulness of spring with an adversative "yet":

> Yet, Dear, though one may sigh,
>> Raking up leaves,
> New leaves will dance on high—
>> Earth never grieves!—
> Will not, when missed am I
>> Raking up leaves.

Personal experience is now and again disentangled from Time (*On the Departure Platform*): "Under the lamplight's fitful glowers" his beloved vanishes; she will "appear again . . . But never as then!"

> —"And why, young man, must eternally fly
> A joy you'll repeat, if you love her well?"
> —O friend, naught happens twice thus; why,
> I cannot tell.

"Nought happens twice thus" has its hopeful opportunity as well as its regretful disappointment. Again, there is the merest hint of a love lasting "in despite / Of Time, and wrack, and foes" (*Her Father*). And an elegiac ballad of the nineties entitled *The Division*, assumed to veil a crisis—and a challenge—in the married life of Thomas Hardy and Emma Lavinia Gifford,[10] looks forward to the profounder elegies of 1912–1913:

> O were it but the weather, Dear,
>   O were it but the miles
> That summed up all our severance,
>   There might be room for smiles.
>
> But that thwart thing betwixt us twain,
>   Which nothing cleaves or clears,
> Is more than distance, Dear, or rain,
>   And longer than the years!

This is indeed a momentous discovery, free of Time and Space, challenging a man and a woman themselves, himself and herself.

We may expect that when the poet puts time and space on one side of his "but" and on the other "that thwart thing . . . / Which nothing cleaves or clears," he is on his way to more courageous investigation and, it may be, a more luminous discovery. Almost in spite of himself he has acknowledged in *The Phantom* that identity is "borne within [the] brain":

> Foremost in my vision
>   Everywhere goes she;

[10] Evelyn Hardy, *Thomas Hardy: A Critical Biography* (New York, 1954).

> Change dissolves the landscapes,
> She abides with me.

Moreover, *Former Beauties*, second poem in the series *At Casterbridge Fair*, suggests that the middle-aged market-dames must have forgotten "what once they were,"

> Or memory would transfigure them, and show
> Them always fair.

We are therefore impelled to ask, by virtue of what power or powers transfiguration is achieved.

The vivid and tenacious memory Hardy had: he was always true to the past. The endurance, too, he had: the present must wear its mask (*The End of the Episode*):

> Ache deep; but make no moans:
> Smile out; but stilly suffer:
> The paths of love are rougher
> Than thoroughfares of stones.

Moreover, he had become aware of the range of metaphorical light and darkness and the scale of transformations to which natural phenomena might be referred. The gloomy wish of *Shut Out That Moon*—

> Within the common lamp-lit room
> Prison my eyes and thought—

is balanced by the truthful testimony of the sun on the letter: its rays "beamed / As brightly" on the page proving the beloved false "as if it had shown her true" (*The Sun on the Letter*). Time itself is allowed a future in which to redeem itself: "Sweet scenes are impending here" (*The Night of the Dance*). Finally, as if to alleviate error and sorrow, human mistakes are sometimes somehow good: the "fine lissom lad" born of a chance encounter brings no grief; "thankful I be / That his daddy once tied up my garter for me!" (*The Dark-eyed Gentleman*). Or, such accidents to maids are useful when they produce "sons for soldiering" (*The Husband's View*). The wanton Julie-Jane, "girl of joy," can laugh on her deathbed, "bubbling and brightsome eyed."

This emergence from the tyranny of Time into the ambivalence of personal character may be observed in *A Dream Question*, with its ethic "fourth dimension"; [11] and the humane action of the wife in *A Wife and Another* redeems the plight of her rival by disclosing their common nature as women and further discovering their spiritual kinship in a spiritual dependency: "I held I had not stirred God wrathfully." In *The Pine Planters* the unregarded wife looks ahead to long life for the tree she plants—the elegiac tree bearing witness to past, present, and future. The old lady in *One We Knew* has the power to overcome Time by bringing the past to life in the present:

> Past things retold were to her as things existent,
> Things present but as a tale.

The wish for what might be (*The Man He Killed*) and the riddling consideration of what might have been (*The Noble Lady's Tale*) further illustrate Hardy's willingness to depose Time, Circumstance, and Crass Casualty in favor of ethical choice and spiritual aspiration.[12]

On what mythic background or ethical system would such more finely human choices and efforts be made? What human values would be discovered? and in what metaphors and symbols would they be presented?

Earlier, in *The Lost Pyx*, he had recourse to ecclesiastical properties and rites faintly recalling Coleridgean romantic balladry. He would now attempt, like Browning, a monologue de-

---

[11] A phrase useful to D. H. Lawrence, a student of Hardy's writing.

[12] As early as 1877 he had acknowledged, with a side reference to Wordsworth, that "the art [in poetry and novel-writing] lies in making [Nature's] defects the basis of a hitherto unperceived beauty, by irradiating them with 'the light that never was' on their surface, but is seen to be latent in them by the spiritual eye" (*The Early Life of Thomas Hardy*, by Florence Emily Hardy, New York, 1928, p. 151).

pending on the structure of Christian doctrine; but this doctrine he would read with a skeptical eye. According to an old legend germane for a rational age and coming to Hardy possibly through Haeckel,[13] a Roman centurion named Panthera, in charge of Golgotha during the crucifixion of three malefactors, recognized in the weeping mother of one of them a maiden he had formerly known at Nazareth. There, thirty years ago, with this maiden he had formed a "true union, yea, / To the pure eye of her simplicity." Inferring the malefactor to be his son, he directed a legionary to pierce the young man's side and bring his end. "Thus Panthera's tale."

The world's greatest story as it unrolls through the mind of a merely natural man is an irony indeed, a tissue of shrewd inferences and near-discoveries. Lacking an epiphany, it suggests one; and, indeed, without the unspoken Christian legend as referent, the poem would be only one more harsh change of fortune, provoking "morbid dream or memory" without *anagnorisis*, peripety, or catharsis. Panthera's mind became "disarranged" in what are called "phantom-like" shocks: had his son not been a criminal, taken by the law? This is the "natural" assumption.

> "Fors Fortuna! He who goes fathering
> Gives frightful hostages to hazardry!"

In its bearing on Hardy's literary predicament *Panthera* is clear evidence of the need for a frame of reference less imitative of the Christian story but more exalted than Natural Man in a monistic All. For his total scheme he must henceforth look elsewhere. He had been reading Schopenhauer and von Hartmann as well as Haeckel; [14] in their hypotheses he might find a wider

---

[13] Prefatory note to *Panthera, Collected Poems*, p. 262.

[14] *Later Years*, p. 97; J. O. Bailey, *Thomas Hardy and the Cosmic Mind: A New Reading of "The Dynasts"* (The University of North Carolina Press, 1956), pp. 9–10.

symbolic opportunity for the interpretation of man in groups, Social Man.

For several years he had been planning "an Iliad of Europe," Homeric balladry without the gods; and by 1892 this had become a kind of puppet show in which the "characters" were not allowed to act "under the influence of reason." Although *The Dynasts* (in three parts, published in 1903, 1906, 1908) was announced as an epic-drama, it proved to be neither dramatic nor epic: in it the agents were given no responsible choice, and the action appeared as the irresponsible activity of an Urging Immanence. Hardy acknowledged that he had made no attempt "to create that completely organic structure of action, and closely-webbed development of character and motive, which are demanded in a drama strictly self-contained." His Napoleon confesses himself a puppet of the Immanent Will: "I have ever known / That such a Will I passively obeyed." Likewise caught in "It's" tissue, Wellington is shown "as acting" while discovering his "intention to act." [15] These assumptions are far more poetically disabling than those of the epic century of Milton and Daniel, for instance, when the energies and sympathies of humanity were at their height and all knew

> that unless above himself he can
> Erect himself, how poor a thing is man.[16]

Even for the purposes of a mighty chronicle Hardy's spurious plot breaks down into epylls and idylls. Although these are undeniably graphic, the spectacle of puppet-like men and women and societies has a merely superficial verisimilitude. There is no peripety likely and there is no valid discovery in sight. Napoleon discovers—and Hardy must have suspected—that

[15] *The Dynasts*, pp. 505, 519–520.
[16] Daniel's translation of Seneca in a poem for the Lady Margaret, Duchess of Cumberland—a passage that Wordsworth quoted in *The Excursion* (IV, 330–331).

> To shoulder Christ from out the topmost niche
> In human fame, as once I fondly felt,
> Was not for me.

To extricate these persons from mere juxtaposition in time and space, and as a way of compensating for the rational and spiritual values of which he had depleted them—and also as a device for accomplishing symbolic tension—the poet envisaged "supernatural spectators," "impersonated abstractions or Intelligences, called Spirits." These would discuss the nature of the Immanent Will: might the Unconscious be developing toward Consciousness and Compassion? Meanwhile Humanity would suffer. "Why?" "why?": "Last as first the question rings." With the dispassionate Spirit of the Years to preside over their metaphysical speculations, the Spirits Sinister and Ironic argue against the Spirit of the Pities, who has a kind heart as well as a "sceptic eye." The monistic "All" is thus split up into puppetry on the one hand and on the other a fantastic extrahuman machinery performing the functions denied to men and women.

Like the elegist Wordsworth a century ago, Hardy the elegist has resorted to dialectic. Yet, whereas the long debate between the skeptical Solitary and the compassionate Wanderer of *The Excursion* was carried on man to man, now in *The Dynasts* all has been brought into an abstract scheme. The best Hardy can accomplish in the way of an elegiac *anagnorisis* is the familiar discovery of identity in superficial appearance and behavior: such is Napoleon; such is human life. Nor is Hardy's momentous record of the plight of Natural Man more hopeful for Social Man: men in groups, too, are merely what they are. And, yet, as participants or readers we suffer.

That Hardy had Wordsworth in mind is suggested by the quotation for the Preface to *The Dynasts* from the lines composed on the banks of the Wye: "the burthen of the mystery." That he had *The Excursion* also specifically in mind is probable. A phrase quoted in his Hymn of the Pities in the After Scene, "fulfil their joy," has a Wordsworthian ring; and when we turn back to the Hymn of the Pastor to the Eternal Spirit at the end of the ninth and last book of *The Excursion,* among other similarities in matter and form we find the following:

> Almighty Lord, thy further grace impart!
> And with that help the wonder shall be seen
> *Fulfilled,* the *hope* accomplished; and thy praise
> Be sung with transport and unceasing *joy.*[17]

A century later Hardy's Pities sing to the "Great and Good":

> We hold that Thy unscanted scope
> Affords a food for final Hope.
>
> . . . . .
>
> And these pale panting multitudes
> Seen surging here, their moils, their moods,
> All shall "fulfil their joy" in Thee,
> In Thee abide eternally!
> Exultant adoration give
> The Alone, through Whom all living live,
> The Alone, in Whom all dying die,
> Whose means the End shall justify.

When the Wordsworth and Hardy Hymns are studied together in their context of the French and English dynastic wars, we gain a sense of elegiac similarity along with further evidence that a hundred years have passed by.

Nevertheless, we should beware of saying about *The Dynasts* what Jeffrey said about *The Excursion:* "This will never do." Hardy's poem has supplied the literature of our century with its characteristic cruces. In it yawn all the mighty schisms and fissures of modern life and modern art. In its skeptical shadow have flourished satire and irony. It prefigured vast cinematographic marvels. Above all, it introduced an epoch whose gen-

---

[17] My italics. The word "fulfil" should be related also to Mary's Magnificat (Luke, I.55): "He hath filled the hungry with good things." In a footnote Hardy quotes the Greek Testament for another line of his Hymn: "Who hurlest Dynasts from their thrones."

erations are still oppressed with monstrous conflicts and grandiose adventure. It repays study as an effort to fit social disasters with appropriate symbols of darkness and dim light. More profoundly, it arouses although it can scarcely relieve our feelings of pity and terror. We suffer, but we see only in part.

Much of Hardy's attendant imagery is stage direction to open and shut scenes as it were with sunrise and sunset. For instance, day breaks and night darkens under all conceivable weather conditions. In Spain the sun is sultry and there are fogs of dust; on the snow-disastered retreat from Moscow, "the stars come out in unusual brilliancy." At worst the actual weather is compounded of rain and mud and rimy mist below and clouds and gloom above.

How far is such imagery metaphorical? To quote the Third Servant in Part III, Act IV, scene iii:

> Dost know what a metaphor is, comrade?
> I brim with them at this historic time.
> . . . My metaphor is one may'st
> have met with on the rare times when
> th' hast been in good society. Here it
> is: The storm that roots [uproots] the
> pine spares the p–s–b–d [pissabed,
> i.e., the dandelion, bluet, oxeye daisy].

We can infer, therefore, that Hardy's natural storms are metaphors of the tempestuous chronicle they help to interpret. On the face of Napoleon, darkening as he walks in his wedding procession, sunny with joy at the birth of an heir, we have a figurative hint as to the emotional temperature; and from his eyes as they flash or deaden we infer the state of his energies.

Is this metaphorical language characteristic of an elegy? Yes, it goes from ignorance to discovery. At first, in the words of the boisterous French "crowd," their Emperor will show himself

> Unwavering, keen, and irresistible
> As is the lightning-prong.

In the "sunlight piercing the clerestory windows" of Milan Cathedral he is assured by the Archbishop Caprara that his entrance has "streamed radiance on [their] ancient capital." Under later disasters, however, he makes a rare acknowledgment of dependency, exclaiming "Not Russia but God's sky has conquered me!" At Charleroi he has in his sleep a vision of reproachful skeletons and corpses rising from his various battlefields in various stages of decay. "He jumps up in a sweat and puts out the last candle." Again, on the field of Waterloo, he cries out from stupefied sleep:

> A horrible dream has gripped me—horrible!
> I saw before me Lannes—just as he looked
> That day at Aspern: mutilated, bleeding!
> "What—blood again?" he said to me. "Still blood?"

This further acknowledgment, that war is horrible, comes as near to a proper discovery as any *The Dynasts* affords, but it is not attended by a proper reversal. Instead the confirmed warrior, puppet-twitched, "takes snuff vehemently, and looks through his glass" to say:

> All my star asks now
> Is to break some half-dozen of those blocks
> Of English yonder.

This is not to be. Wandering forlorn and listless "on a jaded horse" through the moonlit Wood of Bossa, he falls into a fitful sleep, from which he is "stung by spectral questionings" to confess that

> Great men are meteors that consume themselves
> To light the earth. This is my burnt-out hour.

"The moon sinks, and darkness blots out Napoleon and the scene."

There are also frequent instances of effortful man-made light to accompany revelations of strength or weakness, good or ill fortune. Beacons, rockets, bivouac fires, torches, riding-lights of ships in harbor, "the flashing of the priming-pan and muzzles" on fields of battle contrast grimly with the brass chandeliers of the Assembly Rooms at Brighton, the "many-candled saloon" in Paris, the fête at Vauxhall Gardens to celebrate the success of Wellington at Vitoria with "a blaze of lamps and candles . . . a great artificial sun"; in the London opera house are "wax candles"—and the candle snuffers; "the light of a thousand candles" blazes up into the eyes of Marie Louise at Vienna; the "candles" are extinguished in a ballroom in Brussels. While the Kremlin burns, "cocks crow, thinking it sunrise, ere they are burnt to death." The faces of the crowd are "brass-bright" while Napoleon is burned in effigy at Casterbridge. Before Coruña under a dark sky Sir John Moore rallies the English out of despair to victory; except for his death

> the hour had shone
> A star amid these days of gloom!

And it may be that, when Sir John is hurriedly interred by the light of a glimmering "lantern," the skeptical Hardy furnishes his reader with the most traditionally significant discovery of the poem, and a kind of epiphany: "I am the resurrection and the life, saith the Lord: he that believeth in me, though he were dead, yet shall he live."

Spyglasses have their horizontal place in the chronicle: Napoleon and the Emperor of Austria make persistent albeit unavailing use of them. But it is not often that Hardy allows himself, his persons, or his reader to look up. Rather, he takes us to a "lofty point of vision" whence we can minify earth and its creatures rather than magnify the constellations. Thus, terrestrial life becomes an ironic spectacle instead of an aspiring drama. "Europe is disclosed as a prone and emaciated figure, the Alps shaping like a backbone, and the branching mountain-chains the ribs, the peninsular plateau of Spain forming a head." The peoples are seen "writhing, crawling, heaving, and vibrating." Militant humanity appears as "files of ants crawling along a strip of garden matting," "a school of mackerel," the "insect-creep" of "molluscs on a leaf," "swans [in] a creek at feeding-time," "a thicket of reeds in which every reed should be a man." This device, familiar to satirists and ironists and elegists of all times—witness Swift and Kafka, for instance—permits the better reduction into focus of wide areas of experience. It tells us more about Hardy's poetry than do his pseudophilosophical "-isms."

There also occurs here and there during the course of events a revelatory "unnatural light," usurping that of the sun, "bringing into view"—elegiac view—the brain tissues of the Immanent Will, "a brain whose whole connotes the Everywhere." In such a seeming "transparency, . . . exhibiting as one organism the anatomy of life and movement in all humanity and vitalized matter included in the display," we have a theatric equivalent of the monistic "All." This we owe chiefly to the Spirit of the Years, who has the gift "to visualize the Mode." Unnatural light, however, proves less effective as an elegiac device than celestial luminaries; and abstract Intelligences accomplish less for Hardy's metaphorical range than the older Pantheon of gods or the Christian hierarchy had done for previous elegists.

Recalling that *The Excursion* was a dead end in Wordsworth's poetical career, and that he went back from it to simpler elegies and elegiac balladry or to gnomic sonnets, we note without surprise that *The Dynasts* was a dead end for Hardy, too. In summoning him back from puppetry and argumentative Intelligences to the portraiture of natural Man in a spiritual dependency, his personative and ethical genius was to serve him well. We need not avoid the conviction that Hardy's Spirit of the Pities, for a brief moment reaching up out of the grip of the Immanent and yet Unconscious Will to

> The Alone, through Whom all living live,
> The Alone, in Whom all dying die,

owes a debt to Wordsworth's Wanderer and Pastor. But we must note that this debt seems to have been repudiated when, according to his second wife, at the Treaty of Versailles the completely disillusioned poet said that, had *The Dynasts* been written later, he would have omitted from it even a faint evolutionary hope.

Four years after Part III of *The Dynasts* was published, Emma Lavinia Hardy died unexpectedly in November of 1912. This ending to what is thought to have been an ambivalent experience in Hardy's own life demanded review; henceforth his writing showed him more personally involved than ever before. The unifying of diverse elements in his memory was accomplished through what he calls in the first poem of Lyrics and Reveries of the volume *Satires of Circumstance* the "intenser / Stare of the mind." The landscape in front of him seemed "but a ghostlike gauze" to "infinite spectacles" within, spectacles of "speechful faces, gazing insistent," "scenes miscalled of the bygone." The conviction deepened within him that (*To Meet or Otherwise*)

> Nor God nor Demon can undo the done,
>   Unsight the seen.

The way was ready for a more searching study of elegiac themes and a more successful expression of elegiac feeling.

And so it came about. Deserving consideration along with Propertius' Books of Cynthia and Wordsworth's poems of Lucy, Hardy's memorial series for his first wife, *1912–1913: veteris vestigia flammae*, illustrates elegiac poetry at its finest. Like Cynthia and Lucy, Emma Lavinia, "Em," has been set forth *sub specie aeternitatis*.

> You were she who abode
> By those red-veined rocks far West,
> You were the swan-necked one who rode
> Along the beetling Beeny Crest,

> And, reining nigh me,
> Would muse and eye me,
> While Life unrolled us its very best.

Now that he could no longer see her in the perspective "at the end of the alley of bending boughs,"

> O you could not know
> That such swift fleeing
> No soul foreseeing—
> Not even I—would undo me so!

He recalled her face as recently lit by the borough lights

> —all undiscerned
> To be in a week the face of the dead.

As if he remembered Wordsworth's cry, "oh! the difference to me," he walked "to the hill-top tree,"

> Surveyed around
> The familiar ground
> By myself again:
> What difference, then?

At first it is "darkening dankness," "rain," that furnish the elegiac tone but little by little memories of sunny days come back—

> Soon will be growing
>   Green blades from her mound,
> And daisies be showing
>   Like stars on the ground.

Particularly vivid is the memory of first meeting:

> I found her out there
> On a slope few see,
> That falls westwardly
> To the salt-edged air,
> Where the ocean breaks

> On the purple strand,
> And the hurricane shakes
> The solid land.

"Em" had been born "a little girl of grace," to be forever associated with delicate or powerful motion. She enjoyed parties and junketings and picnics. In a summer shower she "would quicken and quicken each tentative tread." She loved the "blind gales" of the Atlantic, when her cheek was "flapped . . . like a flail" by "a wind-tugged tress." She was a horsewoman:

> Nobody calls to mind that here
> Upon Boterel Hill, where the waggoners skid,
> With cheeks whose airy flush outbid
> Fresh fruit in bloom, and free of fear,
> She cantered down, as if she must fall
>   (Though she never did),
>   To the charm of all.

And as a horsewoman she first engaged his affection—

O the opal and the sapphire of that wandering western sea,
And the woman riding high above with bright hair flapping free—
The woman whom I loved so, and who loyally loved me.

. . . . .

A little cloud then cloaked us, and there flew an irised rain,
And the Atlantic dyed its levels with a dull misfeatured stain,
And then the sun burst out again, and purples prinked the main.

The swing of balladry served Hardy as it had served Wordsworth. Finally, it is as a Phantom Horsewoman that he immortalizes Emma, part of a scene "more clear than today," "an instant thing":

> A ghost-girl-rider. And though, toil-tried,
>   He withers daily,
>   Time touches her not,
>   But she still rides gaily
>   In his rapt thought

On that shagged and shaly
Atlantic spot,
And as when first eyed
Draws rein and sings to the swing of the tide.

After death the look of her—and here we remember the dream of Propertius—has grown more vivid:

Where you will next be there's no knowing,
Facing about me everywhere,
With your nut-coloured hair,
And gray eyes and rose-flush coming and going.

Again, like that earlier poet whose Lucy dwelt more serenely with Nature "beside the springs of Dove," he has recognized a place, Saint-Juliot [18]—"What's Juliot to me?"—as the "key" to much of his life.

Yes. I have had dreams of that place in the West,
And a maiden abiding
Thereat as in hiding;
Fair-eyed and white-shouldered, broad-browed and brown-tressed,

And of how, coastward bound on a night long ago,
There lonely I found her,
The sea-birds around her,
And other than nigh things uncaring to know.

.   .   .   .   .
Does there even a place like Saint-Juliot exist?
Or a Vallency Valley
With stream and leafed alley,
Or Beeny, or Bos with its flounce flinging mist?

Thus, to the gallery of natural men and women in his novels Hardy has added one more elegiac symbol, the horsewoman. D. H. Lawrence would observe this association of woman and

[18] St. Juliot was in West Cornwall, not far from Tintagel: Hardy's Lyonnesse in one of his happiest lyrics, "When I set out for Lyonnesse," 1870, the year of his meeting with Emma Lavinia Gifford.

horse and distort it into less than full human relevance—but that is another story. Unlike the *Woman Who Rode Away* and the mistress of *St. Mawr*, the Woman who rode upon Boterel Hill and out from Saint-Juliot along the beetling Beeny Crest or along the ragged and shaly Atlantic shore was an "instant thing" and would stay put.

This view of everything as "instant" is the chief accomplishment of Hardy's elegiac thought.[19] Enough in itself, vision scarcely needs the "re-enactment" of balladry. Moreover, Hardy's discoveries now take the form of *phantoms*, appearances in which identity is recognized with enhanced meaning and value. It was "for its revelations" that the owner of The Cheval Glass "brought it oversea." "Queries breed" within the lover as to

> whether a phantom
> Had my heed
> On that strange night, or was it some wrecked heart indeed?

The Christmas waits see "a strange phantasmal sight" in the mirror: the lady of the manor, whose "roving spouse" has been reported dead, "dancing alone . . . / Thin-draped in her robe of night." The dead are allowed to speak in their own persons. They revisit the living and ask questions. Even for such violent ballads as *In the Servants' Quarters*, *The Work Box*, and *The Sacrilege*, the past is evoked with intensified humanity; and the "fifteen glimpses"[20] included in a series giving its title to the whole volume, *Satires of Circumstances*, are inferred discoveries of what should have been on the contrasting background of what is. Possibly the two outstanding poems bearing witness by token are *In the British Museum* and *The Abbey Mason*, where "stone" and "ogive" are used to bring to life again "the voice of Paul" and the nameless artist of Gloucester Cathedral.

---

[19] He noted on June 10, 1923 (*Later Years*, p. 231), "that things and events always were, are, and will be (e.g. Emma, Mother and Father are living still in the past)."

[20] First published in a periodical, 1911 (*Later Years*, p. 164).

It is not necessary to seek in *Moments of Vision* for other than the kind of *anagnorisis* indicated by the title, again the Wordsworthian "spots of time." These poems have no specious order or schematic purpose; nor do they reveal any explicit philosophy. Nevertheless, we may observe with profit to our understanding of his art the ways in which this master of revelatory devices modified bold disclosures of fact or startling discoveries of identity into aesthetic awareness of human value. To such an end the renewal of formal feeling is of the utmost importance; and for such renewal the chance occasion or casual object will suffice. Therefore, the poems are teased into being by way of mirror, lighted window, old furniture, portrait, photograph; old psalm tunes, violin, minster clock, chimes; bridge, stile, runic stone, handpost at the crossways; yew, grass, rose; pallid moth, blinded bird. *The Last Signal* with its reflected flash from the fire of the sun on the coffin of William Barnes gives that memorial verse its peculiar glory:

> Looking harder and harder I knew what it meant—
> The sudden shine sent from the livid east scene.
>
>   .   .   .   .   .
>
> Thus a farewell to me he signalled on his graveway,
>   As with a wave of his hand.

"From an old note" Emma Lavinia was sketched as seen and heard—now, alas! too late—near the River Stour, where their early life together had been lived. Or he peered again toward Beeny in the West:

> "It never looks like summer here
>   On Beeny by the sea."
> But though she saw its look as drear,
>   Summer it seemed to me.
>
> It never looks like summer now
>   Whatever weather's there;
> But ah, it cannot anyhow,
>   On Beeny or elsewhere.

The dominant mood is regret, and generally the poems of this series, as often henceforth, are lyrics, lyrical ballads, or lyrical idylls in which feeling is aroused and channeled toward an ever finer *aesthesis*. Although he no longer has the will to challenge or to probe as an elegist, he has thrown down the gage to Time, Circumstance, and Crass Casualty and now and then vanquishes them quite. Let us refer to his own testimony in *For Life I Never Cared Greatly*, where Life, "lifting its hand" over "conditions of doubt,"

> uncloaked a star,
> Uncloaked it from fog-damps afar,
> And showed its beams burning from pole to horizon
> As bright as a brand.

"And so," says Hardy, "thus re-illumed [I] have no humour for letting my pilgrimage fail."

There follows a series of patriotic poems grouped around the outbreak of war in 1914. One of them, written in 1913, before the fact, is an elegiac ballad of high quality (*His Country*):

> I journeyed from my native spot
>   Across the south sea shine
> And found that people in hall and cot
> Laboured and suffered each his lot
>   Even as I did mine.
>   .   .   .   .
> I traced the whole celestial round,
>   Homing the other side;
> Then said I, "What is there to bound
> My denizenship? It seems I have found
>   Its scope to be world-wide."

Even as we note the echoes of Coleridge's rhythms and axioms and the poet's restless dismay in the face of a monstrous new world, wider than the British Empire, we realize that Hardy is yet too near global tensions and their event in war to deal with them. "Phantasmal" are the fears with which he awaits the New

Year; and he looks up from his writing to hear the full moon
say:

> And now I am curious to look
> Into the blinkered mind
> Of one who wants to write a book
> In a world of such a kind.

Technically, these Moments of Vision are still indebted to the
ballad measure and such ballad-like effects as tetrameter or hep-
tameter afford.[21] An exquisite example of the modified ballad
is *The Last Performance;* yet here, too, the beginnings of a more
artful pattern and a more sophisticated use of refrain can be
detected, a pattern deeply affecting, also, in *The Five Students*
but all too likely to harden into metrical type.

The Apology for *Late Lyrics and Earlier,* published in the
notable year of Mr. Eliot's *The Waste Land* and D. H. Lawrence's *Fantasia of the Unconscious,* shows Hardy writing critical prose as vigorous and pointed as that with which his successors took over the second decade of what he called "our
prematurely afflicted century." This Apology furnishes us with
one of the clearest statements of Hardy's own generic purposes.
It represents the poet as an elegist, concerned with—here Hardy
quotes Wordsworth—"obstinate questionings" and "blank misgivings." As in his own earlier *In Tenebris,* he is one to take
his "full look at the Worst" in order to discover his "way to
the Better." He is engaged in the "exploration of reality, and
its frank recognition stage by stage along the survey, with an
eye to the best consummation possible." Such "evolutionary
meliorism" predicates of human destiny what the poet will
record in literary form as *anagnorises,* clearer and clearer as

---

[21] Late in life, November 28, 1927, he confessed that his model for
a poem he might like to contribute to an anthology was " 'Drink to me
only . . .' by Ben Jonson" (*Later Years,* p. 263). Hardy's many modifications of ballad metres have been traced in a careful study by Elizabeth
Cathcart Hickson, *The Versification of Thomas Hardy* (University of
Pennsylvania Press, 1931).

thought probes deeper and deeper. Specifically, he agrees with Matthew Arnold that "the real function of poetry" is "the application of ideas to life." He suggests as causes of a newly threatened Dark Age "the barbarizing of taste in the younger minds by the dark madness of the late war, the unabashed cultivation of selfishness in all classes, the plethoric growth of knowledge simultaneously with the stunting of wisdom, 'a degrading thirst after outrageous stimulation'" (here he quotes Wordsworth again). For the contemporary critic, also, he has a rebuke, because of

"the satirizing of individuality, the lack of whole-seeing in contemporary estimates of poetry and kindred work, the knowingness affected by junior reviewers, the overgrowth of meticulousness in their peerings for an opinion, as if it were a cultivated habit in them to scrutinize the toolmarks and be blind to the building, to hearken for the key-creaks and be deaf to the diapason, to judge the landscape by a nocturnal exploration with a flash lantern."

At this we wonder whether Hardy's own habit as a nearsighted young writer rose up in memory to sharpen his phrases. Now at last he can hope for

an alliance between religion, which must be retained unless the world is to perish, and complete rationality, which must come, unless also the world is to perish, by means of the interfusing effect of poetry—"the breath and finer spirit of all knowledge; the impassioned expression of science," as it was defined by an English poet who was quite orthodox in his ideas.

Thus 1802–1822 has spoken to 1922, Wordsworth to Hardy.

With the poems that follow these sentiments Hardy is in the orbit of Yeats, and "showings beyond our sphere" attract his "vision." The word "phasm" creeps into his verses. Revelation takes place as the result of a series of blindnesses. He experiments with what is contrary to fact, with "as it were." This lessens in his writing the articulate procedure of elegy and in-

tensifies the feeling: there are many Songs. The outer eye and
ear rest while regret wakes the inner eye and the inner ear.
References to music, singing, the rhythm of the dance, or the
choiring in old churches and churchyards bear witness to activities of the poet's young manhood. Although occasional phrases
display his former power to use words as keys to open old doors
on new vistas, he has not the zest of many younger poets to
make diction do all the work of poetry; he holds fast to persons
and situations as elegiac tools. In a critical retrospect this may be
to his advantage.

It would be of no more avail with Hardy than with Wordsworth to regret as a poetical anticlimax what are symptoms of
the failing energies of old age. Thought is less urgent and curiosity less eager in the poems of the twenties. Yet Hardy's long
training in personative writing and his habit of using persons for
symbols gave rise in the series of 1922 and in *Human Shows*
of 1925 and *Winter Words* of 1928 to a notable renaissance of
elegiac balladry, as would be true of Yeats also in his last decade.
Occasional stars light the gloom. In *The Second Night* "a mad
star crossed the sky to the sea"; and when the tardy, faithless
lover learned of the lady's suicide, "Again a star overhead /
Shot through the firmament." *At Shag's Heath, 1685*, where the
"heartless woman" betrayed the "sweet King Monmouth, he,"
the kindly visitor appeared to her at the window on the night
after his beheading,

> All blood and blear, and hacked about,
> With heavy eyes, and rumpled hair.
>
> .   .   .   .   .
>
> "Yes, lovely cruel one!" he said
> In through the mullioned pane, shroud pale,
> "I love you still, would kiss you now,
> But blood would stain your nighty-rail!"
> —That's all, And so to drown I go:
> O wear no weeds, my friends, for me . . .

> When comes the waterman, he'll say,
>   "Who's done her thuswise?"—'Twill be, yea,
>   Sweet, slain King Monmouth—he!

"The sun was shining" when Miller Knox rode to market; "the sun was set" when he ambled "home-along . . . in the gray" to discover his good wife hanged "by her own rash and passionate hand" (*At the Mill*). " 'Twas night-time, towards the middle part" when the bride of *The Forbidden Banns*, destined to bear her husband two idiot children, first learned that he regretted wedding her against his father's wishes.

> She turned from one to the other side,
>   And a sad woman was she
> As he went on: "He'd not have died
>   Had it not been for me!"
>   . . . . .
> "Hearken to me, my son. No: No:
>   There's madness in her blood!"
> Those were his father's words; and lo,
>   Now, now he understood.

In *Winter Words*, published after his death in 1928, Hardy's long preoccupation with human personality is again seen to be no mere sketching of external characteristics. *The Whaler's Wife* and *The War-Wife of Catknoll* probe situations in order to challenge, not circumstance but human unwisdom, as revealed in desertion, infidelity, suicide.

> "She kept her true a year or more
>   Against the young men all;
> Yes, kept her true a year or more,
>   And they were most to blame.
> There was Will Peach who plays the flute,
> And Waywell with the dandy suit,
> And Nobb, and Knight. . . . But she's been mute
>   As to the father's name."

Such are the precursors of Yeats's Crazy Jane and her Jack.
Witness also, Hardy's Jack in *The Catching Ballet of the Wedding Clothes* (1919), where

> 'Twas told that, years after,
>   When autumn winds wave,
> A wealthy old lady
>   Stood long at Jack's grave,
> The while her coach waited:—
>   She mused there; and then
> She stepped in, and never
>   Came hither again.

It is possibly in *The Clasped Skeletons* that Hardy can be discovered most like himself. Here we have his fusing of the present and a surmised date of 1800 B.C. "in an Ancient British barrow near the writer's house": Time and Space both yield to the poet.

> O why did we uncover to view
>   So closely clasped a pair?
> Your chalky bedclothes over you
>   This long time here!
>
> Ere Paris lay with Helena—
>   The poet's dearest dear—
> Ere David bedded Bathsheba
>   You two were bedded here.
>
> .   .   .   .
>
> Ages before Monk Abélard
>   Gained tender Héloise' ear,
> And loved and lay with her till scarred,
>   Had you lain loving here.
>
> So long, beyond chronology,
>   Lovers in death as 't were,
> So long in placid dignity
>   Have you lain here.

"Length of time" is "but dream."

Winter Words ends with an elegiac riddle, a resolve to keep all hidden:

> From now alway
> Till my last day
> What I discern I will not say.

We, however, must go on toward further discoveries, following Hardy's Dora to Ireland "through the drift and darkness" of our study of elegy.

> That was where, yea, Ireland,
>   Dora wished to be:
> When she felt, in lone times,
>   Shoots of misery,
> Often there, in Ireland,
>   Dora wished to be.
>
>   . . . . .
>
> Dora's gone to Ireland
>   Through the sleet and snow;
> Promptly she has gone there
>   In a ship, although
> Why she's gone to Ireland
>   Dora does not know.

CHAPTER XII

Flute Song Yesterday: W. B. Yeats

THE career of William Butler Yeats was a long unresting search for luminous truth, "not abstract truth, but a kind of vision of reality which satisfies the whole being." [1] The very daring of his investigations into the mind of man became the index of his poetry. Not only in his personal habit do we find clear evidence of his elegiac imagination; throughout his writing as a whole he dealt mainly with elegiac themes, love and beauty, transience, death, the inner nature and the ultimate destiny of man. Biographies and autobiographies set forth in abundant detail the speculative course of his amazing energy. Again and again he explicitly revealed himself and his purpose; for instance, in his Diary for August, 1910: "Words are with me a means of investigation rather than a means of action." [2] His notable poems [3] often end with a riddle or a query: witness *Among School Children* (1927), where he walked "through the long schoolroom questioning"—

[1] From a letter to his father, September 12, [1914] (*The Letters of W. B. Yeats*, ed. Allan Wade, New York, 1955, p. 588).

[2] Quoted by A. Norman Jeffares, *W. B. Yeats* (Yale University Press, 1949), p. 161

[3] The poetry of Yeats is quoted from *The Variorum Edition of the Poems of W. B. Yeats*, ed. Peter Allt and Russell K. Alspach (New York, 1957); quoted by permission of Macmillan and Co., Ltd.

> O body swayed to music, O brightening glance,
> How can we know the dancer from the dance?

Meditating at Algeciras not much later, he thought of death as an inquest:

> Greater glory in the sun,
> An evening chill upon the air,
> Bid imagination run
> Much on the Great Questioner;
> What He can question, what if questioned I
> Can with a fitting confidence reply.

And toward the end of his long and persistent search, *The Man and the Echo* puts into memorable form the fate of every elegist:

> All that I have said and done,
> Now that I am old and ill,
> Turns into a question till
> I lie awake night after night
> And never get the answers right.

Preceding him by a mere century, Wordsworth, too, had shaped his experience into autobiographical poetry, *The Prelude*, where the actual course of personal events was examined for the truth about love, love of nature and love of man, love of country, fidelity to poetic insight and religious infinitude. Crises in the progress of the two poets were alike: thwarted love somehow redeemed in marriage, and violence of feeling brought under control by stern discipline; the slow emergence from a vague animism on Wordsworth's part, and the artful organization of a sprawling occultism by Yeats; Wordsworth's involvement in the French and Spanish struggles for liberty (*Prelude* IX, X, XI and *The Convention of Cintra*) paralleled by Yeats's efforts toward a renascent Ireland, with disillusionment to follow; the rededication of both in their maturity as students of the classical and Christian cultures and interpreters of history

(*Ecclesiastical Sonnets* and "Dove or Swan"). Although Wordsworth was earlier deflected toward gnomic poetry and Yeats
became involved during the height of his career with diagrams
and ethical graphs, at their best each is a free-swinging fellow
of Tyrtaeus and Solon and Theognis, very much a skeptical
and didactic citizen of the world. Moreover, and of final significance, by no other recent poet are the great wholesome adventures of Wordsworth, Coleridge, and Blake toward unity more
fittingly re-enacted than by Yeats.

Yeats's expressive patterns grew to be more like those of the
spare Wordsworth than like the bounty of either Coleridge or
Blake, whose facility engendered a kind of spurious language
and spendthrift imagery. Yeats and Wordsworth were economical with words and symbols and rhythms, tireless in revision
even to the end of life. When young, both had reached for the
ballad form as the most fitting vehicle for intense personal experience.[4] Wordsworth came soon into the belief that the "language really used by men" was most appropriate for poetical
composition, and little by little Yeats developed a preference for
"ordinary modern speech." Neither poet was in the Greek sense
dramatic; neither was primarily concerned with external action,
praxis, or with plot, *mythos*. There are differences: Wordsworth went on from investigation into theory and doctrine;
Yeats with not less insight gave new life to ritual.[5] Wordsworth

[4] The interest of Scott and Southey in the balladry of event and of
Wordsworth and Coleridge in elegiac balladry can be paralleled by
Yeats's study, 1887–1889, of Irish balladry, in company with Katherine
Tynan, John O'Leary and his sister, Dr. Douglas Hyde, and Dr. John
Todhunter. Their "ballad book," *Poems and Ballads of Young Ireland*,
was published in May, 1888. On December 21 of that year Yeats wrote
to Miss Tynan: "I do not mean that we should not go to old ballads
and poems for inspiration, but we should search them for new methods
of expression" (*Letters*, pp. 37, n. 1, 98). Modified ballad rhythms were
to be, if not the prevailing music of Yeats's poetry, one of its major
delights.

[5] Yeats to Sturge Moore: "I always feel that my work is not drama
but the ritual of a lost faith" (quoted by Richard Ellmann, *The Identity
of Yeats*, Oxford University Press, 1954, p. 179).

diminished himself as an elegiac *persona;* Yeats emphasized and enhanced himself. Wordsworth clarified; Yeats mystified.

In order to ally the two poets in the service of a common elegiac tradition we shall not lose sight of the earlier even as we study the later. This is an alliance not often mentioned,[6] possibly because they differ in their choice and use of symbols. Whereas Nature's infinite variety served the former, the latter preferred an infinitely various artifice: weaving and goldsmithery, the kinaesthetic arts of dance and sex, theatrical and architectural accoutrements and objects such as mask and sword and tower, mathematical and astrological conceits such as gyres and "phases." Yeatsian references to Nature are usually modes of subjective artifice. A tree is not "a tree, of many, one," as it had been for Wordsworth; it is not even the "Green Tree" of William Morris;[7] it has become a ritual tree with a mask hanging on it or a great rooted symbolic blossomer; or it is the Tree of Life, upon which we must find "some place . . . for the Phoenix nest."[8] Thus, Yeats not only contrived his symbols and his poems; he also contrived his philosophy and his history. Above all—his most important contrivance—he contrived himself. Artists and poets might themselves be "Artificers of the Great Moment";[9] but he begged that the Sages of Byzantium gather him, too, "into the artifice of eternity."

Again, Yeats was more intensely kinaesthetic than Wordsworth, a trait that helped him toward love elegy with its strong pulsations as thought drives through waves of feeling. Dancer and the dance were to contend with tower, bird, and moon as ultimate symbols of his imaginative experience. From the speedy dancing of the hundred merry ladies of romance (*Oisin*) or the

[6] Yet see Richard Ellmann's last paragraph in *Yeats: The Man and the Masks* (New York, 1948); and Donald A. Stauffer, *The Golden Nightingale* (New York, 1949), p. 22.

[7] See Yeats on Morris in "The Happiest of the Poets," *Essays* (New York, 1924), p. 77.

[8] "Discoveries," *Essays*, p. 337.

[9] "Poetry and Tradition," *Essays*, p. 314.

"dreary dancing" of pastoral lament on to the "footstep wary"
and "timid grace" of the Countess Cathleen in Paradise—"What
a dancer glimmering!"—Yeats proved as true to Terpsichore as
to Elegeia. Turning his pages we are always aware of delicate
motion suggestive of the dance form: "moments of glad grace";
Helen treading "so sweetly proud"; loves changed "while dancing"; "golden king and silver lady . . . / Prancing round and
prancing up"; Tom Roughly dancing "a measure" on the grave
of his dearest friend; Sheba leading Solomon "a dance"; the
"cradles that a man must needs be rocked in"; the moon spinning round "like a top" as Minnaloushe lifts his "delicate feet."
It is to be expected, then, that in the greater poems "blood-
begotten spirits" die "into a dance" and the dead still dream
of dancing. Moreover, the elaborate courtesies of *A Vision*—
Will and Mask and Body of Fate and Creative Mask in a kind
of quadrille,[10] antinomies and antitheses, rotating wheel and
whirling gyres—are evidence that for this poet Time keeps on
being wound and unwound. Late in life and notably throughout
his *Last Poems* he continued to be prepossessed by bodily
rhythms:

> Let her finish her dance,
> *Ah, dancer, ah, sweet dancer.*

Finally, Yeats accomplished a crescendo of accented movement in the powerful beat of horses' hoofs.

> Did ever man ride such a race?
> No not until he rode.

And it was the "Riders upon the galloping horses" at Galway
Races who rode again in the last line of his epitaph—"Horse-
man, pass by." Wordsworth had spoken of "spots of time";
Eliot would choose a stance from which to propound his "still
point of the turning world"; but Yeats danced or galloped

[10] Donald A. Stauffer speaks of movement in *A Vision* as a *pavane*
(*The Golden Nightingale*, New York, 1949, p. 11).

through the vacillation of his later poetry to arrive at his Sphere by way of a whirling Zodiac. All three are concerned with transcendence as the mode of vision; Yeats, however, seems more prophetically aware of the symbols likely to impress our own kinaesthetic future.

How early might he have known the Virgilian *Copa Surisca*,[11] the Syrian Dancing Girl? This elegy is associated with the poetry of Virgil, from whom he was to borrow the title of *Per Amica Silentia Lunae;* although not now considered Virgil's own, it was usually found in editions of the poems and would have been accessible in the library of William Morris, translator of the *Aeneid,* whom he met in 1888. It appears in Miss Waddell's *Mediaeval Latin Lyrics* just preceding the elegies of Petronius Arbiter, of whom Yeats spoke familiarly by 1919,[12] and may have read earlier when he was working on *The Player Queen* in 1908.[13] Neither the *Copa* nor Petronius would have

[11] These Latin elegiac distichs were attributed to Virgil by Servius in the fourth century: *Mediaeval Latin Lyrics,* by Helen Waddell (New York, 1929), pp. 2–5, 280–284; quoted by permission of Barnes and Noble, Inc., and Constable Publishers.

[12] *Upon a Dying Lady,* poem I: "Her Courtesy."

[13] There are echoes of Yeats's Latinity, such as it was, in *The Player Queen:* "Some will die . . . like Petronius Arbiter, will tell witty, scandalous tales"; he gave Latin names to the three main persons of the play—Septimus, Nona, and Decima; and into Decima's speeches he wrote the insistent exhortations of the Syrian Dancing Girl—"They had some play they were to perform, but I will make them dance instead . . . I must find somebody who will dance with me for a while . . . my man must be lively on his feet and have a quick eye. . . . Dance, all dance, and I will choose the best dancer among you. Quick, quick begin to dance." More explicitly comparable are the "bankrupt tavern" with *fumosa . . . taberna,* the bray of "the donkey that carried Christ into Jerusalem" with *Cassus . . . asellus,* the bottle of wine and broiled lobster with *vappa . . . defusa . . . vitro . . . crystalli* and—cheeses instead of lobster—*caseoli.* Yeats's Septimus refers to "asphodel . . . much overrated by the classic authors," as if the dramatist had been reading of such garlands as those of the Copa Surisca—*violae . . . purpurea lutea . . . lilia* (*The Collected Plays of W. B. Yeats,* New York, 1935, pp. 417–430).

been hard to come by at school or in conversation with Lionel
Johnson and the Rhymers' Club.

> Copa Surisca caput Graeca redimita mitella,
>   crispum sub crotalo docta movere latus

> Dancing girl of Syria, her hair caught up with a fillet;
> Very subtle in swaying those quivering flanks of hers.

None of Yeats's modern dancers—not Gaby or Ruth St. Denis,
not Pavlova or Loie Fuller (1919)—could have furnished a
more entrancing picture of mobile grace in a more timeless
frame of symbolic places. At the tavern where the Copa danced
there were

> tankards and cups and measures and roses and pipes and fiddles
> And a trellis-arbour cool with its shade of reeds,
> And somewhere somebody piping as if it were Pan's own grotto,
> On a shepherd's flute, the way they do in the fields.—

> En et, Maenalio quae garrit dulce sub antro,
>   rustica pastoris fistula more sonat.

To Michael Robartes such a one appeared (1921) dancing
between Sphinx and Buddha: is not Syria somewhere between
Egypt and India? And when we read Helen Waddell's translation of this remarkably swift and vivid elegy on the theme of
carpe diem—"Here's Death twitching my ear, 'Live,' says he,
'for I'm coming' "—and recall that in 1932 Yeats, Shaw, and
others made Miss Waddell an associate member of the Irish
Academy of Letters,[14] we are alerted to an interesting possibility. During those twenties while this other Irish poet and
scholar was interpreting wandering scholars and erotic elegists,
did her work come under the eye of William Butler Yeats?
The rollicking bawdry and frank zest for immediate experience
of his late and last poems echo the songs of the Latin Archpoet

[14] *Letters*, ed. Wade, p. 801.

and the *vagantes* who set down the MSS of Benedictbeuern,[15] likewise concerned with, or obsessed by, dancing maidens, "choreas virginum":

> ibi fulget mobilis
> membrorum lascivia,
> dum puelle se movendo
> gestibus lasciviunt,
> asto videns, et videndo
> me mihi subripiunt.

Thence the change is slight—anacrusis here or catalexis there—to Yeats's

> Come swish around, my pretty punk,
> And keep me dancing still;

or

> *What shall I do for pretty girls*
> *Now my old bawd is dead?*

What Wordsworth might have accomplished in this mode had he not forsworn erotic poetry we need not guess; but in the tradition of flute song as a vehicle for longing and probing and riddling and possible revelation the two poets are significantly related to each other and to the flute singers preceding them. Here, too, Yeats bettered the accomplishment of Wordsworth and Coleridge—and Hardy more recently—in adjusting Elegeia's long step and short to modern ballad rhythms; he gave her a thrillingly new mobile poise and set her tap-dancing. Wordsworth's English Lucy and Landor's English Rose [16] were more gentle; but Moll Magee and Crazy Jane have an Irish abandon, a special Irish cadence, and in *A Thought from Propertius* the Irish poet who did not wish his son taught Latin seems himself to have been playing with the final line of the

---

[15] *Mediaeval Latin Lyrics*, pp. 170–183, 202–205.

[16] In 1880 John Butler Yeats had read *Rose Aylmer* to Willy (Ellmann, *Yeats: The Man and the Masks*, p. 27).

Latin elegiac couplet: like the Cynthia of Propertius his beloved might have walked to the altar "at Pallas Athena's side,"

> Or been fit / spoil for a / centaur
> Drunk with the / unmixed wine.

Finally, what Yeats did with septenaries in stanzaic groups of three, or four, or six seven-beat units, with or without refrain, allies his art to that of Layamon and native English ballad writers and singers of the thirteenth century—

> Bytuene Mersh and Averil,
>   When spray biginneth to springe,
> The lutel foul hath hire wyl
>   On hyre lud to synge.

Still other traits of classical elegy enriched and invigorated Yeats's balladry. From early years he had thought of poetry as akin to and dependent upon its sister arts of music and acting. "I got great pleasure . . . from remembering that Homer was sung" and regretted that "music and verse began to fall apart when Chaucer robbed verse of its speed that he might give it greater meditation, though for another generation or so minstrels were to sing his lengthy elaborated *Troilus and Criseyde*." Douglas Hyde's "popularity as a Gaelic poet" was remarkable, "mowers and reapers singing his songs from Donegal to Kerry." The Rhymers' Club delighted "in poetry that was, before all else, speech or song." Symons "studied the music halls, as he might have studied the age of Chaucer." [17] Yeats's experiments with Florence Farr in speaking to the psaltery were followed years later by the common effort of Yeats and Dorothy Wellesley to enhance the appeal of their ballads by musical notation. He approved what she said about "poetry being begotten of a tune" and from Majorca in 1935 wrote to her: "I dislike the constant uncertainty as to where the accent falls; it seems to

[17] *The Autobiography of William Butler Yeats* (New York, 1953), pp. 129, 131, 145, 200–201.

make the verse vague and weak. I like a strong driving force."
With F. R. Higgins he collaborated toward "a series of painted
broadsides . . . in each a poem by a living Irish poet and a
traditional ballad and the music for each and a picture for each."
"It is a queer thing," he wrote, "that the folk lilt lost since the
time of Burns has been discovered in our time." Along with the
folk lilt he rediscovered the importance of the flute: "I want to
get one of Turner's strange philosophical poems set, let us say,
for the bamboo flute (now taught in English schools) and I
want Turner (who is a musical critic) to choose other poems
and tunes." [18] Philosophical poems set to the flute or reed are,
of course, elegies in their original mode.

We who cherish the songs of the flutist Stephen Foster, or
Britishers who subsisted on the frolicsome or satirical squibs of
the folks for the folks, Scot or Saxon, during the nineteenth
century, know possibly better than Yeats could that neither the
folk lilt nor the art of piper and flutist had seriously lapsed since
the time of Burns. From his assumed discovery, however, came
at last those flute songs undeniably in both classical and popular
traditions. Lover and Lady and Chambermaid of *The Three
Bushes* go beyond the *Historia mei Temporis* of the Abbé
Michel de Bourdeille to Propertius and Ovid. All is old, yet all
is new; romance has touched the distichs of antiquity. The refrains of these final poems betoken lyric and mediaeval Christendom—*O my dear, my dear* and *The Lord have mercy upon us*
—but the questions are classical—*"What then? sang Plato's
ghost. What then?"*

> *O what of that, O what of that,*
> *What is there left to say?*

No small part of the elegiac flavor of the ritual plays also
comes from the flute associated with zither and drum for the
trio of musicians. We remember that Andrew of *The Unicorn*

[18] *Letters on Poetry from W. B. Yeats to Dorothy Wellesley* (Oxford
University Press, 1940), pp. 32–47.

from the Stars (1908) had a "little flute" of his own. In *Calvary* (1920) flute song is heard

> As though a flute of bone
> Taken from a heron's thigh,
> A heron crazed by the moon,
> Were cleverly, softly played.

Attracta, the Priestess of *The Herne's Egg* (1938), is summoned by a flute:

> A flute lies there upon the rock
> Carved out of a herne's thigh.

To such associations may be due that element in the plays more than lyric and romantic and heroic—the elegiac beauty that distinguishes them from all other plays of their time. "There are three very important persons," Yeats wrote to Ethel Mannin, "(1) a man playing the flute (2) a man carving a statue (3) a man in a woman's arms." [19] His emphasis is on elegist, sculptor, and lover.

Here we must scant our discussion of Yeats's elegiac balladry and ritual plays as renascent forms of flute song and flute ritual, and concern ourselves anew with his mastery of *anagnorisis* as Greek drama had revealed it to Aristotle,[20] that which helps to turn a mere change of fortune into an involved action. The slow steps by which the folk of *The Land of Heart's Desire* (1894) detect the nature of the Faery Child constitute a discovery bringing on a choice. The peripety of *Cathleen ni Houlihan* (1902) is illuminated by the exchange between Peter and Patrick:

—Did you see an old woman going down the path?
—I did not, but I saw a young girl, and she had the walk of a queen.

The Oldest Pupil in *The King's Threshold* (1904) puts the discovery of that play into explicit form:

[19] *Letters*, p. 851, March 4 [? 1935].   [20] See Chap. II above.

Not what it leaves behind it in the light
But what it carries with it to the dark
Exalts the soul.

On Baile's Strand (1904) and *Deirdre* (1907) were furnished
with exquisite gradations of awareness before their disasters
might be declared or exhibited: by questions, inferences, simili-
tudes, the protagonists arrived at the truth in which their respective destinies were to be enacted.

We are told in *The Unicorn from the Stars* (1908) that
Martin's "business is not reformation but revelation"; the play
lacks a thoroughgoing peripety, but in his vision of Heaven we
discover with him the furthest reaches of the Irish imagination:

The lover still loves, but with a greater passion,
and the rider still rides, but the horse goes
like the wind and leaps the ridges, and
the battle goes on always, always. . . .
I saw in a broken vision, but now all is
clear to me. Where there is nothing,
where there is nothing—there is God!

Somewhat more explicit but not less riddling is the discovery
of Forgael of *The Shadowy Waters* (1911), "drunken with a
dizzy light":

I can see nothing plain; all's mystery.
Yet sometimes there's a torch inside my head
That makes all clear, but when the light is gone
I have but images, analogies,
The mystic bread, the sacramental wine,
The red rose where the two shafts of the cross,
Body and soul, waking and sleep, death, life,
Whatever meaning ancient allegorists
Have settled on, are mixed into one joy.

Yet the actual moon presided over *The Green Helmet* (1919),
shining through its obscurities; and in the same year the Figure

of Cuchulain of *The Only Jealousy of Emer* touched Emer's eyes, dissolving "the dark / That hid him from them." "I have not given you eyes and ears for nothing."

As the plays became more like rituals the discoveries deferred more to tradition, both canonical and uncanonical. The epiphany of Christ in *The Resurrection* (1931) is as expected as the return of Jonathan Swift in *The Words upon the Window Pane* (1934) is startling: both, however, are instances of *recognitio*, fitting into old grooves of the mind and associated with familiar agencies. Witness the actual hymn sung at the séance of the latter play:

> Sun of my soul, thou Saviour dear,
> It is not night if Thou be near:
> O may no earth-born cloud arise
> To hide Thee from Thy servant's eyes.

This gradual and probably conscious refinement of elegiac vision in the plays was accompanied by an equally effective gain in the use of *anagnorisis* in the poems generally, very often under the symbol of the darkening and brightening moon, the stars, and the sun. Although poems calling for bulky and elaborate symbolic interpretation may be lost in the thicket of exegesis—a peril Yeats's poetry has not escaped—if we consider these certain symbols not as ends in themselves or as mere ornament but as tokens of the speculative nature of his poetry and his increasing skill with revelatory devices, we may ourselves be enlightened.

The early poems are for the most part graphic or lyric; when they are not visionary dreams they are laments, songs of sorrow more frequently than of joy.[21] One definite elegy is *The Indian upon God*. With its rhymed fourteeners it echoes flute song and its speculations recall those of Xenophanes. Its riddling discovery, in the familiar symbol for vision, shines from the "eyes"

21 Writing to Katherine Tynan in 1888, he acknowledged that his early poetry was "not the poetry of insight and knowledge, but of longing and complaint" (*Letters*, p. 63).

of the Moorfowl, the "eyes" of the Roebuck, "brimful of star-light," the "myriad spots of light" lit in "the languid tail" of the Peacock, even from the sliding drop of rain between the petals of the Lotus. Transience is the theme of *Ephemera* and *The Falling of the Leaves,* set forth in metaphors long ago dear to Mimnermus. The mad King Goll "sat and mused," and his elegiac refrain is a riddle—*"They will not hush, the leaves a-flutter round me, the beech leaves old"*—a Celtic version of many a classical distich.

With their space-adorning Rose and their Rood of Time the poems of 1892 and earlier vary from idylls to epylls. There are no questions in the nostalgia of *The Lake Isle of Innisfree;* but the nostalgia is illuminated by midnight "all a glimmer" and the "purple glow" of noon. The "Love" of *When You Are Old* is carried from the fire on the hearth to hide his face "amid a crowd of stars"; and the young man and maid of *Who Goes with Fergus* are exhorted to lift russet brow and tender eyelids from "love's bitter mystery" and "brood on hopes and fear no more"—does not Fergus rule "all dishevelled stars"? Although at this stage Yeats's thought is shallow, his metaphors are lofty and he is making himself ready for a more skillful use of symbols betokening *recognitio.* The disclosure of the identity of Cuchulain's son in that hero's Fight with the Sea parallels the device in Arnold's *Sohrab and Rustum* and, when the poet writes a Dedication to a Book of Stories from the Irish Novelists, *recognitio* brings "memories / Of half-forgotten innocent old places" until Irish bitterness disappears from "Munster grass and Connemara skies."

That Yeats will move along recognizable generic paths from lyric, idyll, and epyll toward speculative verse is further indicated when the beloved of *The Two Trees* is told to seek in her own heart rather than "in the bitter glass" for answers to timeless questions. Dreams set forth in "fitful Danaan rhymes" will make way for discoveries toward "truth's consuming ecstasy." This is the "ecstasy" as distinguished from mere pleasure of "Anima Hominis" in *Per Amica Silentia Lunae;* it is the word "for the awakening, for the vision, for the revelation of reality." In short, the romantic and lyrist is becoming an elegist.

The tone of regret continues into the poems of 1899 gathered under a title appropriate when the poet lays down his Danaan lyre and picks up his Pre-Raphaelite flute, *The Wind among the Reeds;* but the elegiac purpose is at every turn challenged by the very intensity of the feeling. He cannot disregard "uncomely and broken" things, "unshapely things" crowding in athwart his romantic images. O'Driscoll must awake from his "dream / Of the long dim hair" of his faithless Bridget, to hear —elegiac discovery!—

> high up in the air
> A piper piping away,
> And never was piping so sad,
> And never was piping so gay.

Beyond its memory of Blake's flute songs this promises a fresh Yeatsian treatment of all the old problems of love elegy [22] from Callimachus, Tibullus, and Propertius down the centuries: into the tradition of Delia and Cynthia will soon come a Helen instead of a Bridget. The theme of transience emerges from the images of romance; and awareness of "Time and Birth and Change" provokes in the persons of Yeats's maturing poetry further adventure into traditional literature and hence more recondite beauty.

[22] Yeats knew Propertius and Catullus, although he may not have fully realized the many ways in which his poetry recapitulates Alexandrian and Latin elegy. For illuminating generic discussion see Archibald A. Day, *The Origins of Latin Love-Elegy* (Oxford, 1938), and Georg Luck, *The Latin Love Elegy* (London, 1959). Luck detects in the classical distich an approximation of the waltz rhythm; and in the long-and-short verse pattern Yeats borrowed from balladry and skillfully modified, many of his most memorable poems retain the triple swing of classical love elegy:

> O mind your feet, O mind your feet
> Keep dancing like a wave.

Another form of elegiac awareness is, of course, with Yeats as with Hardy, the recognition of the past. When the Lover Remembers Forgotten Beauty, it is no longer to generalize that "all must fade like dew"; the kisses of the one beloved are metamorphosed into White Beauty's "high lonely mysteries"; and from this transcendent view substantial memory is enabled to play its part in a poetic recognition, taking the place of dreams and fancies: "Remembering hers," young men will find no other face so fair though the Valley be Full of Lovers.

From the awareness of the past comes the discovery of identity: οὖτα ἐκεῖνα, this is indeed she. Possibly the most affecting instance of it in this group of flute songs is the loving friend's acknowledgment that in the poet's heart she sees not her own but another's image. She goes weeping away, but her tears and ours are authentic, shed not for the sake of feeling but for the disclosure of a veritable and indestructible love. We recall the similar devotion of Propertius for Cynthia as he invoked celestial witnesses of his constancy; now in a later time Yeats tells of the Perfect Beauty before whom and "the unlabouring stars" his heart will bow "until God burn time."

> stars climbing the dew-dropping sky,
> Live but to light [her] passing feet.

This emergence of stars in the verses about the beloved is a pleasing reminder of the fidelities of love. The young queen of *The Cap and Bells* sang "Till stars grew out of the air"—an elegiac love song.

Along with the stellar images in *The Wind among the Reeds* we find also one metaphor of the resurgent Phoenix. The winds that

> lingered in the hidden desolate place
> Where the last Phoenix died,
> And wrapped the flames above his holy head

"still murmur and long" in the reeds when the Lover Asks Forgiveness because of His Many Moods. That same lover will in a few years be proud that he "knew a phoenix in [his] youth." Meanwhile there is much to learn and suffer and think. From the sedge allying La Belle Dame Sans Merci of Keats with the beloved of Yeats comes the riddling prophecy of the wind: the lovers will not lie breast by breast

> *Until the axle break*
> *That keeps the stars in their round . . .*
> *And the girdle of light is unbound.*

Yet because of his unflagging devotion the poet has been A Part of the Constellations of Heaven. Once more the classical *caveat* of the Latin elegists has been expressed in their metaphors of light and vision, and now in words of our own day.

The full Propertian analogy with the high cost of faithful love became apparent at the publication, 1904 and 1910, of *In the Seven Woods* and *The Green Helmet*. The disappointed patriot must now "put away / The unavailing outcries and the old bitterness / That empty the heart." And the thwarted lover has no "crumb of comfort, not a grain." Moreover, Yeats has turned still further from Hermetic symbols to classical literature and will subject himself to the discipline of traditional form. As the Cynthia of Propertius was more particularly individualized in comparison with her predecessors, Helen among them, so Maud Gonne has been shaped into unique beauty: she is "tall and noble," queenly with the queenliness of long ago yet with a new loftiness, "fierce and kind." Poems about her sound more spare: witness the octosyllabic couplets of *Never Give All the Heart* with their economical message out of the pagan past—

> He that made this knows all the cost,
> For he gave all his heart and lost—

and witness also the counsel of *O Do Not Love Too Long:*

> Sweetheart, do not love too long:
> I loved long and long,

> And grew to be out of fashion
> Like an old song.

The lyric cry of regret did not, however, muffle the queries of
the elegist. Cryptic refrains, as in *The Withering of the Boughs*
and *The Happy Townland*, were still indulged; but he peered
undeviatingly toward light. References to the moon abound—
"honey-pale moon," "hollow moon," "the famished horn / Of
the hunter's moon." Yeats was on the first stage of his journey
to the lunar ethics of *A Vision*.

On this journey his illumination had come from "the eyes /
Of Cathleen," the daughter of Houlihan (*Red Hanrahan's Song
about Ireland*):

> purer than a tall candle before the Holy Rood
> Is Cathleen, the daughter of Houlihan.

Soon, however, from legendary Ireland the poet's gaze shifted
for its visions to his memories of Ilium. Cathleen would be metamorphosed into *A Woman Homer Sung*. There would be *No
Second Troy*: resisting the blandishments of the epic Muse—like
Propertius—and the tragic Muse—like Ovid—[23] Yeats perse-
vered like both Propertius and Ovid in his celebration of elegiac
love. Without love "helmets, crowns, and swords" would go
"into the pit," he says in *Reconciliation*. Even though he must
still accept with time the wisdom of the early Greek Mimnermus, as he wrote in the same sylvan metaphor—

> Though leaves are many, the root is one;
> Through all the lying days of my youth
> I swayed my leaves and flowers in the sun;
> Now I may wither into the truth—

he would continue in the service of another Helen:

> "Such a delicate high head,
>   All that sternness amid charm,
>   All that sweetness amid strength."

[23] In *Amores* III, i.

Classical analogies come to mind not only for the love elegies. The truth into which Yeats saw himself withering was an aristocratic truth celebrated by Solon and Plato in centuries B.C. The argument of *The Republic* has never been modernized with better understanding or skill than in the passage referring to Lady Gregory's House Shaken by the Land Agitation in the series *The Green Helmet and Other Poems* (1910):

> How should the world be luckier if this house,
> Where passion and precision have been one
> Time out of mind, became too ruinous
> To breed the lidless eye that loves the sun?
> And the sweet laughing eagle thoughts that grow
> Where wings have memory of wings, and all
> That comes of the best knit to the best? Although
> Mean roof-trees were the sturdier for its fall,
> How should their luck run high enough to reach
> The gifts that govern men, and after these
> To gradual Time's last gift, a written speech
> Wrought of high laughter, loveliness and ease?

"The lidless eye that loves the sun" and the "sweet laughing eagle thoughts" take us back also to the elegiac Phoenix of Lactantius as translated by the Cynewulfian poet.[24] This is no mere fascist whim; in rescuing the aristocratic tradition from power politics, Yeats was maintaining the principles of a changeless justice, whence his long effort to improve the destiny of Ireland by raising the condition of her youth and her arts. In the series aptly called *Responsibilities* (1914), he counsels A Wealthy Man as follows (1912):

> Look up in the sun's eye and give
> What the exultant heart calls good
> That some new day may breed the best
> Because you gave, not what they would,
> But the right twigs for an eagle's nest!

[24] See Chap. III above.

Still his thought was running on the elegiac Phoenix, on the "eagle look" of Maud Gonne and all it implied of kinship to the sun. Not Leda's Swan, or the bird on the starlit golden bough at Byzantium, or the Great Herne would ever displace the Phoenix as a symbol of celestial influence and beneficent power.

For the time being his imagination was at work on Irish matters: Goban's wine, O'Leary's grave, curlew answering curlew "in the luminous wind," Synge's plays, the beggars in the palace-yard of King Guare were so many veiled instances of his widening scope and extending sympathies. Even when "indignant at the fumbling wits, the obscure spite" of the old Paudeen in his shop,

> suddenly . . . I thought
> That on the lonely height where all are
>   in God's eye,
> There cannot be . . .
> A single soul that lacks a sweet crystalline cry.

The golden hair of the Player Queen, "Love's moon" suddenly hid away by "a cloud blown from the cut-throat North," the street "whereon a thing once walked that seemed a burning cloud": this poetry like the poet in his Cold Heaven is "riddled with light." Ghostlike he would go "naked on the roads." Having been stripped of his Coat,

> Covered with embroideries
> Out of old mythologies,

and, finding "more enterprise / In walking naked," he could make an ever more candid search into himself. Yeats's imagination, indeed, walked naked to the end of his life. Thus, although he has shared himself more fully than any other poet since Wordsworth, he has missed—or shall we say has avoided?—the philosophical pattern that gave another kind of distinction to *The Prelude.* Discovering himself, he became his own symbol for elegiac vision.

There was still sorrow ahead. Among the elegies of *The Wild Swans at Coole* (1919) there are several poems emphasizing feeling over speculation. Regretful complaints, mournful silence, a sore heart, the waste of breath, fatigue, cries of impotence and dejection and renunciation threaten the characteristic poise of the elegist. Memory of Catullus only deepens scorn for "bald heads." There are occasional proud thoughts of one like the Cynthia of Propertius, but the dreams are "broken," the memories are "vague." Like the pedants of Babylon the poet has seen "the stars fade out where the moon comes." There is the merest hope that he will be brought to birth again when "the Pestle of the moon" "pounds up all anew." Meanwhile he is "caught between the pull / Of the dark moon and the full."

We are not surprised, therefore, that circumstances in personal and professional life during the early years of the new century inclined Yeats to elegiac writing in the narrower sense of the term, too. The poems *Upon a Dying Lady* for Mabel Beardsley use several devices familiar in lyrical elegy, among them the ritual properties—here, the toys—the hortatory phrases, and the catalogue of similarly brave and rare souls. The poem *In Memory of Alfred Pollexfen* has its catalogue of deaths all marked by the appearance of "a visionary white sea-bird." And in the elegy for Lady Gregory's son, first written as a pastoral, the laments of Goatherd and Shepherd concentrate on the grief of those who outlive the dead flutist:

> There's nothing of him left but half a score
> Of sorrowful, austere, sweet, lofty pipe tunes.

Between this idyll in dialogue, reminiscent of Spenser, and the final form of the elegy, *In Memory of Major Robert Gregory*, something has intervened to give fresh vigor and a more modern shape to the poem: Yeats will probe anew into the relation between personality and death.

Without claiming even a partial indebtedness, we may suggest as a matter of generic interest that Wordsworth's *Elegiac*

Musings on Sir George Beaumont had set an admirable pattern for this same theme.[25] Sir George and Major Robert were both painters; and the "graceful manners" of the former,

> Brightening a converse never known to swerve
> From courtesy and delicate reserve,

accord with the Yeatsian "Our Sidney and our perfect man" in that both must suffer what Yeats calls the "discourtesy of death." Wordsworth's picture of Beaumont's world,

> all its spirit-moving imagery
> Intensely studied with a painter's *eye*,
> A poet's *heart;* and, for congenial view,
> Portrayed with happiest pencil, not untrue

[25] In a note of appreciation about Major Gregory, written for the *Observer* of February 17, 1918, some four weeks after the airman's death, Yeats mentioned Wordsworth's *Resolution and Independence* (Marion Witt, "The Making of an Elegy" *Modern Philology*, XLVIII [November, 1950], 112). This poem, like the *Elegiac Musings* of Wordsworth, represents the earlier poet meditating on the dead who have been artists, poets, or painters. For instance, he "thought of Chatterton, the marvelous Boy" and of Burns, "Him who walked in glory and in joy Following his plough." For Yeats, comparably, "Lionel Johnson comes the first to mind" and, next, John Synge. In setting his scene Wordsworth noted the hare "running races in her mirth" and "the skylark"; Yeats refers to "the ford where drinking cattle make a stir" and the "water-hen." The most impressive verbal echo of *Resolution and Independence*, from the line "The oldest man he seemed that ever wore grey hairs," occurs in a line of *Major Robert Gregory*, "What made us dream that he could comb grey hair?" (Professor Witt refers Yeats's line to an Irish folk saying.) Right next to *Resolution and Independence* in Wordsworth's Poems of the Imagination Yeats would have found *The Thorn*.
> There is a Thorn . . .
>   like a stone . . .
> Like rock or stone . . .
> High on a mountain's highest ridge
> Where oft the stormy winter gale
> Cuts like a scythe. . . .
So near is the Wordsworthian scene to the Yeatsian "cold Clare rock and Galway rock and thorn."

> To common recognitions, while the *line*
> Flowed in a course of sympathy divine,

is less particular but not less exquisitely precise than Yeats's sketch of Gregory's world and the joy of friends

> that a great painter had been born
> To cold Clare rock and Galway rock and thorn,
> To that stern colour and that *delicate line*
> That are our secret discipline
> Wherein the *gazing heart* doubles her might.

There is, to be sure, a shift in lexical taste; a century has intervened. "Painter's eye and poet's heart" may be less concentrated than "gazing heart." Instead of "sympathy divine" as a rhyme for "line," "secret discipline" more skillfully begs the question. Nevertheless, Wordsworth and Yeats are describing the same artistic situation and finding words for the same technical procedure. Gregory's "delicate line," associated by Yeats with Samuel Palmer's "delicacy" of line—as Professor Marion Witt has pointed out to me—and Sir George Beaumont's "delicate reserve" (in its ethical and aesthetic implications for Wordsworth) ally this group of painters and poets in the service of one of the great principles of expressive art.

There is also a shift in image, setting, and the way of indicating personality. Yet the "fire of turf" in the Yeatsian "ancient tower" and the "mellow lustre" of Beaumont's "evening lamp" are similar, and Beaumont's "rare accomplishments and varied powers" find similar praise particularized in Gregory—

> Soldier, scholar, horseman, he
> And all he did done perfectly
> As though he had but that one trade alone.

Whereas Wordsworth had recalled the grace of Sir George's "undismantled age," Yeats asks in regard to Gregory: "What made us dream that he could comb grey hair?" Especially in the handling of their activities we detect superficial change and

fundamental likeness. Although both dead painters were scholars, Sir George Beaumont had in himself also the vicarious
power, giving with

> eye, voice, mien,
> More than theatric force to Shakespeare's scene.

Such power is distributed by Yeats into the "Greek and Latin
learning" of Lionel Johnson, the "passionate and simple heart"
of the playwright John Synge, and the horsemanship of "old
George Pollexfen"; and these items are as it were reassembled in
the Elizabethan attributes of Major Gregory.

We may, finally, compare even as we contrast the style of the
two elegists, their choice and habit in the act of composition.
Both have set aside "copious elegy" (Wordsworth) and "commentary" (Yeats). Wordsworth's poem is conceived in the
"grounds" of a dead painter and Yeats's poem in the "tower"
delighting the eye of another dead painter; and the herbs in the
one,

> Whose fragrance, by soft dews and rain unbound,
> Shall penetrate the heart without a wound,

are contrasted with the salt in those quarrels of friends in Yeats's
tower to

> lengthen out the smart
> In the affections of our heart.

Wordsworth's "Shades of the Past" have become, ironically,
Yeats's "breathless faces." The "blast / That shook the leaves
in myriads as it passed" has become a "bitter . . . wind / That
shakes the shutter." Gone is the paraphernalia of marble and
tomb, sylvan bowers, votive tablet, God's judgment and mercy.
Now we have, closer to the hand and heart, old carven stone,
storm-broken trees, Galway foxhounds and horses' feet, "lovely
intricacies of a house," and—instead of Judgment Day—"the
entire combustible world . . . finished in [a] flare." Metrists

will be aware that Wordsworth's heroic couplets, themselves
dexterously modified in various run-on patterns, have been
arranged by Yeats into a mobile stanza, earlier used by Abraham
Cowley, predominantly pentametrical but diminished into four-
beat lines for an inner refrain. Yet who will deny that the
Wordsworthian "Time's vanities, light fragments of earth's
dream" are not still the prepossession of William Butler Yeats?

The *Lines Written in Dejection* in the *Wild Swan* series hint
that Yeats has come to what for Wordsworth would not have
been so serious an impasse:

> The holy centaurs of the hills are vanished;
> I have nothing but the embittered sun;
> Banished heroic mother moon and vanished,
> And now that I have come to fifty years
> I must endure the timid sun.

We may expect that the poet's discoveries will continue tentative or riddling and that they will take form more as changeful
lunar than constant solar symbols and, indeed, that his energies
will now and then distort his revelations. There will be a resolute effort toward the prepossessions of youth, its fancies and
passions, an avid and sometimes vehement appetite for what is
in motion; novel systems of conduct and a renovated philosophy
of culture must be asserted, full of change and contingency.
The Unity of Being desired yet dimly foreseen must be composed out of puzzling antitheses, whirled as gyre and wheel
into millennial cycles before it can become a Great Sphere.

Glimpses of this unity are allowed:

> For one throb of the artery . . .
> I knew that One is animate.

When the real image and the imagined image of the bride bed

> Though several, are a single light,
> When oil and wick are burned in one,

a blessed moon brings Sheba to her Solomon. In the revelation of "terrible beauty" on Easter of 1916, partial views of civic glory have been reconciled. Nevertheless, with Yeats as with Wordsworth the dialectical procedure of the elegist will not be too soon thwarted. The "Hic" and "Ille" of *Ego Dominus Tuus* are entangled in debate about images of self and anti-self; and Michael Robartes has a double vision, detecting between the moonlit eyes of the Sphinx and the moonlit eyeballs of the Buddha—somewhat as in a stereoscope—a dancing girl. There is as yet in the poems of *The Wild Swans at Coole* and *Michael Robartes* no proper epiphany; instead, only the changing moon to brighten the eyes of the creeping cat.

Therefore, we may briefly suspend our search for Yeatsian discoveries in the poems to observe those traits, graphic and diagrammatic rather than elegiac, of the prose work entitled *A Vision*, begun in 1917 although not published until 1925. This record of an "incredible experience" (p. 8) was initiated through Mrs. Yeats's skill as a medium for revelations of spirit instructors; and—thanks to their occult teaching—it soon turned into a monstrous lunar symbol for personal and social change.[26] Little more need be said as to what this strange writing *is;* we may, however, probe further by asking what it is *like.* Was there in the literature familiar to Yeats any other work anecdotal in its beginning, dialectical in its middle, and well-nigh prophetic at its end, dealing with revelation rather than action, tentatively entangled in pastoral scenes and the travels, errors, and disasters of its intervenient persons? A work supplying some twenty-eight instances of ethical variety in some twenty-eight "characters"—what we might now call case-studies? Simplifying the myriad details of history into great cycles illustrative of human destiny? A work generally illuminating, although somewhat weighty and didactic? The answer is, of course, yes; and the work is Wordsworth's *Excursion*. In either case an elegist is

[26] Professor Ellmann, *The Identity of Yeats*, pp. 163–164, concludes that it is "best taken as a symbology."

consolidating his revealed world to permit him a further adventure into the unknown.

The Wordsworth influence thought barely possible in *Major Robert Gregory* is even more likely in *A Vision*. Writing to his father, January 18, 1915, Yeats had said:

I have just started to read through the whole seven vols of Wordsworth in Dowden's edition. I have finished *The Excursion* and begun *The Prelude*. I want to get through all the heavy part that I may properly understand the famous things. At the same time I am not finding the long poems really heavy.

This letter from Stone Cottage, Coleman's Hatch, Sussex, where he was entertaining Ezra Pound and Mrs. Pound, corroborates his thoroughgoing study of and mature judgment of the poetry of Wordsworth: "He strikes me as always destroying his poetic experience, which was of course of incomparable value, by his reflective power." [27] In other words Yeats recognized Wordsworth as an elegist.

It would be enlightening to overhear a conversation between Yeats and Pound about Wordsworth, but that may be left to some Landor of the future. Meanwhile, as we are told in this same letter, Yeats himself was "thinking out a long poem, a conversation upon philosophical subjects between a duellist and a gambler." No such poem has been found, but the plan for it may have derived in some part from the dialectical conversation

[27] *Letters*, p. 590. But is this not the universal tendency of the human mind? Later (p. 603) he acknowledged a "fine" letter from his father "about Wordsworth"; still later (p. 710) to Professor H. J. C. Grierson on February 21 [1926] he spoke of "the lack of natural momentum in the syntax" of "some good Wordsworth." The words "heavy" and "lack of . . . momentum" in these comments and the words "flat and heavy" in "Anima Hominis" (*Per Amica Silentia Lunae*, in *Essays*, p. 497) tell us more about Yeats than about Wordsworth. Even as he acknowledged Wordsworth's latent power he himself wished to sense from poetry the kinaesthetic traits he had discovered in Elizabethan and Jacobean lyric and would continue to furnish in his own late poems.

between the skillful Sage and the unlucky Skeptic of Wordsworth—discipline versus haphazardry. At least we can be sure
that two years before he started on his *Vision* Yeats had read
The Excursion.

A pastoral stroll toward a Ruined Cottage introduced Wordsworth's solar dialectics; in the "Packet for Ezra Pound" at the
front of Yeats's lunar didactics, the writer confesses that *A
Vision* was partly thought out in "empty churches." Both writers, somewhat awkwardly, prepare their readers for weightier
discussions by way of persons casually presented: Wordsworth's
story of Margaret and Robert of the Ruined Cottage as told by
the Wanderer and Yeats's yarn of Mary Bell and John Bond as
seen in the trance of Michael Robartes are comparable, as are
the careers of the Wanderer and Robartes; Owen Aherne is
less impressive than that other ironist, Wordsworth's skeptical
Solitary, although like the Solitary he furnishes for his visitors
a snack of Yeatsian sandwiches and champagne only a bit less
hearty than the Wordsworthian bread, curd, cheese, cream,
butter, and whortleberries passed out by the Solitary at Blea
Tarn—with "wine and stouter cheer" offered to, but refused
by, the Poet and the Wanderer.

There are books prominently displayed in the early passages
of the two works: Voltaire's Optimist as the intellectual fare of
Wordsworth's disaffected Chaplain, discovered by the Wanderer
and the Poet in a mountain recess under a rude penthouse over
a turf-built seat; and the *Speculum Angelorum et Hominum* of
a fictitious Giraldus, left in a wall cupboard by "an unfrocked
priest, who had joined a troupe of gypsies and disappeared,"
and found there by the mistress of the gullible Michael Robartes.
Both books were dilapidated, the former swollen with damp,
the latter torn and ragged, missing some leaves wrenched out to
start a fire. Both had been put to base uses, one as prop for the
toy houses of children, the other as prop for a broken-down
bed. Be it noted that there is also a reference to Voltaire in
the narrative of John Bond. Were it not that the introductory

passages of *A Vision* have their own jocose purpose, as if Yeats were poking a little fun at himself and his "Instructors," we might almost suspect him of a parody on Wordsworth's *Excursion*.

Once these occult Yeatsian "Instructors" declare themselves through their medium, Mrs. Yeats, they are allowed complete freedom to express an ethical and historical doctrine that the poet seems to accept completely: the doctrine of recurrence or periodicity, symbolized by a Great Wheel with its twenty-eight lunar "Incarnations." This Great Wheel has many analogues in cult and in letters, although Blake's lunar heavens or churches, twenty-seven in number, may be a more immediate ancestor of Yeats's Incarnations; [28] but the Yeatsian scheme of psychographs recapitulates also the Wordsworthian treatment of human diversity set forth in the twenty or more *characters* of men and women now earthbound in the Churchyard among the Mountains of Books VII and VIII of *The Excursion*.[29] Wordsworth's Pastor, somewhat less diagrammatically, plays a role similar to the "Instructors" speaking in the script or voice of Mrs. Yeats: both oracles intend to illuminate the kinds and destiny of Man; like the "Instructors," the "Pastor" "epitomise[s] the life"; unlike them he gives "solid facts" and "plain pictures" instead of "abstractions."

This formal relationship between the poem of 1814 and the writing of 1917–1937 is not what Wordsworth would have called an "inevitable circle" (V, 328). Whereas the earlier poet

[28] See Thomas R. Whitaker, "The Early Yeats and the Pattern of History," *PMLA*, LXXV (June, 1960), 323. To Blake's possible influence must be added, of course, that of Indian philosophy and theosophy.

[29] Aside from the *characters* of Wanderer, Solitary, and Pastor, the Pastor gives briefer sketches of the Matron and her Mate, the Botanist, the Miner, the Prodigal, flaming Jacobite, sullen Hanoverian, miserly Matron, Ellen the rueful Magdalene, Wilfred Armathwaite, the Father of six daughters, the rural Priest and his Housewife, the Patriarch of the Vale, Wonderful Walker, Deaf Man, Blind Man, Woodman, Grandfather Green, the Scholar, Sir Alfred Irthing, the Parson's Wife and Daughter, and the pair of lusty boys—well over a score of them.

had arrived at his conclusions through the nice balance of argument in the thoroughgoing debate of Books III and IV, Despondency and Despondency Corrected, Yeats would come to rest in a theoretical dogma of contraries and antitheses and antinomies, opposites and discords. Wordsworth's procedure had been skeptical, dialectic, elegiac; Yeats's "Instructors" were oracular, gnomic, visionary, although during their instruction and the reading of history and biography attendant upon it, Yeats declared that he made "continual discoveries."

The poets are most akin in their mastery of *anagnorisis* as a device. The vision "of a mighty city," "the revealed abode / Of spirits in beatitude," appearing to the Solitary and reminding him of the "Hebrew Prophets" (II, 832–875)—

> Glory beyond all glory ever seen
> By waking sense or by the dreaming soul!—

may be set by the side of Yeats's "glory of changeless metal" in *Byzantium*, the art and architecture of which city suggested "the Sacred City in the Apocalypse of St. John" (*Vision*, 1937, p. 279). Again, the sunset watched by the Pastor and his guests (IX, 601–608)—

> Innumerable multitude of forms
> Scattered through half the circle of the sky;
> And giving back, and shedding each on each,
> With prodigal communion, the bright hues
> Which from the unapparent fount of glory
> They had imbibed, and ceased not to receive.
> That which the heavens displayed, the liquid deep
> Repeated; but with unity sublime!—

is a way of presenting through natural symbols what Yeats would express in his Complete Symbol, with its emphasis on form and forms, through an artifice (pp. 213–214):

Every symbol, except where it lies in vast periods of time and so beyond our experience, has evoked for me some form of destiny, and that form, once evoked, has appeared everywhere, as if there were but one destiny, as my own form might appear in a room full of mirrors.

Wordsworth would have been sympathetic with what Yeats was trying to do. Although leaving it (VI, 170–172)

> to others to foretell
> By calculations sage, the ebb and flow
> Of tides, and when the moon will be eclipsed,

he, too, yearned back to the prelapsarian conversations between primal Man and wingèd Messengers (IV, 638–646)—

> Whether of actual vision, sensible
> To sight and feeling, or that in this sort
> Have condescendingly been shadowed forth
> Communications spiritually maintained,
> And intuitions moral and divine—

and he was not less aware than Yeats that to be human is to accept, reject, or make systems (IV, 603–610):

> If, tired with systems, each in its degree
> Substantial, and all crumbling in their turn,
> Let him build systems of his own, and smile
> At the fond work, demolished with a touch;
> If unreligious, let him be at once,
> Among ten thousand innocents, enrolled
> A pupil in the many-chambered school
> Where superstition weaves her airy dreams.

Above all, he would have agreed with Yeats's desire to "see the world as an object of contemplation": this had been the aim of his own poetry. That he went on to detect in "every form of being . . . an *active* Principle" and concluded that "the food of hope / Is meditated action" (IX, 1–26) aligns him further with the modern poet who, of all others, decried passivity in the face of a mechanized nature, insisted that contemplation is an activity,[30] brought drama and elegy together on the stage of

[30] On this point see Thomas R. Whitaker, "Yeats's 'Dove or Swan,' " *PMLA*, LXXVI (March, 1961), 131–132.

a new ritual art, and gave the best years of his life to a cultural action.[31]

In his Introduction to *A Vision* Yeats put the poems grouped under the titles *The Tower* (1928) and *The Winding Stair* (1929) "into evidence to show that [his] poetry had gained in self-possession and power" by way of or as a result of his communication with his spiritual "Instructors." After their "mummy truths" had been set down the poet appeared as it were free of alien preoccupations. He had come home to Bally-lee as Wordsworth to Grasmere,[32] and henceforth was to sing of "what is past, or passing, or to come" in increasingly humane and natural terms and in a rhythm closer and closer to common speech. Those readers to whom at times his artifices—even "Grecian" goldsmithery—have seemed unconscionable bric-a-brac note with pleasure that the stilted water hen and the owl have a place in his meditations little inferior to that of metallic bird and Sato's sword and that the golden grasshoppers and bees of Phidias have made way for the butterflies and honeybees of Ballylee. They may note further that in "Anima Mundi" (1917) the poet comes to the "line of foam at the shallow edge of a vast luminous sea" reminding him not only of Henry More's *Anima Mundi* but of Wordsworth's "immortal sea which brought us hither" [33]—and doubtless of Arnold and Swinburne as well.

[31] Whether or not Yeats had been spurred on by his study of Words-worth's poetry, the year 1915 saw him "full of new poems." He de-clared himself "free at last from the obsession of the supernatural, having got my thoughts in order and ranged on paper" (*Letters*, p. 595). This clearing of the desk and mind was again and again necessary for fresh composition.

[32] Those who wish to estimate differences between Wordsworth and Yeats at a comparable stage in their literary careers should read the lines ending "Home at Grasmere" (Book I of *The Recluse*). As an elegiac program or as a symbology this passage is matchless. It was a chastening point of departure for Wordsworth and may well have furnished Yeats, too, with themes, purposes, and modes of expression. We know that he read it.

[33] *Essays*, p. 511.

He was still the elegist, continuing on what the mystic would call his "illuminative way," intent like Wordsworth upon seeing "into the heart of things." From his tower he "would question all": ruins, ancient trees; along with the symbolic rose of his youth, elms and thorns and pear trees, mice and cows and starlings. Emblems of adversity were countered with symbols of hope; joy was abstracted. There was also a new compassion for sons and daughters, nuns, mothers, and schoolchildren.

Everywhere the poems of this period reflect symbolic heat and light and not only in the celestial bodies: there is a blessed blazing in the human body; from Purgatorio xxvii into the holy fire of Byzantium comes the "flame that cannot singe a sleeve." Midnight candles may be snuffed, "innumerable clanging wings [may] put out the moon," "the brilliant eye" making a "catch in the breath" may become as "clouds of the sky" among "deepening shades," but

> Whatever flames upon the night
> Man's own resinous heart has fed.

As a result of this discovery, elegiac feeling takes on an optative aspect:

> O would that we had met
> When I had my burning youth!

or

> O may the moon and sunlight seem
> One inextricable beam.

And at last the optative becomes an imperative. The infinite piteousness of age will be amended by the mere resolute striking of a match to burn up time; thanks to the poet's defiant arson, two old crones again don their silk kimonos at Lissadell and, beautiful again, move like gazelles around the table of an old Georgian mansion. In such literary conflagration the "log-book of the sun's journey and the moon's" in Babylon and the "beacon" in the tower of Alexandria yield to the gleam piercing the body of the poet at Glendalough and the Tower of Ballylee: "Everything that is not God [will be] consumed with intellectual fire"—surely the discovery of discoveries for those "poets and artists [who] must . . . live but for the moment when vision comes to our weariness like terrible lightning." [34]

Temporal necessity is again and again transcended in recording what Wordsworth had called "spots of time," moments of heightened energy and sharpened vision for which not even symbolic heat and light suffice.[35] The moon in its hitherto vaunted changes now stands still, bidden by proud memory. Or change itself is changed into the utterance of changeless truth:

> Man is in love and loves what vanishes,
> What more is there to say?

Or change is seen as mobility, and mobility is shaped into the art of dance. Most revealing of all, the lunar Great Wheel has been concentrated into the "brightening glance" of a dancer. "When hearts are full / Of their own sweetness," there is a new "stillness." [36] He had said further in *Per Amica Silentia Lunae* that

When all sequence comes to any end, the soul puts on the rhythmic or spiritual body or luminous body and contemplates all the events of its memory and every possible impulse in an eternal possession of itself in one single moment. . . . Even now we escape from time in what we call prevision.

None other has spoken more vividly of the nature of *anagnorisis*, nor more movingly of the sanctity of human passion. When we hear old Madge sing hushaby to the stone wrapped in her cloak and carried in her arms, we too laugh with the poet "till tears run down / And the heart thumps at [our] side." We have discovered love to be indestructible; mockery is mocked; remorse is cast out—

[34] *Ibid.*, p. 503.
[35] Here, thinking back to Wordsworth, we also think ahead to Eliot.
[36] *Essays*, pp. 524–525, 37–39.

> We are blest by everything,
> Everything we look upon is blest.

Thus, by way of an old human experience that becomes the new poetic experience of all eras, primary or antithetical, Yeats emerges from his circles of change into his proper Great Sphere.

Moreover, in this elaboration and concentration of power, the elegist never forgets the valuable seven-beat rhythm, fours and threes, characteristic of flute song. Many of the briefer poems of the twenties and thirties—*Symbols, Spilt Milk, The Nineteenth Century and After, Statistics, Three Movements*—have the lilt of Greek elegiac epigrams, and Berenice's hair is recalled from Alexandrian elegy. The speed soon to be observed in the *Last Poems* is gathering momentum in *Words for Music Perhaps. A Man Young and Old* and *A Woman Young and Old* echo the music of balladry—

> I'm looking for the face I had
> Before the world was made—

but their franker passion has given them a richer harmony as if, indeed, "the Zodiac [of lovers could be] changed into a sphere."

There may well be circumstantial reasons why Wordsworth as a senescent lacked the energy to resist clichés in rhyme and meter as in theme and maxim: physical old age overtook him early. On the other hand, we must point to the varying length of his line in the stanzaic pattern of *Dion, To Enterprise, The Power of Sound*, and in chief that remarkable *Vernal Ode*, now too little known. Those are metrical forerunners if not actual influences upon section II of Yeats's *Tower*, sections II and III of *Meditations in Time of Civil War*, section III of *Nineteen Hundred and Nineteen, All Soul's Night, A Dialogue of Self and Soul*, and *Byzantium*. Wordsworth had, it may be confessed, neither taste for nor skill in those modifications of rhyme into near-rhyme or assonance that often tease and thereby delight our ears in the late stanzaic experiments of Yeats; yet, thanks to the classical scholarship in which the former surpassed the latter, in lexical variety he was to the end a match even for the finest phrase-maker of our modern time.

For instance, just one hundred years before Yeats was visited by his occult "Instructors," 1917, Wordsworth had received an angelic Stranger whose teachings he set forth in *The Vernal Ode* of 1817. Wordsworth, however, turned from such "prelude of unearthly sound" to contemplate "the soft murmur of the vagrant bee": "And is She brought within the power / Of vision?"

> Observe each wing!—a tiny van!
> The structure of her *laden thigh*,
> How fragile! yet of ancestry
> Mysteriously remote and high;
> High as *the imperial front of man;*
> The roseate bloom on woman's cheek;
> The soaring *eagle's* curvèd beak;
> The white plumes of *the floating swan;*
> Old as the tiger's paw, *the lion's mane,*[37]
> Ere shaken by that *mood of stern disdain*
> At which *the desert* trembles.

As notable examples of speculative insight we may compare, or contrast, Wordsworth's "vision" of the vagrant bee and Yeats's "revelation" of the "rough beast" of *The Second Coming,* that "vast image out of *Spiritus Mundi.*" Wordsworth deals with "ages coming, ages gone"; Yeats, with the sequence of the centuries. While Wordsworth takes comfort from what he sees, Yeats's sight is troubled by

> A shape with lion body and the head of a man,
> A gaze blank and pitiless as the sun,
> . . . moving its slow thighs, while all about it
> Reel shadows of the indignant desert birds.

[37] Note also in Wordsworth's *On the Power of Sound* (1828), ll. 21–22: "the prowling lion's *Here* I am, / How fearful to the desert wide!"

When we set the "laden thigh" by the side of the "slow thighs," "the imperial front of man," by "the head of a man," "the lion's mane" by the "lion body," "the mood of stern disdain" by the sun's "gaze blank and pitiless," the trembling "desert" by "the indignant desert birds," and especially "the soaring eagle's curvèd beak" by the falcon "turning and turning in the widening gyre," we must allow a remarkable common factor in Wordsworth's vision and Yeats's revelation. Could the shape Yeats professed to see out of the corner of his imaginative eye have been in some respects a memory of the Wordsworth bee? If so, his poetical modifications are significant. If not, the symbolic habit of the elegist, arising from the *Spiritus Mundi*, is again and freshly illustrated. We may even hazard a suggestion that in 1915 Yeats had studied Dowden's seven volumes of Wordsworth's poetry to good purpose.

Few readers of the post-Visionary Yeats will have read him at the side of the post-Excursive Wordsworth, yet either helps to interpret and to define the other. One accepted old age and one defied it; but Granddaddy Wordsworth [38] and the Wild Old Wicked Man are the two sides of the same elegiac penny. Wordsworth came to rest as the reincarnate *persona* of a Solon or a Theognis; Yeats, as the Mask of a Propertius. Both old men made "words that can pierce the heart" when daybreak comes and the end of the candle:

> "All men live in suffering,
> I know as few can know,
> Whether they take the upper road
> Or stay content on the low."

[38] In "Anima Hominis" (*Essays*, p. 506) Yeats seems to repudiate Wordsworth, "withering into eighty years, honoured and empty-witted."

CHAPTER XIII

Pipings of Pan:
D. H. Lawrence

IN this, our final essay, we may imagine that, when Elegia
stepped forth from the *incaedua silva* of Ovid, she left behind
her in those *nemoralibus umbris* the sylvan Pan, Pan of the
bright eyes, the horns, and the scampering goatish hoofs, still
to be invoked by those who study flute song and listen to the
wind among the reeds. As a literary symbol Pan remains very
much alive in the twentieth century.[1] As a scholarly symbol,
too, he may serve to introduce our discussion of elegy today.
For better or for worse the imagination has its periodic lapses
into the uncourtly or rebellious expression of elemental modes
of feeling.

A minor sun-god, the instructor of Apollo and the companion
of Dionysus, Pan is neither Apollonian nor Dionysian; rather,
he presides with his retinue of fauns, satyrs, and other mischievous earthy beings over a place that might fittingly be
called—with a glance at the traditional pun on his name—
Pandemonium. Seeming to encourage outlawry and mockery,
he yet keeps close to growing things and feeds on humble green-
ery and acorns fallen from great Dodonian oak trees. He leads

[1] For Pan as a theme in our century see W. R. Irwin, "The Survival
of Pan" in *PMLA, LXXVI* (June, 1961), 159–167.

no pastoral orchestra, but the harsh cries of his following at times suggest a possible new tragic goat-song, at least a wood-wind quintette playing Schuller. He refuses to be tamed or groomed and may well be the perennial source of perennially new songs of innocence.

Son of Hermes, he is the proper custodian of valid messages from the gods. Living in woods and caves near Dryope, his mother, he keeps his ear to the ground. As the god of mirages over the foggy terrain, he has the power to mislead and confuse the unwary and to arouse panic—another traditional pun. Supremely, however, he is the Goat-king of the Zodiac, fellow of the celestial Fish and Ram, the Bull, the Crab, the Lion, and the Scorpion: all lively forms of archetypal energy. Lustful, he still pursues the nymph Syrinx; but he is on the side of the Olympians against the Titans, and forevermore he hunts, fishes, sports, sings, and dances in the vacation land of Arcady.

So far the mythographers.[2] For what the poets themselves think of Pan we may refer to that writer of our century whose pipings take us closest of all to the Arcadian scene, D. H. Lawrence. He and his contemporaries were in need of a chthonian to replace the Delian luminaries who had hitherto presided over the speculations of the elegist; and they would welcome a Syrinx or Persephone instead of the fading Cynthias and Delias bequeathed by Rome to Britain. Black masses and even dark suns were mere negations; to restore Lucifer would only tempt the obedient archangels into further competitive brilliance; rainbows and phoenixes had well-nigh served their purpose. Was there aught symbolic and yet nearer the center of human experience? Pan? Pan had been reported dead at the advent of

[2] Of these one of the most recent, Mr. Robert Graves, in his *White Goddess* (New York, 1948, p. 291), refers to Pan's mother as the nymph Dryope and allows him to be hatched from an egg, thus associating him with woodpeckers of barbed tongue, who portend rain. But this is on the distaff side.

Christ, but the report was obviously much exaggerated.[3] His mighty regenerative power and his reed flute would be helpful allusions for a young poet devoted to Arcadian themes and planning to write love elegies. Let it be Pan. And Pan it was.

When did the sylvan Pan come to haunt Lawrence's imagination? If in his schooldays [4] from Virgil's tenth *Eclogue,* the

[3] For Lawrence on Pan see Irwin, pp. 164–165.

[4] We need a thorough study of Lawrence's classical education. As a pupil enrolled in the North Hingham High School in September, 1898, he may well have been taught by the classics instructor, T. B. Hardy. In the spring of 1908 he was translating the Latin quotations of Schopenhauer's *Essays,* Alan Chambers' birthday present to his sister Jessie (Harry T. Moore, *The Intelligent Heart,* New York, pp. 21, 68). I am grateful to Mr. A. H. Stewart, Senior Lecturer in Education of the University of Nottingham, for furnishing me with a photocopy of Lawrence's notebook for Latin vocabulary among several other pertinent items. He refers to a photocopy, in the Department of Manuscripts at the University, of Lawrence's application for a teaching post at Croydon in September, 1908: "In college I have taken the Inter Arts course as well as ordinary training, my subjects being English, Latin, French, Botany, Mathematics." This "degree" course he later abandoned for the "ordinary" course. Mr. Stewart also notes from E. T. (Jessie Chambers), *D. H. Lawrence, A Personal Record,* 1935, p. 75, that in his first term at college he had some special tuition in Latin. "He told her that he had 'broken the back of the Latin.'" I am kindly informed by the Secretary of the University of London "that David Herbert Lawrence passed the Matriculation Examination of this University in June 1905. He did not, however, offer Latin at that Examination and, in any case, the syllabus in Latin then would not include set books."

In 1910 the inspector of schools, Stewart A. Robinson, knew Lawrence as an assistant master in a primary school in Croydon and twenty years later reported that he "had small Latin and no Greek, which was a pity" (Edward Nehls, *D. H. Lawrence: A Composite Biography,* University of Wisconsin Press, 1957, I, 94). In that same year, however, he was quoting the end of *The Bacchae* to Helen Corke; in April, 1911, to Mrs. S. A. Hopkin he wrote of *The Trojan Women, Oedipus,* and *The Bacchae*—these presumably in translation. During the war years Lady Ottoline Morrell sent books to Cornwall for him: in January, 1916, he requested the Homeric Hymns; in February, 1916, he thanked her for the Virgil (it "isn't very well translated") and asked her whether she remembered "that little round picture at the beginning of Hesiod,

goatish God with Sylvanus and the shepherds and the swine-
herds would be listening to the woes of the elegist Gallus,
"while the flat-muzzled goats crop[ped] the tender underwood." [5]
The main attributes of the Virgilian Pan were his ingenuity and
his interest in musical rivalry—the lyrical equivalent of elegiac
debate. It was Pan who taught Corydon and Alexis to join reed
to reed with wax in the second *Eclogue;* on such a wax-jointed
pipe in the third *Eclogue,* Menalcas competed with Damoetas;
and in the famous fourth *Eclogue,* to salute the *nova progenies,*
Pan was challenged to dispute the prize, with Arcady as judge.
Moreover, in the first of the *Georgics* [6] he was invoked; his
wholesome power was mentioned in the second: "Happy is he
who has knowledge of the woodland gods—of Pan, and old
Silenus, and the sister nymphs"; and, in the third, the Arcadian
god, with the lure of a bright-hued fleece, has charmed the
Queen of Night Herself.

> Pan deus Arcadiae captam te, Luna, fefellit
> in nemore alta vocans; nec tu aspernata vocantem.

After Virgil no other elegiac poet would more memorably
associate similar literary ideas until Lawrence advanced into
"the sightless realm" of Persephone with "the blue forked
torch" of a Bavarian gentian or slipped out of "the dark-red

---

of Dionysus crossing the sea"; and in April, 1916, he commented on the
"Thucydides." In September of the same year he asked Dolly Radford
for Burnet's *Early Greek Philosophers.* Back in Derbyshire in May,
1918, he told Lady Ottoline that he felt "like Ovid in Thrace"; and in
April, 1922, he wrote to Lady Cynthia Asquith: "It is strange and
fascinating to wander like Virgil in the shades" (*The Collected Letters
of D. H. Lawrence,* ed. Harry T. Moore, New York, 1962, I, 65, 76,
416, 421, 444, 473, 552; II, 702). It was Plutarch who had broken the
story of the death of Pan. A very few months before his own death
Lawrence wrote to thank Charles Lahr "for the Plutarch" (*Letters,*
II, 1220).

[5] *Virgil,* tr. John Jackson (Oxford, 1908), pp. 28–30.

[6] Dr. Graham Hough (*The Dark Sun,* New York, 1957, pp. 20–21)
notes that Lawrence "was reading the *Georgics* at the time *The White
Peacock* was taking shape"—i.e., before 1911, its date of publication.

mantle of the body's memories" to round "the great final bend of unbroken dark." The Virgilian Luna and the Lawrencean Persephone are sisters and the Virgilian Pan is elder brother to the Lawrencean Pan; and, although literary indebtedness is not at present concerned, there can be little doubt that Lawrence's laments and love elegies [7] are in the classical tradition.

Lawrence was not yet a "Pan male" when he taught school at Croydon—and still less a primitive man—but he resisted doctrine and formality as a growing root resists inert stone or an imprisoned animal batters itself against an iron fence. His identification of himself with the mass of living, growing, moving, frisking things and his acceptance of vital energy as his theme and the origin of his doctrine were distinctly enunciated in an early series of poems called *The Schoolmaster*.[8] In *The Best of School*, with its metaphors of bird and tree, it is "very sweet" [9]

> while the sunlight waves
> In the ripening morning, to sit alone with the class
> And feel the stream of awakening ripple and pass
> From me to the boys, whose brightening souls it laves
> For this little hour.

> This morning, sweet it is
> To feel the lads' looks light on me,
> Then back in a swift, bright flutter to work;

[7] That he gave to his second volume of verse the Ovidian title, *Amores*, indicates that he may have been familiar also with Ovid's dirge for Tibullus, *Amores* III, 9.

[8] Originally published in the *English Review* for November, 1909; and in the *Saturday Westminster Gazette* for May 11, 18, 25 and June 1, 1912. See *A Bibliography of the Writings of D. H. Lawrence*, by Edward D. McDonald (Philadelphia, 1925).

[9] With a reminiscence of Byron, *Don Juan*, canto I, Stanzas 122–127. The quotations from Lawrence's poetry are taken from *The Complete Poems of D. H. Lawrence*, ed. Vivian de Sola Pinto and F. Warren Roberts (2 vols.; New York, 1964); quoted by permission of The Viking Press, Inc., New York, and of William Heinemann Limited and Laurence Pollinger Limited, London, and the estate of the late Mrs. Frieda Lawrence.

Each one darting away with his
Discovery, like birds that steal and flee.
Touch after touch I feel on me
As their eyes glance at me for the grain
Of rigour they taste delightedly.

As tendrils reach out yearningly,
Slowly rotate till they touch the tree
That they cleave unto, and up which they climb
Up to their lives—so they to me.

I feel them cling and cleave to me
As vines going eagerly up; they twine
My life with other leaves, my time
Is hidden in theirs, their thrills are mine.

When "the thin sycamore in the playground is swinging with flattened leaves"—recall Tennyson's sycamore—and the young refuse his love, he excuses them. They "are busy deep down at the roots, / And love would only weaken their under-earth grip."

I must not win their souls, no never, I only must win
The brief material control of the hour, leave them free of me.
Learn they must to obey, for all harmony is discipline,
And only in harmony with others the single soul can be free.

The word "discipline" serves as title for this poem, surely one of the most remarkable ever written about teaching; but while the disciples must "draw their sap from the Godhead, not from me," the teacher is "broken down like a plant in winter," reduced to "a knowledge of . . . roots in the dark" in an undersoil "quickened with gall."

This is sylvan poetry, not pastoral poetry with inbred, docile flocks nibbling outworn ancient meadows. Rarely has the vital struggle of teaching been made so clear. Cowper's *Tirocinium* and Wordsworth's *Prelude* III are here somehow reduced to their essential terms. Lawrence has dared to invade the classroom

with vegetal and animal life—not specimens. Nevertheless, in
The Punisher, he is one whose words are like a "harsh, cold
wind"; he is "desolate . . . as a church whose lights are put
out."

> The fire rose up in the bush and blazed apace,
> The thorn-leaves crackled and twisted and sweated in anguish;
>   Then God left the place.

And in the *Last Lesson of the Afternoon* Lawrence, too, leaves
the place; whether or not he knows himself already stricken in
health, he seems to make the great refusal.

> When will the bell ring, and end this weariness?
> How long have they tugged the leash, and strained apart,
> My pack of unruly hounds!
>
>   .   .   .   .   .
>
> I will not waste my soul and my strength for this.[10]

Then follow the explosive elegiac queries in a roughening of the
verse: "What is the good of it?" "What do I care?" "What is
the point?" "What does it matter to me?" "Why should
we . . . ?" [11] The latent Pan will soon be off on another scent.
Here in little we have a preview of Lawrence's literary career,
its assets and its liabilities. Teaching in the larger sense was the
pivot about which his actions and rebellions and contemplations
revolved, the core of his destiny.

The teaching episode has a bearing on the form of his poetry,
too. "Think of a quivering greyhound set to mind a herd of
pigs and you see my teaching. . . . There, I won't lament any

[10] His effort to free himself from maternal and conjugal domination
is only one aspect of this central strife. The professional rebellion also
haunted him until the end. Witness the letter to Mabel Luhan written
January 6, 1930, only a few weeks before his death:

My being ill so long has made me realize I had better talk to the young
and try to make a new thing with them, and not bother much more
about my own personal life. Perhaps now I should submit, and be a
teacher. I have fought so against it (*Letters*, II, 1230).

[11] *The Complete Poems of D. H. Lawrence*, I, 74–75.

more. I think I ought to be an elegiac poet: forever singing my own elegy." [12] In his style especially the demonic Pan, animating his prose and verse from the earliest days, helped to furnish what is its main distinction, its sense of movement, *kinaesthesia*. Fits and starts in the animals and incalculable changes in the gestures and expressions of elemental men and women make us aware, as Lawrence was aware, of a vast and mighty subhuman realm of movement and power. Although his early poetry is considered to lack Apollonian polish and Dionysian measure, it does have Panic liveliness: for instance, on the wild common of the poem of that name, placed first in the *Collected Poems*, "crowds of glittering king-cups surge to challenge the blossoming bushes," "the hill bursts and heaves under [the] spurting kick" of the rabbits, "peewits are sweeping" above the "leaping . . . sparks on the gorse-bushes." It is as if the *primum mobile* had come down to earth. And within the frame of diverse natural movement, the naked boy watches his shadow "quivering" on the dark waters of the deep pond and starts to think. He asks "What is this thing that I look down upon?"

But how splendid it is to be substance, here!
My shadow is neither here nor there; but I, I am royally here!
I am here! I am here! screams the peewit; the may-blobs burst out in
    a laugh as they hear!
Here! flick the rabbits. Here! pants the gorse. Here! say the insects
    far and near.

Thus, out of the lyric feeling and the idyll of movement come the query and the discovery: "All that is right, all that is good, all that is God takes substance!" The method of elegiac poetry —even its genesis from simpler forms—is clear to view.

Love on the Farm is another early instance of animal movement passing into human behavior and making way for a Pan-like *kinaesthesia*. "In [the] large, hard hands" of the captor, the captive rabbit "with wild spring / Spurts from the terror of"

[12] *Letters*, I, 31, in a letter to Blanche Jennings from Croydon, October 26, 1908.

the throttling—"piteous brown ball of quivering fears!" Caught in the snare of love, the beloved is caressed with "fingers that still smell grim / Of the rabbit's fur." The rabbit is no mere symbol for the beloved. They partake of a common energy and a common destiny.

When exiled to town from such rural scenes, the young elegist becomes understandably homesick for everything that grows of itself, for the violets under the orchard hedge. The "northern wind-flowers shaken stir."

> You tell me the lambs have come, they lie
>   like daisies white in the grass
> Of the dark-green hills; new calves in shed;
>   peewits turn after the plough—
> It is well for you.

Yet in town there are compensations: the white feet of the Jones baby "beat across the grass"; they "nod like white flowers in a wind." That baby, asleep after pain,

> She who has always seemed so light,
>   Now wet with tears and pain hangs heavily.

"Her soft white legs . . . over [his] arm / Swing to [his] walking movement." He compares her to "a drenched, drowned bee" whose wings "are a heaviness, and a weariness." He will not divorce life in nature from primal life in babies—or in young men.

For to Lawrence the sexual life of both brute and man was in the Lucretian nature of things. It was functional movement, and its *kinaesthesia* must be considered normal, wholesome, and hence proper for literary treatment.

> Look now, through the woods where the
>   beech-green spurts
> Like a storm of emerald snow, now see!
> A great bay stallion dances, skirts
>   The bushes sumptuously.

These lines from *Come Spring, Come Sorrow* bring into focus
the truth of a

> Dim spring that interweaves
> The hidden bodies mating everywhere.
>
> . . . . .
>
> For, sure from the golden sun
> A quickening, masculine gleam floats in to all
> Us creatures, people and flowers undone
>   And opened under his thrall
> As he plants his new germ in us. What is there to shun?

This is the proper elegiac query of the great god Pan, justifying,
if it needs justification, the kinaesthetic imagery of *The Hands
of the Betrothed, Snap-Dragon,* and *Seven Seals.*

Lawrence's grammatical forms and stylistic devices also suggest movement and contingency: progressive verbs and present
participles, gerunds and gerundives, allow for duration and save
"thinking" from becoming mere "thought"; queries, optatives,
exhortations, imperatives continue the present into the future;
the incremental repetition of nouns and phrases helps to
expedite them in a kind of rocketry of both significance and
value. All is yet *natura naturans,* before memory and the gen-
eralizing mind have insisted on preterites and abstractions.[13]

Although Lawrence would scarcely approve a metrical analysis of his poems, we observe in them from the first his effort to
associate meter with impulse and thus to subordinate old patterns to new kinaesthetic experience. Rhyme was on its way out;
even when it started a poem sedately, it was soon kicked aside.
All would be alive, in motion, delightedly free. In 1908 for
Blanche Jennings he quoted and translated Verlaine's "De la
musique avant toute chose" as follows: "Let us have music be-

---

[13] One early exception is the often mentioned *Snap-Dragon,* which
Edward Marsh accepted for the first volume of *Georgian Poets,* 1911–
1912, possibly because its account of deep and powerful feeling was
suitably thrust into the past and hence would be less unwelcome to the
taste of readers and critics of a decorous age.

fore everything, and, to obtain it, we will choose a subtle irregularity with nothing which balances and makes weight." Then the English poet commented: "I like it but will not practice it. Before everything I like sincerity, and a quickening spontaneous emotion." Five years later from Shelley's haunt at Lerici he wrote to Edward Marsh:

I think I read my poetry more by length than by stress—as a matter of movements in space than footsteps hitting the earth. . . . I think more of a bird with broad wings flying and lapsing through the air, than anything, when I think of metre. . . . It all depends on the *pause*—the natural pause, the natural *lingering* of the voice according to the feeling—it is the hidden emotional pattern that makes poetry, not the obvious form.

"Flying and lapsing": Lawrence's figure [14] can be illustrated by the classical elegiac distich or by the English septenarius, the ballad meter, which we have noted as similar to the second line of the distich. Indeed, it was at this very time in 1913 that we find the elegist urging Marsh not to "put my 'Ballad of a Wayward Woman' lightly aside." [15]

[14] Coleridge had spoken of the Ovidian elegiac meter as the rise and fall of "the fountain's silvery column"; but Lawrence was for the space age.

[15] *Letters*, I, 21, 242–243, 237. Although there is little or no deference to artificial conventions, there is a liking for such simple, strongly-accented ballad rhythms as we have pointed out in earlier elegiac writing, in Hardy's ballads for instance, with which we may compare Lawrence's *The Collier's Wife*, *Whether or Not*, *The Drained Cup*. There are many seven-beat clusters in Lawrence's as in Yeats's verse: trochaic and dactylic feet resist the marching iambs; the occasional five-four-three diminuendo is a ballad-like modification of blank verse. Lawrence, like Hardy, took delight in folk songs and psalm-singing; like Blake, he thought in scriptural rhythms. Here we may refer to Professor Frye, *Fearful Symmetry*, p. 185:

[Blake] wanted an English dactylic hexameter, a line spacious enough to carry the role and thunder of apocalyptic visions. This he found in the old mediaeval septenarius, the meter which Chapman had used to reproduce the rhythm of the Iliad, the meter of the ballads and of historical and didactic epics down to Warner's *Albion's England*.

As the poet of life in motion, Lawrence is also the poet of transience. He insists on it, will not change it into aught else; witness *Corot:*

> Since life sweeps whirling, dim and vast,
> Creating the channelled vein of man
> And leaf for its passage; a shadow cast
> And gone before we can scan.

Such transience is never plaintive, as it might be with many another; it is the heart of the revelation, accepted as soon as acknowledged. No writer of this neopagan age, except possibly Yeats, has so sternly refused to dull or deaden the ache of this basic elegiac feeling, or to transform it into hopeless regret or hypothetical comfort. All Yeats's answers turned into questions; so was it with Lawrence (*Michael Angelo*):

> Whence cometh, whither goeth? still the same
> Old question without answer!

Therefore, in his elegies for his mother the poet continues to weep, "like a child for the past," as he says in *Piano*. Very different these from Hardy's reminiscent elegies for Emma Gifford, whom the lover locks up safe in the memory of what has been. And yet both series are shadowed: Hardy's, by the sense of an unresolved alienation; Lawrence's, by the awareness of emotional unsuitability. In neither series does the elegist probe deeply enough to arrive at a satisfying *anagnorisis*. Without this, Hardy's would-be elegies remain idylls of bygone feeling, and Lawrence's memorials are incipient lyrics. Nevertheless, if *Suspense, Endless Anxiety, The End, The Bride, The Virgin Mother, Reminder, The Inheritance, Silence, Listening, The Shadow of Death, Call Unto Death, Grey Evening, Passing Bell,* and *On That Day* might be relieved of their overemphasized Oedipean associations and considered as sincere records of universal dismay at the loss of a beloved, they would be hard to match for their fervor and immediacy. They provoke still an-

other question (*Twenty Years Ago*): "Have we had our in-
nings? God forfend."

Other human questions were forming in the mind of the
thwarted lyrist: (*In a Boat*) "What of me then, O love, me?"
(*A Man Who Died*) "Is this what's become of you?" (*Nostalgia*) "Is it irrevocable?" (*Bread Upon the Waters*) "Will you
come back when the tide turns?" Lawrence is already involved
in the long debate between the cult of the frisky Arcadian God
and those other shadowy worships which were to provoke and
supply the conversations of his exploratory novels. Not yet
quite aware of the contradictions involved, he said in his review
of the first volume of *Georgian Poetry: 1911–1912:* "I worship
Christ, I worship Jehovah, I worship Pan, I worship Aphrodite." [16] Which of these religious loyalties would prevail? At
first view his writing appears to be a modern rendering of that
earliest "-ism" of all, animism. Has he not looked with brotherly
eyes at animals of all sorts—rabbits, puppies, bats, tortoises, ser-
pents, cows, the more noble horse—and babies and schoolboys,
"unruly hounds"? As a lover he has felt of and stroked trees
and fruits and flowers. He has basked intimately in the light of
the sun and shivered intimately in the beams of the moon as if
he were kin to them, too, and, although distinct, in no wise
alien. And he has scurried from continent to continent over the
body of Mother Earth in search of primal man and primal
woman and primal joy.

When the liberated schoolmaster had wandered from Croydon to the Bavarian hinterland and Italian lakes and shores—the
Catullan Garda or Virgilian Benacus, the Shelleyan Lerici, the
Theocritean Sicily—Pan and elegies still ran urgently in his
mind. The next book after *Love Poems and Others* would be "a
book of Elegies." [17] *Amores* was published in 1916 and *Look!
We Have Come Through!* in 1917. Since the latter with its

[16] *Phoenix: The Posthumous Papers of D. H. Lawrence*, ed. Edward
D. McDonald (New York, 1936), p. 307.
[17] *Letters*, I, 189.

genesis in classical Pan-worship is surely the most distinguished
series of English love elegies of our second decade, let us post-
pone it for more careful reading while we glance at *Twilight
in Italy* (1916) [18] and *Birds, Beasts and Flowers* (1923). All four
publications were delayed; all four owed their composition or
their reworking to the Mediterranean influence, the influence of
Pan.

Twilight in Italy vividly records the Mediterranean character.
Its sketches are full of goatish references, mostly idyllic. At
Lake Garda the old woman talked of he-goat and she-goat.
Faustino had a sinister light in his eyes,

like a god's pale-gleaming eyes with the same vivid pallor. And all
his face had the slightly malignant, suffering look of a satyr; . . .
always his eyes had this strange, half-diabolic, half-tortured pale
gleam, like a goat's, and his mouth was shut almost uglily, his cheeks
stern . . . the long, pale, steady, inscrutable look of a goat. . . .
[His gestures as he grafted the vines were] amazingly swift and
sure, like a god. It filled me with a sort of panic to see him crouched
flexibly, like some strange animal god doubled on his haunches,
before the young vines, and swiftly, vividly, without thought, cut,
cut, cut at the young budding shoots which fell unheeded on to the
earth. Then again he strode with his curious half-goatlike movement
across the garden, to prepare the lime.

Faustino "belonged to the God Pan, to the absolute of the
senses." [19]

Lawrence had in 1913 taken exception to James Stephens'
treatment of Pan: "Let him . . . leave the Great God Pan
alone." "Poor Pan, he must be in his second childhood if he talks

[18] Originally published in 1916; more recently by The Viking Press
(New York, 1958); see pp. 134–135, 137–140.

[19] "Against the intellectual, Lawrence sets up the Panic in men; this
is the source which sustains life in fear and in joy. Lawrence, who
wished to be Messiah, wished also to be Pan." See Arthur G. Chater's
translation of Sigrid Undset's chapter on D. H. Lawrence from *Men,
Women, and Places* (New York, 1939); or as reprinted in *The Achievement of D. H. Lawrence*, ed. Frederick J. Hoffman and Harry T. Moore
(University of Oklahoma Press, 1953), p. 57.

as he does via Stephens. Fancy the God from Greece uttering such arguments for his own existence." [20] Quite another existence for the "God from Greece" is suggested in Lawrence's well-nigh unendurably animist sketches of He-goat and She-goat as they came from his pen at Taormina, Sicily, and set the pattern for the collection to be known as *Birds, Beasts and Flowers.* The rhythms illustrate demonic energy in all its irregular violence, and the phonetic result proves that Pan has called the tune on his Arcadian reeds. Here are nature's most mischievous antics, appropriately set forth as no pale court-poet or squeamish satirist could possibly have understood them. Listen to the He-goat "smiting out / The godhead of goats":

> Sometimes he turns with a start,
>   to fight, to challenge, to suddenly butt.
> And then you see the God that he is, in a
>   cloud of black hair
> And storm-lightning-slitted eyes.
> Splendidly planting his feet, one rocky
>   foot striking the ground with a
>   sudden rock-hammer announcement.

> *I am here!*
> And suddenly lowering his head, the whorls
>   of bone and of horn
> Slowly revolving towards unexploded explosion,
> As from the stem of his bristling,
>   lightning-conductor tail
> In a rush up the shrieking duct of his
>   vertebral way
> Runs a rage drawn in from the ether
>   divinely through him
> Towards a shock and a crash and a smiting
>   of horns ahead.

[20] *Letters,* I, 250.

In not less magniloquent terms the poet portrays the lust of the goat; did he remember Blake's Proverb of Hell?—"The lust of the goat is the bounty of God."

Except for *The Evangelistic Beasts,* in this collection the sketches of Fruits, Trees, Flowers, Creatures, Reptiles, Birds, and Animals are idylls rather than elegies. Together, however, they furnish the frame of reference out of which the skeptical human adventure must come. Let us, therefore, consider the strange crux of feeling and of experience set forth on Pan's reed flute [21] in *Look! We Have Come Through!* These love

[21] Moore (*The Intelligent Heart,* p. 40) says that when Lawrence moved to 97 Lynn Croft Road he "would at night hear Tom Cooper's flute piping away from next door." Undeniably in that day of "flautists" the poet conceived of himself, too, as a possible player on the reed flute. Witness his Aaron Sisson, from whose music we may gain a hint of what Lawrence considered Pan's expressive gift to be like. When Aaron played in England on Christmas Eve, "the pure, mindless, exquisite motion and fluidity of the music delighted him with a strange exasperation. . . . The more perfectly he produced [the music], in sheer bliss, . . . the more intense was the maddened exasperation." When, later in Italy, he played for the Marchesa,

it was a clear, sharp, lilted run-and-fall of notes, not a tune in any sense of the word, and yet a melody: a bright, quick, sound of pure animation: a bright, quick, animate noise running and pausing. It was like a bird's singing, in that it had no human emotion or passion or intention or meaning—a ripple and poise of animate sound. But it was unlike a bird's singing, in that the notes followed clear and single one after the other, in their subtle gallop. A nightingale is rather like that—a wild sound. . . . A wild, savage, non-human lurch and squander of sound.

Elsewhere the music of Aaron's flute is likened to "a blackbird's when he calls." When the flute was broken underfoot at the explosion of the anarchic bomb in Florence and thrown nervelessly into the Arno, the flutist "just didn't care any more about anything in life or death":

—There goes Aaron's Rod, then.
—It'll grow again. It's a reed, a water-plant. You can't kill it, you can't kill it.
—And me?
—You'll have to live without a rod, meanwhile. (*Aaron's Rod,* London, 1930, pp. 15, 241, 295.)

elegies are best studied in the classical tradition and gain stature from their association with the poetry of the Latin elegists. The series celebrates mainly Lawrence's love for Frieda von Richthofen, his Teutonic Cynthia or Lucy. Here, if anywhere in his verse, we come upon Arcadian pipings. Seeming metrical flaws establish a new rhythmic rule not predetermined. The melody is clear and thin, at first lyric verve without elegiac sophistication. Then the intervals, filled with thought, become unpredictable.[22] The effect is immediate, and the craftsman knows how that effect should be achieved. When he breaks out of tame metrical patterns and rhyme-schemes into wild changes of pace to follow his shifts in purpose or his veering passion, when the words advance in skittish abandon or the intelligence halts in mid-career, darts hither or yon, or dashes curiously around an alien object, in the kinaesthetic form as in the elegiac feeling Pan is still sounding the reed flute. What does not waver in the poetry is the drive of the alerted mind toward orientation in sunlight or courage in the shadows.

As Virgil's Damon in the eighth *Eclogue* began a song for the Maenalian hills—*incipe Maenalios mecum, mea tibia*—Lawrence will sing a song of the Isar:

> By the Isar, in the twilight
> We were wandering and singing.

Luna and the green star Sirius assist, and Priapus [23] is not forgotten. "Fireflies drift through the middle air / Tinily." The doe springs up out of the corn and flashes "up the hill-side /

[22] Dr. Hough calls this "the general atactic quality" of the verse, corresponding "to the mode of vision—in rapid intuitive glimpses" (*The Dark Sun*, p. 206).

[23] In Chapter III of *Movements in European History* (Oxford, 1928) (first published in 1921), p. 23, Lawrence refers to Pan and Priapus as gods of the "peasant people, [who] loved to take flowers, or a little cake, or a gift, to the shrine of some nymph by the fountain, to Pan among the trees, to Priapus in the orchard, to some fauns or nymphs in a cave."

leaving her fawn," and "bees roll round in the wild-thyme
with delight."

Yet where there should be "almost bliss," while the lovers
sit swinging in the fir tree overlooking the marshes and the Isar
can be seen "eerily, between the pines," "squirrel cocks his
head on the fence, and wonders / What about sin?" "Glimmering fear" is abroad. Pale-green glacier water, dark wild roses,
simmering frogs, snake, all suggest guilt. And "Hark" to death,

> The faint fine seethe in the air!
>
> Like the seething sound in a shell!
> It is death still seething where
> The wild-flower shakes its bell
> And the skylark twinkles blue.

Memories of Priapus remind the shepherd of the twofold action
of love, and he sings:

> Something in me remembers
> And will not forget.
> The stream of my life in the darkness
> Deathward set!
>
> And something in me has forgotten,
> Has ceased to care.
> Desire comes up, and contentment
> Is debonair.

The beloved nymph, the Syrinx, frightened by the night, resists
the comfort of her sylvan lover:

—"I am afraid of you, I am afraid, afraid!
There is something in you destroys me—!"

—Come, you are cold, the night has frightened you.
Hark at the river! It pants as it hurries through
The pine-woods. How I love them so, in their mystery of not-to-be.
—"But let me be myself, not a river or a tree."

Or, aching at separation from her, he invokes the

night folk, Tuatha De Danaan, dark Gods . . .
Gods of the living Darkness, powers of Night.

As their least discovery in Arcady the lovers have "found
the dark wild roses / Hanging red at the river"; as their greatest
revelation they have identified themselves (*I Am Like a Rose*):

> No rose-bush heaving
> Its limpid sap to culmination has brought
> Itself more sheer and naked out of the green
> In stark-clear roses, than I to myself am brought.

Then, *Why Does She Weep?*

> Hush then
> why do you cry?
> It's you and me
> the same as before.
>
> If you hear a rustle
> it's only a rabbit
> gone back to his hole
> in a bustle.
>
> If something stirs in the branches
> overhead, it will be a squirrel moving
> uneasily, disturbed by the stress
> of our loving.
>
> Why should you cry then?
> Are you afraid of God
> in the dark?
>
> . . . . .
> Let God come forth to justify
> himself now.

These love elegies have other than twentieth-century quality,
either English idyllic, French symbolic, or German sentimental.
About them is the reminiscence of Latin elegiac feeling, not
quite Tibullan or Propertian, surely not Ovidian: rather Catul-

lan [24] or as we might imagine the songs of Gallus to be, reported in Virgil's tenth *Eclogue*, where Pan tried to cheer Gallus out of his woes:

"Shall there be no end?" said Pan. "Love cares naught for this. Love is insatiate of tears, as the grass of the brook, as the bee of the clover, as the goat of the leaf." To whom Gallus: "Yet will ye sing, Arcadians, my story to your mountains: out of Arcady there is none can sing! . . . I will away; and the songs I framed in Chalcidian verse, I will tune anew on the pipe of Sicily's swain. My purpose stands. . . . Meanwhile I will scour Maenalus amid the intermingled Nymphs, or hunt down the savage boar. With my hounds [recall schoolmaster Lawrence's "pack of unruly hounds"] will I circle Parthenius' glades nor shall any rigor of winter say me nay!" [25]

The later poet eloping from Nottinghamshire to Bavaria, where he framed his song in "Chalcidian" verse, as it were, was not so hardy; but like those lost and long-lamented elegies of Gallus, his poems were to be "tuned anew" on the very Sicilian spot.

"Speech is the death of Pan," says Lawrence in his *Pan in America;* he "can but laugh and sound the reed-flute." [26] By himself Pan could not have accomplished Lawrence's mature life or writing. Along with animism another "worship" had been secretly at work; the shadow of Jehovah fell across the Arcadian scene.[27] This is most clearly evident in these same elegies of *Look! We Have Come Through!* with their impossible wish:

[24] Writing from Lerici to Edward Marsh in May, 1914, Lawrence discussed Abercrombie's estimate of *Sons and Lovers* as "all *odi et amo*": this implies the familiarity of all three with Catullus (*Letters,* I, 279).

[25] If, as Dr. Hough notes (*The Dark Sun,* pp. 20–21), Lawrence was reading Virgil's *Georgics* when he was at work on *The White Peacock,* published 1911, his knowledge of the *Eclogues,* too, may be safely inferred. So Professor Moore assures me.

[26] *Phoenix,* p. 27.

[27] Richard Ellmann, "Barbed Wire and Coming Through" in *Achievement,* p. 254: "Jehovah, that provincial and tyrannical deity, has replaced great pulpy Pan and dark, broody Osiris."

> Ah, if only
>> There were no teeming
>> Swarms of mankind in the world.

Throughout this poetry lurks the threat of sacrifice. Along with the naive "glimmering fear" of the animist and the only half-conscious rodent-like queries about sin, memories of the man's dead mother and the woman's living children begin to cast their shadows. Instead of animal laughter there are human tears.

Lawrence's "awareness"—a favorite word with him—of transience as the Pagan woe of woes gives to his elegies, as it gave to classical love elegy before him, their characteristic emotional quality. It is the necessary accompaniment of life perceived as movement, acknowledging its limitations even as it records its most intense experience. Any more precious value cannot avoid, must not exclude, death as an aspect of vital life.[28] At this point in his series the Old Testament began to furnish his frame of reference: angels coming to Abraham, apples of Sodom, Balaam's ass, Moloch, the dove bought for sacrifice, and—in the ballad strain—the myth of primal man and woman:

> You are born again of me.
> I, Adam, from the veins of me
> The Eve that is to be.

Finally, "looking back on the withering roses," the lovers choose —not to nestle "like plovers / In the fields of eternity"—rather to

>> storm the angel-guarded
>> Gates of the long-discarded
>> Garden.

"As victors" they "travel / To Eden home":

> Back beyond good and evil
> Return we. Eve dishevel

---

[28] In this he will be found comparable with Rilke. See below.

> Your hair for the bliss-drenched revel
> On our primal loam.
>
> .   .   .   .   .
>
> We have died, we have slain and been slain,
> We are not our old selves any more.
> I feel new and eager
>   To start again.
>
> .   .   .   .   .
>
> What is the knocking?
> What is the knocking at the door in the night?
> It is somebody wants to do us harm.
>
> No, no, it is the three strange angels:
> Admit them, admit them.

Thus, in the angelic symbol that pleased Rilke, too, Lawrence has given us one more "new [literary] heaven and earth." The poem of that name with the poet as "the discoverer," the Adam, and Eve as "the other" is followed by a new birth of Adam at the hands of Eve; thereby the poet is "delivered from the womb of the All," "The monstrous womb / Of time."

> We shall not look before and after.
> We shall *be, now.*
> We shall know in full.
> We, the mystic NOW.

In Lawrence's "mystic now" [29] as well as Wordsworth's "central peace subsisting at the heart of endless agitation" (*Excur-*

---

[29] Cf. T. S. Eliot, "Burnt Norton," *Four Quartets* (New York, 1943), p. 7. Without benefit of Eliot, Lawrence had written during the war years (*Going Back*):

> I am not here.
> I am away, beyond the scope of this turning;
> There, where the pivot is, the axis
> Of all this gear.
>
> .   .   .   .   .
>
> There, at the pivot
> Time sleeps again.
> No has-been, no hereafter; only the perfected
> Presence of men.

sion) or his "spot of time" (*Prelude*) reside all the liabilities of transience; and hence from the rarefied air of eternity the poet must always climb down again into the cycles of seasonal and historical change. So it was with this poet in *Craving for Spring*, the Epilogue to *Look! We Have Come Through!* Now he thinks of himself as akin to Moses and possibly unable to attain his promised land:

> Pray not to die on this Pisgah blossoming with violets.
> Pray to live through.

How did Lawrence get from Moses' Pisgah back to Arcadia? Was it through his sympathy for outcasts and exiles, those homeless or not yet home? In his essay on Pan he bridges the gap for us: Pan was "a sort of Ishmael among the bushes." [30]

Himself a restless wanderer, he came nearest to his land of milk and honey in New Mexico, where he rediscovered Pan alive in a pine tree.[31] Here in the American Southwest and sturdier than the willow that bent for Wordsworth's Lucy, or Tennyson's sycamore, or Arnold's elm, the New Mexican pine is not less than these an elegiac symbol.

The tree gathers up earth-power from the dark bowels of the earth, and a roaming sky-glitter from above. . . . Its raw earth-power and its raw sky-power, its resinous erectness and resistance, its sharpness of hissing needles [32] and relentlessness of roots, all that goes to the

[30] *Phoenix*, p. 22. Cf. Genesis, 16.12. "He shall be a wild-ass of a man, his hand against everyone, and everyone's hand against him, defying all his kinsmen." In the story *England, My England* (1922), Egbert "wandered outside, like Ishmael" (*The Short Stories of D. H. Lawrence*, Compass edition, The Viking Press, II, 325).

[31] *Pan in America:* "evidently written in 1924," says McDonald, *Phoenix*, pp. xii, 22–31. On p. 23 Lawrence has his say about Lucy Gray, who was, "Alas, . . . the form that William Wordsworth thought fit to give to the Great God Pan." Lucy was the "sweet-and-pure aspect of Nature." Alas! Alas!

[32] Did Lawrence remember from his schooldays Ovid's Pan, "his head wreathed with a crown of sharp pine needles," *pinuque caput praecinctus acuta* (*Metamorphoses* I, 699)?

primitive savageness of a pine tree, goes also to the strength of
man. . . . "Give me of your power, then, oh tree! And I will give
you of mine. . . . This is the oldest Pan."

It may be that the terrene and solar energy transformed into
Lawrence's sylvan pine yields more heat than light—does not
a man warm "his thighs and buttocks and loins" before the
blaze of his campfire of logs?—but the Indian with the "inscrutable Pan-smile," "glancing up and seeing the flames flapping
in flamy rags at the dark smoke, in the upper fire-hurry towards
the stars and the dark spaces between the stars," knows that
the honey of the pine "goes straight back to where it came
from." What is in this somewhat ragged prose an apotheosis of
the pine becomes for the poet an epiphany of the Great God
Himself.

Look! There is no more tree. We drank his warmth, and he is gone.
He is way, way off in the sky, his smoke is in the blueness, with
the sweet smell of a pine-wood fire, and his yellow flame is in
the sun. It is morning with the ashes of night. There is no more
tree. Tree is gone. But perhaps there is fire among the ashes. I shall
blow it and it will be alive. There is always fire, between the tree
that goes and the tree that stays.[33]

[33] Pan is frequently an agent in Lawrence's short stories, never more
powerful than as the effective *deus ex machina* of *The Last Laugh,*
where the mystery of sin takes on its final Dantesque form as sin against
life. While its author, Lorenzo, grins "like a satyr," two men and a girl
furnish an unmistakable satyr-epilogue for Lawrence's writing. At the
end of the tale, the deaf girl has been blest with hearing but the two
men are blasted from assumed health into such physical deformity as indicates their cowardice and lust: the policeman is marked with a clubbed
foot "like the weird paw of some animal"; Marchbanks, returned from
his base adventure, gives "a strange, yelping, cry like a shot animal" and
dies in agony. Betokening regeneration, there is a scent of almond blos-
som in the room of the newly-enlivened woman: what its persons really
are, such they are finally discovered to be. This is an elegiac *anagnorisis*
rather than a dramatic peripety, and yet the cleared vision and the rectified feeling make us newly aware that Pan has been abroad (*Short
Stories,* III, 630–646). Others of the short stories exhibit similar recogni-

His classical Pan having been confirmed in the New World, Lawrence wrote in 1924, to his New Mexican friend, Mabel Luhan, during one of her recurrent emotional crises, to bid her grin with a "fierce recklessness, based on trust, like the recklessness of Pan; thrusting deep down to the springs of nature, the sources: and then, the laughter." [34] In his novel of Quetzalcoatl, *The Plumed Serpent*, Don Ramon was allowed to preach the same message to Kate: "We must change back to the vision of the living cosmos; we must. The oldest Pan is in us, and he will not be denied." Nor was this only a doctrinal message; Lawrence illustrated his prepossession. At first sight in 1909 Ford Maddox Ford had discovered in him "the God Pan—or Priapus—peeping round beside the trunk of an ancient oak"; and in 1926 the Honorable Dorothy Brett thus described him asleep in the sun: "Out of your thick hair, two small horns poke their sharp points; the slender, cloven hoofs lie entangled in weeds. The flute slips from your hand." [35]

Yet the scriptural shadow continued to haunt the Arcadian. The following year at the Villa Mirendi, Florence, he seemed to Sir Osbert Sitwell "a fragile and goatish little saint . . . a Pan and a Messiah . . . a curious but happy mingling of satyr and ascetic." [36]

Pending a thorough study of the influence of the Old Testa-

---

tions: e.g., the maenad quality of the "strange, wild creatures" of *Tickets, Please,* their "wild faces" and gleaming eyes and "wild frenzy" (II, 343); Hilda of *The Shades of Spring,* finding that the keeper of her "Arcady" was "very curious" with "some of a wild animal's cunning—in a nice sense" (I, 205–206). Note, too, that Jimmy of *Jimmy and the Desperate Woman* was "a good-looking, smooth-skinned satyr"; "when he seemed most himself, it was a pure Pan face, with thick black eyebrows cocked up, and grey eyes with a sardonic goaty gleam, and nose and mouth curling with satire" (III, 606). In *The Overtone* (III, 755–757) there is talk of Pan: " 'Why was Christ afraid of Pan?' said the girl suddenly." " 'Why was Pan so much afraid of Christ that he died?' asked Mrs. Renshaw bitterly."

[34] *Letters,* II, 771.   [35] Nehls, *op. cit.,* I, 113; III, 42.
[36] *Ibid.,* III, 142.

ment [37] on this goatish little saint and Messiah we may here briefly relate certain hints he drops as to the part played in the growth of his mind by the books of the Bible: not only Revelation, which nourished his own last work, *Apocalypse;* the Prophets, whence he appropriated his habit of invective; and the Song of Solomon,[38] which gave him scriptural justification for his praise of sex; above all in the Psalms,[39] the source of the rhythms of many of his *Last Poems.* The Old Testament [40] served him as a guide on his quest, an authority for his doctrine, a shield in his battles, and the ghostly equivalent of his ordeal.

This had not always seemed to him an asset. "Like any other nonconformist child I had the Bible poured every day into my helpless consciousness," he tells us on the first pages of *Apocalypse;* "year in, year out [it was] expounded, dogmatically, and always morally expounded, whether it was in day-school or Sunday-school, at home or in Band of Hope or Christian Endeavour." His hostile reaction will be understood by the myriads of reverent people still suffering from that same overdose. "The mind becomes stubborn, resistant and at last repudiates the whole Bible authority, and turns with a kind of repugnance away from the Bible altogether."

And yet, like the rest of us, Lawrence reread the Scriptures.[41] In so doing he learned that "some books gain immensely, they

[37] This is not to detract from unpublished theses on the subject; e.g., that by Irving Swerdlow, "Lawrence and Myth," 1938, at Columbia University.

[38] "The Song of Solomon is a great poem" ("Pornography and Obscenity," *Phoenix,* pp. 173–174).

[39] He took comfort from Psalm 91 when first he escaped from the confines of Croydon. See his letter to A. W. McCleod from Germany, May, 1912 (*Letters,* I, 116). In the Epilogue to *Fantasia of the Unconscious* (1922) he noted that "all the psalms wind up with the Gloria.— As it was in the beginning, is now, and ever shall be, World without end. Amen" (p. 291).

[40] See review of *The Dragon of the Apocalypse,* by Frederick Carter, *Phoenix,* pp. 301, 302.

[41] For his final review of the treasury of Jewish literature he used Moffatt's translation.

are a new thing." "Especially," he tells us, "the Jewish poetry penetrates the emotions and the imagination." Thus in the *Last Poems* the pipes of Pan yield to the harp of David. *The Work of Creation, The Body of God, Silence, The Hands of God, Abysmal Immortality, Only Man, Song of Death, The End, The Beginning, Tabernacle, Shadows* are modern elegiac Psalms without which our literature would be much the poorer. Many of the long lines recall Blake and Whitman; but, as with both, the main influence is the English Psalter. Moreover, throughout his writing of verse, from the ballads to the speculative psalms and thence to the final elegy, *The Ship of Death*, his "movements in space" often come as pulses of four followed by pulses of three—the rhythm of the long-lived septenarius:

> Now it is autumn and the falling fruit
> and the long journey towards oblivion.

> The apples falling like great drops of dew
> to bruise themselves an exit from themselves.

In this noble elegy the theme and structure alike derived from the first great mortal crisis of the Old Testament. The building of the ship of death—the "little ark"—the rising of "the dark flood," the "tree of our life," "the flood subsid[ing]," "the little ship wing[ing] home," "the frail soul step[ping] out": surely this modern version of Noah's journey, like that in Lawrence's *Rainbow* of unhappy fate,[42] owes its courage to the Just Man, Lawrence's guide as he steered out upon his own "longest journey." Scriptural allusions are even more numerous in the MS B version of *The Ship of Death:* "the long marginal stretches of existence, crowded with lost souls," "lost souls . . . in millions . . . having no boat . . . no ship of the soul." The elegy has Odyssean traits as the traveller fares

[42] Aldous Huxley (*Achievement*, p. 157), reviewing the Old Testament symbols in Lawrence's *Rainbow*, mentions the Book of Genesis episodes in the novel.

> past the jutting rocks of shadow
> past the lurking, octopus arms of agonized memory,
> past the strange whirlpools of remembered greed,
> through the dead weed of a life-time's falsity; [43]

it remembers Charon, "the ancient boatman with the common barge"; Egyptian burial practice and the Babylonian flood of Gilgamesh are reflected in its waters; but like Noah, the Just Man, the soul is "pulling the oars of a life-time's courage": "row, little soul, row on." The "exit / from the fallen self" leads back to the primal self.

Lawrence's elegiac imagination is as evident in his procedure as in his lilting or vibrant music. No one denies that he was a skeptic with a gift for probing to the center. In the words of one critic, "he was anxious to explore reality." [44] Others speak of his "diagnostic insight" [45] or his "swift X-ray glance." [46] His art is "a deliberate exploration and analysis of discoveries." [47] "He belongs to that school of writers whose work is often more explorative, more interrogative, than affirmative." [48] This he himself acknowledges; the words "revelation" and "discovery" recur in his prose: "The essential quality of poetry is that it makes a new effort of attention, and 'discovers' a new world within a known world." [49] Our suggestion that "elegy" is the convenient term for speculative writing is with no poet more fully illustrated than with Lawrence; let us call him an elegist and then go on to discuss his elegiac accomplishment.

What, then, is the nature of the *anagnorisis* toward which he makes his "new effort of attention"? It is the discovery of

[43] *The Complete Poems of D. H. Lawrence*, II, 959.

[44] William York Tindall, Introduction to *The Later D. H. Lawrence* (New York, 1952), p. ix.

[45] F. R. Leavis, *D. H. Lawrence: Novelist* (New York, 1946), p. v.

[46] Hough, p. 8.   [47] *Ibid.*, p. 11.

[48] Mark Spilka, *The Love Ethic of D. H. Lawrence* (Indiana University Press, 1955), p. 148.

[49] Preface to Harry Crosby's *Chariot of the Sun* (*Phoenix*, p. 255).

identity, of self-identity: for instance, Ursula's elegiac look through the telescope in *The Rainbow:*

Suddenly in her mind the world gleamed strangely with an intense light like the nucleus of the creature under the microscope. Suddenly she had passed away into an intensely-gleaming light of knowledge. . . . Self was a oneness with the infinite. To be oneself was a supreme gleaming triumph of infinity.[50]

In a world of Woolfian lighthouses, Proustian telescopes and microscopes, Joycean epiphanies, Lawrence, too, has his revelatory devices, concerned especially to show what goes on within. In his prose and verse we find uttered or sung what we may call the aesthetic quest, the drive toward *anagnorisis* not as an explicit discovery but as a constantly enhanced, ever more deeply implicit value, *aesthesis* in its original meaning of perception, the refinement of experience. For him ultimate life is more than supreme illumination. Its tools are the senses, not the Thomist potential intellect. Its procedure is tentative rather than rational, *à tâtons*, as the French would say. Finally, when the writer discovers his inner selfhood, he comes not so much to know himself to be himself as to feel himself to be himself; and this is self in its most self-like, the primal self as if fresh from the hands of God.

An early poem, *Lightning*, bears witness to the truth of personal feeling—

> When the lightning flew across her face
> And I saw her for the flaring space
> Of a second . . .
> . . . weeping "Not this! Not this!"

"then darkness shut the lid of the sacred ark." The poet heard the rain "saying: Come / Home, come home, the lightning has made it too plain!" Again, *The Attack*, one of the most memorable of the War Poems, works through a vivid common ordeal towards a religious epiphany:

[50] Quoted by Dr. Leavis, *op. cit.*, p. 118.

When we came out of the wood
Was a great light!
The night uprisen stood
In white.

I wondered, I looked around
It was so fair. The bright
Stubble upon the ground
Shone white

Like any field of snow;
Yet warm the chase
Of faint night-breaths did go
Across my face!

White-bodied and warm the night was,
Sweet-scented to hold in the throat;
White and alight the night was;
A pale stroke smote

The pulse through the whole bland being
Which was This and me;
A pulse that still went fleeing,
Yet did not flee.

In front of the terrible rage, the death,
This wonder stood glistening!
All shapes of wonder, with suspended breath,
Arrested listening

In ecstatic reverie;
The whole, white Night!—
With wonder, every black tree
Blossomed outright.

I saw the transfiguration
And the present Host.

> Transubstantiation
> Of the Luminous Ghost.

And when, in his last years, Lawrence was uttering what often seem to be a priori gnomes, *Pansies, pensées*, these, too, had been arrived at by the severest elegiac processes. Reading that

> The profoundest of all sensualities
> is the sense of truth
> and the next deepest sensual experience
> is the sense of justice,

or that

> You must fuse mind and wit with all the senses
> before you can feel truth.
> And if you can't feel truth you can't have any other
> satisfactory sensual experience,

we come to realize that for this poet there were no abstract discoveries, no anaesthetic revelations.[51]

There can be little doubt that the last *anagnorisis* in Lawrence's literary career was religious. Although his God—like Rilke's angel—was scarcely ecclesiastical, may not have been in all regards scriptural, He was God. One distinguished student of theology, reading what Lawrence told the Brewsters in 1930, the year of his death—"I intend to find God: I wish to realize my relation with Him. . . . I must establish a conscious relation with God" [52]—sums up Lawrence's ideas of God in their original variety:

And what sort of a God was it that Lawrence found? The nearest we can get is to say that He is the mighty, jealous God of the Old Testament—mixed up with other colours taken from Mithraism,

---

[51] *The Deepest Sensuality*, p. 220, and *Sense of Truth*, p. 221, in "More Pansies" of *Last Poems*.

[52] See Nehls, *op. cit.*, III, 405.

Zoroastrianism, apocryphal Judaism, and other pagan religions, plus a generous, if highly eclectic, pinch of orthodox Christianity.[53]

Such a God of shreds and patches, possible to a theologian in retrospect, Lawrence would not have recognized as his. His God was a Living Being, not a conception, an experience rather than an idea or an "-ism." Moreover, this God, "Demi-urge," has attributes not often predicated of the first Person of the Trinity or of Hardy's Immanent Unconscious Will (*Demiurge*):

> Even the mind of God can only imagine
> those things that have become themselves.

Although the Lawrencean Creator—like Lawrence himself—"knows nothing beforehand," He can discover Himself (*The Work of Creation*):

> His urge takes shape in flesh, and lo!
> it is creation! God looks himself on it in
> wonder, for the first time.
> Lo! there is a creature, formed! How strange!
> Let me think about it! Let me form an idea!

Verily, this is more than the God of honest doubters: it is the God of elegists.[54]

In acknowledging Divine Power to be creative—but not providential—Lawrence's familiarity with the Old Testament

---

[53] Father William Tiverton (William Robert Jarrett-Kerr), *D. H. Lawrence and Human Experience* (Philosophical Library, New York, 1951), pp. 114–117.

[54] It seems also to be the God of some of the psychologists. In a recent translation by Richard and Clara Winston from Jung's *Memories, Dreams, Reflections*, recorded and edited by Aniela Jaffé ("Jung on Life and Death," *The Atlantic Monthly*, December, 1962, p. 44), we read:

Our age has shifted all emphasis to the here and now, and has thus brought about a daemonization of man and his world. . . . But man's task is . . . to become conscious of the contents that press upward from the unconscious. . . . [His destiny] is to create more and more consciousness, . . . to kindle a light in the darkness of mere being.

was a mixed blessing, but a blessing. Although it scored indelibly the crux in his nature and thought, it substantiated the scene on which his search was to be conducted and it helped to guide his footsteps. In his travels now backward to Genesis [55] and now forward to the Apocalypse, he tried to restore the human lot by insisting on the prelapsarian innocence of humankind. Beyond the jeremiads and proverbial lore, the chronicles and codes, lay Paradise. In his art the scriptural myths of origin and destiny, the songs and prophecies and visions—indeed, the very welter of generic forms of which his own writing is a modern instance—take on fresh significance, help to explain what is harsh and messianic in his attitudes as well as what is unlovely in his doctrines. With the Gospels and the use made of them by Christendom he was less in agreement; but, possibly because of his own experience of physical suffering and metaphysical conflict, he came at last to a cautious understanding of the Christian paradox; in *The Man Who Died* he tried himself to save the Saviour, himself to redeem the Redeemer.

Encouraged by Moffatt's translation, his prose and verse achieved a final speed and lucidity, a notable ease, the words allowing for the immediacy of thought, which comes naked out of the verbal sheath. No time now for sentimental or sensuous lingering on the phrase: he must speak out and tell what he has discovered. All things have led him to Revelation; and what is at last revealed to him is the nature of man as the living child of a living God. Writing of the novel he has said:

The novel is the book of life. In this sense the Bible is a great confused novel. You may say, it is about God. But it is really about man alive. Adam, Eve, Sarai, Abraham, Isaac, Jacob, Samuel, David, Bath-Sheba, Ruth, Esther, Solomon, Job, Isaiah, Jesus, Mark, Judas, Paul, Peter: what is it but man alive, from start to finish? . . . Even

[55] Lawrence's most unwelcome doctrines come straight from Genesis: the recommended domination of husband over wife, the lack of shame at nakedness, the peril of knowledge, the harshness of a cursing Jehovah, the hunger for a cleansing flood and a new start.

the Lord is another man alive, in a burning bush, throwing the tablets of stone at Moses' head.[56]

Of course Lawrence knew that "man alive"—primal man and woman—constitutes a fiction as incredible as ideal man and woman; but while keeping faith with the holy man of Wordsworth, Coleridge, and Blake, he was pleased to emphasize facets of human power and energy that they had disregarded or undervalued. He was, however, always the heir of their purposes: as can be seen, for instance, when his treatment of the education of the child in *Fantasia of the Unconscious* is compared with that of Wordsworth in *Prelude* I–V. Resembling Coleridge in his verbal fluency and Blake in his visual power, in his grasp of reality and his convictions he is closer to Wordsworth. Again, where Blake and Coleridge were romantic or doctrinal and expressed their beliefs by way of idylls and gnomes, Lawrence, like Wordsworth, was usually dialectic. In all his animosities, cultural challenges, and social rebellions, he must be considered as probing, weighing, testing. To take him to task for inconsistency or to nail him to any of his more absurd assumptions is to mistake the nature of his imaginative career and his literary method. This he acknowledges: "My yea! of today is oddly different from my yea! of yesterday."[57]

The amazing dialectic of his Chapters VII and VIII of the *Study of Thomas Hardy* deserves a place beside Hardy's choruses in *The Dynasts* and Yeats's *Vision;* and when Lawrence's philosophy of history is compared with that of Hardy or of the author of "Dove or Swan," it is seen to be no matter of blind circumstance or formally antithetical cycles but of the vital and pulsing nature of man alive. Witness his Introduction to *Movements in European History:*

[56] "Why the Novel Matters," *Phoenix*, p. 535.

[57] *Ibid.*, p. 536. Leavis, in commenting on Chap. X of *Aaron's Rod*, says that we have "something very like a dialogue intérieure" (p. 32). Mark Schorer ("The Individual Talent," *Achievement*, p. 170) considers that in *Women in Love* "he creates a kind of psychical dialectic."

All that real history can do is to note with wonder and reverence the tides which have surged out from the innermost heart of man, watch the incalculable flood and ebb of such tides. Afterwards, there is a deducible sequence. Beforehand there is none.

This is history as the elegist reads it. And Lawrence's histories of the souls of men and women can also be read as an "incalculable flood and ebb" of surging waters. With possible reminiscence of Arnold's and Swinburne's tides he modified the formal static patterns of *The Excursion, In Memoriam,*[58] and *The Dynasts* into what Virginia Woolf would recognize as elegiac novels, where investigation and rebuttal are unceasing and the action takes place mostly between the acts. In these novels the *personae* are scarcely "characters" or agents in the usual sense of making choices and thus advancing a plot. Are they not rather elegiac tools to help the novelist uncover the truth about man alive and, out of contradictory evidence, to elicit human meaning and value in a scope not permitted to Hardy's folks and a depth not craved by Yeats's nobler ritual actors?

All Lawrence's writing is full of light, actual and metaphorical, the shadows from his dark sun serving only to define various degrees of vital power and aesthetic "awareness." More than any other he has centered our literature in that great field of energy now being tapped by scientists and technicians; for him as for them there is no proper moral opposition between light and darkness. Whereas Wordsworth drew his symbols from a dependable old sun and Yeats scarcely adventured beyond his fierce yet tidy moon, Lawrence plunged into the yet unrealized cosmos of the distant stars, the galaxies of energy not soon to be commandeered even by the greatest of poets. For this poet it was life itself that was immortal in sun, moon, stars, rainbow, and the one sole Phoenix of Araby. Although it is less likely

[58] Allan Danzig, "The Contraries: A Central Concept in Tennyson's Poetry," *PMLA*, LXXVII (December, 1962), 577–585.

that he knew the Old English Phoenix [59] or its origin in the elegiac distichs of Lactantius than that he was an avatar rather of the Sun God Ra, the living truth of resurgent flame and light was akin to his own dynamic experience and no mere literary reminiscence. To illustrate his use of "flame" as a token for emotional experience or to substantiate the propriety of light as a metaphor for his numerous instances of "realisation" and "revelation" [60] would encumber our argument at this point; but plentiful evidence is not far to seek.

In his intense concern as in his rebellions, he is the undeniable elegiac successor of Hardy and Yeats. His erratic course took him further afield actually and imaginatively than Hardy was willing to go and into pits of energy deeper than Yeats could well endure. He was mentally swifter than either and impatient with the delay necessary to work his artless progeny—*nova progenies*—into exquisite form; for all its immediacy and kin-aesthetic power, his verse rarely achieves Hardy's economy or the disciplined repose of Yeats. His major literary affinity is with Hardy, whose novels he had studied and whose interest in the Unconscious he was to bring into the light of a sunnier day. Yet he could not rest with Hardy's natural man and woman, corruptible and corrupted by an unredeemable society, nor with Yeats's *homo faber*, tied to late Greek modes of social and artistic sophistication. He would disregard all the great dispensations—Byzantine, Christian, Mosaic, patriarchal or ma-triarchal; he would settle for nothing less than Eden, which must be stormed and re-entered despite man and God.

In many ways, and never meanly or unwholesomely, he oriented the imagination of our century to what is elemental in us as the physiologist and psychologist understand us, or as the pictorial artist sees us with an unabashed eye. His literary

[59] In January, 1916, he asked Lady Ottoline Morrell to bring him "Anglo-Saxon ballads—like 'The Seaman' translated" (*Letters*, I, 416).

[60] In a letter to Barbara Low, September 11, 1916, he reports of Swin-burne, "He is very like Shelley, full of philosophic spiritual realisation and revelation" (*ibid.*, p. 474).

effort is, therefore, comparable with Joyce's attempt to see Ulysses home and Shaw's search for Superman. Still more than theirs, it is closely akin to the nakedly actual ordeals of modern man on all his cultural levels and horizons. From our world of today he has pointed us to a better one; in which, however, his prophecies and schemes of reform are scarcely more than guide-posts, as he well knew. His "Rananim" now appears to be as inconclusive an enterprise as the Susquehanna of S.T.C.,[61] Blake's Universal Brotherhood of Eden, Wordsworth's Gras-mere gate to the Eternal City, or Tennyson's Parliament of the World. Restive under partial failure, Lawrence has, it may be said, vaccinated us against partial success.

For our literature is not yet a literature of action. We have our stories and our plays but their plots are uninvolved: *praxis* and *anagnorisis* are not often harmonized. Indeed, the usual action is a mere *anagnorisis*, a revelation or a riddle, a shadow or sightlessness. Lawrence's dark sun is not the least characteristic symbol of our century; but it has warmth and energy, where some other great spheres are only bright.

Most helpfully, he has put the seal of his genius on a literary medium freer and more inclusive than court-poets and court-critics have been willing to employ. He has set all expression again in flux: reading his prose we are now and again afloat on a stream of poetry and in his verse we find debris from many an old discursive glacier. We never doubt that in his habit of swift and immediate expression he is peerless: he has unforgettable words for what is alive as he believed life to be. Heaven, Earth, Hell: he has been circumscribed by none of them. He was a

[61] *Studies in Classic American Literature* (New York, 1923), pp. 33, 43-44, his satiric account of Crèvecoeur, who wanted to be an 'intellec-tual savage" and peopled his own pre-determined fancy with noble Children of Nature—"all that gorgeousness that flows out of the un-sullied fount of the ink-bottle. Lucky Coleridge, who got no farther than Bristol. Some of us have gone all the way." He was not less aware of the inadequacies of the noble savage than was the disillusioned Soli-tary of Wordsworth's *Excursion*.

denizen of no continent and no class or caste and no institution. He wanted nothing but life, and his whole intention in writing was to heal and inspirit the mankind of which he was so gifted and so ill-starred a member. He consumed himself in the service of his blood brothers. Although unfulfilled, he appears to be little less than the primal English elegist of our century: no later writer is likely to annul him.

Epilogue

TAMMUZ is dead in Babylon; let the flutes lament. Let the pipes wail for Pan, dead in Arcady. The fluting, however, lives on and the piping does not die; there will be new old flutings and pipings in new old tongues and new old measures; and all the old questions will be asked anew.

Even if such questions are not to be tidily and finally answered, the form in which they will be asked can in some sort be anticipated: to this theoretic end our study has been directed. Moreover, we have followed an exploratory method somewhat like that of the elegist himself when he advances tentatively toward his poetic *anagnorisis*. If our substantial evidence has been rightly interpreted, we too, may say, οὗτα Ἐλεγεία, behold Elegy Herself. For there seems to be a literary genre recognizable down the centuries and never more operative and in need of its proper name than in our own day. This genre is consistently speculative, has its own identifiable themes and procedures and devices, and always looks toward discovery. We may assume, therefore, that explicit reference to elegiac form will in the years ahead prove convenient to scholars and critics on the one hand and on the other to poets learning their important craft.

The closest association and most necessary formal kinship
of elegy is with the literature of self. The revelatory moments
of elegiac poetry symbolize the inner events of personal history,
and hence—as with Propertius, Wordsworth, Tennyson, Yeats,
and Lawrence—elegies in series approximate autobiography.[1] Although we may not equate poetry and experience and must
not suppose the bog of personalized adventure in which we are
now floundering to be an unmixed cultural boon, out of it by
formal discipline we may emerge with something both frank
and clear. If readers must know all, then writers will tell all;
but frenzy for self-exposure results in case-studies, not poems.
Our true stories will be reduced into poetic form, we may suggest, most effectively by attention given to traditional elegy
with its familiar procedures and enabling devices. As long as
man sets store by his identity and hopes for personal survival,
survival as himself, what the *anagnorises* of the elegist reveal
or assure will be precious to him.

The vehicle for such discoveries and the symbols in which
they are expressed will vary with writers and epochs in the
future as in the past. To man's eager challenges there are always
many riddling answers: the metamorphoses of classical story and
the quests of romance are not very distant cousins of elegy, and
the poetizing of the occult is a kind of bastard brother; the
masquerades wherein alien cultures delight the outer eye are
so many challenges to look more relentlessly below what is
different for what is comfortably the same—else the loot
brought home in Pound's Chinese Cantos or Yeats's Byzantine
poems or Lawrence's Arcadian sketches might in time prove as
embarrassing as Lord Elgin's marbles in London. Even more out
of place, in spite of their provocative charm, poems written to
mimic the disproportions of pictorial art and the distortions of
sculptural art defeat the serious purpose of elegy. Then, too, the
elegist has more than a few poor kinsfolk, and when the poetical

[1] In his *Autobiography*, p. 182, Yeats says: "I know now that revelation is from the self."

by-products of disease, folly, and despair are prettified with specious ornament or curious techniques all the Muses are aggrieved, Elegeia most profoundly.

Among the perils of the writer is pride in his own contrivances. "Made" poetry will be found as precarious as manufactured engines in lethal weaponry; both are susceptible to change in fashion and function. Like the best musicians, the best symbolists [2] take us into another world, supposedly fair but not yet tested out on earth. At their worst, when they record hallucinatory or abnormal states induced to provoke unnatural feelings and unwholesome images, symbolist poems will scarcely survive the therapy of the doctors of physical and mental hygiene. The artificer beating time for what he hears with his inner ear needs the skeptical outer eye of the elegist peering at what he finds in the actual world.

This is true of poetical language, too, always threatened by new Towers of Babel. The most curious and valiant attempts to reproduce in word patterns the complicated designs of orchestra or architecture, to climb the trellis of mathematics into a diviner air, do not fit the speaking voice or content the anxious ear. Ever since Solon and Mimnermus gave heed to the surge of the waves on the shore of the loud-sounding midland sea, elegiac poetry has seemed destined to master the feelings in accord with the pulse of a vigorous humanity and to articulate its experience into the simplest possible words and rhythms. Nor are alphabetical signs for vocal music aught but a makeshift; if it is to be understood and loved, poetry must keep true to the habitual melodies of speech. At the end as at the beginning of all composition is human nature. Fortunately, the gods have nodded assent: Krishna's flute for the Orient and Pan's

[2] According to Paul Valéry (*The Art of Poetry*, translated from the French by Denise Folliot, New York, 1961, pp. 42, 70), "What was baptized *Symbolism* can be very simply described as the common intention of several groups of poets to 'reclaim their own from Music.'" Valéry quotes Racan in attributing to Malherbe the comparison of Prose and Poetry to Walking and Dancing.

pipes for the Occident have set the style. In a long and wide
view of flute song we are emboldened to hope that the humble
reed flute will maintain its vehicular and metaphorical primacy.

But to what end? Joy,[3] said Coleridge.

> O pure of heart! Thou need'st not ask of me
> What this strong music in the soul may be!
> What, and wherein it doth exist,
> This light, this glory, this fair luminous mist,
> This beautiful and beauty-making power.
>   Joy, virtuous Lady! Joy that ne'er was given,
> Save to the pure, and in their purest hour,
> Life, and Life's effluence, cloud at once and shower,
> Joy, Lady! is the spirit and the power,
> Which wedding Nature to us gives in dower,
>   A new Earth and new Heaven,
> Undreamt of by the sensual and the proud—
> Joy is the sweet voice, Joy the luminous cloud—
>   We in ourselves rejoice!
> And thence flows all that charms or ear or sight,
>   All melodies the echoes of that voice,
> All colours a suffusion from that light.

Like S.T.C. a century before them, Yeats and Lawrence both
understood well that the end of revelation is joy. Yeats "wished
. . . to discover thoughts that tighten the muscles, or quiver
and tingle in the flesh, and so stand like St. Michael with the
trumpet that calls the body to resurrection." [4] Lawrence goaded
us on to the "mystery of Joy-in-Resurrection," [5] and his quest
for what is primal not unworthily echoes Wordsworth's "primal
sympathy" in the *Immortality Ode.* The inherited burdens of
the elegist are heavy: a long tally of deserted villages, ruined
cottages, shipwrecked vessels, slain heroes, and phthisical heroines left scattered in the valleys and on the shingles of the
world along with transience and death, not to mention the

---

[3] *Dejection: An Ode*, V.   [4] *Essays*, p. 392.
[5] "The Church" in *Last Poems*, p. 104.

metaphysical ills initiated by Lucifer and culminating in hothouses of evil flowers. But the very weight of these burdens provokes greatness in the poet faithful to Eden. Joining the Michaels and Raphaels of an earlier campaign, Yeats's Phoenix, Lawrence's Pan, and not far away Rilke's Angel have engaged in combat and should be a match for the Devil, Death, and Boredom in all the narrow places of our human destiny.

From these essays the names of many distinguished writers of our day have been omitted, except for passing allusion. Among them are the two expatriates, T. S. Eliot and W. H. Auden, and that sometime homeless exile, Ezra Pound. Their speculative poems can best be evaluated in a study of American elegy, not here attempted. There are other reasons, too, for not associating them primarily with the elegiac tradition.

Like George Meredith of a century ago, Eliot is a poet of the νόμοι. To these laws, usages, or conventions of the ages and to codes, choices, ordeals, and actions resulting from them the very ablest minds have by nature and training always been loyal—a group in which the author of *Four Quartets* takes his dignified place with Virgil, Dante, and the several court-poets of the north heralded by Spenser. Like them estimating the past that he may preserve it in a fabric of finely differentiated values, he might be called a liturgical poet, a maker of rituals. He has not ceased from exploration, but the end of all his exploring has been to arrive where he started and to know the place for the first time. Nor are his divinations without sudden illumination and revelatory splendor; yet he seems to imply that his epiphanies have already been instituted. The relation of metaphorical light to elegiac *anagnorisis* in his poems must be studied more carefully than is here possible; from it the student will learn much about generic form. Here, however, near the end of a book of essays on elegy as flute song, we may observe that when the poet climbed the third stair of *Ash Wednesday* and heard the maytime enchanted with an antique flute his silent sister was even then severing from the garden god—

Pan?—whose flute had become breathless, and that he was listening ever more attentively to

> music heard so deeply
> That it is not heard at all, but you are the music
> While the music lasts.[6]

From Eliot's *Quartets* the years will bear away the fiddles and the flutes. The weak pipe and the little drum of *East Coker* will in their turn be silenced by the sea bell's perpetual angelus of *The Dry Salvages*. Nevertheless, Krishna, although surrendering flute song for wise counsel, will urge Arjuna on with the old elegiac cry, Voyagers, fare forward!

W. H. Auden, the impressario of things as they unfortunately are in his world of war and woe, offers his spectators expertly designed settings for an action often without a clear *anagnorisis* or a satisfying peripety. He is a master of metaphor and analogue, and from him we have skillful decorative satire arising out of ironical hypotheses, a modern idyll of maladjustment or disintegration. He seems always on the point of rediscovering Eden or reconstituting his world into exquisite levels of meaning and—possibly—value. With him, however, is affiliated a group of writers who prefer to frame and illuminate rather than penetrate their experience; their reflected light suggests the theater or the exhibit with its diversely angled battery of floods, its lamps incandescent and fluorescent, and its collection of varicolored gels now to be supplied in the psychical as well as in the mechanical realm. If Mr. Auden might be tempted more frequently into the sunshine to take again and again one of his exquisite exploratory rambles, his latent speculative power would serve him well, and those who admire him might be wholesomely invigorated.

Most difficult it is to view the turbulent genius of Ezra Pound through the eye of one paragraphic needle or within the vista of one generic term. Even as we record his youthful sympathy with Propertius, we must remind ourselves how authentically

---

[6] T. S. Eliot, *Collected Poems 1909–1962* (London, 1963); quoted by permission of Faber and Faber Ltd.

he has worked his way to the rostrum of the homilists to find himself made one with the moralists and teachers of the Orient, from which he returns to head the school of American didactic poetry.

In associating these writers primarily with literary genera other than elegy we in no wise intend to slight them. Pound and Lawrence, for instance, are brothers under the accident of nationality, comparable in their frank and undeviating concern, their unresting search for truth and justice. When in his *Last Poems* Lawrence says:

> The profoundest of all sensualities
> is the sense of truth
> and the next deepest sensual experience
> is the sense of justice,

he is in agreement with Mr. Pound, whose ninety-ninth Canto spells out the same lesson. The elegiac faith of these two enterprising poets helps to explain their heads bloody but unbowed. They constitute an Anglo-American alliance of which any century could be proud. Moreover, they are not alone in their resolute brotherhood. To their search for what lies below the accidents of time and place others on both shores are contributing evidence yet to be assessed.[7]

Let us end these *obiter dicta* with one more acknowledgment of delight in and reverence for one other poet. None can surpass the delicacy with which the idyllist Dylan Thomas arranged his outlines and colors for a fresh appeal. His experiments with assonance and near-rhyme give to his stanzas individually and in series their distinctive melodic and graphic quality. An avowed struggler from darkness to light, had he lived he might have reduced into perspicuous order his dim rich symbolism of the heavens and thus clarified and enhanced his poetry.[8] Already

[7] Among them Jeremy Ingalls with her literary journeys on five continents and Robert Graves with his researches into prehistory.

[8] Elder Olson, *The Poetry of Dylan Thomas* (University of Chicago Press, 1954), pp. 19–20, 86, 89. Professor Olson points out the apocalyptic nature of Thomas' *Sonnets*.

Pan had embarked with him in his Welsh Noah's Ark. He was not less acquainted with the Phoenix. And the metaphor of man he associated with the sun both of pagan Antiquity and Christendom. It may well be that his moments of insight and awareness occurred more often than they were sought: at first he was not primarily speculative. No study of elegy, however, should omit reference to his remarkable poem, *After the Funeral (for Ann Jones)*. This is not only character writing and lapidary verse; beneath bone and stone he has probed for something unique. Such is indeed Ann Jones, we say, as we watch him getting at her identical self, deathlessly personal.

Thomas rarely subjected his vital surfaces to celestial sheen or terrestrial murk; for this reason he bade fair to outdo Hardy's personative writing, and in his pipings he still challenges D. H. Lawrence for the mazer of pastoral song. Moreover, like Lawrence, he sought without discouragement their common primal Eden and the upright Adam who sang upon origin! We may go further to say that in his *Vision and Prayer* we have an instance of the authentic procedure of the elegist rewarded by an authentic *anagnorisis*, forthright and apposite testimony for what these essays have been aiming to suggest: [9]

> I turn the corner of prayer and burn
> In   a   blessing   of   the   sudden
> Sun. In the name of the damned
> I would turn back and run
> To   the   hidden   land
> But   the   loud   sun
> Christens down
> The   sky.
> I
> Am found. . . .
> The sun roars at the prayer's end.

[9] Dylan Thomas, "Vision and Prayer" from *Deaths and Entrances* (London, 1947), p. 54, reprinted by permission of the Literary Executors of the Dylan Thomas Estate and J. M. Dent and Sons Ltd.; and from

With Lawrence and Pound, Thomas was open to the storms of circumstantial life and subject to the liabilities of the human condition. Let Lawrence speak for all three.

Man is a thought-adventurer. . . . Real thought is an experience. It begins as a change in the blood, a slow convulsion and revolution in the body itself. It ends as a new piece of awareness, a new reality in mental consciousness. . . . [Man's undying effort at consciousness] is the human destiny. The light shall never go out till the last day . . . the light of the human adventure into consciousness, which is, essentially, the light of human God-knowledge.[10]

However briefly, and in conclusion, we may now look to the Continent. Across the Channel from Lawrence and Thomas two other famous elegists have put their seal on courage in speculation and joy in discovery: Paul Valéry, the poet of the graveyard by the sea, and Rainer Maria Rilke, the elegist of Duino. Both may be invoked to accredit further our long search to discover the nature and form of elegy.

In the symbols of sea and sun serving Lawrence also, Valéry says:

> Brisez, mon corps, cette forme pensive!
> Buvez, mon sein, la naissance du vent!
> Une fraîcheur, de la mer exhalée,
> Me rend mon âme. . . . O puissance salée!
> Courons à l'onde en rejaillir vivant! [11]

His elegiac properties and scene are familiar: pine-trees, sea, and sun. The skeptical imagination at midday ranges vertically between earth and sky. This *Cimetière Marin* should be studied at the side of Blake's *Thel*; but Valéry discovers that the undeniable worm feeds on life, not death. Here he is in accord

---

[10] D. H. Lawrence, *Assorted Articles* (New York, 1930), pp. 226, 252–253.

[11] Paul Valéry, "Le Cimetière Marin," *Morceaux Choisis* (Gallimard, Paris, 1946), pp. 38, 34, 36; © Editions Gallimard; quoted by permission.

with both Lawrence and Thomas: death is not something other, it is the inner face of life.

In his very first stanza the French poet acknowledges elegy as speculative, leading to vision:

> O récompense après une pensée
> Qu'un long regard sur le calme des dieux.

It is the eye that guards peace; the serene scintillation that masters the depths; and a flash or sparkle that recalls the departed. Valéry's spot of time is "Midi,"

> Midi là-haut, Midi sans mouvement
> En soi se pense et convient à soi-même.

His Temple of Time is subsumed in a single sigh. His instant sparkles.

In still another foreign tongue the poet of angelic aspiration has said that under the Stars of the Land of Pain at the very foot of the mountains of Primal Pain gleams in the moonlight the source of Joy:

> es schimmert im Mondschein:
> die Quelle der Freude.[12]

Rilke's inexpressible stars and his elegiac tree on a slope, to be looked at day after day, show him also true to generic form. In his first elegy we are reminded that the aim of angelic effort is "to espy a trace of eternity"; and the last lines of the incomparable ninth elegy reveal that "Supernumerous existence wells up in his heart." This elegist, too, has his spot of time, his moment of insight, with which he has fused his observant vision of the past and his theoretic attention to all kinds of particulars inviting his devotion: the tablet in Santa Maria Formosa (I), that vague look in the faces of pregnant women, Attic steles (II), puppet stages (IV), Picasso's painting, *Les Saltim-*

[12] Rainer Maria Rilke, *Duino Elegies*, with an English Translation, Introduction, and Commentary by J. B. Leishman and Stephen Spender (New York, 1939), p. 84; quoted by permission of W. W. Norton and Co., Inc.

banques (V), Sphinx and Chartres (VII), Etruscan tombs (VIII); but not less, dumb brute and joyful gnat. He does not abstract their essence from their value: he has a better word for it, *Verwandlung*, transformation. Man is still necessary. "Things . . . look for rescue through something in us . . . want us to change them entirely . . . into ourselves!" (IX) [13] And, again, "the most visible joy can only reveal itself to us when we have transformed it, within" (VII).

Meanwhile, we are aware in Rilke's dactylic pentameters of frequent likeness to the second line of the classical distich. He recalls the dirge for Linus as the initial flute song, and in no language are simple phrases more imaginatively set down to evoke more complicated and profound discoveries. He bids Time stand still at the very heart of Transience (IX):

> Einmal
> jedes, nur einmal. Einmal und nichtmehr. Und wir auch
> einmal. Nie wieder. Aber dieses
> einmal gewesen zu sein, wenn auch nur einmal:
> irdisch gewesen zu sein, scheint nicht widerrufbar.

Although this scarcely needs translation, in our faltering words it may serve as a valedictory for the elegist as for the student of elegy.

> Once
> everything, once only. Once and no more. And we, too,
> once. Never again. But to have been
> this once, if indeed only once,
> on earth, may not, it seems, be annulled.

"And we, too, once." Thus Rilke helps us recognize our cultural identity and to take our distinctive place in literary history. Moreover, like other great elegists, he encourages us to

---

[13] Cf. Lawrence (*Phoenix*, pp. 430–431): "It seems as if the great aim and purpose in human life were to bring all life into the human consciousness. And this is the final meaning of work: the extension of human consciousness."

bear genuine witness. Toward such testimony, if it is to furnish an authentic *anagnorisis*, poets and critics alike will purify their matter from what is mischievous and clear their utterance from fruitless ambiguities. "Style is the ultimate morality of mind," says Whitehead; and in the arts generally there is a lack of style if the artist be guileful or shortsighted. Whether our moment on earth, our "irdisch gewesen," reveal us and our writing to be trifles or ultimately moral, in our "once only" we shall deceive no one. So we were: οὗτοι ἐκεῖνοι.

Afterword

IN the summer of 1963 Abbie Findlay Potts wrote to me her desire that this study of elegiac poems, together with her two earlier books concerned with form and mode, the first centering on *The Prelude* and the second on *The Faerie Queene*, should be taken as "a trilogy on literary form, a generic study of three main modes—and, I hope, distinct from either literary history or philosophy in literature or literary biography."

Professor Potts died in Troy, New York, February 19, 1964.

Since I had previously seen the whole work, and exchanged views on it with the author, it has been a pleasure for me to substitute for the author in editing the manuscript. I have been guided by suggestions from Professor Jack Stillinger, but I have tried throughout to preserve the author's own meaning and purpose. Like the two previous books in her trilogy, this is the mellow fruit of a lifetime of reading, teaching, and meditating.

CARL R. WOODRING

Index

DATE DUE